Margaret Zoller 8 I
Washington Clay

SHARING

HOME LIFE

By LAURA BAXTER
MARGARET M. JUSTIN
LUCILE OSBORN RUST

In consultation with Benjamin R. Andrews

Mrs. Baxter is Assistant Professor of Home Economics Education, Kansas State College, and Supervisor of Home Economics in the City Schools, Manhattan, Kansas ❧ Miss Justin is Dean of the Division of Home Economics, Kansas State College ❧ Mrs. Rust is Professor of Home Economics Education, Kansas State College ❧ Mr. Andrews is Professor of Household Economics, Teachers College, Columbia University.

J. B. LIPPINCOTT COMPANY

CHICAGO PHILADELPHIA NEW YORK

18.434.7

Printed in the United States of America

PREFACE

The content. An introductory course in home economics should be broad in scope and based directly upon the needs, interests, and abilities of the pupils. The textbook for such a course must be so planned as to present many phases of homemaking in a manner which emphasizes sound appreciation and understanding of the ideals of worthy home membership. Taking these objectives as guides, the authors have developed the content of *Sharing Home Life.*

Comprehensive and thorough, the material presented in this text provides for the three or four semesters of work usually allotted to the beginning or introductory course in home economics. Provision has been made for the extension of pupil understanding within the various areas of home economics and also for the integrating of these areas into a unified concept of the subject. Significant is the use of the word "Sharing" in the title, for underlying each broad concept and each seemingly small phase of the material is the broad emphasis upon the importance of *sharing* in the home, in the school, and in the community.

All units in this book have been tested through several years' tryout in classrooms. Only those problems have been retained which contributed most to the pupil's advancement in the principles of homemaking, and those which were enthusiastically received by the pupils and teachers.

The unit organization. Sharing Home Life employs the unit-problem method of organization, in accordance with recommended educational procedure. This organization allows the subject matter to be presented in concise units which are directed toward definite goals. Each problem within the units contributes definitely to the reaching of these goals by a discussion of a fundamental sector of the larger whole of the unit. In addition to the logical informational value of this organization, its flexibility is advantageous.

Each problem has been carefully prepared to cover the lesson for one day in schools that use short class periods. For longer class periods two problems may be combined, or greater use may be made of the activities which follow each problem. Some teachers plan their course so that a complete meal is prepared and served in a laboratory lesson. This type of lesson can be easily arranged

The Indian pueblo, the thatched cottage of England, and the modern American house are all "home, sweet home" to some boy or girl. In the home are formed the fundamental traits of character which largely determine the manner in which the individual fits into the intricate pattern of our society. It is the habit of *sharing* which the authors of this book emphasize as being essential in the formation of such traits.

through a fusion of several problems as presented in a single unit. Unit 8, entitled "Helping with the Family Meals," perhaps indicates most clearly the advantages of the organization followed. Here several problems may be combined in order to prepare a complete breakfast in the laboratory:

How shall we prepare and serve a breakfast of orange juice (Problem 8); rolled oats (Problem 14); buttered toast (Problem 18); and cocoa (Problem 11)?

Similarly, in Unit 14, entitled "Selecting and Preparing the School Lunch," the following large problem may be made by combining problems or parts of problems:

How shall we prepare a lunch of cheese sandwiches (Problem 5); stuffed eggs (Problem 7); fruit (Problem 9); and brownies (Problem 12)?

The resourceful teacher interested in this pattern of presentation will have no difficulty in combining problems in this manner.

The activities and references. Adequate opportunity for pupil activity and expression will be found in *Sharing Home Life*. Each problem ends with a group of "Activities" which focus attention upon the essentials of the problem. At the close of each unit are given "Suggested Home Experiences," designed to enable the pupil to evaluate the material of the text in terms of actual home, school, and community living.

The reading lists which also are placed at the close of each unit have been compiled with extreme selectivity. In certain units the lists are purposely brief. The authors have no wish to encumber the teacher and pupil with references to books which are not written primarily for pupils of the introductory course. Consequently those books listed will be found to be of direct and continuous assistance in the use of this text.

The vocabulary. Of primary importance in a textbook for the junior high school is the language in which the book is written. *Sharing Home Life* has been written simply. The authors have followed the suggestion of Dr. E. L. Thorndike, Teachers College, Columbia University, and other leaders in research in reading, and, with few exceptions, have kept the vocabulary within the first seven thousand words of the Thorndike Word List. (This list is based on a count of the actual occurrences of words in children's reading matter.) The exceptions are the more or less technical terms with which pupils of home economics must become familiar. These terms are thoroughly explained whenever they are introduced in the text.

Acknowledgments. The authors wish to acknowledge gratefully the assistance of the following persons in the preparation of *Sharing Home Life:* the members of the staffs of the Division of Home Economics and of the Department of Education, Kansas State College, Manhattan, Kansas, and of the staff of the Manhattan High School; Dr. W. E. Sheffer, Superintendent of Schools, Manhattan, Kansas; R. W. Browning, former Principal of Junior High School, Manhattan, Kansas; and Mrs. Lyla Roepke Schrock.

The authors express their appreciation to the following for permission to reproduce the photographs on the indicated pages:

Norma Albright, 193, 277; American Can Company, 243, 254, 442; *American Consumer,* 322 (bottom), 323, 462, 464, 465, 466; *American Home,* 486; Armour and Company, 220, 256, 258, 427, 439; Atchison, Topeka and Santa Fe Railway, vi (top), 96 (top); Jessie Tarbox Beals, 483; *Better Homes and Gardens,* 147, 158, 385, 387; H. C. Bohack and Company, 28, 284; California Fruit Growers Exchange, 203, 204 (both pictures), 205 (both pictures); Calumet Baking Powder Company, 226, 260; *Capper's Farmer,* 197; *Consumers' Guide,* 13 (top right, bottom left), 16, 27, 280, 322, 333, 334, 369, 414 (left), 472; Consumers Union, 401; *Country Gentleman,* 271; Cream of Wheat Corporation, 216; Dennison Manufacturing Company, 487, 488; Mrs. Clarence Eckleberry, 5; Evaporated Milk Industries, 185, 530, 537; *Farm Journal,* 213; Farm Security Administration, 11; Fuller Brush Company, 389, 391; General Motors, 96 (bottom), 347; *Good Housekeeping,* 262, 263, 308, 318, 319, 376, 506, 558; Great Northern Railway, 30; Greyhound Lines, 97 (bottom); George A. Hormel Company, 365; Richard W. Hufnagle, 20; Iowa State College Extension Service, 196; Kansas Business Association, 13 (top left); Kansas State Board of Agriculture, 13 (center); *McCall's,* 310; Martha P. McMillin, 426, 430; Michigan State Board of Control for Vocational Education, 92, 162; National Apple Institute and Stark Brothers Nurseries, 265; National Association Service, 224, 268, 298, 433, 448; National Safety Council, 553; New York State College of Home Economics, 157; Philco Radio and Television Corporation, 414 (right); Mrs. P. K. Putney, vi (bottom right); Quaker Oats Company, 214; H. Armstrong Roberts, 4, 15, 17, 77, 408, 539, 542, 544, 546; Alma Roudebush, 358; Royal Desserts, 290; Singer Sewing Machine Company, 56, 57, 64; *Successful Farming,* 402, 403, 404, 551, 552; Swansdown Cake Flour Company, 295, 367, 368; Swift and Company, 257, 282, 292; Marguerite Tice, 173, 175; Dorothy E. Tower, 191; Transcontinental and Western Air, Inc., 97 (top); Union Pacific Railroad, 93; U. S. Bureau of Home Economics, 200, 239, 287; U. S. Department of Agriculture, 32; Letitia Walsh, 169, 170, 181; *What's New in Home Economics,* 82, 346, 371, 372, 374, 392; Wheat Flour Institute, 221, 266.

CONTENTS

Unit 1: YOU AND YOUR FAMILY 3
Unit 2: THE FOOD WE EAT 25
Unit 3: USING THE SEWING MACHINE 55
Unit 4: WHEN WE ARE AWAY FROM HOME 75
Unit 5: PLANNING AND MAKING A MORNING DRESS . . 101
Unit 6: MAKING OUR OWN ROOM LIVABLE 145
Unit 7: MAKING AND KEEPING FRIENDS 167
Unit 8: HELPING WITH THE FAMILY MEALS 183
Unit 9: HOW TO LOOK OUR BEST 307
Unit 10: CARING FOR OUR CLOTHING 321
Unit 11: IF WE HAVE GUESTS 341
Unit 12: HELPING TO CARE FOR THE HOUSE 383
Unit 13: FUN FOR THE FAMILY 407
Unit 14: SELECTING AND PREPARING THE SCHOOL LUNCH . 423
Unit 15: HELPING TO SELECT AND PURCHASE OUR CLOTHING 451
Unit 16: EXPRESSING FRIENDSHIP FOR OTHERS 477
Unit 17: WHEN THERE IS SICKNESS IN THE HOME 495
Unit 18: THE FAMILY'S MONEY. 509
Unit 19: HELPING TO CARE FOR YOUNGER CHILDREN . . . 527
Unit 20: PLANNING AND MAKING A SCHOOL DRESS . . . 555

INDEX 589

SHARING HOME LIFE

UNIT 1

YOU AND YOUR FAMILY

MOST PEOPLE IN OUR OWN COUNTRY live in family groups. The same is also true of the people who live in other countries. If we were able by some magic to look in turn at families in Iceland, Sweden, Mexico, Brazil, the Philippines, and this country, we would find each concerned with problems of food, shelter, and clothing for the family and with the care of children. The father or mother or both would be found teaching their children to talk, to walk, to help themselves, and to do some simple task in the home. Although the homes would be different, we would find that each provides shelter of some sort for the family members.

Every home, no matter how simple, holds a place in the hearts and memories of the family members that continues even after they are grown up. For each of us, the members of our family are the ones whose understanding and love mean most to us. It is important that we understand our families and be able to live with satisfaction in our own. Perhaps the first step in attaining this is to understand ourselves and what we possess by being a member of our own family. Our first problem, then, will deal with ourselves and may be expressed in words one hears often on the streets and on the schoolgrounds: "Who are you?"

Problem 1: WHO ARE YOU?

"I am Sarah Lee Duncan."

When this question is first put to you the natural reply is somewhat like this: "Oh, I am Sarah Lee Duncan. My father is a lawyer. We live on Leonard Street. My grandfather is the judge at the Courthouse, and I am thirteen years old."

Almost without thinking, you present your family as the basis for explaining who you are and what you are. You tell the generations of your family that are still living in the community almost as directly as is done in the old song:

There is old Sam Simons,
And young Sam Simons,
And young Sam Simons' son,
And young Sam Simons
Will be Sam Simons
When old Sam Simons' gone. . . .

You know that one generation follows another in this order. You like to hear your mother or your grandmother tell of the days when she was a little girl. Perhaps then you ask, "And what was it like when *your* grandmother was little, and *her* grandmother too?" You hear stories of great-great-grandmother's courage when the Indians came to her home and tales of the bravery of some more remote ancestor in Revolutionary days. As you listen you may think of your family as a stream that flows on and on.

The part of your family that you will know best in days to come is that which lives in the span of your own days. It

Five generations of this small girl's family are pictured here—her father, grandmother, great-grandmother, and great-great-grandfather.

is right that you should try to learn about the others of your family—what they looked like, what they thought, and how they lived. By so doing you can understand yourself better.

Certain things about you were determined before you were born because of what you inherited from your parents, your grandparents, your great-grandparents, and so on back. All have shared in giving you your physical characteristics. Your hair is yellow, black, or red because of your family heritage. It is straight and smooth like the strings in a harp or a mass of waving curls for the same reason. Your skin is fair or dark, your nose is short or long, your fingers short and thick or long and tapering, because that part of you reflects some qualities of your ancestors. Even your height, within certain limits, is governed by the fact that you are *you,* and that your ancestors were of a certain stature.

Knowing this, it becomes easy when you are told how tall you are or how short you are to answer as did the little elf when asked

Why he was so small,
And why he didn't grow.
He slightly frowned, and with his eye

He looked me through and through.
"I'm quite as big for me," said he,
As you are big for you."[1]

There is some evidence that not only your physical characteristics but also certain mental ones are inherited. Your musical interest and mechanical skill and your ability to learn are all believed to be limited, if not determined, by your heredity.

"Who are you?" is a more complicated question than it first appeared and should be given more consideration. You must place yourself in relation to your family as the beginning of the answer.

Activities:

1. Make a list of your ancestors up to your grandparents.
2. Does any physical characteristic such as brown or blue eyes, curly hair, or short or tall body build appear in a number of your family members and grandparents? Select one characteristic and put a check by those persons that have it.
3. What other characteristics are said to appear frequently in your mother's family? In your father's family? Do you or any of your sisters and brothers have any of these characteristics?

Problem 2: WHAT HAS MADE YOU WHAT YOU ARE?

You have seen that the basis or the beginning of the real *you* lies in your family heritage. But important as you know this is, you surely realize that it is only part of the story. You are as you are today partly because of your mental and physical growth. Perhaps it is hard for you to remember a time when you were any different. It may be that you think of yourself as being the same now as you were when you entered school. No doubt your mother or your grandmother has a collection of snapshots that will help you to see what part growth has had in making you as

[1] John Kendrick Bangs, "The Little Elf." Reprinted by permission of the publisher, D. Appleton-Century Company.

you are now. As you look at these photographs, you may smile at the big-eyed baby looking at things in wonder, and chuckle over the toddler intent on pulling a flower to pieces. You may even remember, as you see the picture of the little girl starting off to school, how lonely you were that first day at school. Those days seem far away now. They have been pushed back by your growth which makes you different as the years go by.

The steps in your growth and your sense of the importance of the present year may be like that of Anne Darlington, who looked back over her life at the age of six.

When I was one,
I had just begun.
When I was two,
I was nearly new.
When I was three,
I was hardly me.
When I was four,
I was not much more.
When I was five,
I was just alive.
But now I am six, I am clever as clever,
I think I'll be six now forever and ever.[1]

Of course no one would want to be six or even sixteen "forever and ever," but you will find that whatever stage of growth you are in seems right and normal.

The growth that has changed you from a round and plump baby to your present size and shape, making you as you are now, has required certain things. The food you eat, the exercise and rest you take, and the care you give your body all help determine what you are like and are going to be like. The thin, poorly nourished girl who does not give her body the food it needs, either because food is

---

1 A. A. Milne, "The End," *Now We Are Six,* p. 102. E. P. Dutton & Co., New York.

lacking or because her food habits are poor, stunts herself. She becomes less sturdy than her heritage would provide. The nervous, tense child who spends at the movies hours needed for refreshing sleep also takes from her heritage. She makes herself less vital and strong than she might be.

Growth, food, rest, play, and proper care of the body—these have all helped make you *you*. However, this is not all. The real you is partly determined by all that may be seen and felt in the world about you. Edwin Markham, one of the well-loved American poets, wrote of Lincoln and described the influence of the world about him, his environment, in these words:

The color of the ground was in him, the red earth;
The smack and tang of elemental things:
The rectitude and patience of the cliff;
The good-will of the rain that loves all leaves;
The friendly welcome of the wayside well;
The courage of the bird that dares the sea;
The gladness of the wind that shakes the corn;
The pity of the snow that hides all scars;
The secrecy of streams that make their way
Under the mountain to the rifted rock;
The tolerance and equity of light
That gives as freely to the shrinking flower
As to the great oak flaring to the wind.[2]

Of course, this environment that helps to make you as you are is largely determined by your family life. From your family, then, comes the basis for what you are and many of the influences that direct your growth. More than school, church, or community, your family life determines what you become.

Activities:

1. What things and experiences might a city child have that a rural child might not?

---

[2] Edwin Markham, "Lincoln, the Man of the People," *Lincoln and Other Poems*. Doubleday, Page and Co., New York, 1902.

2. What things and experiences might a rural child have that a city child might not?

3. How might each of these children be influenced by these things and experiences?

Problem 3: HOW ARE YOU INFLUENCED BY YOUR FAMILY?

You have just learned that among the things that make you as you are, the family life you share is perhaps the strongest. You should now understand the different ways in which you are influenced by your family. It may be difficult to know just where to start. Suppose we consider first the influence that your family life has had on your standard of living. If you were the daughter of a Welsh coal miner, the standard of living in your family would be very simple. You would not have a comfortable house heated by a furnace, a motor car for trips, nor could you go to the movies every week. These would be entirely beyond what was possible for your family. If you were the daughter of a Kansas or Nebraska farmer, probably you would not include hand-woven draperies, Oriental rugs, or a big car driven by a chauffeur among things you must have. Telephones, automobiles, vacation trips, and other conveniences and pleasures are so familiar to many that they seem to be "must haves" instead of being merely "would like to haves." To a large extent, we regard as "necessary" that which we have become used to in our childhood.

Another way in which your family influences you is in your use of the English language. If your family is from the South, your speech is what is called "Southern." If your father and mother came from some foreign country, your speech may show words and phrases not common to the English language. If your family members have been careless in their speech, you will find it difficult to free yourself from the "ain'ts," the "have wents," and the "gits."

The manners and customs which you hold as right are

those that your family call good. If these are such as are common in the community, you will find that your home training is a help to you. On the other hand, even simple acts such as eating soup, greeting an acquaintance, and introducing a friend become difficult and trying if your manners and customs differ from those of the rest of the community.

Your religion and your religious beliefs are for the most part determined by your family. One girl may say that her family "has been Catholic ever since the Church was established;" another may say her family "has always been Scotch Presbyterian." In each case the family has passed on its religious beliefs to its members. Much the same is true about political beliefs. You often hear some heated argument about politics backed by the statement, "Well, my father says———." Religious and political beliefs formed when we are children are usually so strong that they tend to remain the same no matter what later experiences may be.

Your friends are often largely determined by your family. As a child, you were most often with children of your mother's friends. Later you knew the boys and girls of your father's associates. Neighborhood picnics and church festivals tend to keep you in the circle of family friends. There is something pleasant in the thought, "Her grandfather knew my grandfather," or "His mother and my mother were in school together." Through the years the families seem to belong together.

Your ideals and attitudes are influenced by those held by your family. If such values as honor, personal integrity, honesty, tolerance, and many others matter more to your family than making money, acquiring land or goods, or obtaining comforts, you are fortunate. Your own ideas of those things that are best in life cannot help but be colored by the ideas of your family. If your family believes in living within its means, you are influenced away from lavish spending for show and display. If your family has good teamwork in the doing of its tasks, you will know something more about helpfulness than how to spell the word. The satisfactions and pleasant relationships that come from working together will be matters of true worth to you.

Working and sharing with other family members develops worthwhile attitudes.

Knowing that your family believes in you and loves you is of great worth to you. If this feeling of belonging and being valued were taken away, you would find yourself shaken if not broken by its loss.

You will find that your attitude toward responsibility is largely determined by the attitudes held in your family. If your father and mother work for the good of the community earnestly and thoughtfully, you know that such duties are important. From them you have lessons in being a good citizen that make a far greater impression than any amount of flowery talk by speakers.

If your father and mother in their living together express mutual affection, generous loyalty, and loving consideration, you may learn more of the meaning of love than you can get from volumes of silly love stories. On the other hand, it may be that you have seen one person in your family spoil the happiness of all the members for an afternoon or evening by jealousy, selfishness, or even a fit of temper. Such experiences should make you more critical of your own demands and moods, and more eager to be a good family member.

Activities:

1. List the churches to which your grandparents went and those to which your family members go. To what extent does family influence appear?
2. Name one or more customs of your family that have come from the family of one of your parents.
3. Describe two families that have different ideas about the use of their money.
4. How many of your close friends are children of close friends of your parents?

Problem 4: WHAT ARE THE FATHER'S RESPONSIBILITIES TO HIS FAMILY?

The father is the head of the house. He sits at the head of the table, of course, but his responsibilities as head are far more than this. They differ with each family, and with the stage of the family's life.

A little boy just entering school was asked what his father did. After thinking a moment he replied, "He tends the furnace, shovels the walks, takes care of the car, and then goes to his store." Most people listing a father's responsibilities would put his wage-earning work first, for generally the father supports the family by his work. What he does as a farmer, a merchant, a mechanic, a teacher, or a lawyer brings in the income that provides the food, shelter, and clothing for the family group.

There is a certain strain about earning the living that is more difficult perhaps than the labor itself. The farmer must know what to plant and when and where, and also

From many fields of work comes the income for the family. The father, for example, may work in a salt mine (top left); in a research laboratory (top right); in the wheat fields of the West (center); in a postoffice (bottom left); or in a meat-packing concern (bottom right). Money he earns will be used for his family's needs.

when to buy and sell, if his labors are to bring the money to buy the things his family needs. The merchant must know whether prices of articles he sells are going up or down, what people will want, and who may safely be allowed to have charge accounts. The automobile mechanic must know how to locate the parts of a car that are out of order and how to repair any car that may be brought to him.

Any occupation a father may follow presents many problems. He has pleasant contacts and some that are not pleasant. He cannot always consider what he himself would like to do, but must think of what will be best for his family. The father shares with the mother in the plans for spending the family income. Working together, they decide whether the family shall own or rent its home, whether it shall have a new car or new furniture or save for the education of the children.

The father's influence on the speech, courtesy, and manners of the family is strong. If the father's speech is a strange mixture of oaths and "ain'ts," some of these will show in the children's talk. If the father is courteous and polite in his treatment of the family members, his influence in this will be far greater than his many warnings, "Now be polite!"

Many fathers find great satisfaction in helping plan for the social and educational life of the family. Hours spent together reading aloud by the fireside, playing games, or hiking over the hills help the family know each other better and know more of the joys of living.

Fathers often help with the work of the home. This is more frequently one of father's responsibilities now than it was a couple of generations ago. Then there were maiden aunts, older sisters, and often employees to carry part of the home duties. Today relatives less frequently share in the home and fewer families have employees. Now the working day has been shortened to six or seven hours so the father

Fathers are helpful in the more difficult household tasks.

has more free time for helping than he did long ago. One of his responsibilities to the family may be the care of the furnace, the preparation of Sunday breakfast or supper, or any or all of the jobs of "fixing" that a house requires. If there is a lawn or yard, its care is usually his. This is also true of the care needed to keep the automobile oiled, greased, and shining brightly.

There are other jobs which the father carries because he has a family and is interested in the community in which his family lives. These include helping with the Boy Scouts, serving on the school board or the city council, and being a member of the church board. All these are important and are responsibilities which good citizens gladly carry.

Activities:

1. Make a list of the occupations of the fathers of your friends. How many different ones do you find?
2. What community jobs does your father do? How does your list compare with the lists of the other members of your class?
3. Describe something which you enjoy doing with your father. Why do you enjoy it?

Problem 5: WHAT ARE THE MOTHER'S RESPONSIBILITIES TO HER FAMILY?

We tend to group the mother's responsibilities under several large main topics. These were given by one girl as "taking care of the house; taking care of the family; planning and preparing the meals; answering the door and the telephone; feeding the bird and Rover; seeing that we are all doing what we are supposed to do, that we are having a happy time, and that she looks pretty and sweet." If you were to name all the separate tasks included in this statement, they would be many and different. You would no longer wonder, if you ever have wondered, why mothers do not have more time to do things with their children.

Choosing food for her family is one of the mother's responsibilities.

These and many other tasks may make up the day's work for a mother. Some of the tasks are what we call routine, that is, they are repeated day after day until one can do them with ease and speed. Other tasks are done only once in a while. The needs of the family change during the year and so the tasks change also. The birthday party, the Christmas festivities, the making of father's favorite preserves. and the making of your party dress are done so seldom that they do not become routine.

What must a mother know to carry her responsibilities well? She must know what foods you should have; how to provide them on the money she has for food; how the food can be prepared so as to be interesting and attractive; what can be done with the leftovers so that no food will be wasted; how to care for all the utensils, dishes, silver, and linen used in preparing and serving the food; how to plan

The event of the birds' returning in the Spring is made more enjoyable when Mother helps her children to look at nature with seeing eyes. The songs of birds, the color of flowers, the fluttering of butterflies, and the leafing of trees all may become matters of interest if Mother or Father will spend time with the children in enjoyment of these things.

her time so that she can get everything done; what provisions should be made for your growth from a baby to an adult; how to select and care for all the furnishings of the home; and how to keep all the family members happy.

Knowing all this, she then has the difficult task of doing much of this herself and getting the family members working together to do the rest.

Perhaps the responsibility the family dislikes most to have mother turn over to paid help is that of caring for the sick. When we are ill, we all seem to feel that we will surely get well more quickly if mother is on duty. Home nursing is a responsibility mothers usually carry, except for serious illness that requires expert care.

In addition, many mothers have, in the past few years, shared in the wage earning for the family. Then, often, after the work in office or store is done, the mother tries to carry as much as she can of the usual homemaking responsibilities. In such case, if mother is not to be sadly overworked, the family members must help to lighten her load of home duties.

Mothers have always taken the major responsibility in caring for and guiding the children. The mother helps them become adjusted to this strange world; answers millions of questions; joins in their play; directs their reading and music; and keeps a thoughtful eye on their friends, manners, and speech. All this she must do without seeming bossy or keeping the children from being independent. With the father and the other family members she should build a satisfying and happy family life.

The mother, too, has responsibilities in the community. These may be much the same as those of the father. She may spend time in club work, in PTA activities, and in church organizations. All in all, the mother is indeed a very busy person with many responsibilities, often heavy and difficult.

Activities:

1. Make a list of all the unusual responsibilities that your mother had during the past month. Did they make for any difficult situations? How?

2. Assume the responsibility for answering the telephone and the door for a given time, such as Saturday or Sunday morning or afternoon. Note the number of calls made and the time required for each.

Problem 6: WHAT ARE THE CHILDREN'S RESPONSIBILITIES IN THE FAMILY?

The children, as well as the father and mother, have a responsibility for family living. On first thought this may seem strange. You look at a toddler trying to step his way about the room. You wonder what his responsibility can be and how he can possibly carry it. You see some high school girl step out of her home where there are many jobs to be done and hear her call back, "Well, I don't want to help with the dishes tonight—tell Susie to do them." You wonder who ought to do the dishes, and what the sister's attitude should be toward Susie. Of course the toddler cannot be held for sharing the dishwashing or earning money to support the family. We judge his conduct quite differently than we do that of his high school sister. The responsibilities of children differ with their ages.

Both the toddler and the high school girl can help by lessening the amount of work to be done. If the toddler has learned to pick up his toys and put them on the cupboard shelf or back in the toy box, he is sharing in the responsibility of lessening the work of keeping the house in order. If the high school girl picks up her clothes from the bedroom floor when she dresses and undresses and if she cleans up the bathroom after using it, she is carrying her responsibility of helping keep the house in order. Both children have helped in their own way.

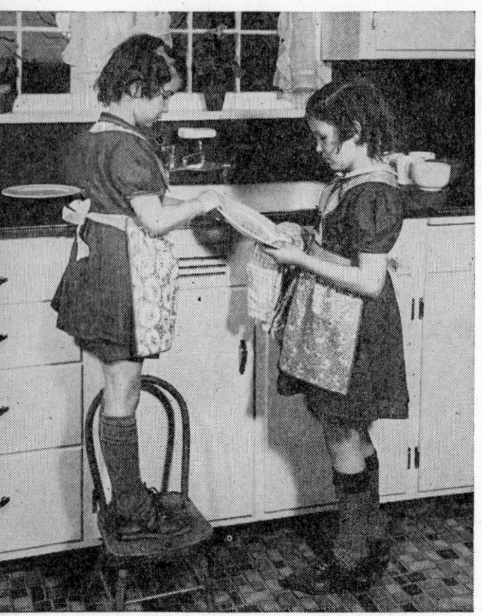

These little girls doing dishes know that every member of the family should share in the work of the home.

As the children grow from toddlers to school age and then to adults, they have increasing responsibilities for the work of the home. Some of this will be most interesting, some will not. The children learn many things from both kinds of tasks. They find that skill reduces the time required for a task, that those who do not do their share are not popular, that there is satisfaction in doing a job well, and that working together counts. They learn the joy of doing something for someone they love, and of being appreciated for what they have done.

The children's share in the work of the home varies with the age of the child—from the task of feeding the goldfish or the canary done by the four-year-old, to the difficult task of canning and preserving food for the year sometimes done by the high school girl, or the task of caring for the floors and woodwork assumed by a high school boy.

Sometimes situations arise that make it necessary for the children to carry extra responsibilities in their family life. A mother's illness may throw the care of young children on the oldest daughter; a father's death may put the burden of family support on the high school son. There are many heroic stories of the way children have met such emergencies.

There are certain responsibilities that come from sharing in a group that give the children affection and a feeling of worth and security. The children have an obligation to help not only by work but by attitudes and thoughts, so that the family will be "a going concern." There are certain customs, traditions, and ideals that are important to the family. The children have the responsibility of being loyal to these. Being members of the family, they have no right to act without considering the other members. They must understand and respect the desires, needs, and rights of the other family members if they are to be good members of the group.

Last but not least, the children have the responsibility of becoming worthy persons. Day by day they build themselves a little more this way or that way. They may become more patient, more kind, more self-controlled, and more generous—or just the opposite. The family wants the best for its children and is eager that each accept his responsibility to become a fine individual.

Activities:

1. Make a list of your responsibilities in your home.
2. What others could you add to the list? How would it affect your family life if you took over these responsibilities?
3. Give examples of things children have no right to do without considering the other family members.
4. What home responsibilities should be assumed by a four-year-old child? A ten-year-old boy? A fourteen-year-old girl?

Problem 7: HOW WOULD YOU DESCRIBE A GOOD FAMILY MEMBER?

If one is to be a good family member, one must be more than a good lawyer or teacher and more than a good person. One's wage-earning life may be very different from one's personal life or one's life in the family group. A man may be an able surgeon, lawyer, or contractor and may have a fine reputation in his occupation, but still not be successful as a member of a family. A woman may be a brilliant teacher, a fine secretary, or a well-known clubwoman, and still fail to be a good mother. In case of failure as a family member, the meaning of much of the other success one may have in life is lost. The person still misses happiness in daily living.

Because you are interested in a rounded life, satisfying at home as well as at work, you want to know what a successful family member is like. Perhaps the first item in your description of a good family member is that she have the capacity for loving people and appreciating things outside herself. She is willing to share her thoughts, her enthusiasms, and her affections freely with the members of her family. Feeling her own need for love, she will know that others, too, have this need.

The successful family member gives other family members appreciation and courage. She recognizes their worth and esteems them for it. She helps them by giving *generous* recognition of their personal qualities and their efforts. A good family member appreciates the security her home offers and *adds* to it rather than *subtracts* from it. In her comradeship and her courage, other members feel a sense of new strength. Teasing, belittling, and annoying others makes them more shy and less secure, so such practices are on her "Don't" list.

A good family member is democratic. If you have never done so, look up the meanings of *autocratic* and *democratic*. By comparing the definitions, you will see why you would prefer to have democratic persons as members of your family group. A democratic person will recognize the rights of others as well as her own; she will make no unreasonable demands on the other family members; and she will be willing to sacrifice for the good of the family. For her, "ours" will always be above "mine."

A good family member assumes her responsibilities cheerfully. She does not have to be driven or coaxed to carry her share of the work. She does her tasks without whining or pouting. There is something about cheerfulness that is contagious, so the good cheer and the sense of pleasure in work spreads from her to her younger brothers and sisters, and to her parents.

A good family member has respect for what is hers. She values the good name of the family, its standing in the community, and its traditions and ideals. The regard in which she holds her family does not mean that she will worship them, and talk about being "descended from the Mayflower." Rather, it means that she finds a certain challenge to her personal worth in the long stretch of years that members of her family have lived good lives and have served their communities, bringing regard to the family's name. The name may not appear in *Who's Who* nor in the registry of noblemen, but it may have records of achievement and stories of nobility that may well make each person eager to make her family proud of her as a good member.

Activities:

1. Choose a person that you consider a good family member. Write a brief description of him or her.
2. How does he or she measure up to the standards given in this problem?
3. How does being a good family member help us in our personal life? In our occupation?
4. In what ways are you a good family member? In what ways are you a poor family member?

REFERENCES FOR THE UNIT

Calvert, Maude Richman, *The New First Course in Homemaking.* Atlanta: Turner Smith Co., 1932.

Friend, Mata Roman, and Shultz, Hazel, *Junior Home Economics: Living in Our Homes.* New York: D. Appleton-Century Co., 1933.

Kinyon, Kate W., and Hopkins, L. Thomas, *Junior Home Problems,* Revised Edition. New York: Benj. H. Sanborn & Co., 1938.

Talbot, Nora, and Others, *Practical Problems in Home Life for Boys and Girls.* New York: American Book Co., 1936.

SUGGESTED HOME EXPERIENCES

1. Decide what qualities you need to improve yourself as a family member. Make a plan for your procedure and follow it for a given time. Check your results.

2. Decide what responsibilities you should take over to be a better family member. Assume these responsibilities and note the effect on you and others in your family.

UNIT 2

THE FOOD WE EAT

THE FOOD YOU AND I EAT SEEMS TO US "right and proper." We accept orange juice, cereal, egg, and toast as a matter-of-course breakfast. Perhaps we never stop to think that only a small part of the people of this world would expect or enjoy such a meal. The Eskimo in the cold North has for his breakfast caribou meat and seal or salmon. The French child enjoys a breakfast of hot milk, slightly colored and flavored with a mixture of coffee and chicory. A Chinese boy likes a large bowl of rice, eaten without the addition of cream, sugar, or butter. In far away Africa, the dark-skinned son of a native tribe devours his roast sweet potato and lump of sheep fat.

If the maps in our geography pictured the food habits of the people as they do the stretches of their lands, we would find in no two countries exactly the same foods used. In each country there might be some foods eaten which to us would seem not good to eat. Snails, bird's-nest soup, shark fins, locusts, and fried snake are some of the foods we might not think of eating, although many people like them. Why are there such great differences in the food habits of different countries? Food habits are influenced much by what the people of a land have always done. Also, people tend to eat those foods which they can get easily.

Problem 1: WHERE DO WE GET OUR FOOD?

A small boy was asked not long ago where his food came from. He replied, "Mr. Smith's grocery store." When questioned further, this seemed to be all he knew about the source of his food. Of course the grocery store is important in obtaining food, but there is much more to the answer than just going to the store.

Plants and animals are our chief source of foods. With the exception of table salt and water, all our food comes from these sources. Plants used as food include vegetables, fruits, and grains. Sometimes we eat the leaf, sometimes the stem, sometimes the seed, and sometimes the root.

A grouping of some common plant foods according to the part used is as follows:

Bulb	*Root*	*Stem Tuber*	*Stem*
onion	carrot	Irish potato	asparagus
garlic	turnip		celery
	beet		rhubarb

Leaf	*Flower*	*Fruit*	*Seed*
spinach	cauliflower	tomato	corn
lettuce	broccoli	squash	peas
cabbage	French artichoke	peach	wheat
mustard greens		banana	

Animals used chiefly for food are cattle, sheep, hogs, poultry, and fish. In some places even today elk, deer, bear, opossum, birds, and rabbits are common foods. The early pioneers depended largely for their food upon such game as these. Certain products which make up a large part of our diet are also included among the food from animal sources. These are milk, cream, cheese, butter, eggs, and lard. In almost any meal, two or more of these foods are used.

Early in man's development he depended upon wild

plants and animals that grew near by for his food. He gathered wild rice from the swamps, robbed birds' nests of their eggs, and killed the deer with his crude axe. Later, he planted grain and, although he journeyed far during its growth, he returned later to harvest the ripened grain. Next he began the raising of animals for work and for food. Efforts to improve the wild plants and animals above their wild state were made early and have continued through the centuries to the present time.

These cattle are being carefully fed before being shipped to the stockyards of the city. Much of the meat we eat is beef from the cattle ranches of the West.

Today in only a few isolated places, such as the Arctic regions and the South Sea Islands, are wild plants and wild animals an important source of food. Planning the production of food, curing and storing it for future use, and transporting it from one place to another are now a regular part of our daily living.

At one time in this country each family produced nearly all its own food, buying only such things as salt, coffee, and tea. This is no longer the case, not even on farms. Now a farm or a given region produces chiefly those foods which will grow best there. Because of this, certain sections supply the market with certain foods only.

The foods produced in any section tend to be eaten by the people living there. People on the seacoast eat much

Important to us all is the modern grocery store, spotlessly clean and neatly arranged for our convenience in shopping. Notice the canned and packaged foods, attractive and pleasing.

fish, people in the western grazing states eat much lamb, and those in California and Florida use many citrus fruits and green vegetables. However, foods from other places are being used more and more. Orange juice has become a part of the American breakfast everywhere. Many a small inland town café boasts of the seafood it serves. Modern methods of transportation and communication have enabled us to have foods from everywhere quickly and safely.

There are many interesting food stories in the long freight trains that puff across the country and in the large trucks that hum along our highways. These stories may also be found in the ships that sail the seas. Because of progress in keeping foods cold and safe, apples, oranges, lettuce, cream, and other perishable foods may be shipped over long distances and be kept in good condition.

Some foods are not grown in our own country and must be obtained from far-off lands. Among these foods are spices, coffee, tea, cocoa, and tapioca. If you check your day's food you will probably be surprised to find how many regions and countries are represented.

Activities:

1. Make a list of the foods you ate yesterday. For each food give the state, region, or country from which it came.
2. How many of these foods were produced in your own community? How many were produced by your family?
3. Name the states or countries which are known for the production of the following foods: grapefruit, pineapple, cane sugar, beet sugar, lamb and mutton, beef, corn, wheat, lettuce, coffee, chocolate, butter, and tea.

Problem 2: WHY DO WE NEED FOOD?

Perhaps sometime the call to luncheon or dinner came when you were at an exciting point in an interesting game or story. What you were doing seemed much more important than such an ordinary thing as eating. You may have said, "Oh, I don't want any lunch," and when further urged by your mother, you may have added, "—and I don't need any." Whether you knew it or not, your body did need the food.

Because you are alive you have certain food needs. Only when you stop living will you stop needing food. Being alive means "being in a state of activity." The activities connected with being alive are many. Boys and girls walk, run, jump, lift, push, play, and work. Their whole bodies seem to be in motion. When they stop, panting for breath, and throw themselves down on a couch for a rest there is still motion in their bodies. Their chests rise and fall while they are breathing, the blood pulses through their bodies, and many slight movements of the body may be noted. The body needs food that will provide sufficient fuel for all this motion. The more motion there is, the more fuel is

These men are loading apples in refrigerator cars. Every day thousands of carloads of fruit are shipped in such cars, which carry the fruit, fresh and unspoiled, to its destination. People who are careful about their diets eat some fruit every day.

needed, just as the more miles a car is driven, the more gasoline is required.

The body does other work that requires fuel. The digestion and absorption of food, the circulation of the blood, and the maintaining of the normal body temperature are some of the examples.

The body is constantly growing both in height and in weight, from its beginning as a tiny cell until it is full-grown. This growth period includes about the first twenty-five years of life. At certain periods the rate of growth is more rapid than at others. The infant doubles his weight at six months and trebles it at twelve months. At two years he is said to be one-half as tall as he will be when he is grown up. Food is needed for this increase of body tissue and for the energy required for the growing.

The body must keep itself in repair and good condition throughout life. Even when one's growing is over, as is usually the case when one is twenty-five years old, there is still a need for repair and upkeep if the body is to be in good condition. So thoroughly, constantly, and easily is this work done that we are scarcely aware that it is going on. Certain foods are needed for this repair and upkeep just as they are for growth.

Food has another use in the body: that of regulating many of its activities, such as the building of blood and bone, the digestion of food, and the elimination of body wastes.

Food helps to protect the body and keep it in good condition. Certain foods aid in protecting against colds and other infections. Certain foods prevent the decay of teeth, others help keep the nervous system in good condition, and others prevent rickets. Good health is the body's best protection against disease. Good food is necessary for good health.

Food may also give us pleasure and enjoyment. Then in addition to meeting our body's needs, the eating of food together may add to the satisfaction of our everyday living.

Activities:

1. Write a paragraph explaining to a fifth- or sixth-grader why our body needs food.
2. With what could you compare our need of food?

Problem 3: WHAT FOODS MEET THE BODY'S NEEDS?

Already we have found that our body has certain food needs. Now we wish to know what foods we should eat to meet these needs. We turn to the foods used by man the world over and find the list so long and varied that the study of the value of each separate food seems almost impossible. A grouping or classification that will list like with like makes the choice of the needed food easier.

In such grouping, there are few foods that belong in only

These foods are important in meeting body needs. How many of them can you name? How many of them do you include in your own meals?

one class. A food is placed in a group because it is especially rich in a given substance; thus it may be listed in more than one class.

A common grouping is based on the source of the food, such as *plant* and *animal*. These two main groups may be further divided, the plant foods into vegetables, cereals, and fruit; and the animal foods into meat, fish, milk, eggs, and cheese. Foods are also grouped according to their function as *go, grow, regulating,* and *protecting* foods. The scientific basis for this grouping is their composition and nature, such as carbohydrates, fats, proteins, minerals, vitamins, roughage and bulk, and water.

Because the body needs energy, the go foods must be supplied to it. The composition of a food determines its energy yielding or its go quality. Carbohydrates and fats are both high in this quality.

The building and repair of body tissue requires a different type of food than is needed for the production of energy. Foods that meet this need of the body are the grow foods, which include proteins and minerals. Protein supplies two of the body's food needs. Not only is it absolutely essential as a grow food for building and repairing of tissue, but it is also a source of energy. So important is the grow function that we generally consider protein as a body-building rather than a go food.

Certain minerals are needed for the body tissues. Important among these are calcium and phosphorus, needed especially for the building and maintenance of bones and teeth; iron for the blood; and iodine for the proper development of all the body tissues.

Foods high in the properties of regulation and protection are the minerals and vitamins. The minerals that are needed for body building and repair are also needed for body regulation and protection. The vitamins are extremely important in these functions. They protect against certain diseases, they stimulate growth, and they keep the tissues in good condition. The best known and probably the most important are vitamins A, B_1, C, D, and G.

The following list classifies the common foods according to their principal food values.

GO FOODS: *Carbohydrates*—Starches, potatoes, sweet potatoes, wheat, oats, corn, rice, barley
Fats—Butter, cream, lard, peanut oil, cottonseed oil, olive oil

GROW FOODS: *Proteins*—Cheese, meat, eggs, fish, chicken, milk

REGULATING FOODS: *Calcium*—Milk, cheese, dandelion and mustard greens, clams, molasses, celery, cabbage
Iron—Oysters, lean meat, beans (shelled, fresh, or dry), dandelion and mustard greens, egg yolk, liver
Phosphorus—Lean meat, milk, fish, beans (navy and Lima), liver, cheese, poultry
Iodine—seafoods, seaweeds

PROTECTING FOODS: *Vitamin A*—Fish liver oils, butter, cream, eggs, liver, yellow and green vegetables, apricots

Vitamin B_1—Yeast, whole grain cereals, beans, peas, pork, chicken, kidney, liver

Vitamin C—Citrus fruits, berries, cantaloupes, tomatoes, leaf and green vegetables, liver

Vitamin D—Fish liver oils, salmon and other oily fish, egg yolk

Vitamin G—Milk, cheese, eggs, lean meat, liver, kidney, heart, greens, beans, peas, wheat germ

Anti-pellagra Vitamin—Lean meat, chicken, liver, green and leaf vegetables, beans and peas (shelled, fresh, or dry)

Water, of course, is needed by the body for maintaining body tissues and for regulation. Though not always thought of as a food, no food is more important or essential than water.

The body requires a certain amount of roughage and bulk. These are the parts of the food that the body does not digest. Roughage and bulk are needed for regulation and stimulation of certain body processes and should not be omitted in the food of the normal person. Foods high in roughage and bulk are the leafy vegetables, whole grains and seeds, raw fruits, and potatoes with skins.

Activities:

1. Make an outline of the grouping of foods according to go, grow, regulating, and protecting foods. Include examples of each group.
2. How many of the groups of foods did you include in your yesterday's food?

Problem 4: WHAT FOODS SHALL WE EAT DAILY?

A person's food requirements should be considered in terms of her needs for the day. If we are to meet our needs properly, we must know what foods we should eat daily. Rules which guide us in wise choice of food will help us meet our daily needs.

All classes or groups of foods should be represented in the day's diet. Go, grow, regulating, and protecting foods should all be included in the food of the day. If we wished to use more scientific terms, we would say that carbohydrates, proteins, fats, minerals, and vitamins should all be included in our daily food. Whether the rule be stated in popular or scientific words matters little. The important thing is that the rule be observed.

Vegetables should be an important part of the day's food. They are especially valuable in furnishing minerals and vitamins. Some are rich in the go foods. The vegetables are often spoken of as starchy and green leafy vegetables. Starchy vegetables include potatoes, sweet potatoes, beets, and carrots. Green leafy vegetables include lettuce, cabbage, spinach, and endive. Vegetables of both types should be eaten each day.

Grain products are needed daily. These are the foods that are made from such grains as wheat, oats, corn, and rice. Wheat bread, cornbread, oatmeal, macaroni, and various "breakfast foods" are all made from grains. Some of these foods should be those that contain the whole grain, such as cracked wheat, rolled oats, and bread made from whole wheat flour.

Fruits should be an everyday food. We have a long list from which to choose. Apples, pears, oranges, bananas, plums, peaches, strawberries, and many more can be had in most places, either fresh or canned, throughout the year. The citrus fruits, which include oranges, lemons, and grapefruit, are especially important, for they are rich in vitamin C.

Meat should have a place in the day's diet. It is one of our best protein foods and hence is a grow or building food. Beef, pork, lamb, poultry, and fish are classed as meat, and any one may be used as the grow food in the diet.

Other valuable protein foods are eggs, cheese, and dried beans. Because they are high in protein and frequently take the place of meat in a meal, they are sometimes called meat substitutes. Eggs are so important that they should be included in the diet every day.

Milk is an essential food for everyone, young or old. The day's diet is not complete without it. Milk is a good source of the grow, protecting, and regulating foods. It contains calcium and phosphorus and several of the vitamins. Although milk is popular as a beverage, it is included in the diet in many other ways, such as in cream soup, gravy, ice cream, and custard.

Butter is important and is more widely used than any of the butter substitutes, even though it is somewhat higher in cost. However, when the money for food is limited, a good butter substitute may be used if plenty of green leafy vegetables and milk are included.

Seafoods, the most common of which is fish, are extremely valuable in the diet, not only for their protein or grow content especially, but for the mineral they contain. They are rich in iodine, an essential mineral that is sometimes lacking in our diet. The rule of including a seafood in the diet once each week is a good one, both for the sake of health and for variety.

Water is a necessity. It should be taken at mealtimes and between meals. Our food, of course, contains some water, but not enough to meet the body's needs. We should regard water as an important food that should be taken just as regularly as any other essential food.

A certain amount of roughage and bulk is needed in our day's food. Therefore, we should choose some food each day that furnishes these. Green leafy vegetables, fruits, and whole grains are high in roughage and bulk.

The foods that we eat daily should include vegetables, grain products, fruit, meat, eggs, milk, butter, and water.

Activities:

1. Check your yesterday's food to see if you included all the essential foods. What ones were omitted? Would this be true of your other days' meals?

2. Why should we try to include all the essential foods in our day's meals?

Problem 5: HOW MUCH FOOD DO WE EACH NEED DAILY?

The amount of food we need daily is quite as important as the kind of food. However, it is difficult to state exactly "how much" food, for we all differ. Some of us are old and others are young; some of us are small, others are large; some of us like to sit and read, others enjoy swimming and hiking; some of us live in Florida, and others in the North. The day may be warm and sticky, or it may be cold and snappy. All these things affect our food needs.

We need enough food to care properly for all the body's activities. Though starches, sugars, and fats are highest in go or energy value, practically all foods have some of this quality. Therefore, our go or energy needs are not met entirely from foods high in starches, sugars, and fats. Grow, regulating, and protecting foods, too, have a share in meeting these needs. Adequate provision for go or energy foods will be made if the following foods are included:

1. Grow, regulating, and protecting foods in the right amounts daily.

2. Bread, two or more slices at each meal.
3. Butter, one or two pats at each meal.
4. Cereal at least once daily.
5. One potato daily.
6. Moderate amounts of sugars and fats used in the cooking and serving of various foods.

We need enough of the grow foods. If we are still adding to our stature and building body tissue we need grow, or protein, and mineral foods. Also, these same foods are needed to maintain the body tissues already built. It is estimated that our need for protein foods will be well met if we include daily one quart of milk, one egg, and one serving of either meat, poultry, or fish. If these foods cannot all be had in these exact quantities, each food should be represented, and the amount of one or more increased if others are decreased. If, in addition, whole grain products, vegetables, fruits, and butter are included in generous amounts, the need for minerals will be met, as well as the need for other protecting and regulating foods.

The following guide will help us choose the amount and kind of food needed each day:

1. *Milk:* One quart.
2. *Fruit:* Twice daily. Canned, dried or stewed, with one fresh fruit, preferably citrus or tomato. (Tomato may be canned or fresh.)
3. *Vegetables:* Two, other than potato. At least one should be of the green leaf variety. One should be raw.
4. *Grain products:* At least twice daily. Whole grains are desirable frequently.
5. *Meat, poultry, or fish:* One of these each day.
6. *Egg:* One daily.
7. *Butter:* Moderate amounts at each meal.
8. *Water:* At least six glasses daily.

9. *Other foods:* Bread, cereals, and moderate amounts of sweets and fats, enough to satisfy the appetite and keep the body in good condition.

Providing the body with sufficient food for its daily needs is important. Eating too little food presents a dangerous health hazard. If continued for a long time, one may become underweight and lack resistance to disease. Tissues may lose some of their important substances. Under such conditions, one cannot do her best. There are ways of knowing whether or not we are eating enough. A continued feeling of exhaustion although we are not exerting ourselves greatly is a sign that our food is not adequate. Loss of or failure to gain in weight, sallow-colored skin, dull and brittle hair, and poor appetite are other signs of improper diet.

Boys and girls who are still growing are more apt to eat too little food than too much. The body requires a large amount of food for obtaining energy, for building tissue, and for maintaining itself. It is better to be on the safe side and eat a little more than is needed than to eat too little.

Eating too much food may be harmful also. If more food is eaten than the body actually needs it is stored in the body as fat. We do need a certain amount of fat distributed throughout the body, but not too much. Some of our organs, the heart, for example, are greatly hindered in their work when surrounded by too much fat. The foods most likely to cause an excess storage of fat are the starches, sugars, and fats. Candy and sweets of all kinds, whipped cream, and rich pastries belong in these groups. If too much food is being eaten each day, it can be readily told by a needless increase in weight. Pimples, acne, and other skin eruptions often indicate the eating of much rich food.

Activities:

1. What word is used to describe a meal that contains the right kind and amount of food?
2. How nearly did your yesterday's food meet the standards for amounts of the essential foods?
3. How would you decide that you were not eating enough food, or that you were eating too much food?

Problem 6: WHY SHOULD WE EAT A WIDE VARIETY OF FOOD?

There are many people everywhere who eat the same foods day after day with little change. They "must have" meat and potatoes, pie, fried eggs, or certain other foods. When the "must have" is one of the daily essential foods the situation is not wholly bad, but it lessens the possibility of an adequate diet. Even the foods in one class, such as vegetables, are not exactly alike in what they contain. One food contains more iron, another more calcium, and another more vitamin A. For this reason variety is desirable to make sure that the body's food needs are adequately met. When the "must have" is not an essential food, the situation is much worse, for the essential foods may be crowded out entirely. Eating a variety of foods makes it much easier to obtain the foods needed by the body.

Satisfactory meals are more easily planned when people enjoy a variety of foods. It is much easier for the one in charge of planning meals to do a good job if she appreciates variety and if the family members like many foods. Satisfactory meals are almost impossible to plan if the family members will eat only those foods which are low or lacking in some essential. A certain schoolgirl eats only these foods: potatoes, bread, cheese, oranges, butter, green beans, and ice cream. With this small variety her diet cannot be satisfactory. Much pleasure comes from planning meals with different foods. There is fun, too, in going to a meal knowing that it will not be quite like the last meal nor like one yesterday.

The old saying that variety is the spice of life may well be applied to our meals. The same foods day after day with little or no change tend to become tiresome and uninteresting. A high school girl, upon her return from camp, was asked about the food. "It was not exactly bad," she said, "but I was so tired of the same plain boiled potatoes, roast beef, and cornstarch pudding that I don't want to see them for a long time."

The use of a variety of foods helps make our meals attractive. One food may add color, another flavor, and still another texture. If a person will eat only plain boiled potatoes, the fine flavor of one baked golden brown will never be known. If carrots are on the black list, their cheery and inviting color and their pleasing crispness will never be enjoyed. Not all our foods are attractive in themselves. Sometimes they are made so by combining them with other foods.

The person who likes a wide variety of foods finds it much easier to adjust when away from home. One with a limited food list rarely, if ever, finds another whose taste is like hers. Because she cannot find a place where her especially desired foods can be obtained, she usually has a hard time. Mary Alice, a rather spoiled and indulged high school girl, seldom has an invitation out for meals. She eats so few foods that all she can do is sit and stare as others eat. When on a trip she is "just miserable" because "her foods" are not always on the menus. Instead of having fun trying the new and different foods that might be served to her, she is unhappy and others are too. By the use of the "don't care for any" behavior she spoils the pleasure of all.

Knowing and using many foods not only adds to our pleasure, but to our education. Eating foods that are eaten by people in other regions and countries increases our interest and knowledge of their life. One of the valuable experiences in travel is becoming acquainted with the foods of other people. Each country and often regions and localities have some delightful food peculiar to them.

We in this country are eating a wider range of food all the time. Our remarkable transportation service has had much to do with this and our increased knowledge of nutrition has helped, too.

Activities:

1. How nearly are your meals alike day after day?
2. Are there any foods that you must have for every meal? Write these down. Are they essential foods? Are there other foods that could be substituted for these?
3. Try eating and liking a new food during the next two weeks. Report your experience to the class.
4. Describe some food that is common in another region or country. Would it be a good dish for us to serve occasionally? Why?

Problem 7: WHAT IS OUR DAILY MEAL PATTERN?

In the days long ago, when man hunted, fished, and gathered wild game and fruits for his food, his meal pattern was one that boys and girls today would not enjoy. When hunting was good or when the fish bit well, he feasted; when the hunting was not good and other food was scarce, he fasted. "Today a feast; tomorrow, and perhaps for many days following, a famine," made up his life. "The tightening of the belt," a practice used then to deaden the feeling of hunger, remains still a way of saying that the food supply is short. When man began to tame wild animals and grow grain, he began to gain control of his food supply. Meat was dried, grains were harvested and stored, and man turned from irregular gorging at the kill to a more regular plan for his eating. The meal became a daily event, and later a twice-a-day event. In some lands today two meals a day remains the food pattern, in others as many as six meals are served. In our country the pattern of three meals daily is generally followed, except for young children, aged persons, and those who are ill. Their needs require a pattern of five or more meals a day.

We have already learned rules to guide us in the choice of adequate daily food. The importance of variety, too, has been emphasized. Now we will consider the day's food in terms of the three meals: breakfast, luncheon or supper, and dinner.

The day's food should be divided rather equally between the three meals. A good plan to follow is to eat about one-third of the day's food or slightly less at breakfast, one-third at luncheon or supper, and one-third or slightly more at dinner. Though we judge whether our food is adequate in terms of the whole day's supply, we should have the essential foods well represented in each meal. Many years ago, a good meal was described as one that would "give the body something that would stick to the ribs, stay the stomach, give power to go on, and be pleasant to eat." In a homely way, this states that each meal should include a fair share of the essential foods and should provide pleasure by its variety and appeal to the appetite.

Probably the most frequently broken of these rules is the one concerning the amount of food that we should eat for breakfast. A meal of an orange and a glass of milk is far from being equal to one of soup, steak, potatoes, gravy, string beans, fruit salad, bread and butter, and chocolate pudding. The difference is so great as to be serious. A bowl of cereal, an egg, and a slice or two of buttered toast are necessary to bring this light breakfast into balance with the heavy meal.

A division of the day's food into three fairly even-sized meals is given in the following list:

Breakfast	*Luncheon*	*Dinner*
Fruit	Protein dish or meat substitute	Meat
Cereal	Two vegetables	Two vegetables
Egg	Bread and butter	Bread and butter
Bread and butter	Milk	Milk
Milk	Dessert or fruit	Dessert or fruit

Other foods, such as soup, relishes, and sweets, are added as desired and needed. The rules on the amount and kind of food needed daily should, of course, be followed. For example, the vegetables should include one of the green leaf variety and one raw.

You notice that no provision is made for eating between meals or "piecing." Except for drinking a glass of milk or eating fruit when really needed, eating between meals is regarded as an undesirable addition to the meal pattern.

Activities:

How shall we judge the following days' meals for schoolgirls in regard to the division of the day's meals and the rules for the day's foods?

Menu 1

Breakfast

Orange juice ...... 1 *tumbler*
Buttered toast ..... 1 *slice*

Luncheon

Scalloped macaroni and cheese . 2 *servings*
Creamed potatoes .... 1 *serving*
Bread ....2 *slices*
Butter ....1 *pat*
Jelly ....1 *tablespoon*
Chocolate pudding ....1 *cup*
Milk ....1 *tumbler*

Dinner

Swiss steak . . . 1 *serving*
Mashed potatoes . . . . 1 *cup*
Buttered green beans . 1 *cup*
Banana salad . ½ *banana*
1 *lettuce leaf*
Bread . . . . 2 *slices*
Butter . . . . 1 *pat*
Canned blackberries . . . . . ½ *cup*

Menu 2

Breakfast

Baked apple 1
Oatmeal . . . . ¾ *cup*
and thin cream . . ¼ *cup*
Soft cooked egg . . . 1
Buttered toast . . . . 1 *slice*
Milk . . . . 1 *tumbler*

Luncheon

Hamburger sandwich 1
Chocolate bar 1

Dinner

Clear meat soup . ½ *cup*
Roast beef . . . . . . 2 *thin slices*
Gravy . . . . ½ *cup*
Steamed rice . . . . ½ *cup*
Head lettuce salad . . . . ¼ *head*
Rolls 2
Butter . . . . 1 *pat*
Pineapple slices . 2

Menu 3

Breakfast

Orange . . . . ½
Cornflakes . . . . ½ *cup*
and thin cream . . . ¼ *cup*
Scrambled egg 1
Whole wheat bread . . 2 *slices*
Butter . . . . 1 *pat*
Milk . . . . 1 *cup*

Menu 3—*Continued*

Luncheon

Baked beans ...	1 *cup*	Butter	1 *pat*
Combination vegetable salad	1 *cup* 1 *large lettuce leaf*	Cherry preserves	1 *tablespoon*
Bran muffins ...	2	Raspberry gelatine	⅔ *cup*

Dinner

Breaded veal chops ..	1
Buttered cabbage	¾ *cup*
Wilted spinach	1 *cup*
Bread	2 *slices*
Butter	1 *pat*
Apricot sherbet	⅔ *cup*
Vanilla wafers	2

Problem 8: HOW SHALL WE JUDGE OUR MEALS?

Any discussion about food and meals soon turns our thoughts to our own food. We are always interested in seeing how nearly the food we have eaten meets the established standards. This can be done by rating our food for the past day on a score card prepared for this purpose. A common way is to judge our daily meals in relation to the essential foods. A score card for this purpose is suggested on page 47.

In preparing to find your own score, list the food eaten at each meal and between meals during the day before, considering the following amounts as servings:

½ cup raw or cooked vegetable
1 whole orange, apple, peach, or banana
½ grapefruit
4–5 prunes
⅓ cup tomato juice
½ cup cereal

	CREDITS	SCORE
Milk: 4 cups whole milk or 4 cups skimmed milk plus 1½ tablespoons butter (1 cup of either—4 credits) Count also milk in cooked food.	15	
Vegetables: At least twice, other than potato 1 green leafy, or yellow 1 raw	 5 5 5	
Fruits: Twice or more (once—5 credits) Include orange, grapefruit, or tomato (fresh or canned).	 10 5	
Meat, fish, poultry, cheese, or dried legumes: Once	 10	
Eggs: One	 5	
Whole grain bread or cereal: Twice (once—5 credits)	 10	
Butter (in addition to above): 2 tablespoons	 10	
Water or other fluid: 8 glasses (6 glasses—5 credits)	 10	
No food between meals except fruit or milk	10	
TOTAL	100	
Deduct: 10 credits if you ate no breakfast 10 credits if you drank more than 1 cup of tea or coffee, or more than 1 "cola" drink		
CORRECTED SCORE		

Rating of day's meals: Good ____. Fair ____. Unsatisfactory ____.

This may take a little time, but we should do our best to recall everything and to make the list complete and accurate. When this is done we should estimate as correctly as possible the amount of each food eaten, such as 3 slices of bread, ½ cup of gravy, 1 orange, and ½ cup of cereal. A better way is to plan our food record for one day and list the foods and their amounts as we finish eating them.

The foods and their amounts should then be rated by means of the score card. If the score is high, between 85 and 100 with no zero for any point, the day's meals are good. If the score is average, between 75 and 85, the day's meals are fair; if the score is low, 75 or below, the day's meals are unsatisfactory.

After the rating is done, a study should be made of the results. Both the strong points and weak points should be noted. Suggestions for improving the day's meals should be made.

Activities:

On this page and the next two pages are the reports of the meals of four schoolgirls for one day. What is their rating by our score card?

Menu 1

Breakfast

Cream of wheat and dates .... 1 *cup*
and thin cream .... ¼ *cup*
Bacon and eggs . 1 *slice bacon*
1 *egg*
Bread .... 2 *slices*
Butter .... 1 *pat*
Plum butter ... 1 *tablespoon*
Cocoa (made with milk) .. 1 *cup*

Luncheon

Lemon pie ......1 *large piece*
Milk ....1 *tumbler*

Mid-afternoon

"Cola" drink 1
Peanut bar 1

Dinner

Salmon loaf	1 *serving*
Breaded tomatoes ..	1 *cup*
Buttered peas and carrots	⅔ *cup*
Rhubarb sauce	½ *cup*
Coffee	1 *cup*

Menu 2

Breakfast

Dried peaches ..	½ *cup*
and puffed rice	⅓ *cup*
with thin cream	¼ *cup*
Milk toast	2 *slices bread* 1 *cup milk* 2 *pats butter*

Luncheon

Cream of pea soup ...	1 *cup*
Crackers	2
Bread-and-butter sandwiches	2 *large*
Fruit salad	1 *cup*
Baked potato	1
Butter	1 *pat*
Rice pudding	½ *cup*

Dinner

Fried chicken	2 *pieces*
Gravy (milk)	1 *cup*
Mashed potato	½ *cup*
Buttered carrots	½ *cup*
Shredded cabbage salad	¾ *cup*
Bread	2 *slices*
Fresh strawberries ...	¾ *cup*
and thin cream	⅛ *cup*

Menu 3

Breakfast

Buttered toast ..	1 *slice*
Coffee	2 *cups*
and cream ...	2 *tablespoons*

Luncheon

"Hot dog" sandwiches	2
"Cola" drink	1

Dinner

Fried ham	1 *large slice*
Fried potatoes ...	1 *cup*
Sliced tomatoes ..	4 *slices*
Hot biscuits	3
Butter	2 *pats*
Orange marmalade	1 *tablespoon*
Apple pie	1 *large piece*
Tea	1 *cup*

Menu 4

Breakfast		*Luncheon*	
Orange slices	1 *orange*	Cottage cheese	⅔ *cup*
Whole wheat mush	½ *cup*	Baked potato	1 *medium*
and thin cream .	¼ *cup*	Butter	1 *pat*
Poached egg	1	Tomato, lettuce, and cucumber salad	1 *cup*
on toast	1 *slice*	Whole wheat rolls	2
Milk	1 *tumbler*	Butter	1 *pat*
		Canned cherries ...	½ *cup*
		Oatmeal cookies ..	1

Dinner	
Roast pork	1 *slice*
Gravy (milk)	½ *cup*
Baked sweet potato	1 *medium*
Mashed turnips ...	½ *cup*
Apple sauce	¼ *cup*
Bread	1 *slice*
Butter	1 *pat*
Grapefruit and pineapple salad	¾ *cup*
Devil's food cake ..	1 *serving*

Problem 9: WHAT FOOD HABITS SHALL WE FORM?

One of the best ways to secure good health for ourselves is through the forming of good food habits. Once we have established good food habits we do not have to think every time whether we will eat this vegetable, drink this glass of milk, or include citrus fruit in the meals of the day. We eat these foods as a matter of course every day.

The earlier we can form good food habits the better it is for us. We are not as yet influenced by foolish notions or wrong ideas. The time required for forming or breaking a habit is much less when we are young. Thoughtful parents today begin building good food habits in their children's babyhood and continue with this on through the preschool years into those that follow. Children whose food habits are thus started are usually in good health. They are fortunate in having few, if any, bad food habits to be broken in later years.

What are some good food habits that we should form? Probably the most important ones are these:

1. The habit of washing hands and face thoroughly in preparation for eating.
2. The habit of eating three regular meals a day.
3. The habit of going to the table in a happy and relaxed frame of mind.
4. The habit of not hurrying in the eating of food.
5. The habit of thoroughly chewing all solid food, never bolting food or swallowing it hurriedly.
6. The habit of eating food as served, without evidences of food prejudices or food fancies.
7. The habit of not eating between meals.
8. The habit of drinking plenty of water.
9. The habit of including each day the needed amounts of essential foods, such as milk, raw vegetables, and citrus fruits.
10. The habit of eating candy and sweets only at the close of a meal.

We should always keep in mind that all the food groups should be represented in the day's diet, and the right amount of each should be eaten. One quart of milk should be consumed daily. It is very difficult to secure the needed calcium and phosphorus when the amount of milk used is low. A wide variety of food should be eaten. One should try all the time to increase the number of foods eaten. No between-meal piecing should be done. When food is necessary between meals, milk or orange juice should be taken. Candy and other sweets should be eaten only at mealtime.

Drinking plenty of water each day is most important. This should be done both at mealtime and between meals. Water aids in the digestion of our food as well as in the other body processes.

There are other habits that affect our health which, though not strictly food habits, are closely related to them. These habits, too, should be formed early and continued throughout life. The body should have sufficient sleep and rest to keep it in good running condition. Though individuals vary somewhat in their need for sleep, it is known that boys and girls between the ages of ten and fifteen require about nine hours of sleep daily.

> When we start to form a habit, we should want to do it very much. Then we should work out a plan for forming the habit. We should practice and practice until the habit is a part of us, permitting no exceptions as we are practicing. When this is done, almost before we know it the habit is formed.

Some time for rest should also be allowed during each day. The amount depends upon the individual and the conditions under which he lives and works. Short rest periods after meals are recommended, and in some cases a similar period before meals. If one can completely relax at these times, the rest will be much more effective.

The habit of taking plenty of exercise and fresh air is important. An hour of recreation each day which includes exercise in the open is highly recommended. Some suggest this in the afternoon following school. Others would have it after the evening meal. Working and sleeping in a well-ventilated room also contribute to health.

Keeping the body clean is a desirable habit to form. It makes for our own comfort as well as that of others, and contributes to our general health.

A person's habits are influenced greatly by the family's

habits. The forming of good habits is much easier when everyone around us is interested in forming good habits, too. For this reason, we can say that good food habits are a family matter.

Activities:

1. Decide upon the food habit that you need most to form.
2. Make a plan for forming this habit.

REFERENCES FOR THE UNIT

Calvert, Maude Richman, *The New First Course in Homemaking.* Atlanta: Turner Smith Co., 1932.

Friend, Mata Roman, and Shultz, Hazel, *Junior Home Economics: Food.* New York: D. Appleton-Century Co., 1933.

Jensen, Milton B., Jensen, Mildred R., and Ziller, M. Louisa, *Fundamentals of Home Economics.* New York: The Macmillan Co., 1935.

Kinyon, Kate W., and Hopkins, L. Thomas, *Junior Foods,* Revised Edition. New York: Benj. H. Sanborn and Co., 1938.

Matthews, Mary Lockwood, *The New Elementary Home Economics.* Boston: Little, Brown and Co., 1937.

Talbot, Nora, and Others, *Practical Problems in Home Life for Boys and Girls.* New York: American Book Co., 1936.

Trilling, Mabel, Williams, Florence, and Reeves, Grace G., *Problems in Home Economics.* Chicago: J. B. Lippincott Co., 1939.

SUGGESTED HOME EXPERIENCES

1. Develop the food habit for which you made the plan in class.
2. Develop other needed food habits.
3. Encourage other members of your family to improve their food habits.
4. Help in planning the daily food for your family so that the essential foods are included in the right amounts.

UNIT

3

USING THE SEWING MACHINE

THE CHILDREN OF COLONIAL DAYS watched with wide-eyed interest Indian squaws sewing soft leather into shirts and moccasins. For thread, the Indians used the cords that hold the muscles of an animal to the bone, and for their needle, a sharpened bone or horn. To the Puritan boys and girls this seemed a strange and awkward way of making clothing. Their mothers sewed all their clothes with fine steel needles threaded with linen thread which they had made by spinning. Many hours went into the labor of stitching seam after seam by hand. The young girls early shared in this work and no doubt were thankful that their equipment was so greatly improved over that of the Indian squaw and her daughter.

The girl of today would find little to be thankful for in such a situation. The invention of a usable sewing machine in 1846 by Elias Howe marked the beginning of a new and easy way of making seams. The use of the sewing machine is commonplace to the modern girl. With it she is able to stitch up a seam a yard long, securely and neatly, in a few minutes. If she had to sew that seam with the tools of the colonial maid or those of the Indian squaw, the task would take hours.

The modern sewing machine which has so greatly increased the ease and speed of such work is, of course, harder to understand than the simple equipment of earlier days. Just as the colonial girl mastered her tools, so the modern girl must master the sewing machine if she is to be skillful in the use of this labor-saving machine.

Problem 1: HOW CAN WE KNOW THE GENERAL PARTS OF THE SEWING MACHINE?

The most obvious part of the sewing machine is the frame and the cabinet which supports and protects it. The cabinet is made of wood, often beautifully finished. It may include two or more drawers for holding sewing essentials. Its shape has changed with the development of the sewing machine. In the sewing machines of a quarter of a century ago, the head of the machine was securely fastened to the cabinet. When not in use, the head was covered with a nicely finished box of the same wood as the cabinet. This afforded protection from dust and marring. Later, the machine with the flat top was invented. This is often spoken of as the drop-head machine, because of the way in which the head goes below the surface of the machine when it is not in use.

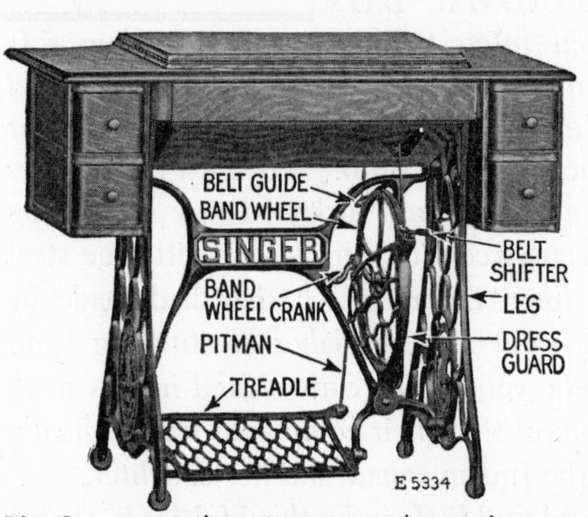

The first step in learning to use the sewing machine is to get acquainted with the general parts of the machine.

There are two types of the drop-head machine. In the one type, the head of the machine is lifted into place by merely raising the closing board and letting it down in the opposite direction flat with the surface of the machine. The belt and all working parts are then in position for the operation of the machine. In closing this machine, the closing board is raised and lowered in the opposite direction into position over the machine.

The other type of machine is opened by raising the closing board and lowering it in the opposite direction, but in this machine the front board must be raised with the left hand and the head raised to a position that slants back; while held in this position, the front board is lowered and the head is then allowed to come down and rest on the front board. The belt must then be placed in position on the large wheel which is on the right side below the surface of the machine. The machine is then ready for operation. In closing this machine, the belt must be released from the large wheel, the front board raised, the head lowered, and the closing board raised and then lowered in the opposite direction.

The parts of the sewing machine are delicately adjusted and should be thoroughly learned and understood in order to get the best results from the machine.

When the machine is uncovered or opened, one sees the metal *head,* comprised of the *arm* which contains many working parts and on which the thread is placed; the *bed* or flat base which is attached to the cabinet; and the *balance wheel.*

Below the cabinet, which holds the head, is the *treadle,* the platform on which the feet rest. It is set into a rocking motion when the machine is being operated.

To the right below the cabinet is the *band wheel,* which carries the belt that connects this wheel with the balance wheel on the head. The *belt shifter* is the lever at the front of the band wheel by which the belt may be thrown off this wheel.

A well-kept machine should be carefully wiped with a clean, soft cloth after it is opened and again before it is closed. A clean machine will not soil whatever we may be making and should be desired by everyone. Oiling the machine is important to keep it in good condition. Should oiling of machines be deemed a desirable class activity, instructions will be given by your teacher.

Activities:

1. Examine a sewing machine and see how many of its parts you know.
2. Practice opening and closing a machine until you can do it easily and well.
3. Locate the places on a machine which are to be oiled.

Problem 2: HOW SHALL WE TREADLE THE MACHINE?

The "whirr" of the sewing machine may be a pleasing sound if it is done smoothly and without sudden starts or stops. Smooth treadling is as essential to good sewing as smooth pedaling is to good bicycle riding. Those who ride a bicycle know that it takes much practice to pedal and ride a wheel skillfully.

In learning to treadle a sewing machine, one must be sure to seat oneself the correct distance from the machine, and to sit erect and well back in the chair, with the arms in an easy position when on the table of the machine. The chair should be of comfortable height; the feet should be flat on the treadle of the machine. The worker must determine the correct distance of the chair from the machine, as it varies with each individual. When the feet are placed on the treadle of the machine, the right foot should be placed toward the lower right-hand corner of the treadle and slightly below the left foot, which is placed toward the upper left-hand corner of the treadle. One should be sure that the feet are flat on the treadle, with the treadle being forced up and down in rhythmic motion by pressure first from the left foot and then from the right foot. When this position is established, the right hand should give the balance wheel (the small wheel on the right side of the head of the machine) a start toward the worker. This is done with the palm of the hand, bringing it from the top of the wheel and pulling down; this starts the machine, and the motion of the feet should keep the wheel in motion.

Practice is needed for skill in treadling. It is best to practice with the belt removed from the balance wheel. The belt is removed by holding the belt release in the right hand and pushing the balance wheel back; this in turn pulls the belt from the band wheel, and if the balance wheel is turned with the left hand, the belt will be completely released from the band wheel. In this way one may learn to treadle without danger of injury to the machine. Sudden starting and stopping will result in poor stitching and is harmful to the machine.

The electric sewing machine operates in the same general way as the hand machine. A book of specific directions is furnished with each machine and may be studied for a thorough understanding of its use.

Activities:

1. Find the correct distance for you to have your chair from the machine when sewing.
2. Practice treadling a machine, not threaded, until it goes easily and smoothly.
3. Practice starting and stopping the machine.

Problem 3: HOW SHALL WE PRACTICE STITCHING ON THE MACHINE?

Just as the colonial girl found much practice necessary before she could make small, even hand stitches, so the modern girl finds much practice necessary before she can stitch evenly and neatly on the machine. When properly seated at the open machine, we will make it ready for operation by seeing that the belt is connected with the balance wheel. For our practice stitching we will use an unthreaded needle and ruled paper. The paper is placed under the presser foot, with the needle coming down on the first ruled line. The presser foot is lowered, and the machine started and set in motion by treadling. The paper is guided with the hands so as to keep the line of stitching on the ruled line.

As the stitching nears the end of the paper, treadle slowly, and when the end is reached, place the palm of the right hand on the balance wheel, bringing the machine to a stop. If one is stitching a long seam and desires to stop before reaching the end, the machine may be stopped in the same way as described. Care should be taken that the machine does not go backward.

After the stitching has been stopped, the machine should be started slowly and any backward motion avoided. Similar care should be taken when turning a corner. In this case the machine is brought to a stop, the presser foot is raised, the material turned in position to continue stitching, the presser foot lowered, and the stitching continued.

Good sitting position at the sewing machine makes it possible to do satisfactory work; an incorrect position would give difficulty even to an experienced sewer.

In practice stitching, the machine should be set to have twelve stitches to one inch. Your teacher will help you adjust the machine for proper stitching, if adjustment is needed.

Activities:

1. Practice stitching on a piece of ruled paper until you feel you can stitch evenly on a line.
2. With the help of your teacher, adjust the length of the stitch until there are 8 to an inch, 10 to an inch, and 12 to an inch.

Problem 4: HOW SHALL WE WIND THE BOBBIN?

The first sewing machine had no bobbin; only one thread was used, which was placed on the top of the machine. Doll sewing machines of today have this type of construction. Regular sewing machines of the present time use two threads, one being on top and one being underneath the upper part of the head. The lower thread is wound on a piece of metal which is called the bobbin. Bobbins are of two types: rotary and oscillating. These are wound in a similar manner, but the differences are in the shape and in the movement while in operation.

In winding the bobbin, it is necessary to release the balance wheel, which is done by turning the large hand screw toward the worker. This permits the needle to remain motionless during the process of winding the bobbin. The empty bobbin is placed on the bobbin carrier, being carefully fitted on to the small projection extending out from the inner side of the carrier. The thread is wound around the bobbin a number of times or caught at the side of the bobbin as it is placed on the carrier. The spool from which the thread is to be taken is placed on the carrier on the top of the machine, with the thread coming over the thread guide. Treadling is then begun and continued until the desired amount of thread is wound on to the bobbin. Steady, smooth treadling results in a well-wound bobbin with even layers of thread. If the bobbin is wound unevenly, the thread may be broken during the sewing process, and not so much thread can be placed on the bobbin as if it were wound well. After the bobbin is wound, it is removed from the carrier, the thread is broken or cut, and the bobbin is ready to be placed in the machine.

Activities:

1. Examine the bobbin and the carrier until you understand how the bobbin fits on the carrier.
2. Wind the bobbin.

Problem 5: HOW SHALL WE THREAD THE MACHINE?

The properly threaded machine is necessary to good stitching, and should be carefully studied and understood by all who would use a sewing machine. A properly threaded machine will sew so that the stitching appears the same on each side.

Threading the upper part of the machine is best done in the following way:

1. Place the spool of thread on the spool pin.
2. Raise the thread take-up lever to the highest point.
3. Carry the thread across the thread guide down the arm to the tension.
4. Place the thread between the tension discs, going from right to left.
5. Place the thread under the take-up spring, then back and under the thread regulator.
6. Follow the arm down through the thread take-up lever, through the thread guide, and on through the needle. The thread goes through the needle from left to right.
7. Pull out at least four inches of thread from the needle.

Threading the lower part of the machine should be done in the following way:

1. Place the filled bobbin in the shuttle, if a shuttle is required.

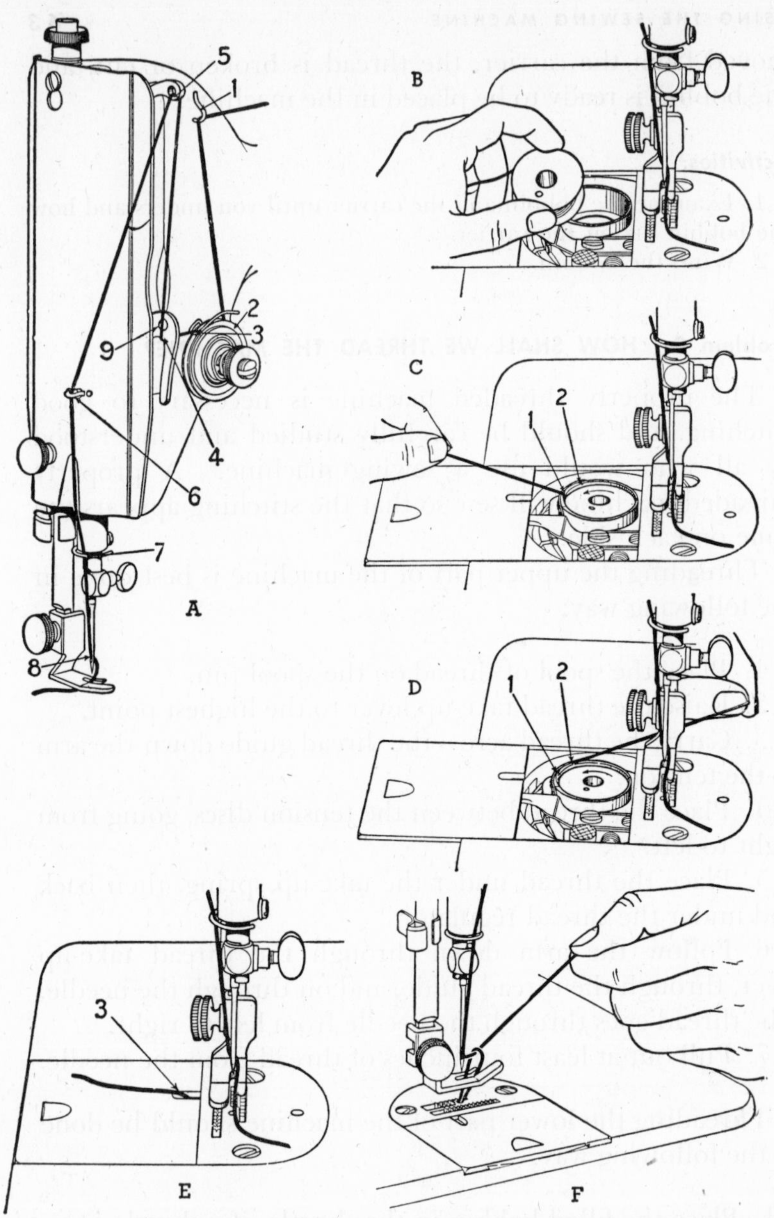

These diagrams show the threading of one type of lockstitch machine. Read the directions for threading a machine on pages 63 and 65.

2. Pull the thread through the slit in the shuttle and up to position place.

3. Place the filled bobbin in the bobbin case and pull the thread back through the slit and into place with at least four inches of the thread on top.

4. Close the bed slide, having the thread through the groove at the side.

In completing the threading of the machine, the balance wheel is turned and one stitch is taken to bring the lower thread to the top. Both threads are pulled to the back. It is a wise procedure to test the stitching on two thicknesses of material before stitching on our tea towel. If one has not become accustomed to stitching, it is always good practice to do some stitching on two thicknesses of waste material.

Activities:

1. Examine the machine until you recognize the path that the thread should follow.

2. Thread the machine.

Problem 6: HOW SHALL WE PREPARE A TEA TOWEL FOR HEMMING?

In making a tea towel we should choose material that is soft and will take up moisture. Some like to use flour or sugar sacks, while others prefer to use a loosely woven muslin, or cotton or linen toweling.

Many of you have seen your mother carefully straighten the edges of cloth in preparation to making some garment or household article. This is necessary if one wishes to have a neat product. The material for the towel may be straightened with the thread of the cloth. The easiest and quickest way is to pull a thread from each side that is to be hemmed, and then cut on the line where the thread was pulled. This will insure a towel with straight edges, easy to hem.

The hem is then made by turning the edge over between 1/8 inch and 1/4 inch and pressing it in place. Then another turn is made, 1/4 to 3/8 inch wide, and pressed in place. The hem should be kept as even as possible while turning, thus making the basting and hemming that will follow easier.

Activities:

1. Straighten the material for a tea towel.
2. Turn and pin a hem in the tea towel according to directions.

Problem 7: HOW SHALL WE BASTE IN THE HEM IN OUR TOWEL?

In earlier days, when hand sewing was a valued art, basting was but one important step in a series of hand processes. The other hand processes have been replaced by machine stitching, but the importance of basting still remains. Basting is done to hold the cloth in place until it is stitched. It should be done as carefully as possible. In this Problem we are going to baste the hem in our towel.

First we will thread the needle with a thread about sixteen or eighteen inches long. The thread is placed through the eye of the needle and pulled through one-third the length of the thread. With the thumb and first finger of the right hand, a knot is made in the end of the longest piece of the thread. In making the knot, the end of the thread is placed around the first finger and with the thumb holding the thread against the first finger, the end of the thread is brought over and under the thread, thus tying the knot.

The thimble, usually thought of by beginners as awkward to use, is a necessary piece of equipment for hand sewing. The thimble is placed on the third finger of the right hand.

It should be tight enough not to fall off while in use, yet loose enough to feel comfortable on the finger. One can learn to use the thimble well only by practice.

After the hem is pinned in place, the needle threaded, a knot tied, and the thimble placed on the finger, we are ready to baste the hem. Place the threaded needle in the material and push it through by means of the thimble. Thus a stitch is taken in the side to be hemmed. Holding the towel with the wrong side toward you and in such a position that you will baste from right to left, take basting stitches about 1/4 inch long and just far enough from the edge so you will be able to stitch between the basting and the edge of the hem. When each side of the towel has been basted, it is well to press the hems with a moderately hot iron, pressing on the wrong side without the use of water.

Activities:

1. Practice threading the needle and tying a knot in the thread.
2. Baste the hem in the tea towel.

Problem 8: HOW SHALL WE STITCH THE HEM IN OUR TOWEL?

Some people like to have the hems of their towels put in by hand, but this is neither necessary nor a practical procedure, especially for the busy person. Stitching a hem in neatly with the machine is wholly satisfactory. In doing this, the machine must be properly threaded. You will recall that four inches of both threads are pulled toward the back of the machine. The towel is placed under the presser foot and the needle is brought through the hem in such a position that the line of stitching will be just inside the edge of the hem. The presser foot is lowered, the machine is started in motion, and the hem is stitched the length of the side.

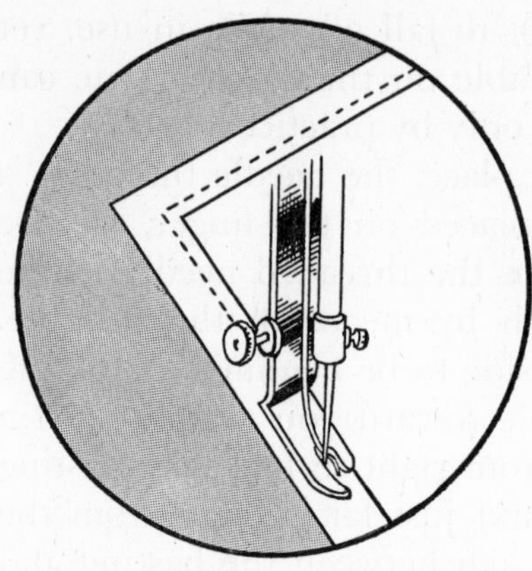

Good workmanship is shown by a straight edge and even stitching on the hem of the tea towel.

When this is finished and the presser foot is raised, the thread is cut about three inches from the hemmed end. In order not to unthread the needle, the thread should be pulled out six inches before cutting.

When the sides are hemmed, the threads at each end are tied, and the thread ends are then clipped. All basting threads are then removed.

Activities:

1. Wind the bobbin, thread the machine, and have threads pulled into place.
2. Stitch the hem in the tea towel.
3. Tie the thread ends and remove the bastings.

Problem 9: HOW SHALL WE PRESS AND FOLD OUR TEA TOWEL?

The neatly pressed and folded tea towel shows that careful work has been done. The first step in pressing is to dampen the towel with a wet cloth. Place the towel, right side down, smoothly on the ironing board with one edge near the edge of the board. Press on the wrong side with a moderately hot iron, then move the towel and press another portion. Continue this until all the towel has been pressed. Fold the towel in the middle with the wrong sides together and press the one side. Fold again and press both sides. The towel may be folded in any shape desired. Care should be taken that the corners and edges are even.

Activities:

1. Dampen and press the tea towel.
2. Fold and press the tea towel until you have the desired shape.
3. Figure the cost of your tea towel.

Problem 10: HOW SHALL WE PURCHASE MATERIAL FOR A PILLOWCASE?

The fabrics most commonly used for pillowcases are pillow tubing, muslin, and sheeting. All are made from cotton by the same method of fabric construction. Pillow tubing is woven in tube form and requires only a seam at one end and a hem at the other to make the pillowcase. Tubing comes in 36-, 40-, and 42-inch widths. The size of the pillow for which the case is being made determines which of these widths should be used. The width of tubing and pillows means the distance around. The tubing should be two inches wider than the pillow. The length of tubing needed for a case is estimated by measuring the length of the pillow and adding to that length an allowance of nine inches. This provides for the seam and a three-inch hem.

Muslin is slightly less expensive than tubing. It is woven flat, not tubular, in just one width, 36 inches. If a 36-inch pillowcase is wanted, the estimate for the muslin pillowcase is made in the same manner as that for a tubing case. To the length of the pillow is added a nine-inch allowance. With this material there will be an end and a side seam. If the case is being made for a 40-inch pillow, the width of the muslin must be used for the length of the case. The amount to be purchased is estimated by adding an allowance of three inches to the measurement of the width of the pillow.

Sheeting is not as commonly used as either muslin or tubing, but might be economical if odd-sized pillowcases are desired or if the width of the sheeting divides evenly into a given number of pillowcases.

Activities:

1. Examine some pillow tubing and muslin to see if you can determine any difference.
2. Determine the amount of material you will need for a pair of pillowcases.
3. Figure the cost of pillow tubing for a pair of pillowcases.
4. Figure the cost of muslin for a pair of pillowcases.

Problem 11: HOW SHALL WE PREPARE OUR MATERIAL FOR THE PILLOWCASE?

In preparing the material for making a pillowcase, the material must be straightened. A thread is pulled across one end, and from this line the proper length is measured and another thread is pulled. The material is then cut on the lines where the threads were pulled. This procedure is followed for cases made from muslin and tubing. When sheeting is used, it is necessary to pull and cut threads for both the length and the width of the case. When the proper size is obtained, the fabric should be pulled into the correct shape. It is a good practice to press the material free from all wrinkles.

Activities:

1. Straighten the ends of the material for a pillowcase.
2. Pull the material into the correct shape.
3. Measure the length of the material after the ends are straightened.

Problem 12: HOW SHALL WE MAKE THE SEAM IN OUR PILLOWCASE?

In making the pillowcase, tubing, muslin, or sheeting is used. Muslin and sheeting require both a side seam and an end seam, while tubing needs just the end seam. A desirable seam for the pillowcase, whether end or side, is the plain seam stitched twice. This type of seam is simple to make and is strong. For the beginner it gives good practice in stitching.

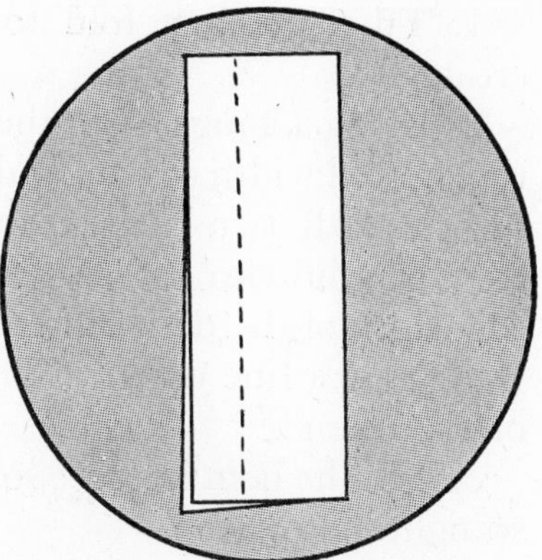

This shows a plain seam, ready to be stitched. The first line of machine stitching should follow closely the line of basting.

Making the plain seam is best done in the following way:

1. Fold the material in the proper shape with the right sides together.
2. Pin the edges in place with the pins at right angles to the edge and three or four inches apart.
3. Baste ½ inch from the edge with small basting stitches.
4. Remove the pins.
5. Stitch close to the basted line.
6. Stitch a parallel row, ¼ inch from the first stitching.
7. Remove the bastings and tie the threads.
8. Press the seam flat.

Activities:

1. Make the seam in the pillowcase.
2. Press the seam.

Problem 13: HOW SHALL WE HEM OUR PILLOWCASE?

The hem of a pillowcase may add to or take away from the appearance of the case. Generally the wide hem of three inches is regarded as desirable. The hem should be made carefully and accurately.

The procedure in making the pillowcase hem is as follows:

1. Turn the first fold to the wrong side 1/4 inch and crease.

2. Using a gauge, turn the second fold to the wrong side the desired width of hem and crease. (The gauge is a piece of stiff cardboard cut two inches longer than the width of the hem and two inches wide. Measure on the cardboard the width of the desired hem and cut a straight slit 3/4 inch in. Draw a line down to the end of the 3/4-inch slit. Cut on the line.)

3. Pin the hem in place so that the threads of the hem are straight.

4. Baste close to the edge of the fold.

5. Remove the pins.

6. Stitch on the edge of the first fold.

7. Remove the bastings and tie the threads.

The pillowcase is now ready to be pressed and folded.

Activities:

1. Try different widths of hems for the pillowcase and determine which one you like.
2. Make the hem in the pillowcase.
3. Remove the bastings and tie the thread ends.

Problem 14: HOW SHALL WE PRESS AND FOLD OUR PILLOWCASE?

Many of you have seen bed linens folded and carefully put away in a closet and have admired the orderly stacks of neatly folded articles. You would like the pillowcase just made to be ready to be placed in such a stack.

The same method of dampening will be used as that used when we pressed the tea towel. Our next step in pressing will be to press the hem on the wrong side, holding the pillowcase open as we press. With the hem pressed, place the edges of the hem together with the side seam straight, or the fold straight if tubing has been used.

Beginning at the closed end, press on the right side the entire length and width of the case. Then fold it in half, parallel to the hem, with the pressed side folded in. Press on the side of the closed end, then fold in thirds lengthwise, pressing each side as you fold. This is an easy and desirable way of folding pillowcases, although there are several other ways that may be used. The storage space for the pillowcases might determine the manner of folding them.

Activities:

1. Examine one of your mother's pillowcases and see how she has it folded. Do you like this method?
2. Choose a method of folding for your pillowcase.
3. Fold and press your pillowcase by the method chosen.

Problem 15: HOW SHALL WE JUDGE OUR PILLOWCASE?

There is always great satisfaction in knowing that a piece of work has been well done. Even though we may be just learning to sew, it is desirable to judge our work if we are to know how to improve it. Whatever we may make, there are certain items to be considered when we score the finished piece of work. The following score card is suggested:

Material 25
- Firm
- Soft
- Free from starch

Workmanship 55
- Seams on the straight of the material
- Stitching straight
- Second stitching parallel to first
- Straight hem
- Hem stitched evenly
- Neatly folded
- Well pressed
- Bastings removed

Cleanliness 20

Activities:

1. Examine several pillowcases and judge them according to your standards.
2. Score your pillowcase according to the score card made.

REFERENCES FOR THE UNIT

Donovan, Dulcie Godlove, *The Mode in Dress and Home.* Boston: Allyn and Bacon, 1935.

Jensen, Milton B., Jensen, Mildred R., and Ziller, M. Louisa, *Fundamentals of Home Economics.* New York: The Macmillan Co., 1935.

Matthews, Mary Lockwood, *The New Elementary Home Economics.* Boston: Little, Brown and Co., 1937.

Todd, Elizabeth, *Clothes for Girls.* Boston: Little, Brown and Co., 1935.

SUGGESTED HOME EXPERIENCES

1. Examine the machine you have at home. Is it the same kind as the one you use at school? How are the machines alike? How are they different?
2. Practice stitching on the machine at home with the needle unthreaded; stitch with the needle threaded and the bobbin wound.
3. Make several tea towels at home.
4. Make a pillowcase to match the one you made at school.
5. Plan and make a cover for your best dress.

UNIT

4

WHEN WE ARE AWAY FROM HOME

"AWAY FROM HOME" ON FIRST THOUGHT means to most of us a trip to some faraway city or town. At once we think of the many interesting hours that will be spent on the train, in a bus, or in a car, watching the scenery rapidly change as we are whisked along the road or highway to the end of our journey. Because there is so much excitement connected with our leaving and with all the things we do while gone, we forget about the daily comings and goings that take us away from home. When we go to the store we are out in the community away from home. When we stop at our chum's home we are in her home and away from ours. We go to school, to the library, and to church, and though the time spent there may be short, we are "away from home." When we attend a football game, cheering noisily for our side, or when we splash merrily in the city swimming pool, we are likewise away from home.

All of us spend much time away from home, often more than we realize. In this we differ greatly from the people of our grandparents' and great-grandparents' days. Very little of their time was spent away from home. If we were to stop and figure the amount of time we spend away from home, we might be surprised. As much as one-third or one-half of our time may be spent thus, even though we take no trips and see no strange land.

Problem 1: WHY IS OUR CONDUCT AWAY FROM HOME IMPORTANT?

In the hours when we are away from home we still remain persons who live, feel, think, and act. In doing this we so behave ourselves that we are said to have this or that sort of conduct. Because these hours away from home make up such a large part of our day, our conduct during them is important. When our conduct at home and away are the same, our habits become better established and are more completely a part of us.

A friendly greeting, a calm acceptance of a slight inconvenience, and an expression of concern over some accident to another all help fix these habits of thoughtfulness and courtesy that the home deserves. In this way our life at home and away from home are kept in harmony and made to strengthen each other in our personal living. If our conduct away from home is rude, harsh, and without consideration of others, quite the opposite of our conduct as a good family member, we are brought into war with ourselves by these conflicting habits. This may make it difficult, if not impossible, for us to be happy.

When we are at home, our families may show patience and an understanding of our little weaknesses. When we are away from home, we are expected to act our age. We are not mother's baby, but Sue Jones, age fourteen. Baby tricks do not appeal to others as they may to our family.

It is important to consider our conduct away from home because it helps us to see ourselves clearly. We are away from the family and the influence of the family's opinion. No longer can we depend upon what an aunt or a parent says we should do. We must make our own decisions and accept the results. Soon we learn that back of the Ten Commandments and the rules of living advocated at home there is much human experience. "Thou shalt not steal"

Much of the time boys and girls spend away from home goes into trips to and from school. A streetcar ride or a bus trip may be necessary, but usually some time is spent walking in the fresh air.

and "Thou shalt not covet" are not just words to be learned, but facts found true through thousands of years. Our belief concerning these and our ideas as to what is good conduct are tested by our life away from home.

Our conduct away from home determines somewhat the character of our friends. An old proverb states, "A man is known by the company he keeps." If we are rude, noisy, and bad-mannered, we will attract only those who are the same. We will repel those whom we might wish to make our friends.

We are ambassadors of good-will or ill-will for our families, whether we wish it or not. Praise and blame alike are attached to the family as well as to the person. Such statements as, "You can trust all of that family" or "The Smiths never pass on unkind words" are merely ways of expressing a family code. A member of the Smith family who took part in unkind gossip would do damage not only to the person discussed and to himself but also to the regard in which his entire family was held.

Impressions about people hold far longer than we often

realize. A rude act, thoughtlessly done, may persist in the minds of those who saw it long after the doer has forgotten it. Conduct should be such that if it is remembered, it shows our real selves favorably.

Activities:

1. Have you ever formed your opinion of a person by the way you saw her or him act away from home? Give the incident.
2. Was this opinion a correct judgment of the person?
3. Is it fair to judge a family by the way one member conducts herself away from home? Give reasons for your answer.

Problem 2: WHAT ARE OUR RESPONSIBILITIES AS GUESTS?

Knowing how to be a desirable guest is important to all of us. Guests have much to do with the success of the hospitality offered them. In every community there are certain persons who are always welcome guests. There are others of whom this is not true. There are many things that determine whether or not a guest is welcome.

The first responsibility of the guest comes upon the receipt of the invitation. Invitations should be answered at once or within a short time after they are received. Many hostesses are greatly disturbed because guests do not reply until nearly time for the party or dinner. We should never make it necessary for the hostess to inquire about our reply to an invitation. We should be reasonably sure of the nature of the function before accepting. Invitations from strangers and those to doubtful or unknown places should be declined.

The guest should fit in the group as easily as possible, whether it be made up of people younger than herself, older, or of the same age. The nature of the contacts to be made in each group may differ, but all will be enjoyed and be of value if we permit them to be. We should be courteous and polite to other guests. All of them may not be our close friends and perhaps we do not wish them to be. However, as guests, it is our duty to respect the friends of the hostess and to help her make the event a happy one.

The guest should try her best to enter into what has been planned, as long as the entertainment and the activities are desirable ones. To refuse to take part in the entertainment or to let the hostess know you are not pleased with what has been planned is rude and bad-mannered. If we cannot adjust to the group or situation happily, we had better excuse ourselves as graciously as possible and depart. If we find it difficult to adjust to groups made up of people other than our own friends, we should busy ourselves with the matter of "growing up." We cannot go through life with a closed circle of friends without doing great harm to ourselves.

Respect for the hostess should be shown at all times. Accepting an invitation means that we will be courteous and will show proper regard for the use of her home and furnishings. The mother of a thirteen-year-old daughter not long ago made this remark, "Mary Jane may have no more parties. Her guests are perfect 'ruffians.' They are the worst-mannered people I ever saw. They respect neither people nor property, and carry no responsibility as guests."

The dress of the guest should be suitable for the type of function, the group, and the locality. The guest places herself at an unnecessary disadvantage if she is dressed much differently from the other guests. To be the only one wearing a short street dress when other guests are dressed in long dinner gowns is just as embarrassing as it is to appear in an evening dress when other guests are in school clothes.

Guests should be prompt in arriving at a function. Teas, receptions, and other events for which a range of time is given should be attended during that period. Meals, parties, and other events set for a stated time should be attended at that time. There is no excuse for being late to one of these. Guests should also stay the full time at such events as meals and parties. Unless you are convinced that the hostess does not object when the reply to the invitation is made, you should decline if you must leave early.

Guests should assure the hostess that they have had a good time. This is done by both attitudes and words. Except at large receptions, the guest should speak to the hostess before leaving. A brief, well-worded, and courteous statement of her enjoyment and appreciation of the invitation should be made. Exaggerated praise and extreme flattery are not in good taste. The hostess may feel that they are not true, and they take away from instead of adding to her pleasure. The guest should conduct herself that her hostess will want to entertain her again.

Overnight, week-end, and longer visits require a written "thank-you" note. This is often called the "bread-and-butter" letter, and should be sent at once upon one's return home. It should never be overlooked or forgotten.

Activities:

1. A schoolgirl recently said this: "You can't pay any attention to the rules of etiquette at a party and still have a good time." Would you agree with her? Give reasons for your answer.
2. Plan what you would say to your hostess when leaving at the end of a party or a tea.
3. What is prompt arrival at a function?

Problem 3: HOW SHALL WE REPLY TO INVITATIONS?

Invitations that have been extended must be answered. (See page 351 for the correct form for extending invitations.) Everyone should know the correct way to do this. Replies to informal invitations are given orally or are written. Replies to semiformal ones are written, using specific names in the wording instead of "I," "you," or "we." Both oral and written replies should be worded in correct English. Written ones should be properly spelled and neatly written. Black ink and white or light-colored stationery should be used.

Informal invitations may be answered orally, either in person or by telephone, or they may be written. No matter which method is used, the reply should be courteous and friendly. Appreciation of the invitation should be expressed. The invitation given orally in person or by telephone receives an immediate answer, such as "Thank you, Mary; I shall be glad to have supper with you tomorrow," or "I am so sorry, but Mother and I are going to Aunt Jane's tomorrow evening."

Sometimes it is necessary to ask for a brief delay before giving the reply. When this is done, some reason should be given. A reply of this type then is in order: "May I give you an answer tomorrow morning? Mother and I have been considering going to the concert. I must see first if our plans can be changed."

In accepting an invitation orally, it is well to repeat the date, the time, and the place, especially when the invitation is given over the telephone. This affords a check on possible mistakes. One should always make a written note of the invitation unless the event occurs within the next few hours. It is so easy to forget, and all sorts of difficulties may arise.

Informal replies that are written should be cordial and friendly. These are examples of written informal replies:

Dear Ruth,

I am happy to accept the invitation to your party, Wednesday night at eight. I am looking forward to meeting your cousin Ann. I have heard so many pleasant things about her.

Sincerely yours,
Marybelle

Dear Helen,

I am sorry to tell you that I cannot spend the week end with you. Some friends from New England are coming for a visit and will

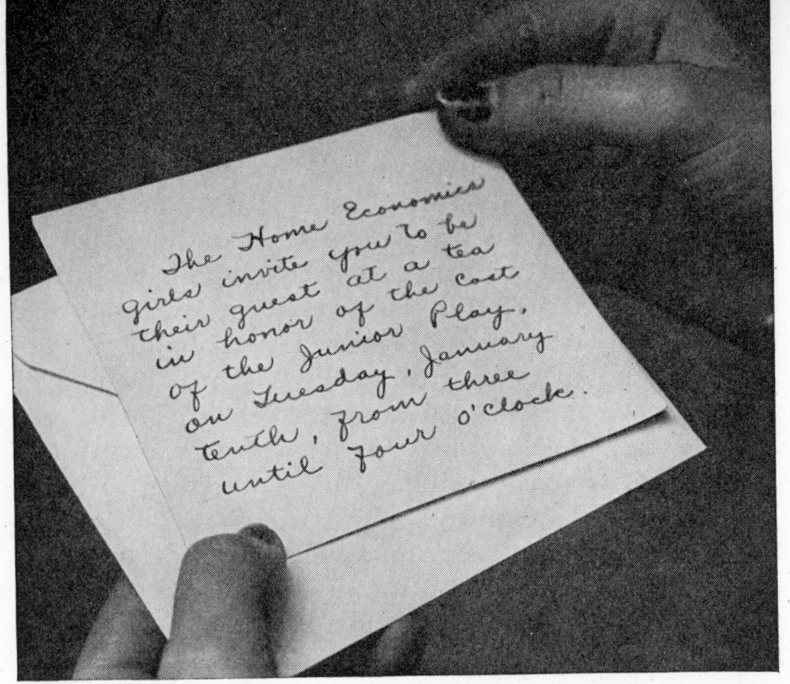

The invitation to a tea should be neatly written on stationery chosen for its good taste.

arrive during this time. My last visit in your home was so delightful that I feel cheated in not being able to come this time. I am thinking of what I will miss.

With regrets,
Betty

Dear Margaret,

I shall be pleased to have dinner with you Thursday evening. It will give me a grand opportunity to hear all about your trip. I hope you haven't forgotten a single detail.

Your friend,
Luella

The form and wording of the semiformal invitation suggest the form and wording of the reply. The third person is used, as in the invitation. However, friendliness and cordiality may be expressed even though the more intimate forms "you and I" are not used.

The two examples that follow illustrate the form and wording that may be used in a semiformal reply.

Miss Mary Moore
accepts the kind invitation
of Miss June Roberts for
Friday, January 6
8 P. M.

Mrs. John Greene regrets
that illness prevents her
acceptance of the kind invitation
of the Girl Reserves to their
Mother-Daughter dinner
Tuesday, March 10, 6:30 P. M.

A semiformal tea generally requires no reply other than attendance. Many guests, however, follow the thoughtful practice of informing the hostess if they cannot come. It helps her in making her plans, especially if the guest list is not large. When this is done, either a semiformal regret card is written, or a personal note is sent. Here is an example of the semiformal card of regret:

Miss Frances Hibbs

Regrets

Tea and Exhibit
Friday, March the first

The "thank-you" or "bread-and-butter" letter is longer than a reply to an invitation. It is always informal in nature because it is very personal. It should express sincere appreciation for the hospitality offered, as this one does.

Dear Jane,

I arrived home about six-thirty yesterday. Father met me at Burlington Junction and we had a pleasant ride home over the hill road. All the way I had much to share with him as I told him of the wonderful time I had in your home. He laughed and said that if the visit had been much longer, he might never have had his daughter back.

You had so many things planned. Everyone was most thoughtful of me. I thank you for everything. Now please do visit me soon. Give my regards to your Aunt Bell and your Uncle Will.

Sincerely yours,
Margaret

Extending an invitation is extending an honor. It should be so regarded by the person receiving it. An invitation should be accepted only when you can do so honestly and with appreciation. If this is impossible, a regret is far better in every way.

Activities:

1. State an acceptance that you would give orally in person to an invitation for a theater or line party.
2. State an acceptance that you would give over the telephone to an invitation to a picnic.
3. Write a reply to an informal invitation to a Sunday evening supper.
4. Write a reply to a semiformal invitation to an evening party.
5. Write a "bread-and-butter" letter to your hostess after a week's visit in her home.

Problem 4: HOW SHALL WE CONDUCT OURSELVES IN OTHER PEOPLE'S HOMES?

Our manners when we are in other people's homes should be an expression of our best selves. We should be courteous, polite, and thoughtful of others. This means that we should remember to use "Thank you" and "Please" frequently, and to observe such manners as rising when older persons come in the room, standing aside for them to pass, and waiting for others to go first. We should also avoid being loud or noisy, for this behavior is as out of place here as it is in our own homes. We should make our conduct such that no matter how short or how long the stay, our hostess will be pleased to have us again as a guest.

Courtesy and consideration should be shown all members of the family, even though we regard ourselves as the guest of only one member. If we are staying a day or more, it is well to give some time to each family member unless we have reason to think that this is not desired. Much as we may enjoy reading, we should not keep our nose in a book all the time. We should offer to assist with small home duties, such as setting and clearing the table, drying the dishes, and dusting a room or two. By all means, we should make our bed and keep our room in order.

Our clothing, rubbers, galoshes, shoes, coats, hats, as well as dresses and underwear, should be put in the proper places. Nothing is more disturbing than the disorder created by a careless guest who strews her things everywhere. All toilet articles should be kept in a neat and orderly condition. We should wash the tub and lavatory after each using, and hang the towel and washcloth in their proper places.

We should do our best to follow the customs and habits of the home. Seldom do any two families have exactly the same habits and customs. We should be at meals on time and accept the food pleasantly. We should come in at night at an hour agreeable to the family, and take part pleasantly in those activities approved by the family.

We should do nothing that would be considered snoopy. Trying to pry into other people's affairs is rude and never well received.

We should avoid helping ourselves to things unless definitely invited to do so by someone in authority. The guest who raids the refrigerator or pantry for food soon wears out her welcome, as does the one who helps herself to soap, perfume, and other toilet articles. Even less appreciated is the guest who raids clothes closets and wears other people's clothing. Using the stationery, postage stamps, and postcards of the hostess is another bad practice. Borrowing money of the hostess or her family members is never a good thing to do, no matter how small the amount. If such help is absolutely necessary, we should pay the debt promptly and express our appreciation of the kindness.

Visiting friends whose parents are away from home for even as much as two or three hours is not wise unless a chaperon has been provided. Many difficult situations have resulted when no responsible adult was present. If a proper chaperon is lacking, we should excuse ourselves and leave as soon as we can do so gracefully without making a scene or disturbance.

Activities:

1. Recall someone that you like to have call or visit in your home. Write the things that she does which make her a pleasing guest.
2. What are some habits and customs in your family that a guest would have to understand or follow?
3. List some things that a guest should avoid doing. What might be the results if she did do them?
4. Give an example of an unpleasant situation which might happen with a group of young people when in a home or other place with no chaperon or adult person present.

Problem 5: HOW SHALL WE CONDUCT OURSELVES AT SCHOOL?

The standard for our conduct at school should be the same as that for our conduct at home. This is much easier said than done. We come in contact with many people at school. They come from a variety of places and from many types of homes. Some are wealthy; some are not. Some homes emphasize desirable personal conduct, manners, and social forms; some do not. Because of these differences there is not the common sharing of standards which we have in a home. Some of the people must learn the accepted standards for conduct at school; others must maintain the standards of conduct they have; all must share in the life and conduct of the whole school group. Here individual and group conduct are both important.

The standards for our personal conduct should be high. A safe rule is to act at school as we would in our own homes, that is, if our standards of conduct at home are high. Regardless of what anyone else does, we should keep in mind that good manners are good manners no matter where we are. They should be observed in our contacts with our teachers and classmates. "Thank you" and "Please" and other expressions of natural courtesy are terms that should be used frequently at school just as they are at home.

Standards for group conduct are often more difficult to maintain than are those for personal conduct. People do not always behave the same in a group as they do as individuals. Sometimes the mob spirit asserts itself and then the standards that have been accepted by individuals are thrown aside. When this happens, the person acts more like a beast than a human being, and the conduct of the group becomes of the worst type.

The established rules and customs of the school should guide the individual and also the group. Many schools have adopted creeds and codes of conduct as standards and guides for the actions of their pupils. Does your school have such a code? Organizations, too, have codes. Two of the most widely known of these are the Girl Scout Laws and the Campfire Girls' Laws:

The Girl Scout Laws

1. A Girl Scout's honor is to be trusted.
2. A Girl Scout is loyal.
3. A Girl Scout's duty is to be useful and to help others.
4. A Girl Scout is a friend to all and a sister to every other Girl Scout.
5. A Girl Scout is courteous.

6. A Girl Scout is friendly to animals.
7. A Girl Scout obeys orders.
8. A Girl Scout is cheerful.
9. A Girl Scout is thrifty.
10. A Girl Scout is clean in thought, word, and deed.

The Campfire Girls' Laws

Seek Beauty.
Give Service.
Pursue Knowledge.
Be Trustworthy.
Hold On To Health.
Glorify Work.
Be Happy.

Being extremely loud and noisy should be avoided at school. Of course, school cannot be as quiet as the home because of the larger number of people. However, shouting and loud talking in the halls and classrooms are not in good taste.

Honesty is a fundamental trait for desirable conduct of all persons and groups. It should be expressed all the time. Cheating, the telling of false tales, and taking other people's things are familiar ways of being dishonest.

Whether a leader or a follower, our conduct at school is important to us. Of course a leader has more responsibility for group conduct than has a follower, but both are respon-

> Every pupil should respect school property and give proper care to it. The school belongs to the community and everyone has an interest in it. Therefore, we all should do our best to keep the building and equipment in the best of condition. The finest school buildings in the world have been built for the girls and boys of our country. We should show our appreciation by helping to keep them in excellent condition.

sible for their own individual conduct. To be remembered as a kindly, well-behaved, and well-mannered person at school who worked well with others is a worthy goal for us all.

Activities:

1. Write a code for the conduct of your class.
2. Make a list of "don'ts" for your conduct at school.
3. Name specific ways in which your conduct at school differs from your conduct at home.
4. Give examples of good conduct at school that you have seen in the past week; give examples of bad conduct.
5. What suggestions can you give to aid in having less undesirable conduct in the future?

Problem 6: HOW SHALL WE CONDUCT OURSELVES IN PUBLIC?

Our conduct at home and at school tends to be much the same each day. We know many of the contacts we will have and whether or not they will be pleasant. Of our public contacts we are not so sure, for they vary so much. This uncertainty may affect our conduct. We are somewhat outside the influence of our home and family, as well as that of our school and classmates. We must make decisions almost constantly in regard to our conduct.

The first person we meet may be a crippled old man; the next may be our father's business partner; then a toddler of uncertain step, pursued by his anxious mother, may cross our path.

A parade may pass, with the flag waving proudly and the band playing loudly. You may stop at the grocery store, at your mother's request, to return some purchase that was not satisfactory. You may take the streetcar or bus home and find in the rush hour that vacant seats are few. If you obtain one, you must soon decide whether to give it to an elderly woman or just look out of the window as she sways clutching the strap.

If in your trip downtown you go to a show, you must decide whether your pleasure in eating freshly buttered pop corn should prevail though you annoy those near you. You must decide whether your enjoyment in explaining in loud whispers what is happening on the screen is worth the disturbance it causes others. If in the rush your ticket was not collected, you must decide whether it is right to turn it in or to use it at a later show.

As you leave the show, you may be pushed or crowded by the milling crowd. You must decide whether you will elbow just as hard, speaking hatefully of the people about you, or whether you will be polite and refuse to add to the pushing and bad manners of the crowd.

It may be that a classmate calls to you loudly from across the street, attracting everyone's attention. You must decide whether you will respond in kind or merely wave a friendly greeting.

These descriptions indicate the wide variety of situations in which you may find yourself, even in the brief time of an hour or so. Your public conduct, then, is the sum total of all your responses to these and similar situations.

How you conduct yourself in public is important both because of its effect upon you and its effect upon others. If your public conduct shows self-respect, personal honesty, consideration of others and of accepted social customs, and regard for a given situation, it can well be called *good,* both for yourself and for others.

General rules for public conduct have been established. They vary with the function, place, and community. People should be quiet and give attention at church and at concerts; they should not keep others from enjoying the services and the musical programs. At football games much freedom is allowed. You are expected to cheer, shout, and have a more or less noisy time. We should know the rules for conduct and follow them without being a slave to them.

If we are not certain of the established custom, we should ask others who may know, or stand back and observe for a short time and then do as others are doing, or do as we would in a similar situation at home.

Activities:

1. Tell why this statement is true or untrue: "Good conduct in public means no fun."
2. Suggest for a schoolgirl some rules for her conduct at church; at a basketball game; at a movie theatre; at a lecture.
3. Describe briefly good conduct on a bus; at a school carnival; at a music recital; and at a Girl Reserve Convention.

Problem 7: WHAT SHALL WE DO WHEN EATING AWAY FROM HOME?

People in America eat away from home a great deal. Places to eat are found everywhere. They vary from the cheap to the costly, from the simple to the elaborate. Each has its particular way of doing things. Though some places are more formal than others, good manners should be used when eating away from home, regardless of the place or the informality of the meal. Good table manners and the accepted ways of eating should serve as a general guide at a picnic, or even at a lunch counter.

Dining in restaurants, cafés, tearooms, and hotel dining rooms is much the same. Tearooms and hotel dining rooms usually have more elaborate menus, service, and equipment, and the food is more expensive than in many other eating places. A printed or typed menu card is provided from which a choice of food is made. The food is usually grouped in menus for a complete meal to be served at a set price. Choices of meats, salad, and desserts are often permitted. In addition, a list of foods that can be prepared on order is often given. A meal selected on order is generally more expensive and less likely to be balanced.

These girls are putting into practice the correct restaurant etiquette that they have learned in class. The high school lunch room furnishes the setting. Members of the class serve as waitresses.

When we enter one of these places, a waitress or waiter seats us. We are then brought a menu card and our water glasses are filled. When we are ready to give our order it is taken, and soon the food is served. We may wait to choose our dessert until we are ready for it to be served. When we have finished our meal and the statement is brought, it is customary to tip the waitress, usually ten per cent of the price of the meal but never less than ten cents.

Cafeterias are popular food services in this country. They are cheap in price and the service is quick. The food is displayed on a counter from which it is served. We pass along this counter, carrying our tray and choosing the food desired. A checker gives us a slip indicating the price of the food we have selected. Our tray is carried to the dining table. As we leave we pay the cashier.

Lunch counters, drugstores, snack shops, and hamburger stands are food services that reach large numbers of people. The menus are quite limited, and in many cases the food is prepared after it is ordered. The service is simple, quick,

Dinner on the train is an enjoyable experience if we know the rules for the etiquette of traveling and dining. The menu card is planned to make ordering easy, the waiter is attentive and courteous, and there is charm and interest in the passing scene.

and very informal. The food service at these places usually consists of one food, or maybe two, sold at a low price. An adequate and balanced meal is often difficult to obtain in such places. Also, good table manners are not encouraged.

Many trains have convenient food services. Of these the dining car is the most formal. The meal is announced by a waiter going from car to car. If you wish to be served, you go to the dining car. The steward seats you and from then on the service is similar to that in a tearoom or hotel dining room. Instead of giving your selections verbally, you write them on an order card. Prices are likely to be much higher in a dining car than in other food services. Some trains have a buffet service. Menu cards are distributed, your order is taken, a table is set up at your seat, and the food is brought to you. A tip of ten per cent of the price of the meal, or more, is expected by the waiter. For example, if the price of the meal were ninety-five cents, you would tip the waiter ten cents or fifteen cents.

The food service on a ship is interesting. Eating is an

important part of the day's activities, as it gives you something to do. Much food is served and eaten. In addition to the three usual daily meals, bouillon is served about eleven o'clock in the morning, tea at four or five in the afternoon, and snacks at ten or eleven in the evening. The price of the ticket includes the cost of the food, as well as that of rooms and transportation. The tipping on a boat is done at the end of the trip rather than at each meal.

Picnicking is a favorite way of eating away from home. The great out-of-doors invites us to pack our food and take it away from home. A meal in the woods or on the open plains cannot be equaled for enjoyment. Like the picnic itself, the service of the food is most informal, too.

Meals in the homes of friends are greatly enjoyed by us all. As guests we should observe the social customs of the family and use our best table manners. In every way we should be pleasing and well-mannered guests.

Activities:

1. In what ways does eating away from home differ from eating at home?
2. Make a set of rules to observe when eating away from home. Does the place make any difference in the rules? How?
3. Select some place for eating, such as a restaurant, coffee shop, tearoom, dining car, or cafeteria. Outline the procedure you should follow in eating at this place.

Problem 8: HOW SHALL WE ACT WHEN TRAVELING?

We are great travelers in this country, going by automobiles, buses, railroads, and airplanes. These have all been made so comfortable, convenient, and attractive that traveling is a great pleasure. No matter what the mode of transportation, good manners should be shown by the traveler. She should not make herself conspicuous, and should avoid being loud, noisy, or rude.

The traveler should be as well poised as possible. Adequate information concerning the details of the trip help in this. Assurance that arrangements have been made for one to be met helps, as does plenty of money for any likely emergency, such as a delay over a meal hour or the need to take a taxi.

The traveler should plan to enjoy the trip. Her dress should be suitable and comfortable, with due regard to the weather and the mode of travel. If she is sensitive to variations in temperature, she may require a wrap to wear in air-conditioned trains, buses, and hotels. She should not demand services out of the ordinary, nor should she be complaining all the time. The traveler who is selfish and unreasonable spoils the trip for herself and annoys others.

Making the acquaintance of strangers when traveling is a bad practice. One may engage in a casual conversation with the person sitting next to her, but the discussion should not be personal, nor should a chance acquaintance go any further.

When traveling by car one should not require more than her fair share of the space for baggage. She should be willing to change places in the car, to eat at places selected by the group, and to make stops for rest as the others decide. Patience and a sense of humor are most important when traveling in a car.

The person traveling by bus should take the least possible amount of baggage, unless she is willing to check most of it. For a trip by bus a ticket is purchased, and when the bus is called the traveler takes her seat, making herself as comfortable as possible. On a long trip the bus makes occasional comfort stops for five or ten minutes, and stops of twenty or twenty-five minutes for meals. On long trips, pillows are sometimes provided. The back of the seat can be lowered to make one more comfortable in resting or sleeping. The porter or the bus driver should be asked to assist in this at a bus stop.

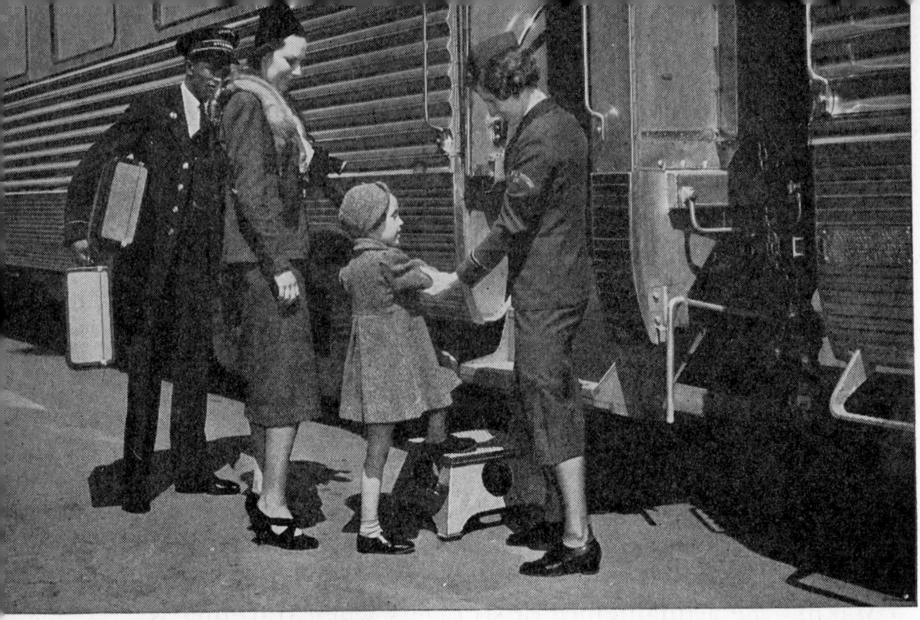

(Above) For all of us there is a thrill in traveling. This little girl and her mother are boarding one of the swift streamliners that are featured today on many railroads. The lady to the right is a stewardess, who sees that the coach passengers are comfortable during the trip. (Left) Thousands of families take week-end trips in automobiles, or spend vacations touring.

When traveling by train, the traveler should check all heavy and large pieces of baggage and carry only the pieces essential during the journey. The checking is done at the baggage room after the ticket is purchased. In cities, the services of a porter can be obtained to assist one in boarding the train and in carrying baggage from the train. A tip is given for this service, ten to fifteen cents for each bag or package the porter carries.

The traveler takes her seat after boarding the train and settles herself comfortably. If one is traveling in a Pullman or tourist sleeping car, the special Pullman or tourist ticket purchased in addition to the train ticket indicates the space one is to have. The traveler should plan something to oc-

(Above) Becoming more popular every year, air travel is also governed by rules of travel etiquette. Most air lines employ hostesses, such as the girl standing at the top of the steps; these girls make the trip pleasant and comfortable for the passengers. (Right) Bus lines cover the country and are popular with thousands of people who like this form of economical, safe transportation.

cupy the time on a long train trip so that she does not become too restless. Some travelers read, knit, or even play solitaire.

If the trip requires a night or more on the train, the traveler should plan to sleep as much as possible. In the chair car, the porter will adjust the back of the chair and furnish a pillow or two. In the winter time, a shawl or car robe to throw over one might well be carried.

If traveling in the Pullman or tourist sleeper, the traveler goes to the dressing room and makes ready for bed as soon as her berth is made up. She puts a dressing gown over her night clothes and bedroom slippers on her feet, collects her day garments and toilet articles, and comes to her berth.

She draws the curtains, buttons them securely, and turns out the light. In the morning after putting on her house slippers and dressing gown and gathering her day clothes and toilet articles, she goes to the dressing room and makes ready for the day. When she leaves the train, she gives to the porter of the sleeping car a tip of from 25 to 50 cents per day, according to the service he has rendered.

The lure of far horizons has attracted this girl to a cruise by boat. Well-poised and confident that she knows the etiquette of travel, she can count on having a good time with her fellow passengers.

On arrival at a hotel, a porter takes the bags and the traveler goes to the room desk and registers for a room. She may ask: "Do you have a quiet room with a shower on an upper floor? What are your prices?" When she is registered, a bellboy carries the bags to the room, checks the room and its equipment, and hands her the key. She tips the bellboy for this service. When she leaves the hotel, she tips him again for carrying her bags to the hotel entrance.

The superior tourist camp furnishes the traveler by automobile a most satisfactory place to spend the night. It is informal and not expensive. Many people prefer these camps to hotel rooms because there is no lobby through which one must pass in a disordered and soiled state; the service is simple; and one's departure is easily and quickly made. Though the services provided are much less than those in a hotel, one should be just as courteous and well-mannered in one place as in the other.

Activities:

1. Describe what you consider the correct dress when traveling on a train; on a bus; in an automobile.

2. Prepare a leaflet called, "Do's and Don'ts for Travelers."

3. Give some examples of desirable and undesirable actions of travelers.

REFERENCES FOR THE UNIT

Allen, Betty, and Briggs, Mitchell Pirie, *Behave Yourself!* Chicago: J. B. Lippincott Co., 1937.

Black, Kathleen, *Manners for Moderns.* Boston: Allyn and Bacon, 1938.

Clark, Mary E., and Quigley, Margery C., *Etiquette, Jr.* New York: Doubleday, Doran and Co., 1935.

Faculty of South Philadelphia High School for Girls, *Everyday Manners.* New York: The Macmillan Co., 1935.

Leaf, Munro, *Manners Can Be Fun.* New York: Frederick A. Stokes Co., 1936.

McLean, B. B., *Good Manners.* Peoria: Manual Arts Press, 1934.

Pierce, Beatrice, *It's More Fun When You Know the Rules.* New York: Farrar and Rinehart, 1935.

SUGGESTED HOME EXPERIENCES

Decide on a standard for your personal conduct at various places away from home. Follow this standard for a given length of time. Study the results. If your standard is still low, make needed changes and follow the improved one.

UNIT 5

PLANNING AND MAKING A MORNING DRESS

IF YOU WERE ASKED TO DIVIDE THE DAY into familiar parts, the first division would be into day and night. The day would again be divided into morning, afternoon, and evening—evening leading on into the night. The morning is the time of clear, bright light, in which one feels gay and hopeful. It is the time of work, enjoyable, active, and perhaps necessary. A dress that would be suitable for morning wear would have little in common with the clothes worn for an evening party.

By afternoon the main tasks of the day are supposedly done. The house is clean and in order, the laundry is on the line, or the ironing is finished and the linen stacked in neat piles or the garments hung away in the closet. For the homemaker, afternoon usually brings some free time for a walk in the out-of-doors, a cup of tea with a friend, or occasionally enjoyment of a concert or lecture. For the schoolgirl, the late afternoon at least brings freedom from school routine, and possibly an opportunity to skate, hike, or ride for an hour or so with her chums. Perhaps the late afternoon may be spent helping her mother entertain her friends.

Evening, when the dark folds one in, seems a time for friendliness and gay sharing of interesting happenings with friends and family.

Our clothes seem to reflect the spirit of the time of day.

These cut-out paper dolls show the lines of the kimono dress.

Problem 1: HOW SHALL WE CHOOSE THE PATTERN FOR OUR MORNING DRESS?

If you will look at yourself in a long mirror you will see that your figure has definite shape, the outlines of which are roughly sketched by your height and breadth. These outlines must be considered when you choose a pattern. They really are the basis for determining the size that should be purchased. Since we are just learning, we should choose a pattern that is the right size, is simple, and is as easy as possible to make. A dress made by such a pattern is easy to take care of if minor details are kept in simple form. A simple dress suitable for morning wear may be made without difficulty if a one-piece dress pattern with kimono-style sleeve is chosen.

Does this sound complicated? It really is not. Do you remember when you cut out rows of paper dolls, somewhat like the sketch at the top of this page? That was your first venture in making a simple dress with a kimono-style sleeve. Because fit is more important to you than it was to your paper doll and because you must be covered on both sides rather than just one, the dress you will make this time will be made of two large pieces, one being the front, the other the back. There is a shoulder seam and an underarm seam to hold the garment together. The sleeve is cut with the front and back, seeming to be an extension of the shoulder line. Fullness is often adjusted at the waist by means of gathers, pleats, or darts. For the beginner, it is usually advisable to let the belt or sash hold the fullness in place.

In making this style of dress, individuality may be shown by having different styles of neck and sleeve finishes. The neck may be bound or faced, or finished with a collar. In this dress we shall make a collar. Material of other colors for binding or facing, or rickrack, or a finished edge of the same material may be used. The pockets may vary in size, shape, number, and location. They may be finished in the same way as the sleeves and neck, or they may be finished with a hem at the top. The belt may be made of the same material. It may be straight and narrow, or a long sash tied in a knot with long ends, or tied in a bow. Whatever our choice of a finish may be, we should be careful to carry out our idea consistently.

Activities:

1. Select some patterns of dresses that would be good for a morning dress.
2. Draw three pictures of different styles of neck shapes or finishes.

Problem 2: HOW SHALL WE BUY THE MATERIAL FOR OUR MORNING DRESS?

For the dress that we are going to make, we should choose material that is easy to launder and requires no unusual care. Fortunately we may choose from many different cotton materials that are easily laundered. The ease of laundering can be determined only by seeing that the material is free from starch, is firm, and is of desirable weight. We should insist upon fast colors that launder well and when possible buy preshrunk material. We should avoid wiry, sleazy material that tends to ravel and is difficult to

Simple to make is the attractive and comfortable kimono-sleeve dress.

keep in place, and should choose material that is easy to work with and easy to keep fresh.

We all know that we look better in some colors than in others, so we must know what will be the best color for us to buy. Each one of us will want to choose colors that blend with our own coloring, and are also suitable for a morning dress. If we are large, we will not want too bright a color, nor material with a large conspicuous design.

We will want to avoid large figures in the design and will not want a heavy-appearing material. The design in the material should be one that will not give a problem in the construction of the dress, such as the matching of stripes or plaids. Material with a small design going each way or having no "up and down" is highly desirable for the simple morning dress.

In buying materials one should choose simple, all-over patterns. There should be no definite "up and down" to the design.

When we go to the store to buy our material we will want to know what material to ask for. The ones commonly found that are suitable for the morning dress are gingham, percale, and prints. Gingham is made in plaids, stripes, or plain colors. Percale may be plain or figured and usually has a rather stiff finish. Prints come in figured patterns and are firmly woven. Ginghams and prints vary in width, ginghams being from 26 to 32 inches wide, and prints being from 30 to 36 inches wide. Percales come only in the 36-inch width. Varying grades of each of these may be found and give approximately the same service for the money spent. Percales or prints will be best suited for our work at this time.

Percales and prints suitable for our dress have a wide price range and we should choose an attractive inexpensive material. The cost should not exceed twenty cents or twenty-five cents a yard. Some satisfactory materials may be had for fifteen cents a yard. The amount of money we plan to spend for the dress should be decided before we go to buy the material.

In buying material one needs to know the amount to buy. For the design of dress we have chosen, it will take just twice the desired length of the dress plus six inches for hem. The material needed for belt and pockets will come from the pieces left at the side when cutting out the front and back.

Activities:

1. Wash a piece of cotton material and determine whether it has been filled with starch.
2. Determine by the method given how much material you will need for your dress.

Problem 3: HOW SHALL WE BUY THE PATTERN?

Since we have chosen a one-piece kimono sleeve design for our dress, the problem of selecting a pattern is somewhat lessened. We may not be able to find a pattern that will correspond to the lines of the design we have chosen, but we can find one not greatly different from it. Each pattern in the various pattern books has a number, and when buying a pattern one calls for the number. So we must find the number of the pattern that is most nearly like the design we have chosen. In addition to this, we must know the size of pattern desired.

Pattern sizes are expressed either by age or by bust measurement. At no time is the purchase of patterns by age wholly satisfactory, since this does not allow for individual differences. A mother buying a coat pattern for a young child can only estimate whether the four-year-old or the six-year-old pattern will prove more satisfactory. Those of us who are more than ten years old need not depend wholly on guesswork. The manufacturers of patterns have set up a table that expresses the bust measurements that they have accepted for the various ages from ten to twenty years. By taking our bust measurement we can determine just what size pattern we need. We should not be concerned if the size does not coincide with our age.

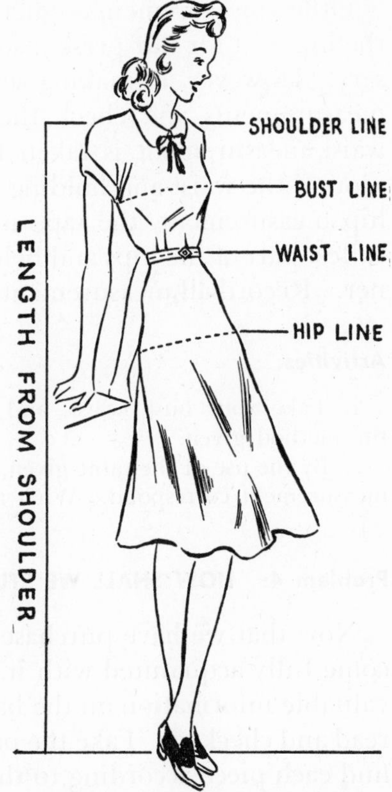

These measurements will determine the size of the pattern you will buy.

The bust measurement is taken by placing the tape measure over the fullest part of the bust, around to the back, raising it one inch as it comes from under the arms to the back, and holding the tape measure just tight enough to stay in place.

The following table may be helpful in determining the size of pattern to buy:

Size (age)	10	11	12	13	14	15	16	17	18	20
Bust	28	29	30	31	32	33	34	35	36	38

Other measurements sometimes taken are the waist and the hip, but for our present selection this will not be necessary. However, in making the dress, you must know these measurements and check them with your pattern. The waist measurement is taken by placing the tape measure around the waist and holding it in a firm position. For the hip measurement, the tape measure is placed around the fullest part of the hips and held in a firm but not tight manner. Record all measurements as they are taken.

Activities:

1. Take your bust, waist, and hip measurements according to the method given.
2. By the use of the table given, check to see if your age and bust measurement correspond. What age pattern will you buy?

Problem 4: HOW SHALL WE STUDY THE PATTERN?

Now that we have purchased our pattern, we should become fully acquainted with it. All pattern envelopes have valuable information on the back which should be carefully read and checked. Take the pattern from the envelope and find each piece according to the pieces on the guide as they are numbered. The pieces that are not going to be used in the construction of your garment should be folded and placed back in the envelope. The various makes of patterns have different markings and we should familiarize ourselves with those of the one we are going to use.

When studying a pattern, it is well to answer the following questions:

1. What pieces will I use?
2. How may I recognize the back?
3. How may I recognize the front?
4. What markings indicate the fold of the material?

5. How may I know that the pattern is correctly placed on the material?

6. How may I know if two identical pieces are needed?

When the above questions are answered correctly, we should note the markings on each piece of the pattern and consult the guide to know their meanings.

Activities:

1. Examine all the pieces of your pattern and decide what part of the dress each piece represents.
2. How do the markings on your pattern differ from those on the pattern of one of your classmates?
3. Study the guide sheet until you are familiar with the pieces you are to use.

Problem 5: HOW SHALL WE CHECK AND ALTER OUR PATTERN?

We have often heard the remark, "She is a perfect 34." This means that all the individual's measurements correspond to those used in commercial pattern-making for a pattern with 34 as the bust measurement. Few individuals have such measurements, and since patterns are usually designed and made for the average figure, it is essential that we check and alter our pattern to meet our individual needs. The measurements to be taken are those of the bust, waist, hip, and length of dress front and back. These measurements are taken over the clothing to be worn with the garment. The bust measurement is taken by passing the tape measure around the fullest part of the bust, bringing the tape measure up about an inch as you cross the back. The measurement should not be tight, but close enough to the body so that the tape measure does not fall.

The waist measurement is taken at the waistline and the tape measure is held very firm, but not uncomfortably tight. Each individual can locate her own waistline.

The hip measurement is taken over the largest part of the

hips, extending all the way around the body, usually varying from seven to nine inches down from the waistline. This measurement is also taken close but not tight. To allow for freedom of movement, add two inches to the hip measurement. The length of the back measurement is taken by placing the end of the tape measure at the upper part of the bone in the middle of the back at the neck and extending it to the floor. From this measurement subtract the number of inches the finished garment is to be from the floor and add three inches for the hem.

The length of the front measurement is taken by placing the tape measure at the base of the neck in front and proceeding as for the length of back measurement. All measurements are recorded as taken and saved for future use.

After having taken our measurements we are ready to check these measurements with corresponding measurements on the pattern. In checking the bust, waist, and hip measurement, it is well to locate these lines on the pattern, and with one-half of these measurements check the pattern, front and back, to see that each is one-half of the measurement desired.

The measurement for the length of the front and the length of the back is taken on the center front and center back edge of the pattern.

When it is necessary to make alterations on the pattern, the following method has proved satisfactory:

1. If the pattern is too small in bust and hips, increase as needed at the underarm edge. The increase should be evenly divided between the two sides of the front and the two sides of the back.

2. If the pattern is too large in the bust and hips, fold over the underarm edge the needed amount. This decrease should be evenly divided between the two sides of the front and the two sides of the back.

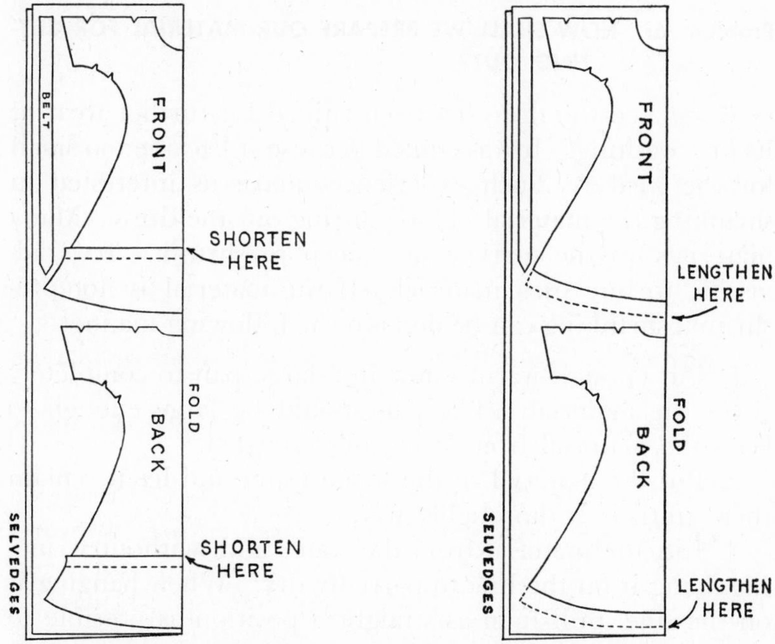

The pattern may be shortened or lengthened by making the alterations shown above.

3. If the pattern is too long, fold out the necessary amount five or six inches above the hem line.

4. If the pattern is too short, add the necessary amount below the hem line. When alterations are necessary, it is well to write them on the pattern.

If body measurements are carefully taken and the pattern purchased accordingly, great changes will not be necessary.

Activities:

1. Take the body measurements that are necessary to check your pattern.
2. Check your pattern with your measurements.
3. Make the alterations necessary, according to the directions.

Problem 6: HOW SHALL WE PREPARE OUR MATERIAL FOR CUTTING OUT?

Many a cotton dress has been ruined for further wear at its first washing. It was ruined because it became too small for the wearer. Such experiences make us interested in shrinking the material before cutting out the dress. Many materials on the market have been preshrunk. It is advisable to buy such material. If the material is not preshrunk, shrinking can be done in the following manner:

1. Put enough warm water in a large pan to completely cover the material. The pan should be large enough to keep the material from being overcrowded.
2. Put the material in the warm water and let it remain there until it is thoroughly wet.
3. Lift the material from the water and, without wringing, hang it on the line to partially dry. When hanging it on the line, pull it in as straight a position as possible to prevent unnecessary wrinkles.
4. When partially dry, remove the material from the line and iron it smooth and dry. In ironing, be sure to iron with the thread of the material.

When the material is ready for the pattern, the thread of the material should be straight throughout the piece. Straightening can be done by pulling the material diagonally along the edge, until the threads are pulled in position. Straight material, free from wrinkles or creases, is necessary for good workmanship.

Activities:

1. Measure a four-inch square of your material and wash it to see if it shrinks.
2. Straighten both ends of your material, either by pulling it into shape or by drawing a thread.
3. Press the material to be sure there are no wrinkles or creases.

Problem 7: HOW SHALL WE LAY THE PATTERN ON THE MATERIAL?

When our material is in proper condition and the necessary alterations have been made on our pattern, we are ready to place the pattern on the material. Your pattern guide will show some ways of placing the pattern on the material, and it is well to try these. There are some additional points that may prove helpful.

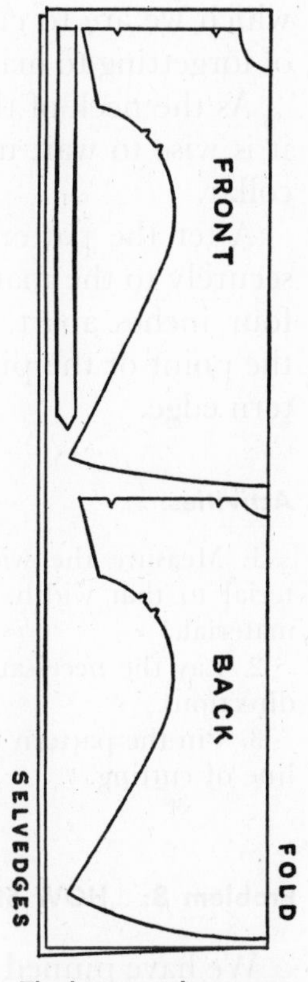

The kimono-sleeve pattern is placed on the fold of the material.

The largest pieces of the pattern should be laid on the material first. The material is folded as wide as the widest part of the pattern, and the pattern is laid according to the markings on it. If the design of the material has an "up and down," it is necessary for the pattern to be laid so as to permit the design to go in the same direction for all pieces of the pattern. If the design does not have an "up and down," it is usually advantageous to place the shoulder seam edge of the front and back so that the neck points touch. If the pattern is so laid, the material left after the cutting is of such a size that it can be used for pockets, collar, or belt.

It is wise to lay all pieces of the pattern on the material before doing any cutting. In this way we can assure ourselves of having enough material and can know that the placement is economical. When we are sure of adequate material and have planned our placement, we may find it advisable to cut out some pieces before pinning others on, thus permitting us to fold the material economically.

If a pattern requires no alterations other than seam allowance or addition for the hem, after pinning the pattern down, a few pins should be placed to indicate the line on which we are to cut. If this is not done, there is a danger of forgetting to make needed allowances when cutting.

As the neck of the dress often requires some adjustment, it is wise to wait until the neck is fitted before cutting the collar.

After the pattern is properly laid, it should be pinned securely to the material. The pins should be placed about four inches apart, perpendicular to the cutting edge, and the point of the pin should be about 1/4 inch from the pattern edge.

Activities:

1. Measure the widest piece of your pattern and fold the material to that width, being sure it is folded on the thread of the material.
2. Lay the necessary pattern pieces on the material according to directions.
3. Pin the pattern in place, being sure the pins will not be in the line of cutting.

Problem 8: HOW SHALL WE CUT THE DRESS?

We have pinned our pattern to the material, and are now ready to cut out our dress. If we are to have straight, smooth, even edges, it is necessary to have scissors with a good cutting edge. Scissors or shears made of good steel have a sharp cutting edge and will keep this edge if properly cared for. Good scissors or shears will cut the length of the blade and will move easily. The cutting is done at the edge

The pattern is carefully pinned to the material before the dress is cut out. In cutting out the dress, follow the pattern edge, except for notches, which are cut away from the pattern. Care must be taken to cut the notches correctly, as they are important guides in putting the garment together.

of the pattern or just outside the alteration line, using the entire length of the blade of the scissors or shears on a long straight or curved edge. When cutting on a short straight or curved edge, it is best to use the tips of the scissors or shears. This is also true when turning corners. The notches at the edge of the pattern should be cut out rather than in. This is done to avoid the danger of cutting into or beyond the seam line.

As each piece is cut from the material, it should be folded and laid in a box or at one side of the table. After all pieces have been cut, the scraps should be rolled and pinned together or folded and placed in a box of convenient size. This will keep them in good condition in case they are needed at some future time. It is very important that the pattern remain pinned to the material until all necessary markings are made and we fully understand the next step in our procedure.

Activities:

1. Practice cutting material to see if your scissors or shears are in good condition. Can you cut the length of the scissors or shears? Can you cut a curved edge?
2. Cut out each piece of your dress.
3. Put the scraps of material in a box.

Problem 9: HOW SHALL WE REMOVE THE PATTERN FROM THE MATERIAL?

When the dress has been cut out and the scraps have been put away, we are ready to make the necessary pattern markings on the material. If the garment is to have the crosswise threads of the material horizontal to the floor, we must keep the center front and the center back lines perpendicular to the floor. Careful marking will help us to do this. We will put a basting thread on the fold of the center front and the center back. This basting may be made with long stitches, fastening the stitching well at the neck and at the bottom.

If the dress has darts, the markings for these will be made by means of tailor tacks. Tailor tacks are made by threading the needle with a thread twice as long as usual and knotting the two ends together so that the thread is double. We then take a small stitch through the marking, leaving a length of thread of about three inches where the needle went into the cloth. A second stitch should then be taken in the same place and a loop of three inches of thread left. If another tailor tack is to be made a short distance from the first one, a long stitch may be taken and the second tailor tack made in the same manner. If there is only one tailor tack needed, or if the next one is some distance away, the thread is cut about three inches from the material when the tack is completed.

When all markings are made, pins are removed and each pattern piece is folded and returned to the envelope. When tailor tacks have been made, the two pieces are pulled apart only enough so that the threads from the loops may be clipped. Care should be taken that the markings are not pulled out. It is wise not to remove the pattern until you are ready to use the piece.

Activities:

1. Make all the necessary markings shown on the pattern.
2. Put a basting thread on the fold of the center front and the center back.
3. Remove pins, fold up the pattern piece, and place it in the envelope.

Problem 10: WHAT STEPS SHALL WE FOLLOW IN MAKING OUR DRESS?

In making a dress—as in any other piece of work—if one understands the task and the procedure is well planned, the results are likely to be satisfactory. Also the work will proceed with less difficulty. When we are ready to make our dress, it is helpful to study the pattern picture and list the problems involved, thus making our plans of procedure. The patterns we are using are similar and our plans of work will be very much alike.

A good plan to follow in making a dress with the kimono-style sleeve is:

1. Pin and baste in all darts.
2. Baste the front and back together for the first fitting.
3. Cut down four inches on the center front line, making the neck opening.
4. Fit and make any necessary alterations, including lengthening of the neck opening.
5. Stitch the darts and finish the seams.
6. Fit the neck.
7. Cut the collar and finish the neck.

8. Finish the sleeves.
9. Make the belt.
10. Make the pockets.
11. Sew on the pockets.
12. Hem the garment.
13. Press the garment.
14. Score your garment, according to the score card suggested on page 142.

This plan of procedure presents in their order the problems involved in making the dress. As you finish one problem, you can prepare for the next one.

Activities:

1. Examine your dress and list the tasks to do.
2. Decide the best order for doing these tasks.

Problem 11: WHAT PRACTICES SHALL WE FOLLOW IN MAKING OUR DRESS?

No matter what our task may be, we should maintain desirable standards of work. We all want the dress we are making to be clean when it is completed. This necessitates good care during the construction of the dress. When making a dress at school, it is necessary to put it away many, many times. This should be done carefully to keep the dress in good condition. If the dress is folded in thirds lengthwise and then crosswise to a size suitable for the box, our packing will be neat. The dress will not be wrinkled as it would if it were piled or jammed into the box carelessly when the bell rings for dismissal.

As we work we should keep the basting threads removed from those parts of the dress where the stitching is completed. Threads at the end of the machine stitching should be tied as soon as possible after the stitching is completed. This prevents ripping of the stitching. The easiest dress to press when completed is the one that has been pressed at various times during its construction. Pressing the different parts, such as shoulder and underarm seams, after they are stitched and the bastings removed helps greatly in keeping the garment in good condition.

We well know that our best and most efficient work is done when we have it planned carefully. In making our dress, we should know the sequence of tasks and should plan a definite amount to accomplish each day. We should be careful not to set more than can be accomplished in the given amount of time that we have. In class work, as in any contact with others, it is necessary to be cooperative and to maintain a helpful attitude. Much more pleasure is derived when work is done under such conditions. Each day as we work we should try to improve upon the work of the previous day. By so doing we will improve our ability to sew and be able to undertake the more difficult tasks of the next problem.

Activities:

1. Write down the tasks you expect to finish today.
2. Fold your dress in the best way for it to fit the box you are using.
3. Time yourself and see how long it takes you to put your work away carefully.

Problem 12: HOW SHALL WE BASTE OUR DRESS FOR THE FIRST FITTING?

When our dress is cut out we are ready to put the various pieces together. Our first step will be to baste in the darts. This is done on the wrong side of the material. You will note that the two rows of markings form a triangle. Fold the triangle so that the markings coincide. Baste on the line of the markings.

The type of dress we are making has two principal seams, the shoulder seam and the underarm seam. To baste these seams, the front and back of the garment should be held so

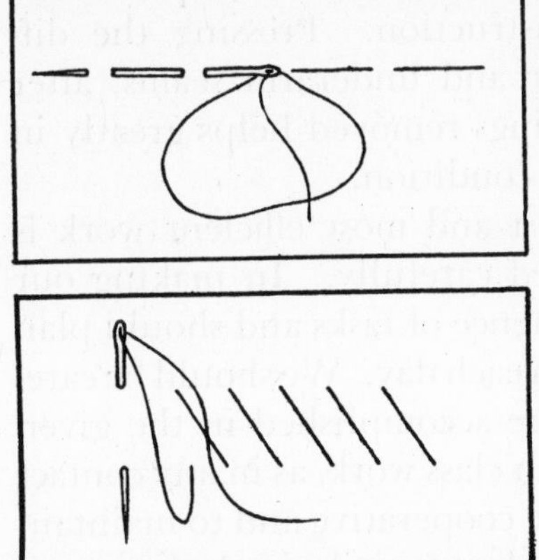

Basting may be done with even stitches (top) or with diagonal stitches (bottom). Even stitches are used to baste the seam. Diagonal stitches are used to hold two pieces of cloth together.

that the right sides are together and the edges of the seams are even. When the material is thus placed, pin it together, placing the pins perpendicular to the edge and about six inches apart. When this is done we are ready to baste. Bastings should be done on the line of seam allowance with stitches about ¼ inch in length. Stitches of this length will hold the garment firmly for the fitting.

We have all seen dresses with necks that were too large. This is often caused by the material at the neckline being stretched during the construction of the dress. To prevent this, run a basting with a double thread around the neckline. This is done by placing stitches, of about ¼-inch length, ¼ inch from the edge of the neckline. We must be sure to fasten the ends of the thread securely. The thread should be slightly shorter than the neck edge so that it will pull it in slightly without gathering. Such precaution helps us avoid ill-fitting necklines.

Activities:

1. Place the right sides of your dress together with the shoulder seam of the front and back and the underarm seam of the front and back coming together.
2. Pin the two pieces together.
3. Baste the two pieces together on the line of seam allowance.
4. Put a basting thread around the neckline ¼ inch from the edge.

Problem 13: HOW SHALL WE FIT THE SHOULDER AND UNDER-ARM SEAMS?

The desirability of cooperation has been stressed several times. Now we have reached the place where we need cooperation of a classmate to help us fit our dress. Fitting is a procedure that each of us should be anxious to understand. An understanding of fitting is necessary both in making clothes and in purchasing ready-made clothing.

In order to insure a well-fitted dress, it should be fitted over the garments with which the dress will be worn. The person being fitted should stand with the body erect, weight on both feet, and the arms hanging loosely at the side. To stand erect means to stand tall. Standing tall brings the body into an erect position with the abdomen in, the chest out, and the shoulders up.

The person fitting the dress should be sure that the center front and center back lines are in place, truly perpendicular to the floor. If the darts that are to take out excess fullness at the waistline are not in proper place, bastings are removed and the darts are pinned in the correct place. This adjustment will put the darts on the right side of the material, which means they will have to be changed later.

The location of the shoulder seam is usually determined by imagining a line that passes up the middle of the arm to the neck. This line is found to be on the middle of the shoulder and is the place for the shoulder seam. If the shoulder seam does not fall where this line would come, the bastings are removed and the pieces are pinned together on this line, thus making a correct shoulder seam from there.

The underarm seam should bisect the armpit and fall from there in a straight line perpendicular to the floor. If it does not do this, it is corrected, following the same procedure used in correcting the shoulder seam. Remove the

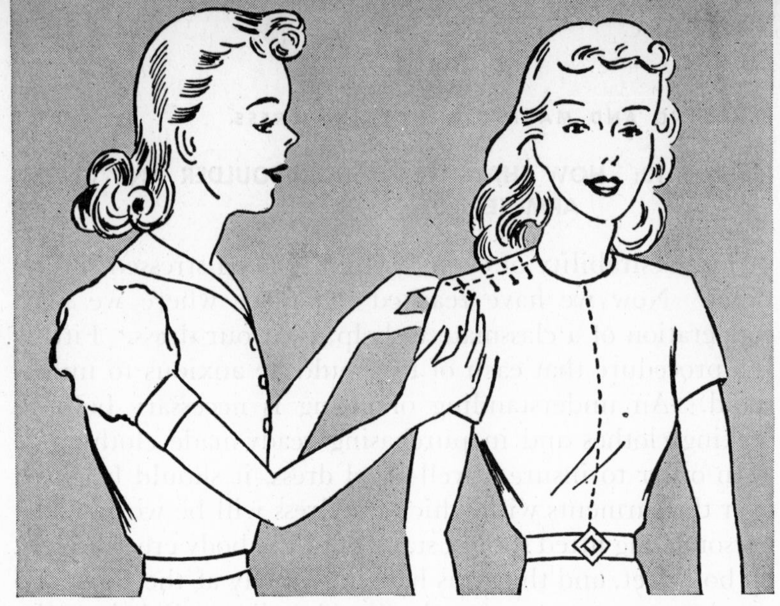

This kimono-sleeve dress is being fitted at the shoulder seam.

dress after the fitting is completed and mark all alterations with a basting thread. Turn the dress to the wrong side and rebaste. Remove the pins after the basting is complete. A second fitting is desirable. This should give a well-fitted garment. The dress should be large enough to go on and off easily without an opening in the underarm seam.

Activities:

1. Put the dress on, being sure the center front and center back are in the correct position.
2. Stand in a natural position, weight on both feet, and as tall as you can.
3. Have your partner fit the dress, marking places for alteration.

Problem 14: HOW SHALL WE MAKE THE SHOULDER AND UNDERARM SEAMS?

We have all seen dresses that had crooked seam lines or gaping seams caused by broken stitches. Such seams give to that garment a careless appearance that may be avoided by careful stitching. The plain seam which we will use in this garment is simple to make, yet it will give a good appearance to our dress if properly made.

The underarm seam of this kimono sleeve has been fitted with pins. Note that the pins are placed "heads up."

In making the plain seam, the right sides of the material are put together and basted along the line for stitching. With the sewing machine in proper condition and ready for use, place the end of the seam to be stitched in under the presser foot of the machine, having the seam edges to the right and the dress to the left. Have the threads to the back of the presser foot, and bring the needle down through the seam line one stitch from the end of the seam. Lower the presser foot. Stitch as close to the line of basting as possible, but avoid stitching in the basting. Guide the material with the left hand, and as you near the end of the seam stitch very slowly. Stop just at the end of the seam. Raise the presser foot, have the take-up lever at the highest point, and pull the threads out six inches from the needle. Cut the threads three inches from the material. When the two shoulder seams and two underarm seams have been stitched, the bastings may be removed and the seam trimmed to 1/2 or 5/8 inch.

We will use only one row of stitching on the seams of our dress instead of the two rows used in making the pillowcase. There are two reasons for this: the material we are using does not ravel excessively, and the seams are curved. In order to keep them flat we must press them open. To press the seams open, the first step is to have them trimmed to the proper width. Next, with the fingers fold the seam open, pressing the edges back as you go down the seam. Now you are ready to press with a moderately hot iron and a damp cloth. Dampen the seam a short distance at a time and with the point of the iron press over the dampened portion.

Proceed with the dampening and pressing until each seam has been finished. There should be no creases on the right or wrong side. The garment can be slipped over the board, making the pressing of the underarm seams easy. The neck opening is not large enough to permit the shoulder seams to be placed on the board. It is well to press them first; then when the neck, sleeves, and hem are to be finished, the seam ends will lie in proper position.

Activities:

1. Practice stitching on a piece of scrap material to see that your stitching is just as you want it.
2. Stitch the seams as directed.

Problem 15: HOW SHALL WE CUT A BIAS STRIP?

We have all seen facings on sleeves or neck finishes that were scarcely visible. They seemed neat and gave the garment an appearance of good workmanship. This was in part due to well-cut bias. Bias should be cut on the true bias, which means that the line for cutting should be made when the material is so folded that the lengthwise threads are parallel to the crosswise threads. A piece of true bias can be stretched to fit curves and will make a smooth, flat finish. After folding and marking the line for true bias on the material, we will use a ruler or gauge to mark the other side of our strip. To make a bias strip one inch wide, keep the gauge at right angles to the line which marks the true bias. Measure down one inch and place pins on a line parallel to the true bias one inch apart. Then cut, following the line of the pins. If possible, the bias strip should be the length necessary for facing the neck, one of the sleeves, or the neck opening. The last will of course require double its length. All bias strips may be cut at one time; we should be sure of the length needed in each case. An allowance of one or two inches more than the actual measurement should be made.

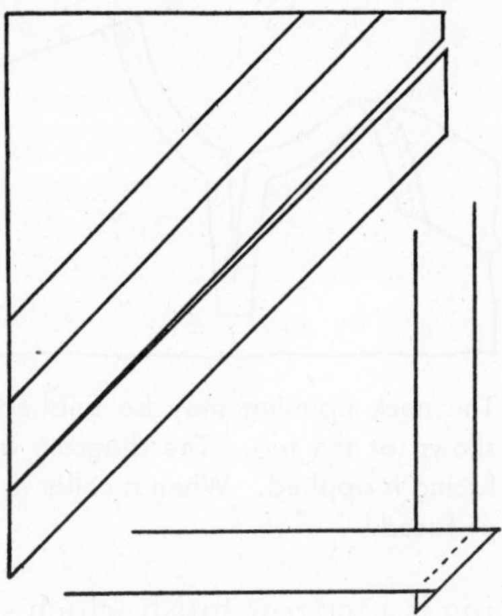

Bias is cut diagonally and placed at right angles with the right sides together for joining.

Activities:

1. Fold a piece of your notebook paper on a true diagonal and cut two bias strips one inch wide.
2. Fold a piece of material as you did the paper, and cut the bias you will need for your dress.

Problem 16: HOW SHALL WE FINISH THE OPENING AT THE NECK?

We found when we fitted our dress that it was necessary to cut down from the neckline a distance of four to six inches on the center front to permit us to put the dress on. We must finish this opening in such a way that it will look well and wear well. We will finish it by binding. A bind-

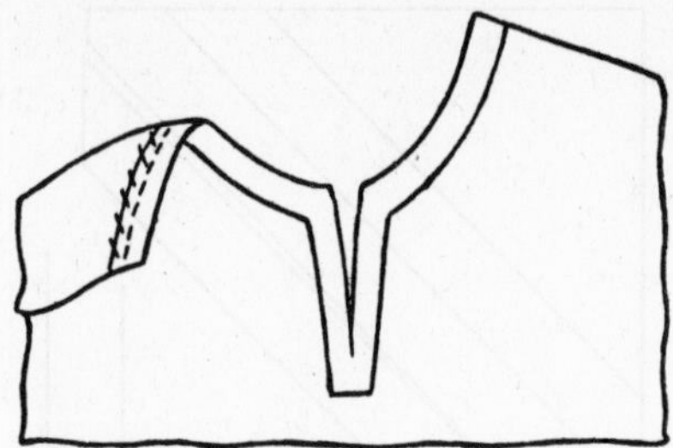
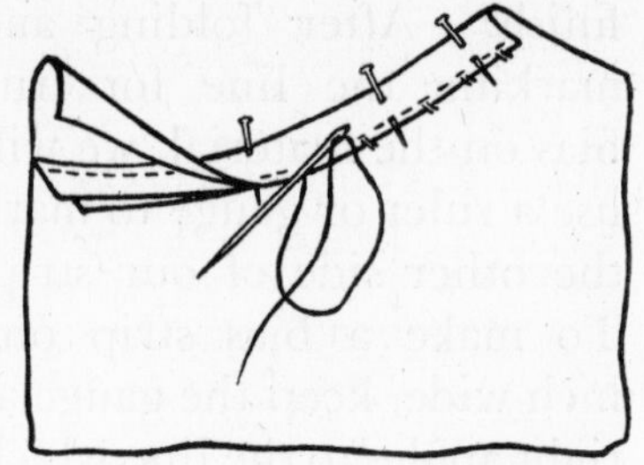

The neck opening may be finished with a simple binding or facing, as shown at the left. The diagram at the right shows how the binding or facing is applied. When a collar is used, only the center opening is bound or faced.

ing is a narrow finish which shows the same amount on both the right and wrong sides. In the previous lesson we cut a bias strip one inch wide and twice the length of the neck opening. With this bias strip we are now ready to bind the neck opening. Binding is done as follows:

1. With the right side of the binding held against the right side of the opening, pin the bias in place, beginning at the right upper end.
2. As you reach the lower end of the opening, ease the bias in slightly and place the pins close together.
3. Baste $\frac{1}{4}$ inch from the edge of the opening.
4. Remove the pins.
5. Stitch close to the basted line.
6. Remove the bastings.
7. Press or crease the bias over the wrong side $\frac{1}{2}$ inch.
8. Turn the bias under $\frac{1}{4}$ inch and pin in place to the line of stitching.
9. Baste at the rows of pins.
10. Remove the pins.
11. Stitch close to the edge of the turned-under edge.
12. Remove the bastings.
13. Press the binding.

The line of the neck is changed by placing the tape to conform to the figure, marking the new line with pins, and cutting out along this line.

If a narrower binding is desired, the bias strip may be cut narrower and the ¼-inch fold may be reduced slightly. The narrowest binding in common use is about ⅛ inch. Narrow binding, however, is difficult to work with. If we desire bias to serve as a trimming, a contrasting color may be used. If the entire neck opening is to be bound or faced, the neckline is marked and cut first (Problem 17).

Activities:

1. With a piece of bias about four inches long, bind an opening cut 1¾ inches long in a scrap of material.
2. Bind the opening at the neck of your dress.

Problem 17: HOW SHALL WE MARK AND CUT THE NECKLINE?

Marking and cutting the neckline can only be done with the dress on. Again we will work with a classmate. With the dress properly adjusted for wearing, we will decide just how high or low we desire to have the neckline.

Most people find the slightly V neckline is desirable when a collar is included. Place a row of pins in a line 3/8 inch from where we plan to cut the neckline. This row of pins should be placed end to point entirely around the neck, with care taken that they are at the proper place on both sides. The opening should measure the same on both sides. When the pin line is in proper place, remove the dress. Trim the neckline 3/8 inch up from the pin line. Place a basting thread on the line of pins and then remove the pins.

Activities:

1. Put the dress on and adjust it as it will be worn.
2. Mark the neckline with a row of pins.
3. Measure from center front to center back on the row of pins, to be sure they are the same length.

Problem 18: HOW SHALL WE MAKE THE COLLAR?

You will recall that we did not put the collar pattern on when we were putting our pattern on the material. We wished to check the collar pattern with the neck of the fitted dress before cutting out the collar. To check the collar pattern, pin the center back of the collar pattern to the center back of the neck of the dress. Keeping the neck edge of the pattern even with the neck edge of the dress, pin them together around the neckline at one inch spaces. If the collar pattern extends about 1/4 inch beyond the opening edge, it must be shortened that amount by creasing back or cutting off. If it does not reach the opening, add the necessary amount to the pattern.

With the material folded lengthwise on a thread, place the center back of the pattern on the fold. Pin in place and cut out the collar. Two identical pieces will be needed,

Many different effects are possible with the plain collar. Each collar shown is particularly becoming to girls of certain types. The styles may be varied both as to shape and to the width of the collar.

since the collar is to be double, so it will be necessary to place and cut the collar pattern twice. Any markings on the collar pattern should be cut in a similar manner to that used in cutting out the other pieces of the dress.

When the duplicate pieces of the collar have been cut, remove the pattern and place with the remainder of the pattern. Put the right sides of the two pieces of the collar together so the edges are even and pin the collar around its outer edge. Baste $\frac{1}{4}$ inch from this edge, leaving the neckline open. Remove the pins. The collar is then stitched close to the basted line and all basting threads removed.

The next step is to turn the collar, and crease along the stitched edge so that the seam line forms the outside edge of the collar. Baste close to the outside edge of the turned collar. Press the collar with a moderately hot iron. Remove the bastings and press again. The first pressing is to establish the crease. Care should be taken that it does not leave signs of the basting.

Activities:

1. Check the collar pattern with the neck of the dress.
2. If alterations are necessary, make them on the pattern.
3. Place the pattern on the material and cut out the collar.
4. Make a collar for the dress.

Problem 19: HOW SHALL WE JOIN BIAS STRIPS?

In a previous problem we cut sufficient bias for our dress. Now we find that some of these pieces will have to be joined in order to be long enough to use on the neck. Two pieces must be joined. The joining of bias is important and requires careful thought and practice.

If the following procedure is used, well-joined bias will result:

1. Place two strips of bias facing with right sides together.
2. Have the ends so placed that the bias edge of one is at right angles to the other.
3. Have the point of one extend ¼ inch beyond the other.
4. Baste in this position a ¼-inch seam, beginning at the point where the two edges meet.
5. Stitch across very close to the line of basting.
6. Remove the basting, and open and press the seam flat.

If one joining does not give sufficient bias, another joining will have to be made.

Activities:

1. With the paper bias you cut in Problem 15, pin the two pieces together and crease the seam open.
2. Join two pieces of the bias material and press.

Problem 20: HOW SHALL WE ATTACH THE COLLAR TO THE DRESS?

When the collar and the bias strips are made, we are ready to put the collar on the dress. The center back of the dress and the center back of the collar are held together and pinned on each side from this point to the front. The pins should be placed one inch apart. Baste the collar and dress together, allowing a ⅜-inch seam. With the collar basted in place, we will begin at the right side of the neck to apply the bias facing. A facing differs from a binding in that it shows only on one side. In our dress it will show only on the wrong side. The facing should be placed on top of the collar and basted with a ¼-inch seam, to be turned under ¼ inch at each end of the seam.

The facing and collar are stitched to the dress close to the basted line. The threads of machine stitching are tied and all bastings removed.

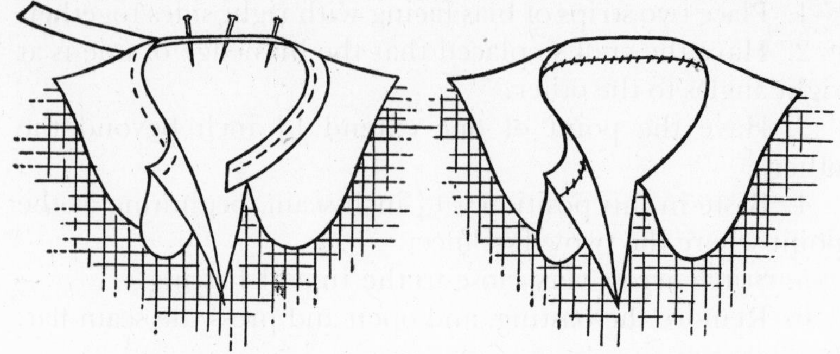

The collar is neatly attached to the dress with a strip of bias.

Then the facing is turned over and down, and is pinned flat to the dress. It is basted close to the seam edge and pins are removed. The edge of facing is turned under 1/4 inch, pinned to the dress, and basted. Pins are removed. A line of stitching is then made close to the second basted line. The threads of machine stitching are tied, all bastings are removed, and the dress is pressed.

Activities:

1. Measure the neckline of the dress and that of the collar to insure that they are of equal length.
2. Attach the collar to the dress.

Problem 21: HOW SHALL WE FASTEN THE NECK OF THE DRESS?

The neck of the dress may be fastened with a hook and eye or ties may be used. Hooks and eyes, if selected properly, are a desirable way of fastening the neck. They should be well made, rustproof, and large enough to fasten easily, yet not so large as to appear awkward. As this hook and eye will be sewed on where there are several thicknesses of material, no extra precautions need be taken to keep it from pulling out.

Hooks and eyes should be sewed near enough to the outer

edge that the opening will be held shut, but far enough from the edge of the opening not to be seen when the dress is fastened.

The location for the eye should be marked by a pin on the left-hand side of the neck opening. Just across from it another pin should be placed on the right-hand side, marking the location for the hook.

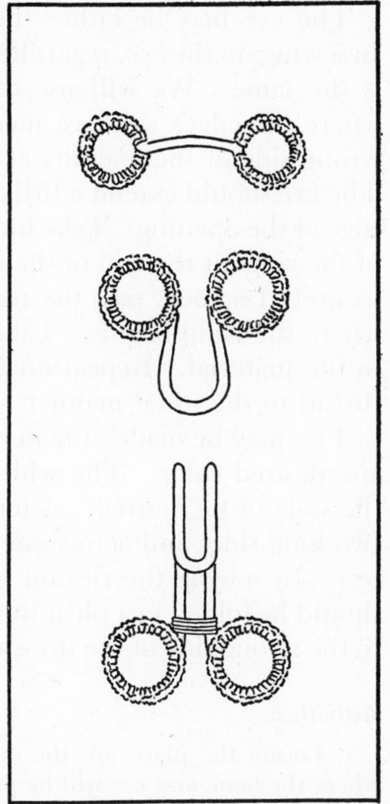

The hook and eye should be sewed on securely. The over-and-over stitch or the buttonhole stitch shown here may be used.

With the positions of the hook and eye marked, we are ready to sew them on. We will thread our needle with a thread about two feet long and of the desired color. Have a knot in one end of the thread and take a stitch in the material where it will be covered by the hook. Put the hook in the place marked by the pin. Hold it in position and take four or five parallel stitches over each circle of wire at the end of the hook. In taking these stitches, care should be used that the stitches do not come through to the right side. With the base of the hook securely fastened, pass the needle under the hook to the opposite end and take four stitches through the base of the hook to hold it to the material. Take several small stitches in the same place to fasten the thread. Cut the thread close to the material.

The eye may be either the round or the straight type. In sewing on the eye, regardless of the type used, the method is the same. We will use the round eye, since it is best where the edges will just meet. The eye is placed on the wrong side of the opening at the place marked by the pin. The eye should extend a little less than $1/16$ inch beyond the edge of the opening. Take four or five stitches through each of the rings at the end of the eye. With the base of the eye securely fastened, pass the needle up one side of the hook where the bend begins. Take four stitches to hold the eye to the material. Repeat on the opposite side. Fasten the thread in the usual manner.

Ties may be made of material the same as the dress or of any desired color. The width and length will depend on the style of tie desired. After cutting the ties, hem on the two long sides and across one end, using a hem $1/4$ inch or less. In sewing the ties on to the neck of the dress, they should be folded in a pleat in the middle and sewed securely to the wrong side of the dress with several overhand stitches.

Activities:

1. Locate the places on the opening at the neck of your dress where the hook and eye will be placed. Mark these places.
2. Sew the hook and eye on the places marked.
3. If ties are used, make them and sew them on.

Problem 22: HOW SHALL WE FINISH THE SLEEVE EDGE?

The edge of each sleeve is finished with bias facing. In a previous lesson, bias strips one inch wide were cut and joined together for the necessary length.

The facing at the sleeve edge is done in the following way:

1. Start at the underarm seam, allowing $1\frac{1}{2}$ inches extension of the facing.

2. Place the right side of the facing to the right side of the dress.

3. Pin the facing in place around the sleeve edge.

4. Baste with small stitches with a $\frac{1}{4}$-inch seam.

5. Remove the pins.

6. Join the two ends of facing by means of pins, so that the facing lies flat on the sleeve.

7. Baste and stitch the seam of the joined ends, and crease it open.

8. Baste the facing carefully to the dress at this seam.

9. Stitch, holding the facing seam at the bottom of the sleeves very close to the basted line, and remove the bastings.

10. Turn the bias facing to the wrong side of the sleeve, creasing so that the seam makes the bottom edge of the sleeve.

11. Baste into place.

12. Turn under $\frac{1}{4}$ inch of facing and baste it in place.

13. Press the facing.

14. Stitch close to the edge of the facing.

15. Remove the bastings, tie all thread ends, and press.

In facing the two sleeves, we may either complete one sleeve and then do the other one, or we may take each step on both sleeves, thus finishing the two sleeves at about the same time.

Activities:

1. Face a short edge of material with bias.
2. Face the sleeve edge of each sleeve.

Problem 23: HOW SHALL WE MAKE THE BELT?

Belts are a necessary part of this type of dress; they help to hold the dress in place, and they may be used as a trimming.

We will make a plain straight belt cut from the lengthwise

or crosswise of the material. The belt should be as long as your waist measurement, plus two to three inches for lapping. The piece of material cut should be twice the desired width of the finished belt, plus 5/8 inch for seams.

In making the belt, the following procedure is suggested:

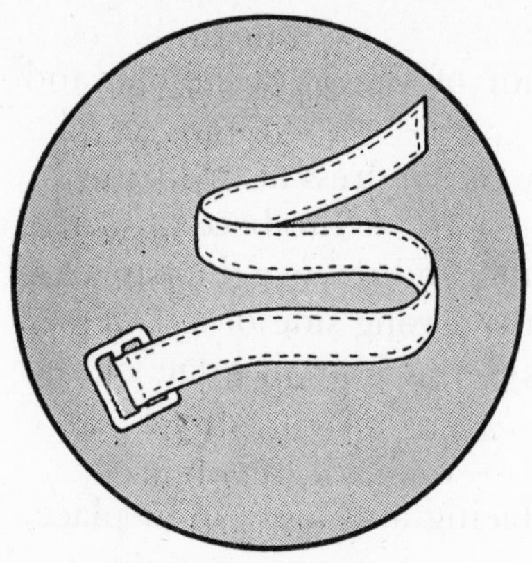

A neatly made belt adds much to the dress.

1. Place right sides together and fold lengthwise so that the edges are exactly even.

2. Pin into place.

3. Baste with 1/4-inch seam, starting at the folded side of one end, going across the end and entire length, leaving the other end open.

4. Stitch very close to the basting line.

5. Remove bastings.

6. Clip off the corners 1/8 inch from the stitching to avoid bulkiness at the end of the belt.

7. Turn the belt to the right side, using a safety pin or yardstick to pull or push the material through.

8. Crease at the seam, and fold and baste into place.

9. Turn in the unstitched ends 1/4 inch, baste in place, and stitch in by hand.

10. Sew on hooks and eyes for fastening, using method learned in previous lesson.

11. If a buckle is desired as a finish, one end of the belt may be folded in and sewed to a point. The other end of the belt will be drawn over the center of the buckle, folded over, and then stitched securely in place.

12. Press the belt lightly, remove the bastings, and press again.

Activities:

1. Measure your waistline over your dress and decide how long to cut the material for your belt.
2. Cut the piece of material for your belt.
3. Make the belt for your dress.

Problem 24: HOW SHALL WE MAKE AND SEW ON PATCH POCKETS?

The patch pockets for the dress may be made any desired shape, and of a material to match the collar, ties, or belt. The size of the pockets should be such that they will look well on the dress. They should not be so small as to be useless, nor so large as to look unbalanced. If the rectangular-shaped pocket is used, it may be four inches deep and four and one-half inches wide. If some other shape such as round or oval is used, these proportions usually serve as a general guide.

In cutting out the pocket, an allowance should be made for the finished size plus 1/4 inch on the two sides, 1/4 inch at the bottom, and 3/4 inch or more at the top for a hem. The pocket should be cut so that the horizontal threads of the pocket correspond with those of the dress.

The first step in making the pocket is to hem the top. This is done by turning under 1/4 inch to the wrong side, then making a 1/2-inch turn which is pinned, basted, and stitched in the usual manner. Remove the bastings and turn under 1/4 inch on the other three sides, baste, and press lightly.

The dress should be put on, the belt adjusted, and the pocket or pockets located in the desired position. They are pinned into place. The dress is removed, the pockets basted into place, and the pins removed.

In stitching the pocket onto the dress, start at the lower edge of the hem and stitch across the hem diagonally to a

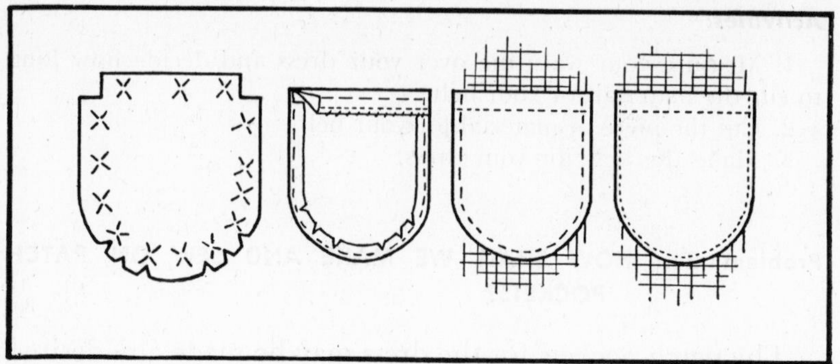

There are four major steps in making the patch pocket: (left to right) marking for folding; hemming and basting down the fold; pinning the pocket into place and basting it to the dress; and stitching the pocket into place.

point ½ inch from the upper edge of the hem. Stitch across from this point to the outer edge of the pocket, on around the sides, across the bottom, and up the opposite side of the pocket; this makes a triangle which prevents the stitching from ripping. When you reach the top of the hem, at the opposite side from which you began, make a triangle like the one made in the beginning. Cut the threads three inches from the material and from the needle. Pull threads to the wrong side and tie them. Remove the bastings and press.

Activities:

1. Cut three or four paper pockets that you think are a good shape.
2. Place the desired pattern on the material and cut it out.
3. Make the pocket or pockets.
4. Sew the pocket or pockets onto the dress.

Problem 25: HOW SHALL WE MARK THE HEM LINE?

Again we have another cooperative task that takes care and patience. The dress must be put on, the neck fastened, and the belt adjusted. In marking the hem, the equipment needed is a table, a yardstick, and many pins. The wearer of the dress stands on a table in a natural position with arms at the side. The classmate who is to mark the hem assumes a comfortable position with eyes about even with the edge of the hem line. If the wearer moves during the time the hem is being taken, she should be careful to assume the same position as at first.

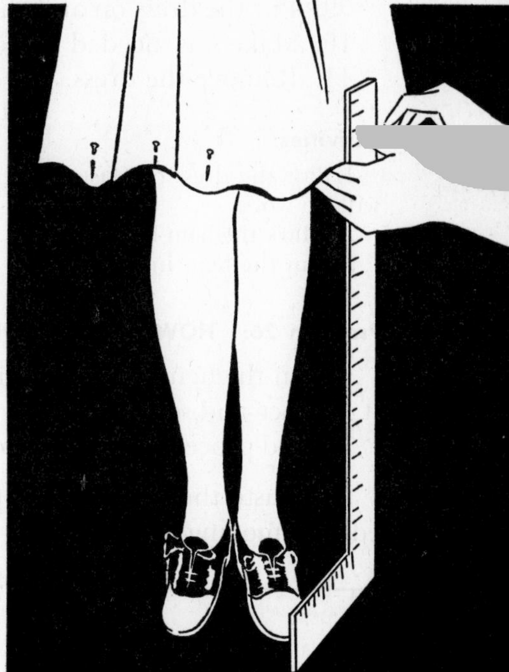

The hem line is checked to be sure it is an equal distance from the floor at all points.

The hem is marked as follows:

1. Decide how many inches from the floor the dress will be.
2. Mark this number on the yardstick with chalk or a rubber band.
3. Hold the yardstick, perpendicular to the floor, against the dress.
4. Place pins in the dress at the point even with the mark on the yardstick and parallel to the floor.
5. Pins should be placed about 3 inches apart and with the heads on the right side of the garment.
6. Recheck the line of pins.
7. Remove the dress, turn the hem on the line of pins, and crease.
8. Pin the hem into place.

9. Put the dress on and check.
10. Make any needed corrections.
11. Remove the dress.

Activities:

1. Put the dress on, fasten at the neck, and adjust the belt as it will be worn.
2. Mark the hem line.
3. Pin the hem in place.

Problem 26: HOW SHALL WE PUT IN THE HEM?

When the hem has been pinned in, we are ready to baste it in place and sew it in.

A good procedure is as follows:

1. Baste the hem line in place ¼ inch from the lower edge, removing all pins when you have completed the basting.

In putting in the hem, the line of machine stitching comes close to the upper edge of the folded hem.

2. With a gauge, measure up from hem line the desired width of hem plus ⅜ inch for a turn-in. Measurements should be made at intervals of two inches and marked with a pin at each point.
3. Trim along the line of pins and remove the pins.
4. Turn under the edge of the hem ⅜ inch and baste with small basting stitches, starting with a new thread at the center front, center back, and each side seam.
5. Pin the hem in place at the center front, center back, and each side seam.
6. With basting thread, adjust fullness between the pins and pin the hem in place.

7. Baste the hem in place and remove all pins.

8. Try on the dress and make any needed alterations.

9. Press the hem.

10. Stitch close to the edge of the hem.

11. Remove the bastings, tie the threads of the machine stitching, and press the hem again.

Activities:

1. Put a basting line $\frac{1}{4}$ inch from the edge of the hem line.
2. Make a gauge for marking the width of the hem.
3. Practice using the gauge.
4. Put the hem in the dress.

Problem 27: HOW SHALL WE PRESS THE DRESS?

Pressing adds much to the appearance of a dress, and it should be done carefully. As pressing is the last step in the completion of our dress, we should now check to see that all basting and guide threads have been removed. When the dress is free from these it is spread over the ironing board and dampened. It is then pressed on the right side with a moderately hot iron, in the following order:

Pressing—the last important step in making a dress—should be carefully and neatly done.

1. Press the belt and collar first.

2. Press the sleeves, pressing up to the neck.

3. Press the dress over the board and press with the threads of the material, keeping the iron moving up and down or crosswise, parallel to the crosswise threads.

Special care in pressing should be given the pockets, the facing on the sleeves and neck, and the hem. When the dress is pressed, it should be placed on a hanger, fastened at the neck, and hung in a closet until needed. Hanging in a closet prevents dust from collecting on the dress, and keeps the garment out of the light.

Activities:

1. Examine the dress and see what places will need special attention in pressing.
2. Press the belt and put it on the hanger.
3. Press the dress, place it on the hanger, and hang it in the closet.

Problem 28: HOW SHALL WE JUDGE OUR DRESSES?

Everyone enjoys wearing a neat and well-made garment. It is only by knowing what we have done well, or where we have failed to do well, that we are able to improve our workmanship. The appearance of a dress is determined by the choice of material; the fit of the dress; the workmanship; and the condition of the garment. In studying the dress to know its strong points and weak points, it is helpful to use a score card.

The following items are suggested for making a score card:

Choice of material:
- Color
- Design
- Texture

Fit of dress:
- Neck
- Waist
- Hem line

Workmanship:
- Stitching of seams
- Finish of neck and sleeves
- Belt
- Fasteners
- Pressing

Cleanliness

Activities:

1. Examine your dress and see if all finishes have been cared for.
2. Decide points for each item in the score card.
3. Check the dress according to the score card you have decided to use.

REFERENCES FOR THE UNIT

Donovan, Dulcie Godlove, *The Mode in Dress and Home.* Boston: Allyn and Bacon, 1935.

Friend, Mata Roman, and Shultz, Hazel, *Junior Home Economics: Clothing.* New York: D. Appleton-Century Co., 1933.

Jensen, Milton B., Jensen, Mildred N., and Ziller, M. Louisa, *Fundamentals of Home Economics.* New York: The Macmillan Co., 1935.

Kinyon, Kate W., and Hopkins, L. Thomas, *Junior Clothing,* Revised Edition. New York: Benj. H. Sanborn and Co., 1938.

Matthews, Mary Lockwood, *The New Elementary Home Economics.* Boston: Little, Brown and Co., 1937.

Todd, Elizabeth, *Clothes for Girls.* Boston: Little, Brown and Co., 1935.

SUGGESTED HOME EXPERIENCES

1. Choose patterns suitable for a morning dress for your mother.
2. Make a dress for your mother, planning and making it with the supervision of your mother and teacher.
3. Figure the cost of four such dresses for your mother. Compare this cost with four similar ready-made dresses.
4. Follow the same procedures in making a dress for yourself.

UNIT 6

MAKING OUR OWN ROOM LIVABLE

WE ALL WANT A ROOM OF OUR VERY own: a place where we may enjoy our treasures (which may not seem like treasures to anyone else), have our favorite books, or experiment with colors we think we will enjoy; a place to be alone; a place where we may rest, study, grow, and dream our dreams of what tomorrow will bring. Perhaps not all of us are so fortunate as to have such a room yet. We may have to share a bedroom with a sister.

Such an arrangement may present some difficulties, as we may not have the same ideas of what the room should be like. We may not like the same colors, we may not choose the same arrangement, nor even have the same ideas about order and cleanliness. Even so, because the room is part our own, we have a pride of ownership in it. We may use the need to arrive at an agreement with sister on matters about the room to help us know more about getting along with people successfully. To think in terms of "ours" instead of "mine" means growth for us.

We want our own room to be convenient and attractive, clean and orderly. We want it to express our personality and to give us real pleasure. We know that wanting doesn't bring results. We must study and work to build the sort of room we want. We must learn to solve the many problems to be faced in making the room we wish for out of the room we have.

Problem 1: WHAT MAKES AN ATTRACTIVE AND CONVENIENT ROOM?

To be attractive, a room must be orderly. More important than its fine furniture, beautiful window curtains, and modern carpets is *order*. Yet this costs nothing but effort to obtain. We may well say with the poet:

Order is a lovely thing,
On disarray it lays its wing,
Teaching simplicity to sing.
It has a meek and lowly grace,
Quiet as a nun's face.
Lo—I will have thee in this place.[1]

Cleanliness also affects the appearance of a room; it always seems to be related to order. Cleanliness and order make for health and peace, we are told. Cleanliness, like order, costs little but effort to maintain.

Furnishings which are in good taste help make the room attractive. There should be a pleasing use of color that would add to our enjoyment. Since our room is a bedroom, meant to be a place of rest, the main color note should be light, simple, and restful.

If the room is to be convenient, it must have the furniture and furnishings needed for the purpose it serves. Our own room is a place for sleeping, resting, dressing, and caring for clothes. It is a place where we will study, read, and write letters, and frequently, when some member of the family or a chum comes in for a chat, a place where we will visit.

So we will need furniture for sleeping and resting: a bed, a bedside table, a rug, and a lamp. We will need furniture that will make dressing convenient: a dresser or a dressing table with storage space for our toilet articles, a mirror, such small things as we enjoy, and a clothes closet for storage of

---

[1] Anna Hempstead Branch, "The Monk in the Kitchen," *The Shoes That Danced*. Houghton Mifflin Co., New York, 1905.

clothing. We desire furniture that will make study and reading easy. For this we will want a table or a desk; a chair; a study lamp; and real equipment of books, ink, paper, pencils, pen, and such other articles as are necessary for our "brain work." A comfortable chair and a bookshelf add to the appearance and convenience of the room, and provide for the comfort of the family member or chum who drops in for a chat.

In this attractive, neat bedroom a comfortable covered cot has replaced the bedstead. How does the arrangement of the pictures enhance the appearance of the room?

The curtains we put at the windows, the rugs we put on the floor, and all the "gimcracks" we put about or put away affect the sense of repose in the room. If we have too many extra, meaningless things, we will create a sense of confusion that will be wearying.

Activities:

1. List the furniture you have in your bedroom.
2. What do you do to care for your room before you come to school?

Problem 2: HOW CAN WE IMPROVE THE FURNISHINGS IN OUR ROOM?

A few days ago a girl commented about her room: "It looks awful! Now, if I could just have a new maple set such as I saw in the window at Burter's!" The "new maple set" costs so much that it is out of the question for most of us.

We have the more interesting and difficult task of planning to improve the furnishings in our room at little if any cost. How shall we go about it? Perhaps the first thing to do is to look critically at each article in the room to see if it is useful and if it is beautiful. If we find that one wall holds a collection of canes and a Betty Boop doll won at a school carnival last year, we can say

Beautiful, what?
Useful? No!
All of it's trash—
Out you go!

Just clearing away useless, ugly articles helps to bring a sense of quiet into the room and improves our furnishings.

Perhaps as we look at the furniture that we really need we find the various pieces are quite different in type. There isn't much we can do to fit a walnut dresser, a bird's-eye maple bed, and a painted rocking chair into a "happy family" group. Then we can go to the attic, the basement, the sleeping porch, and the back hall, looking for "relatives" of the pieces of furniture we like best in our room. If we find pieces that seem to fit together better than those the room now has and it will not interfere with any other family member's interests, we may ask permission to make the change.

We may get a comfortable cot from the sleeping porch in exchange for the bird's-eye maple bed. Then we will see if we can get father to unscrew the upper part of the dresser and make a chest of drawers with the mirror separate above it. The painted chair may have a cushion and a tie-on back cover made of fabric in some color that fits it into the color scheme for the room.

If we do not have a desk and bookshelves, possibly father or brother will help us make them from an old commode or from some boards and an old kitchen table. These may be made fresh and attractive by the use of paints. Even a wide study shelf, put on substantial brackets with smaller, narrower shelves for books placed conveniently above it, will serve our needs nicely.

Next we can give thought to the pictures and small furnishings that we have used to make the room our own. There are three questions which we will ask:

Does this have beauty?

Does it fit here?

Is it one thing too much?

Too many pictures and too many trinkets will spoil the effect we desire, so we will keep only a few of the best. We will check the height at which the pictures are hung. If they are too high, they will seem to pull us up; if they are too low, the effect is not pleasing. They should be hung so we can seem to look right into the center of them. If we wish to use two or more smaller pictures instead of one large one in a wall space, those should be grouped together to make a unit. They may have the same line for the upper edge of the frame and be so placed that we do not have to go "hop, skip, and jump" in our minds when we look at them.

Now let us look at our clothes closet to see if it could be improved. It may be that our room has no closet space. Then it is our problem to arrange to have some. Later we will learn some ways that girls have followed to provide a substitute for a clothes closet. Perhaps there is a clothes closet which has no place for hanging clothes except on hooks around the walls. In such case, we will want to put in a clothes pole and some racks for our shoes. A shelf for hat boxes will help us to keep our hats in good shape, and a hook on which the laundry bag hangs will surely keep much litter from the floor.

After we have thrown away everything that is neither lovely nor useful, have checked to see if there is furniture in the home that would match up better for our room, and have seen that the pictures and other ornaments have been well placed, perhaps it is time then for us to think of what we would do to our room if we had some money to spend. Let us plan what fifty cents would do; what two dollars would do; and what five dollars would do. If we can plan the spending of these sums wisely, and are really interested in improving our furnishings, perhaps we will find a way to earn the money to go ahead, step by step. That is a slow way, of course, but it really brings the most fun.

Activities:

1. With the list of furniture made, check the articles really needed in your room.
2. How could you improve your room to make it more easily cared for?
3. Make a plan for improving the furniture you have in your room.

Problem 3: HOW CAN WE IMPROVE OUR ROOM THROUGH RE-ARRANGEMENT?

We have already said that our own room should have furniture in it to meet certain needs. Do you remember what these needs are? Sleeping, dressing, studying, and often reading. For sleeping we need a bed, a bedside table, a rug, and a lamp. For dressing, we need a dresser or a dressing table, a mirror, a stool or chair, the small ornaments that make the room cheery, and a clothes closet. For writing and study, we need a table or desk, a chair, a study lamp, and some shelves for our books. For reading and for friendly visiting, we need a comfortable chair, possibly a magazine rack or an end table with bookshelves, and a lamp.

We want the arrangement of furniture to be such that it will be convenient. We want good lighting for each activity in which light is important, such as studying, reading,

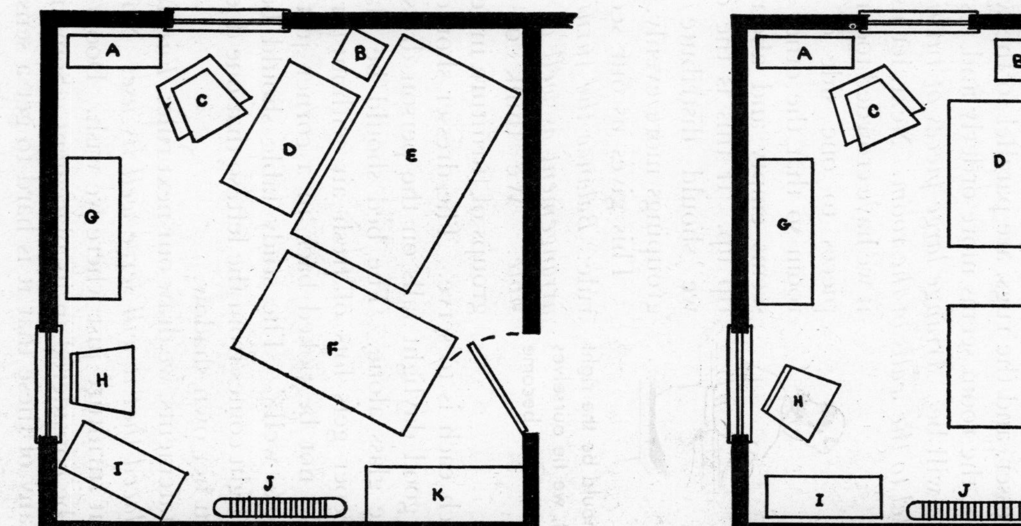

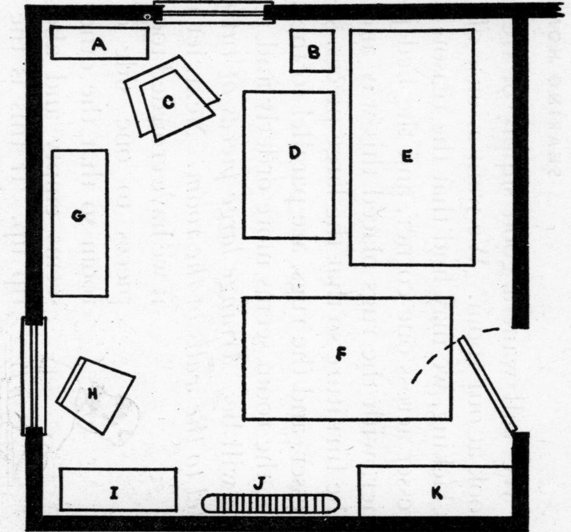

Can you explain why the chart at the left illustrates a poorly arranged room, and the one at the right a well-arranged room? The letters represent the following pieces of furniture: *A,* bookcase; *B,* bedside table; *C,* easy chair; *D,* rug; *E,* bed; *F,* rug; *G,* dresser; *H,* chair: *I,* desk; *J,* radiator; *K,* closet.

and dressing. We will want a good supply of fresh air.

Now let us look at our room. We want a sense of order in it. If this is lacking, we may find that the reason is that we have the dresser across one corner, and the bed jutting out from another, with the rugs placed this way and that. If we arrange the furniture so that the large pieces, such as the bed, the dresser, and the rugs, are parallel to the walls, we will find that the room seems more orderly and restful.

Our first rule will be: *Arrange large pieces of furniture and rugs parallel to the walls of the room.* Next, let us see if we have crowded too many pieces to one side of the room so that the other side seems empty and about to tip up. If this is the case, we should distribute the groupings more evenly.

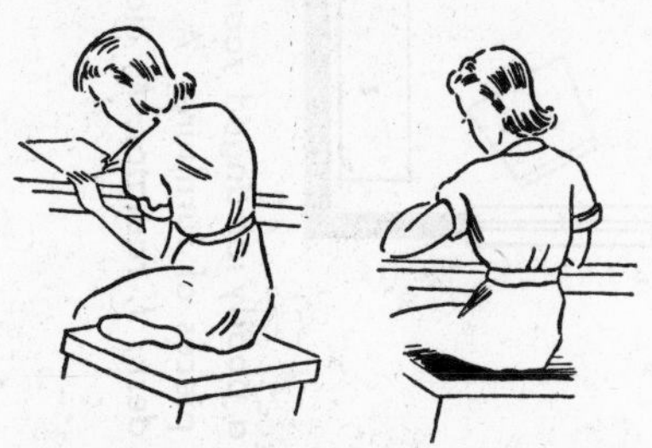

The study table should be the right height. If it is not, we tie ourselves in hard knots and soon become weary.

This gives us our second rule: *Balance the furniture arrangement as well as possible.* We think of the groups of furniture in terms of the use which each is to serve. The dresser should be placed so that good daylight falls on the person dressing, and not on the glass alone. The bed should be placed so that the sleeper gets lots of fresh air without drafts. The bed should not be poked back in a corner just because that "looks well." The study table should be so placed that the light comes from the left, so that one doesn't need to write in her own shadow.

From these statements, we draw our next rule: *Furniture should be so placed that it will serve well its use.* Not always can we put furniture just where we wish. Doors and windows must be considered in its placement. Sometimes there are so many of these that it is hard to get a sense of being alone; sometimes the openings are so few that a room seems to be a cell. We are fortunate if our room is pleasantly supplied with well-placed windows and has only two doors—one to the closet and one to the hall.

> In arranging any room, we may have to try several times in order to find the grouping that is fully satisfying. But if we find one arrangement we like very well, that is worth all the pulling and tugging.

Activities:

1. Make a drawing of the arrangement of furniture in your room.
2. Make a drawing showing a different arrangement.
3. Which arrangement is better for you? Why?

Problem 4: HOW CAN WE MAKE OUR ROOM EXPRESS OUR PERSONALITY?

If we look around at our classmates, we will see many different personalities. Mary Jo is athletic. She likes things that smack of the out-of-doors. No frills or elaborate trimmings for her! Janice is studious, a regular bookworm. She likes the quiet order and the soft, subdued colors of the library. Rosemary is little, dainty in face and person, and has a secret desire to be a moving picture star some day. Every once in a while she breaks her mother's rule that she is not to "play" with perfume yet. She is interested in her hair, her skin, her eyelashes—everything that seems to offer any promise of making her face more beautiful. There are many other different personalities among us.

Now, what have we all in common that we want our room to express? We all enjoy freshness, cleanliness, and order. We all seek peace and rest, cheerfulness and joy. We make our room express these things first; then next we will want it to say something about each of us as a different person from the other persons. Fancy, calm, romantic, or full of odd notions, we want our real selves to be reflected in our rooms.

In the expression of peace and rest, cheerfulness and joy, color plays a large part, just as it does in expressing our individual selves. So the most important thing in making our room express our personality is the choice of a color scheme.

Soon we find that colors also have "personality." Red and yellow are termed "warm colors" and blue is called a "cool color." If our room is sunny, we will not wish to add warmth. If our room is on the north and has only one window, we will not wish to add "coolness" to its effect. We find that colors are quiet, strong, dull and soft, or bright. With colors, as with people, we can have much more of the quiet than we can of the noisy or strong without becoming weary of it. As we study the room, we will decide what general color effect we think will be most desirable. Then we find out what we have to build on in the walls, woodwork, and floor of the room. If these are not to be changed, we will see what colors there are already in the room and then build the rest of our color scheme about these. If our color scheme is good, it will contain several colors.

There will be some one color that will be more outstanding than the others. Perhaps yellow is the color we plan to use as our keynote. If the walls are a soft tan and the woodwork is ivory, both will have some yellow in them. If the floor is oak or waxed pine, it will have some yellow in it. The window curtains may be of sheer material in a soft yellow. If we do not have any contrast, but have the whole room in yellow or green, we would feel as if we had been trapped in the cap of a daffodil or in a dense thicket in the woods. We would struggle for release and not enjoy our room at all.

To keep the room from giving this effect and becoming

It is difficult to think and live in an organized way when one occupies an untidy room.

tiresome, small amounts of color most unlike yellow may be used for contrast. Perhaps as we look at our room we may find that contrast is lacking to make it cheery and bright. Then we plan to provide contrast in our choice of small furnishings and ornaments. Pillows, dresser scarfs, table runners, and chair pads may all be used to give a note of contrast, or to repeat, perhaps in a stronger way, the color of the room. What color you want, what color the room will take, and how contrast can be given are all questions we must decide if we are to express ourselves successfully.

Our choice of pictures, vases, and small pottery figures ranks next to the color scheme in our plans for self-expression. We may choose to use enlarged photographs of scenes in the mountains where we spent our vacation, dainty colored prints of flowers, or copies of famous paintings.

The picture should please us in subject and in color, or it does not really "belong" in our room.

If we have opportunity to select new furniture, we express ourselves in our choice. A simply designed article of good lines, workmanship, and wood tells of our belief in sincerity and steadfastness. The choice of an article adorned with many patches of different wood shows our belief in surface values. Our choices do reveal our personalities.

We know, too, that the care we give our room expresses our own selves, just as truly as do the things we buy to put in the room. If we live in a room with pictures to one side, dust everywhere, soiled clothes kicked under the unmade bed, and the study table in a litter, we become indifferent to order and cleanliness. If we keep our room tidy, clean, and orderly day by day, we express our appreciation of tidiness, cleanliness, and orderliness, and our desire for the rest they help to bring.

Activities:

1. What do you have in your room that really expresses you?
2. How can you make your room more enjoyable through color?
3. What ornaments do you want in your room? Why?

Problem 5: HOW SHALL WE ARRANGE THE TOPS OF OUR STUDY TABLE AND DRESSER?

We have all studied with some girls whose desks were so arranged that the business of studying seemed easy. There was space to work, the supplies needed were conveniently at hand, and the light was good. Perhaps some of us have studied with other girls and have had a very different experience. Only the edge of the table was free from piled-up papers and books; the pencil sharpener was in another room; there was no paper at hand; and the light was so dim that our eyes became tired before an hour had passed. Experiences such as these should make us look more carefully

An orderly dresser top with only a few articles on it adds much to the charm of the room.

at the working surfaces of our study table and other flat surfaces in our own room. Before anything is given a place on study table, shelf, or dresser, we should know that it is useful or beautiful or both. If we accept the "useful or beautiful or both" rule we can make short shift of such a litter as last semester's examination papers, railroad timetables from last summer's trip, and empty ink bottles.

Next we should ask, "Does this belong *here?*" A handkerchief box may be both beautiful and useful, but it should not be on top of the study table. A dictionary is very important to the schoolgirl, but it does not "dress up" her dresser. It does not belong there. When we have right things in the right places, we should look at them to see if there are too many things for the space. A dresser top crowded with articles that may belong in or on the dresser still does not present a pleasing appearance. Let's put some of the stuff away in drawers and leave only a few things out. A few articles can be brought into a simple, orderly arrangement which has good balance. You remember that if all the heavy pieces of furniture were placed on one side of the room it seemed as if it might tip up. The same effect will be felt if we place most or all the articles on one side of the top of our dresser or table. We may balance one heavy article by another, or by two lighter ones. We want to place the articles far enough back from the edge so that they will not fall off or appear to be ready to fall off.

A snug corner of this cheery room has been set aside for a desk, which is well lighted for day or evening work. The bookshelves are close at hand.

In order to find the arrangement that we will like best, several different arrangements must be tried. When we find one that satisfies our sense of balance and our desire for pleasing color combination, we should consider it carefully. If it is simple, orderly, and well balanced, we will enjoy living with it and can regard it as a success.

Activities:

1. How are the tops of your study table and dresser arranged?
2. How can you improve this arrangement?

Problem 6: HOW SHALL WE ARRANGE THE STORAGE SPACE IN OUR ROOM?

Perhaps the term "storage space" seems strange when applied to our own room. Some of us may think of storage space for desks and other school equipment in the furnace room at school. Others may think of the storage space in the basement at home where the porch swing and lawn chairs are stacked in the winter. Of course, we have nothing like these in our room. The storage space we need is different, because of the sort of things we want to store or put away. The storage space in our room includes the drawers of the dresser and dressing table, and the clothes closet. The dresser drawers and chiffonier drawers usually hold the toilet articles, including comb and brush, powder and rouge, handkerchiefs, and gloves; such dress accessories as beads, bracelets, and clips; and underwear, including panties and slips, pajamas, hose, and similar articles. Possibly certain drawer space is given over to the storage of the past season's clothes. Our question is how we can arrange the available drawer space so as to take care of all these things, and have them easy to find and convenient for use. The following rules will help us work out a satisfactory arrangement:

1. Things frequently used should be put together in a place easy to reach.
2. Similar articles should be put together.
3. Small articles should be put in boxes or containers.
4. Things easily soiled should be wrapped or put in boxes.
5. The arrangement should be such that "pawing" is unnecessary.

As we apply these rules we find that the top dresser drawer is well suited to the storage of the comb and brush, cold cream, powder, and other toilet articles. They are alike in their purpose and are used frequently. It would be absurd to bend double several times a day to reach for a comb or a powder puff. We can well make a plan of the arrangement of the top drawer so that it will also contain

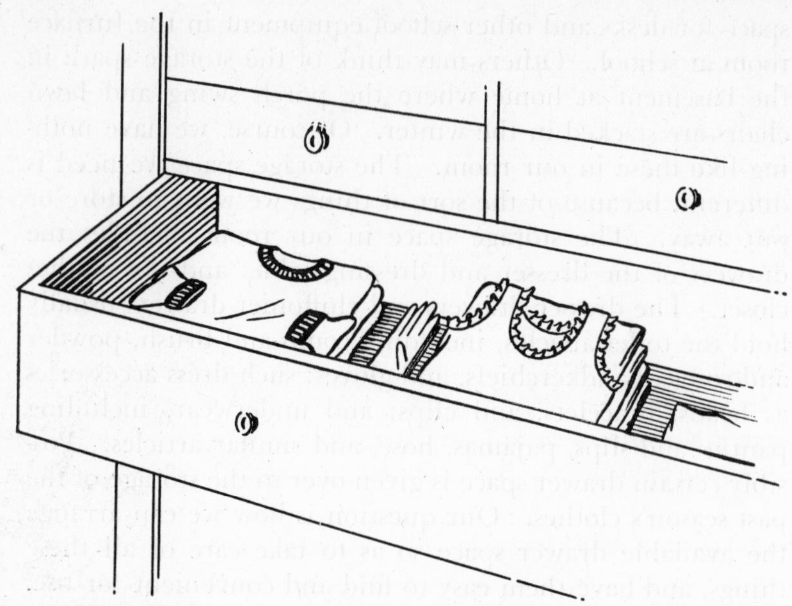

A well-arranged dresser drawer helps us to keep our room in order.

a handkerchief box and other necessary boxes. Possibly there will be room for a glove box if we plan carefully.

The second drawer is a convenient place for the storage of such things as hose, panties, pajamas, and slips. These we will stack neatly so that when the drawer is pulled out we can see what we want to take out without "pawing."

Because the lower drawer is the least convenient, it can be used to store garments of the past season. It may be packed full of neatly folded garments and covered with tissue paper or a towel to help keep out dust.

Careful thought should be given the arrangement of the closet. Provision should be made for all the clothes that are to be kept in it. Dresses, coats, blouses, and skirts are hung on hangers and placed in the closet. Best dresses and those used only occasionally should be hung to the back so as not to be brushed against when dresses are taken out and put in daily. Shoe racks or shoe boxes are useful for the storage of shoes.

Hats may be stored in boxes placed on shelves, put on hat stands, or hung on hooks. They should be placed high enough so they are not likely to be knocked off when clothes are being taken from the closet.

Both the drawer space and the closet space should be kept in order. Order saves time, fuss, and worry, and adds greatly to the appearance of the room.

Activities:

1. Plan the best way for you to arrange the storage space in your dresser drawer or in any other drawer.
2. Plan how to make the best use of the closet in your room.

Problem 7: WHAT CARE SHALL WE GIVE OUR ROOM DAILY?

The appearance of our room will depend upon the care it gets each day. In a well-kept room the bed is made each day. A satisfactory method for making a bed is as follows:

1. Place the mattress pad on the mattress.
2. Place the sheet over the mattress pad, with the center of the sheet being in the center of the bed.
3. Fold the sheet well under the mattress at both the head and the foot.
4. Pull the sheet tight at the sides and tuck it in, making the corners as square as possible.
5. Place the second or top sheet on, allowing enough length at the top to permit the sheet to be turned back over the covers.
6. Make mitered corners at the foot and on each side.
7. Put on the blankets or other covers. They should be placed straight on the bed and tucked in well at the foot.
8. Pull the top sheet over the upper portion of the covers to keep them from being soiled.

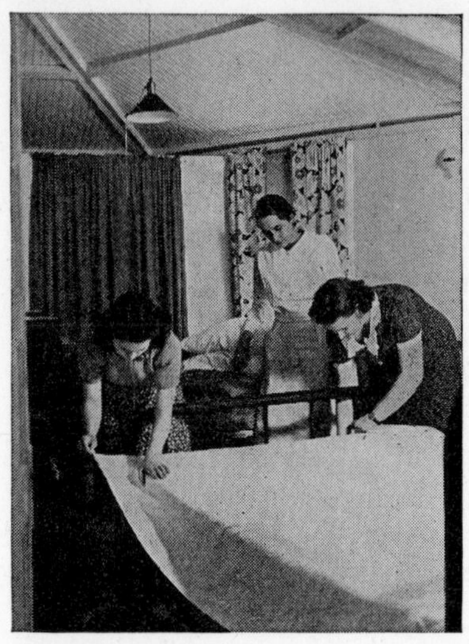

These schoolgirls are learning how to make a bed neatly with square corners.

9. Place the spread on evenly and straight. Tuck it in at the bottom.

10. Shake or press the pillows into form and place them on the bed as desired.

In making the bed, work from each side to be sure the covers are straight and even and free from wrinkles.

With books and magazines put in place and our clothing properly put away, the room begins to have an orderly appearance. The tops of the dressers and tables will have to be straightened and dusted. The amount of straightening will depend upon how many things we keep on the table surfaces. A few well-chosen articles on the dresser make it easier to keep and will give a better appearance.

Shades and curtains should be adjusted in such a way as to give an appearance of good order and to give the amount of light desired.

Sometimes our wastebasket needs to be emptied daily, so the contents are placed in a larger basket in the basement or in a trash burner in the yard away from the house. The wastebasket is then dusted and returned to the room.

With this care, our room will appear well and we will enjoy living in it.

Activities:

1. What do you do to care for your room each day?
2. List the steps for some daily job in the care of your room other than making a bed.

Problem 8: WHAT CARE SHALL WE GIVE OUR ROOM WEEKLY AND SEASONALLY?

Each household seems to have a time set aside each week when there are special tasks to do. For many of us that time is Saturday, when we are home from school and have more free time. We can carry our home responsibility by giving our room and closet a thorough cleaning. Such a cleaning means sweeping the rugs; dusting floors, woodwork, furniture, and ornaments; and wiping the windows. Perhaps the curtains may need to be dusted. However, this is difficult for a schoolgirl to do by herself, especially if her curtains must be taken down to be shaken and hung on the line.

The steps in sweeping a wood floor are as follows:

1. Use a good, firm broom that is not too stiff and scratchy.
2. Sweep with the length of the flooring as much as possible.
3. Overlap the broom strokes and sweep the dirt and waste to one place, going back to get any left wastes.
4. Give special sweeping to the corners.
5. Take up all dirt and waste on a dustpan.
6. Do not sweep dirt and waste from one room to another.

The following steps are used in sweeping carpets with a vacuum cleaner or sweeper:

1. Run the sweeper slowly lengthwise and then crosswise of the rug.
2. Repeat this again and again until the dirt is removed.
3. Empty the bag of the vacuum cleaner, or the bin of the sweeper, after each thorough weekly cleaning.

The following steps are used in sweeping carpets with a broom:

1. Sweep evenly, going across the width of the carpet.
2. Overlap the broom strokes.
3. Sweep the ends and edges well.
4. Keep the broom on the carpet while sweeping.
5. Sweep the dirt to one place, going back to get any left wastes.
6. Take up all dirt and waste on the dustpan.
7. Do not sweep dirt and waste from one room to another.
8. Use bits of moistened paper to reduce dust and brighten the carpet.

Often when thorough sweeping is done the furniture and small objects are covered or removed from the room. The steps in dusting are as follows:

1. Use soft cloths that do not shed lint.
2. Use oil sparingly on the dust cloths.
3. Wipe the dust off surfaces carefully, taking the dust up into the cloth.
4. Dust high things first and then the low ones.
5. Use a dust mop for uncarpeted floors, wiping well the corners and the surfaces under the large pieces of furniture.

Sometimes it is desirable to use the sweeper on carpets after the dusting.

The bed should be made up with fresh linen each week. When the mattress is stripped ready to be remade, we should turn it, with the help of some older member of the family. This will equalize the pressure which sleeping on it has caused, and help prevent sunken places in it.

The dresser scarf and table runners should be changed each week.

There is additional care to be given seasonally or at long intervals, which we can hardly give ourselves. This care includes washing windows, curtains, bedspreads, pillow covers, and dress covers; polishing furniture and fixtures; waxing floors; and cleaning the bed springs.

Activities:

1. How do we care for our room weekly? How do we care for our room seasonally?
2. What are the steps in dusting woodwork? What are the steps in wiping windows?
3. What are the steps in dusting furniture?

REFERENCES FOR THE UNIT

Jensen, Milton B., Jensen, Mildred R., and Ziller, M. Louisa, *Fundamentals of Home Economics.* New York: The Macmillan Co., 1935.

Kinyon, Kate W., and Hopkins, L. Thomas, *Junior Home Problems,* Revised Edition. New York: Benj. H. Sanborn and Co., 1938.

Matthews, Mary Lockwood, *The New Elementary Home Economics.* Boston: Little, Brown and Co., 1937.

SUGGESTED HOME EXPERIENCES

1. Do the weekly cleaning of your room and keep a record of how much time is needed to do it well. Make a list of the successive steps in the work. Can you improve the process in any respect?
2. Rearrange the furniture in your room and compare it with the original arrangement.
3. Plan and rearrange the top of your study table and dresser.
4. Plan a new color scheme for your room.

UNIT 7

MAKING AND KEEPING FRIENDS

HAVING FRIENDS IS VERY IMPORTANT to all of us. We all need friends—"persons to whom we are attached by esteem and affection." People speak with pity of a friendless dog; the state of a friendless person is much more sad. Perhaps you have experienced some part of the loneliness of being without friends at one time or another. Your family may have moved to a new town where you knew no one. You saw other girls pass by in two's or three's, laughing and chatting. Perhaps they paid no attention to you, and you became homesick or "friend sick" for the familiar streets and friends of your old home.

For the moment, you wanted friends more than anything else in the world. You needed their interest and companionship. Probably you ran quickly to your mother or father and found yourself partly comforted by the loving attention shown you. If you were very shy, you may have tried to make the love of your family fill its own place in your life, and also fill the empty place caused by your lack of friends. Some boys and girls do this. It saves them from the hurts of possible cold treatment and disappointments in friendships. However, using your family to take the place of friends is not a good idea. Boys and girls who do this seldom fully "grow up." They remain "mothers' babies."

The persons who do without friends are never fully happy, nor do they get the most out of life. In the heart of each of us there is a strong desire for friends.

Problem 1: WHY DO WE WANT FRIENDS?

Why do we want friends? It might be easier for you to tell why you want a certain person as a friend. Suppose we start that way and you give the reasons why you desire Mollie or Sue for your friend. You might say, "Well, I want her as a friend because she likes me and thinks I'm fine. I can trust her, she gives me courage, she is always seeing something new, and she is such fun to be with!"

Stated just a little differently, these are among the reasons why we all want friends, whether we are high school girls and boys, college students, or white-haired businessmen. Being liked by someone makes us feel worthy. Even a little child feels the need of the esteem of others and of being highly valued by them. As one grows older, this need for esteem grows, and with it the need for friends.

Being able to trust another person adds to our sense of security and safety. When the whole day seems to go wrong, when we have slipped on wet stones, tripped over sticks, and been hurt by schoolmates, it is comforting and deeply satisfying to have a friend who understands and can be depended upon.

We want friends because they give us courage. You may have heard a speaker say, "I would never have had the courage to go on had it not been for my friends." Explorers, scientists, statesmen, and musicians all have found the encouragement of friends to be at least part of the reason for their continued struggle and success. We want a friend who is "always seeing something new." We all want friends because they help us to see things in the world about us. Through friends we come to have interest in many things. One may interest us in stamps, another in stories, another in music, and still another in flowers and trees. They give us their eyes and we see things we have missed before.

We want friends because they are "fun to be with."

This group of young people has met together for an afternoon of conversation about books. Sharing with others the joy of good books is one of the most pleasant delights of friendship.

They share with us their joy in living. Have you not had friends who could make a hike over the hills seem an exciting adventure, and a trip to the grocery store an amusing journey? We want friends, then, because they bring color and fun into daily living.

Most of all, perhaps, we want friends because we have the capacity for loving. If we are to grow, we must use this as we use our capacity for seeing or walking. If we are not to waste our love on ourselves, we must have friends for whom we can feel admiration and affection.

Activities:

1. Can you think of other reasons for wanting friends? If so, what are they?
2. State the kind of a picture each of these statements brings to your mind: "Everyone loves her." "He hasn't a friend in the world."

Problem 2: WHAT QUALITIES HELP BUILD REAL FRIENDSHIPS?

Jean was talking to her aunt, whom she had not seen for several months. She told about her new books, her school

Be a good loser. A poor sport never makes good friends. If the girl at the right were a good loser, she would offer congratulations to the girl who won fairly in the archery contest.

work, and her music lessons. Then her aunt asked, "Do you still have Bess for your chum?" Jean replied, "No, I don't like her very much any more. She just didn't wear well." In friendships, as in hose or shoes, the matter of "wearing well" is important. It depends on whether or not certain qualities are present. Although the person appears ever so attractive, if these important qualities are lacking, an effort at a friendship with her just will not "wear well." It will be soon ended, usually with some hurt to one or both persons. The shortest possible statement of what is important in friendships *that wear well* is shared confidence, shared understanding, and shared love.

What gives you confidence in another person? No one word will cover the whole matter. Confidence is placed in one who is honest, truthful, loyal, and reliable, and has self-control. If a person has these qualities, she will be one whom you can safely trust.

Perhaps you have known a girl who had all these qualities, but still you did not wish her for a friend. You seemed to have little in common. You had no *shared understand-*

ing. To build a shared understanding one must be appreciative, patient, and thoughtful. One must have sympathy and be a good companion; and last but not least, one must have a good sense of humor. A girl who has all these qualities may be great fun, but if she lacks honesty and loyalty, there would not be much chance of building a real friendship with her. The first time you needed to count on her, she might fail you. You need both confidence and understanding if the friendship is to last.

Shared love is more difficult to analyze. You know quite well that sometimes your heart goes out to some other person. You find it easy to like her, and look forward to a real friendship with her. As time passes and your acquaintance deepens, the attraction and respect changes to affection, and you have a friend.

In the same way, sometimes you feel a dislike for a person from the first, much as was felt toward Dr. Fell in this rhyme:

I do not like you, Dr. Fell.
The reason why I cannot tell.
But only this, I know full well
I do not like you, Dr. Fell.

If you find nothing to share with a person, it will be difficult to develop a liking. However, you may cheat yourselves out of interesting acquaintances and, perhaps, friends, if you follow your first impressions. Certain qualities lie too deep to be seen at first meeting.

It is well to remember that you must bring to a friendship the qualities you seek in your friend. There is an old saying, "One finds what he brings." Perhaps there is no person who is wholly truthful, wholly loyal, or wholly not selfish all the time. There are many people who have grown to be more truthful, more loyal, and less selfish, just as they have grown in height and learning year by year. If you value these qualities yourself, choose for your friends persons who feel as you do about them. Then your friendships will help you all to grow.

Activities:

1. Make a list of the qualities you like or desire in your friends. Check these with yourself and see how many of them you have.
2. What qualities do you think will prevent the building of real friendships? Do you have any of these qualities? If so, what can you do about it?
3. Can a real friendship be built if one of the persons is domineering and selfish? Give reasons for your answer.

Problem 3: HOW SHALL WE CHOOSE OUR FRIENDS?

It is a difficult matter to choose something and be sure that you will be satisfied with your choice. You may puzzle quite a while over the choice of a handkerchief or a hat. Before you spend your cash for it you can see the color, inspect the material, and check in several ways whether it is suitable, durable, and desirable. Even then you are sometimes disappointed in your choice. Choosing friends is even more difficult. There is no way in which you can get your hands on the personal qualities of another girl to determine whether she is suitable, durable, and desirable as a friend. However, there are certain points which may serve as our guides when we choose friends.

We should choose friends who have the qualities already discussed as important in friendship. Few, if any, persons are 100 per cent honest, loyal, sincere, and so on through the list of qualities we discussed. Many, if not most, people are interested in possessing these qualities. We want to choose our friends from the group to whom these qualities are important.

We tend to choose as our friends persons who have the same interests that we have and like to do the same things that we do. If we have never studied music and know too

Interest in games has led many girls into warm friendships. These girls are absorbed in the tense finish of a game of checkers.

little about it to find it interesting, we may be bored by a person whose only thought is of music. If we are bookish, we may find little to share with the person who never reads and never thinks. *Sharing* is really the secret of a successful friendship, and if we have nothing to share with another person in interests and activities, a friendship can scarcely grow between us. Fortunately, most of us have not one but many interests, so there are many possibilities of making contacts that may lead to friendships.

Personal standards should be considered in choosing our friends. You may quickly reply, "Oh, I would never choose as a friend a girl who had poor standards of cleanliness, dirty nails, and hair not combed. My friends must be neat and clean." It is easier to see low standards in the care of the body than it is to see low standards of thinking and living. Yet the standards one holds for thinking and living matter most in making a person a good friend. We want our friends to be clean in body and mind. We know the person with low standards has little to share.

> We should choose not one friend but several. Many girls limit their chance for comrades and growth by having only one person with whom they share their interests and activities. This is much like climbing a hill and looking at the view only in one direction. It may be fine on all sides. One needs to view life from various angles, through the eyes of many friends.

In choosing friends, we should seek those who want to *share,* not those who want to boss us or lean on us. If we can find sharing friends, there will be growth for us all. If we have a bossy friend, we almost become "things" for her to manage instead of sharers with her in plans and activities. If we have a "leaner" as our friend, we are likely to tell her what to do and what to think. So, we ourselves may become bossy. Such friendships do not help us to grow. We should choose as our friends persons who will *share* with us, so there will be equality in our relationship.

Activities:

1. Consider two or three of your friends, and write for each an account of how you and they came to be friends.
2. When would you say a person had made the right choice of friends? What would you consider a bad choice?
3. Can you give examples of a good choice of friends and of a poor choice?

Problem 4: HOW SHALL WE MAKE FRIENDS?

In a school one day a shy, lonely girl watched her classmates go to the game room by two's or four's, chattering merrily on the way. She made one or two slight efforts to get into one of the groups without success. At last she went to the teacher in charge and said, "Can you help me? I'd like to be friends, too, but I just don't stick." Many of us

Many schools set aside afternoons for school parties. Participation in such activities helps to make boys and girls feel at ease in meeting and talking with others. Pupils should have the opportunity for social experience of this kind and should take part in such events gladly.

are like her. We would like to find a way that would help us to "stick" in making friends. We may think it would be fine if we could find a short cut or a magic way of drawing friends to us and holding them there. This might be possible if we were magnets and other people were bits of steel. However, friendships are between live people, not between magnets and steel. In the making of them, nothing is more important than consideration of people as people.

A girl who has many friends suggests the following qualities as important in making friends.

Be sincere and trustworthy. Real friendship is impossible unless we can trust one another. Trust goes when we find we have been deceived. Deceit and double-dealing soon are discovered and the double-crosser is held off at arm's length by people as a protection from her. Not only does the friend who has been deceived become wary of her, but others as well. On the schoolground we sometimes hear words like these: "Well, I told her I wouldn't tell, but I'll tell you." "I said I'd go with her, but I'll tell her that mother kept me in; I'd much rather go with you." This is cheating, isn't it? When one cheats all the time, soon her word means nothing to her and to others. Then her friendship also means nothing to others.

Be kind and generous in speech and thought. Unkind words have a way of being repeated, added to, and emphasized so that their hurt goes on and on. Said in a careless and thoughtless manner, they are often repeated as if they were reasoned thinking. We all need to remember the warning of the poet, Will Carleton:

> Boys flying kites
> Haul in their white-winged birds.
> You can't do that,
> When you're flying words.
> Thoughts unexpressed
> May sometimes fall back dead,
> But God, Himself, can't kill them,
> When they are said.

Saying pleasant things isn't enough; we must think pleasant things. What we think determines what we are and what our attitude will be. That in turn affects our friends. Our words and our thoughts both affect our success in making friends.

Be considerate. Courtesy and consideration bring good returns, not only in building good habits, but in drawing friends to us.

Be interested in the interests of others. Having interest in the interests of others is a good way to grow in wisdom and in friends. This is very different from having interest in other people's business. This last, which is merely being nosy, destroys friendship, while the first builds friendship. People like to talk about their hobbies, their work, and their play. Friendship deepens as you listen. Being a good listener is said to be one of the characteristics of a friend. We must listen if we are to understand and share the thoughts of our friends and the things they are doing. Possibly you may learn to like the special interests of your friends. *Your* interest then will help you to make friends and increase your own capacity for pleasure.

Avoid boasting and pretense. Sometimes we make the mistake of bragging about our family, our home, our car, and so on, in an effort to impress our classmates with our importance. Sometimes these claims become so absurd that they amuse rather than impress. The same thing is true of reckless spending of money to make a show. People are seldom deceived by extravagance in talk or spending. They will doubt our wisdom and our training if we try to brag or spend our way to attention. We lose rather than gain friends when we rely on pretense and display.

Bring your best self to the friendship. "We will find what we bring." If we bring envy, jealousy, self-pity, and a whining discontent with life, we will not rise above that level in our friendship. If we bring generosity, happiness, and enthusiasm for living, we will make friends at that level.

Activities:

1. Imagine that you are the editor of a girls' page in a newspaper. A schoolgirl writes you that she is lonely and wants to know how to make friends. Write a paragraph or two in which you tell her how to do this.
2. Make a list of "Do's for Making Friends" and one of "Don'ts for Making Friends." How do they compare?
3. Think of a person who has many friends. What qualities does he or she have that are responsible for these friends?

Problem 5: HOW CAN WE KEEP OUR FRIENDS?

Choosing friends is the first step, making friends is the second step, and keeping friends is the third. Perhaps it would be more nearly true to say that keeping friends includes a number of steps. To make the friendship worthwhile, the keeping must continue over a much longer time than is required for the making. What we will do to keep anything depends upon what it is we will keep. If it is money, we may put it in the bank; if it is a bracelet or a watch, we may put it in one of our boxes or a drawer; if it is a dog, we may tie it on a leash and take it with us. You can do none of these things with friendship. It is not a material thing that can be put away and when taken out be found the same. It either increases or decreases. It gains in strength or loses.

In order to keep our friends, then, the bond between us and them must be alive and growing. *Sharing* is important in keeping the friendship alive and growing. Sharing is not dividing something into smaller parts; rather, it is possessing and enjoying something together. That is what we want in friendship. Shared confidences, shared understanding, and shared love all help us to keep our friends. Being true to our friends helps us to hold them. Being true to them doesn't mean agreeing with them at every point and taking their side in school squabbles. Shakespeare speaks of being true in these words:

> This above all, to thine own self be true,
> And it must follow as the night the day,
> Thou canst not then be false to any man.

If we are true to ourselves, we will be fair and honest to our friends.

Being thoughtful and considerate will help us keep our friends. With friends, as with our family, it is important that thoughtfulness and consideration should characterize our every contact. It is easy to presume on friendship. We can all think of many examples of this. Anne and Rachel were in the high school hall talking about plans for a school party, and Jane was waiting for Anne at the door. Anne suggested to Rachel that they go to the class sponsor to talk about the favors. When asked if Jane were not waiting for her, she replied, "She can wait; she's my friend." Friendship does not give us the right to be demanding, hurtfully frank, brutally rude, or unkind in our remarks and action. Ugly comments on hair that cannot be changed, clothes that must be worn, or the peculiarities of some family member are not excusable.

In China, it is believed that "keeping one's face" is necessary for living. By "keeping one's face" is meant holding one's self-respect and carrying one's head with pride. The sharing involved in friendship may give us information about our friend that, if widely circulated, might cause her to "lose face." Perhaps her clothes are all "made overs" and the other girls think they are new. Perhaps her loved father has lost his job and the family soon must go to live with the grandmother. Perhaps there is some member of her family mentally sick. If we know such facts because we are friends, we should be careful not to hurt our comrade, either directly or by causing her to "lose face."

Perhaps the most important thing in keeping friends is being worthy of them. A poet, thankful for friends, puts his desire to keep them into these words:

> It is my joy in life to find
> At every turning of the road,
> The strong arms of a comrade kind,
> To help me onward with my load,
> And since I have not gold to give,
> And love alone must make amends,
> My only prayer is "While I live,
> God, make me worthy of good friends." [1]

[1] Frank Dempster Sherman, "A Prayer," *High Tide—Lyrics of Joy.* Houghton Mifflin Co., New York, 1916.

Keeping our friends will be made easier if we constantly remember what friendship really is. We should not use our friend to keep us satisfied with ourselves. If we want her to act as a mirror in which we can see a flattering reflection of ourselves all the time, we will not be able to keep her friendship. She must be true to herself, and we should not demand that she be otherwise.

Activities:

1. Talk with your mother or father about some friend that she or he has had for years. Obtain from her or him reasons why the friendship has been a lasting one.
2. What great friendships do we know of through history and literature?
3. How far would the Golden Rule aid in keeping friends?
4. A young man recently said, "I expect my friends to do something for me. I want no other kind." What is his likelihood of keeping friends? Why?

Problem 6: WHAT ARE CAUSES OF DIFFICULTY IN MAKING AND KEEPING FRIENDS?

Sometimes girls are lonely, lacking friends just because there are no persons of their own age around with whom to be friends. A mountain home, far away from any neighbors, might be a happy place, and the brothers and sisters in it might enjoy playing together, but there would be little chance for them to make friends. An American girl, with her parents in Paris, but lacking any knowledge of the French language, would have small chance of making friends with other girls. There have to be other girls and boys about if one is to make friends among them.

Another difficulty, perhaps more common, is that we just do not know the rules of playing and being together which are accepted by the crowd we would like to be in. Sometimes our manners are different from theirs, and that holds us apart. A carefully reared southern girl, always thought-

The girl at the left must do her part, too, if she wants to be included in friendly companionship. If she pouts or acts "uppish" she will be left out of the good times the others are having.

ful of her "Yes, ma'am," "Thank you, ma'am," and "If you please, ma'am," was for a long time shut out of friendships in a midwestern high school because her classmates thought her "ma'ams" seemed unnatural and put on for show.

Kate, a tomboy, always one of the group in grade school days, found herself left out when the class entered high school. Kate couldn't understand the reason for this. When her teacher inquired of the other girls, they said, "She just doesn't know anything about behaving. She is like a bull in a china shop. She wants to wrestle and scuffle even when we are all dressed up." Kate failed to keep up with the rules accepted by the group. She was lonely and lacked friends until she accepted and began to follow the rules of her school group.

Sometimes a person knows the rules of the group and follows them, but has difficulty in making a friend out of an acquaintance. She is unable to trust people. Perhaps back in her childhood a friend failed her and now she refuses to trust anyone. She doesn't want to be hurt again. A child who refused to walk because he might tumble would miss much joy in living. Once a tumble doesn't mean always a tumble. This girl must be adventurous and take her chances on friends, else life will be rather flat.

Another difficulty sometimes found in making friends is that the person does not know what friendship is like or how to help it to grow. If one thinks that a friend must be an owner or a guardian, she will find her ideas are not accepted by others, and she will always be disappointed. Sometimes the difficulty in making and keeping friendships is that one or the other tries to boss or rule the other. For example, a girl was asked by her older sister where the friend was who had been always about some weeks earlier. The girl replied, "She thought being friends gave her charge of an army, and I was it—and I didn't think so." When we try to boss or rule, we forget that friendship is based on *sharing* for the equal satisfaction of both.

Most of our difficulties in making and keeping friends arise in what we and our friends are, in our failure to understand what friendship is, and in our lack of skill in handling our contacts with people.

Activities:

1. Outline a program of conduct for yourself that will aid you in making and keeping friends.
2. When a difficulty arises in a friendship, what should the persons do?
3. To what extent should outsiders influence us in our friendships?

SUGGESTED HOME EXPERIENCES

Try to be a better friend yourself. Work out a plan of procedure. Then follow it. Make changes as necessary. After a few weeks, check yourself and find out how much you have improved.

UNIT

8

HELPING WITH THE FAMILY MEALS

HAVE YOU EVER THOUGHT HOW MUCH time and energy go into providing the family with three meals each day? It is often stated that at least one-half of man's time and energy go for this purpose. There is the raising of the food or the earning of money to buy it, the planning for purchasing the food and using it, the care of the food after it reaches the home, the preparing and serving of it, and the clearing away and the cleaning up necessary after each meal. All of these together make the job of preparing and serving the family meals a large and responsible one.

The meal in most homes is more than just a means of obtaining food. It is a happy time for the family group. Usually all the family members are together for at least one or two meals each day. Over their food they share the happenings of the day. In the give-and-take of such discussion and planning each one has an important part in the family life.

Certain ways of doing things have come to be associated with the serving and eating of food at mealtimes. Certain of these are generally accepted as the correct ones to follow, and are known as rules for table service and table manners. To the extent that these rules are observed in the home, the meal offers training to the family members.

Each member of the family has important responsibilities in the family meals. If we can learn to do our part and help in making our family's meals successful, we will add to the happiness of our family.

Problem 1: WHY ARE THE FAMILY'S MEALS IMPORTANT?

Family meals are the means of providing, at regular times, the food needed by the family. Planned and prepared with the individual members in mind, family meals should care for food needs better than is done in any other way. Mother is interested that the baby shall have the grow foods he needs, that the high school son shall have not only adequate grow foods but the go ones needed by the captain of the football team, and so on through the special needs of each member of her family. Her interest leads to the planning and preparation of meals that are adequate and right for her family.

Mealtime gives an important opportunity for the family members all to be together as a group. In these days of many individual activities and interests, families often find "getting together" or having time for family life somewhat difficult. Mealtimes seem to offer one answer to this problem. People are then usually in good spirits, eager and ready for food. Sitting close together around a table seems to give a oneness of feeling that is good and fine for the family. Through these times of being together, the family members come to develop deep bonds of love and loyalty.

The family's mealtime gives an opportunity to renew the happenings of the day. Here it is possible for each one to tell something of what he has been doing. Each then has a share in the other's experience. Interest in one another's activities is developed, and all feel better acquainted. The discussion is usually extended to include events in the community, state, nation, or world. All this helps in the education of the family.

Mealtime also gives opportunity for the establishment of family ideals. These may be shown in our manners, standards of living, consideration of others, interests, and character. Eating, thinking, working, and playing together help

Mealtime is enjoyable when the table is neat and orderly, the food tastily prepared, and the members of the family contribute to happy conversation.

in the forming of common ideals. You have heard comments similar to the following: "The Browns have such strong family loyalty." "Everybody knows the Smiths are honest; you can trust any of them anywhere." Such observations make us realize that families should give more time to their ideals.

Family meals offer a place for the teaching of manners and social forms, especially those connected with the serving and eating of food. Good manners and other social graces are learned chiefly through actual doing. Mealtime offers one of the best opportunities for their practice. Our table manners are said to express the family's standards more than anything else. Surely families should not be blind to the need of proper training along this line.

Family meals should be the happiest times of the day.

The family members should look forward to mealtime with joy, quite as much for the time together as for the food. Families that use mealtime for corrections, however necessary these may be, or for disputes and quarrels, are making a mistake. Good times together during family meals will do much toward keeping us in good health and making us worth-while persons.

Activities:

1. Why should mealtime be more than a means of obtaining food?
2. Give examples of the use some families are making of mealtime for the improvement of the family members.
3. Find and bring to class some reference in literature concerning the importance of meals or mealtime in family life.

Problem 2: WHAT INFLUENCES THE FAMILY'S MEALS?

If we were to take a trip in which we spent a day or two with several different families in our neighborhood, we would probably find that no two served identical meals. Though the meals of two homes might be alike in some respects, we would find some differences. Perhaps this would be shown in the beverages or dessert served, or in the service of the food. If we would extend this trip to include other sections, we would probably find the difference in the meals even greater.

What makes this difference in families' meals? Why do they vary so? Families differ in their food needs. One family may be composed of young adults and children, another of middle-aged members, and still another may be composed chiefly of aged people. The activities of the families vary, too. In one family the members may engage in heavy outdoor work; in another, they may have light indoor work. The interests of a family also make a difference. Outdoor sports and exercise produce certain needs for food.

The *income* of the family is an important influence on the meals. The food must be selected and purchased in relation to the family's money. Families with lower incomes must purchase less expensive foods. Careful planning, then, is necessary if the essential foods in proper amount are to be supplied to the family. Some families with low incomes extend their food allowance by raising fruit, vegetables, and animals for food.

The *likes and dislikes* of families influence the character of the meals. Just to what extent this should be encouraged is, of course, a question. We do want to serve foods that the family likes and enjoys. However, if the dislikes are so numerous that many essential foods are omitted, a change in the family's likes and dislikes should be made. Foolish notions about food are poor guides for meal planning.

The *time, energy, and help* that those responsible for the family meals have are other important influences on meals. Elaborate meals served at too great an expense of some person's time and energy do not contribute to satisfying family life. Families with plenty of help, either from family members or from paid helpers, may be able to serve elaborate meals and to have dishes that require much work in preparation. However, there is some question as to whether, after all, the simple meal is not more to be desired than the elaborate meal.

The *equipment* on hand determines to some extent the character of the family's meals. Certain foods and dishes cannot be prepared if essential equipment is lacking. In many instances another piece of equipment than that called for can be used. However, to make an angel food cake, a special pan is needed; to freeze ice cream, a freezer is essential; and to fry croquettes, a deep-fat frying kettle is required.

The *standards and customs* of the family have a strong effect on the character of the meals served. Many of these habits have their beginning far back in the history of the family. A family may serve Swedish breads because some of the ancestors of the mother came from Sweden. In another family, because the father's ancestors were from Italy, spaghetti served with strong cheese is enjoyed. Likewise, another family, whose ancestors lived in England, frequently serves roast beef and Yorkshire pudding. There are wide differences in the standards affecting the family's meals. One family serves all its meals informally; another, more formally. One family always has chicken for Sunday dinner, and another, baked ham. One family always has bacon and eggs for breakfast, and its neighbor across the street has toast and fruit. In one family all the members must eat breakfast together; in another, breakfast is a "help-yourself" meal. If the practices followed are satisfying to the family and give its members no disadvantage in their life outside, they may be regarded as desirable.

Community practices exert an influence on the character of the family meals. The same type of meals are served generally in a given place. Certain foods and dishes and ways of serving the food are also in common use. The three meals of the day usually follow a given pattern, such as breakfast, dinner, and supper, or breakfast, luncheon, and dinner. In some communities any breaking away from the food customs brings all sorts of difficulties to a person. Sometimes community practices are strong influences in preventing people from improving their diets and food habits.

Activities:

1. Make a list of the things that influence your family's meals. Compare your list with the lists of the others in your class.
2. What things do you consider should be the most important influences? When is an influence an undesirable one?
3. What special customs in regard to family meals exist in your community?

Problem 3: WHAT IS OUR RESPONSIBILITY FOR THE FAMILY MEALS?

If the meals are to be truly a family affair, every member must have a share in them. Just what this share is depends upon the family itself. Even the preschool child may have a part, though it be as small as wiping the spoons or placing the silver on the table. Older members have a larger responsibility in keeping with their larger ability.

The responsibilities for the preparation and serving of the meals should be divided as evenly as possible. The whole responsibility should not rest upon only one family member. This not only overburdens one person but causes the others to miss fun and pleasure that comes from sharing and working together. Usually some one member must be responsible for planning and directing the work. The others then have some special part, such as a particular job, or they may render general assistance. Tasks that are common in meal preparation and service include gathering food from the garden, shopping, preparing and serving of food, and cleaning up afterwards. Accepting one's share of such duties cheerfully and willingly is highly desirable on the part of everyone.

Being on time for meals is an important responsibility. Nothing is more upsetting to the family's daily routine than frequent tardiness at meals. Those who have had to wait are upset and disturbed, and the meal is seldom a pleasant one. Food is rarely at its best when it stands for any length of time after it is ready to be served. Being late to meals becomes a habit and is in most cases unnecessary. Many families have an understanding that the meal will be served at a set time, whether everyone is present or not. Should a member be late, he slips quietly into his place when he comes, or, if the table is cleared away, goes to the kitchen and serves himself.

Family members should come to the table with their faces and hands washed and their hair combed. Their clothing should be clean and in satisfactory condition. They should be fully dressed. Sleeping garments and bathrobes are not suitable garments for the dining room. Many families follow the custom of "dressing" for dinner several times during the week. They find this practice adds to the pleasure and satisfaction of the meal.

The family members should be cheerful and in a pleasant mood when they come to the table. It is far better to stay away from the meal than to come in a sulky or grouchy manner "carrying a chip on one's shoulder." One unpleasant person can mar the mealtime pleasure of the entire family.

The food served should be accepted without fuss and complaint. If one does not care for a particular food or dish, he should quietly leave it alone and do nothing to call attention to his own shortcomings. Unkind remarks are apt to hurt the feelings of those who prepared the meal. If some dish is a failure, the person responsible for its preparation already knows the fact. Further talking about it will cause an unhappy time for everyone at the table.

All of you know homes where you like to be invited for meals. The chief reason for your enjoyment is not the food that will be served but rather the good spirit that exists at the table. Every family member has a responsibility for the development of a fine family spirit and should do his best to make each meal a happy time. Only through effort to this end can mealtime become a time of real pleasure for the family and their guests.

A further responsibility which we all have is to increase our knowledge and skills so that as we grow older we may be able to assume a larger share of the work of preparing and serving family meals. Our school kitchens and dining rooms are not identical with those of our homes, but they give us opportunity for instruction and practice in food preparation and service. If we take advantage of this and apply at home what we have learned at school, this increased knowledge and skill should be ours.

Activities:

1. What responsibilities do you assume at the present time for your family's meals?
2. What other responsibilities could you and should you assume?

Problem 4: HOW SHALL WE WORK IN OUR SCHOOL KITCHEN?

The dress and personal equipment suitable for work in our school kitchen or laboratory is that which is suitable for work in the home kitchen. An apron is essential. It should be made of cotton material that is easily laundered. Plain colors or prints are preferred. They add cheer to the group, and soil less easily than white. The design and style should be such that the apron covers one's dress well, and gives real protection. The apron should be put on the first thing after entering the kitchen.

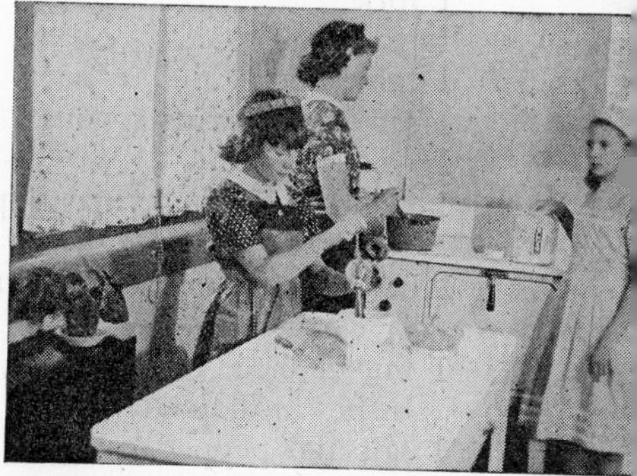

These young girls are at work in their school kitchen, making a pudding for their luncheon.

Some girls like to wear a headband or hairnet to keep the hair in place and prevent loose hairs from falling into the food. If one of these is worn, it should be put on at the same time as the apron.

One or more pot-holders are necessary. These can be made from scraps of cotton material and should be well padded. A small hand towel, colored or white, is also needed.

The school kitchen or laboratory is divided into work units where two, three, or four pupils work together. Each unit includes a working surface of some kind, a storage cabinet, a sink, a stove, and certain small equipment needed for food preparation. In some laboratories, the work unit includes a small kitchen and dinette combined, much like those in small apartments.

The small equipment which is used regularly and frequently is kept in each of these units all the time. It usually includes most, if not all, of the following pieces:

Equipment for Each Girl

1 spatula, 6-inch blade
1 steel paring knife
1 knife
1 fork
1 teaspoon
1 tablespoon
1 set of measuring spoons
1 wooden spoon
1 glass measuring cup, ½-pint capacity
1 baking cup, enameled, Pyrex, or earthen
1 fine-meshed wire sieve, 6 inches in diameter
1 salt and pepper set
1 biscuit cutter
1 double boiler, 1- or 1½-quart capacity
1 saucepan with cover
1 stew kettle with cover
1 frying pan
1 plate
1 cup and saucer
2 mixing bowls, 6 and 8 inches in diameter
1 pie tin, 6 inches in diameter
1 cake pan, 6 inches by 6 inches
1 breadboard
1 small bread pan

Equipment for Each Two Girls

1 rolling pin
2 dishpans
1 Dover egg beater, center-geared, double-wheeled, small size
1 wire whisk
1 6-hole muffin pan
1 soap dish
1 match holder
1 scrubbing mesh
1 asbestos mat
1 baking dish, 1-pint size
1 small flour sifter

This equipment should be arranged conveniently in the work units and then kept in this order all the time. A good procedure is for each group or the class to discuss and plan a method of arrangement that seems desirable for all.

The *stove or range* should be correctly used and cared for, according to the directions supplied. It should be thoroughly cleaned and left in proper condition each time after use. The wicks of kerosene stoves should be wiped daily. The burners of gas stoves should be taken apart frequently and cleaned. The heating unit of electric stoves should be wiped, and any grease, food, or other particles removed. The oven should be cleaned after each using. A dirty stove is ugly and cannot give the best results.

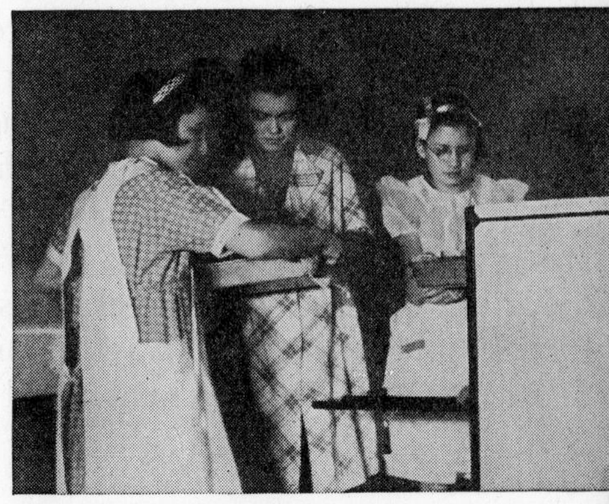

The finish of a baking lesson in the school kitchen. Hot rolls are being taken from the oven.

The refrigerator should be kept dry and clean. Whether an ice refrigerator or a mechanical refrigerator is used, it should be washed once a week with water and washing soda and thoroughly dried. If an ice refrigerator is used, the drainpipes should be cleaned with a brush and water and washing soda. The mechanical refrigerator requires defrosting one each week, at which time it may be conveniently cleaned. No food should be allowed to spoil in the refrigerator. All dishes should be kept perfectly clean. Strong-odored foods should not be kept in the refrigerator.

The *pantry and supply room* should be kept clean and in order. The shelves should be frequently wiped, and washed thoroughly when necessary. The floor should be swept and mopped frequently. The supplies and equipment should be arranged so that good use of space can be made and things can be found easily.

Cupboards and all storage centers should be kept orderly and clean. They should frequently be washed and wiped. Occasional washing of the dishes, glassware, and equipment not frequently used is necessary. Some care should be given them each day. Cupboards, closets, and shelves in disorder prevent the school kitchen from being attractive. They also make good work difficult.

A general schedule of work should be made out for the group and for each individual. Provision should be made for daily tasks, weekly tasks, and less frequent ones. If we have a regular way of doing many of these tasks, our work in the school kitchen will be better done.

Activities:

1. Make a schedule of work to be followed in the school kitchen.
2. Plan the arrangement of the equipment in the units.
3. Decide on the rules that will be followed.
4. Practice cleaning various pieces of equipment.

Problem 5: HOW SHALL WE WASH THE DISHES AND UTENSILS?

The washing of dishes and utensils is an important part of kitchen work. Our health, the appearance of our kitchen, and our ability as workers are affected by the way this task is done. Dishwashing is one of the jobs in home-making that must be done frequently and regularly. It should be so done that the least possible amount of time and energy will be required. Proper equipment and satisfactory methods are essential if this is to be accomplished. Necessary equipment and supplies are given below:

Equipment	*Supplies*
Two dishpans, or one pan and the drainboard	Soap
Wire drainer or rack	Silver polish
Dishcloths	Aluminum polish
Plate-scraper	Scouring powder
Dishmop	
Metal dishcloth of steel wool	
Dish towels	

To do dishwashing well we must have good standards of cleanliness and management. A carefully planned way of doing the dishwashing will help the worker in performing the task. The following method of procedure is efficient:

1. Remove all grease and scraps of food from the dishes and utensils.
2. Pile the dishes and utensils in the order to be washed.
3. Place the dishes in a convenient position for the person washing them.
4. Put to soak the dishes and pans with food sticking to them.
5. Fill the dishpan $\frac{2}{3}$ full with hot, soapy water.
6. Wash in order: glassware, silverware, china, greasy dishes, and kitchen utensils.
7. Change the water as often as necessary.
8. Rinse with clear, hot water.
9. Allow the china to dry in the dish rack or wipe dry with a clean towel.
10. Dry the glassware, silverware, and utensils thoroughly with a clean towel.
11. Wash the sink, drainboard, dishcloth, and dishpan.
12. Hang the dishcloth and towels on a rack to dry. If longer service is desired from dish towels, wash them out in hot suds, rinse, and hang on the rack to dry.
13. Put all the dishes, utensils, equipment, and supplies in their proper places. If this is done each time, there will be no disorder in the storage spaces or in the kitchen. Kitchen disorder is also lessened by washing and putting away, while the food is cooking, as many as possible of the dishes and utensils used in food preparation.

Most people when washing dishes like to work with someone. When dishwashing is a joint undertaking, the tasks should be divided equally so that good will prevails.

Activities:

1. (*Class activity*) Work in groups of two, and practice washing dishes and utensils according to the suggested method.
2. Make a time study of washing dishes, in which you try to reduce the time used.
3. After using the suggested method, state any changes you would make to improve the procedure.

Problem 6: WHAT GENERAL METHODS SHALL WE FOLLOW IN COOKING?

In cooking, as in traveling, there are certain guideposts that point the way. The success of the traveler is determined by his ability to read signs and follow their directions. The success of a cook, likewise, depends on her ability to understand and her readiness to follow the directions on her guidepost. She must not only know "what" and "how much," but "how," if she is to be skillful in food preparation.

The first guidepost directs our attention to the necessity of *standard equipment.* Only measuring cups and spoons that have been made and tested according to government

Results in cooking cannot be the best unless standardized measuring equipment is used. Here are shown the spatula for leveling ingredients; the set of spoons for measuring; and the graded cups, one for dry ingredients and one for liquids.

standards should be used. These have the various divisions indicated upon them. The spoons are in sets of three or more, a spoon for each different measure: 1/4 teaspoon, 1/3 teaspoon, 1/2 teaspoon, 1 teaspoon, and 1 tablespoon. These are all inexpensive items and can be purchased almost anywhere.

This little girl is learning to make accurate measurements.

Accurate measurements are very important in cooking if we wish successful results. This is our second guidepost. Reliable recipes are based on such measurements. Because there is no way of estimating "rounding" and "heaping," all measurements should be level. This is done with dry or soft foods, such as flour or butter, by pushing the back of a knife along the surface of the spoon or cup. Accuracy in measuring liquids is obtained by following exactly the markings on the cup.

When we first see a recipe it looks strange and queer. The funny combinations of letters and figures do not seem to make sense. Just as *St.* stands for *street, Mass.* for *Massachusetts,* or *Nov.* for *November,* so certain other abbreviations have been accepted for terms used in recipes. An understanding of these abbreviations is necessary if we are to use recipes successfully.

The recipe should be carefully read and followed. Only by doing this can we know the correct method to use for each food. For example, we learn from the recipe that milk is easily burned, so it should not be cooked directly over a high flame; that cabbage, turnips, and other strong-flavored vegetables should not be cooked in a covered vessel. Sometimes a recipe is blamed for a poor product when the difficulty lies in how the recipe is followed.

We should be familiar with the following terms and their abbreviations:

cup	c.	pound	lb.
teaspoon	t.	square	sq.
tablespoon	T.	quart	qt.
pint	pt.		

There are also some equivalent measurements that we should know:

1 c. = 16 T.
1 T. = 3 t.
1 pt. liquid = 2 c.
1 qt. = 2 pt. or 4 c.
1 egg = 9 t. or 3 T.

In writing a recipe, the ingredients and their amounts are given first, then the method of preparing, and next the combining and cooking. An example follows:

Rice Pudding

4 c. milk, scalded	¼ c. sugar
¼ c. rice	¼ t. salt
¼ t. cinnamon	½ t. fat for oiling baking pan or dish

Wash the rice. Combine the milk, rice, sugar, salt, and cinnamon. Pour into an oiled baking pan. Bake in a slow oven (325°F.) about 2½ hours. Stir frequently (every 15 or 20 minutes). When done, the rice will have taken up all the milk and will be soft and plump.

Sometimes we need to divide or enlarge a recipe. Either process is easily done. If a division is to be made, such as ½, ⅓, or ¼, all ingredients in the recipe are divided alike.

One half of the above recipe would be:

2 c. milk	1/8 c. sugar
1/8 c. rice	1/8 t. salt
1/8 t. cinnamon	1/4 t. fat for oiling baking pan or dish

If the recipe is to be enlarged two or three times, all ingredients in the recipe are increased two or three times.

Twice this recipe would be:

8 c. milk	1/2 c. sugar
1/2 c. rice	1/2 t. salt
1/2 t. cinnamon	1 t. fat for oiling baking pan or dish

The finished product should be cared for properly. The care required, of course, varies with different foods. Some foods should be kept warm or hot, and others cold. Usually the care needed is described in the recipe or in the general information given on the care of the various kinds of foods.

Activities:

1. Practice measuring accurately.
2. Read a number of recipes to see that you know the abbreviations used.
3. Read two recipes. What information concerning the procedures to use is given in each?
4. Practice dividing recipes (1/4, 1/3, and 1/2), and enlarging recipes (2 and 3 times).

Problem 7: WHAT IS A GOOD BREAKFAST?

Breakfast is a most important meal. Coming after a long period of fasting, its importance in maintaining bodily wellbeing can hardly be overestimated. Not only should we never go without breakfast, but we should always have a

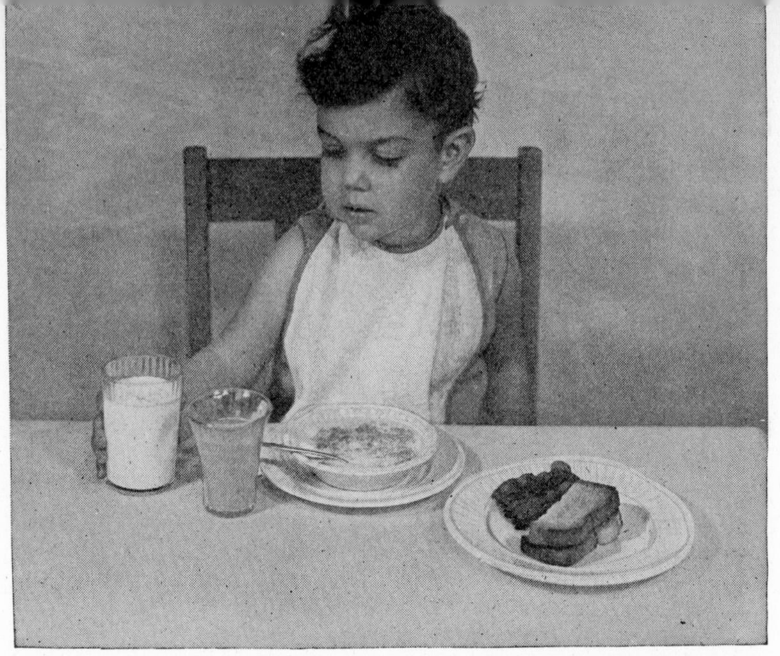

A good breakfast gives a good start to the day. A well-balanced breakfast for a child includes orange juice, cereal, milk, toast, and bacon.

good breakfast. There are certain standards by which we can judge our breakfast so that we can easily give ourselves a proper one.

A good breakfast *has all the food groups* represented. Thus, we should have the go, grow, protecting, and regulating foods in our meal. In other words, carbohydrates, proteins, fats, vitamins, and minerals will be included in foods of the meal. Though there are two other meals in which the necessary foods may be included, it is much easier to obtain the needed amounts if our breakfast contains a fair representation of these foods.

We use a smaller number of foods for breakfast than for any other meal. In fact, people tend to eat much the same breakfast day after day. The foods that are considered suitable for breakfast are fruit, cereals, breads, milk, beverages, eggs, meat, vegetables, and sweets. The fruits include oranges, grapefruit, apples, pears, peaches, grapes, berries, and dried prunes and apricots. These are served either raw or cooked. Cereals include rolled oats and wheat, Farina, corn meal, rice, and ready-prepared cereals. Breads include yeast bread, toast, rolls, griddle cakes, muffins, and biscuits. Milk is served as a beverage and in combination with other foods. Cocoa and chocolate are popular breakfast beverages. The grownup family often prefers coffee and tea. Eggs are a favorite breakfast dish and are served in many ways. Probably the most common methods used are frying and cooking in water. Breakfast meats are limited to bacon, ham, sausage, fish, dried beef, and occasionally lamb chops. Vegetables served for breakfast are potatoes and tomatoes. Sweets include such foods as jelly, preserves, jam, marmalade, and honey.

Milk is such an important food for everyone that a safe rule is, "Always include milk in some form in the breakfast." In this way, a good start is made to obtain the needed daily quart. Including milk in one's breakfast is not difficult because many foods served at this meal require milk. People who have milk for their morning beverage find little difficulty in meeting their day's requirement for milk.

A good breakfast is *sufficient in quantity.* It includes one third, or slightly less, of the day's food. We really need a good supply of food for the body's activities and to give us a good start for the day's work. When we eat too small a breakfast, we are likely to feel lifeless and weak, and to be unable to do our work in a satisfactory way. Of course, the needs of all people are not the same. Some are more active than others; some are growing and others are already grown. Season and climate, too, affect the food needed.

Breakfasts are classed as light, medium, or heavy, according to the quantity and kind of foods included. Light breakfasts, as well as other light meals, are for adults who do very light work and need little food for body building. Medium and heavy breakfasts are for boys and girls who are growing and are very active. Boys playing football, and boys and girls playing such games as basketball, tennis, and hockey, require a medium or heavy breakfast.

Typical patterns for medium and heavy breakfasts follow:

Medium Breakfast	*Heavy Breakfast*
Fruit	Fruit
Cereal or main dish	Cereal
Bread in some form	Main dish
Beverage	Other hot dish
Sweet	Bread in some form
	Sweet
	Beverage

A good breakfast is *attractive and appealing* to the appetite. Pleasing and colorful food combinations, good flavor and seasoning, and interesting contrasts all help in this.

The breakfast should be served in a pleasing manner. Although this meal is the most informal of all, a nice, simple, and easy way of serving should be worked out by the family. Plenty of time should be allowed for breakfast. If this is not done, a half-eaten, bolted breakfast is likely to result and we will be less than our best throughout the day.

Activities:

1. Judge the following breakfasts for schoolgirls:

Menu 1	*Menu 2*
1 glass of orange juice	Corn flakes and whole milk
1 slice of dry toast	Two soft-cooked eggs
	Coffee

Menu 3

½ grapefruit	1 tablespoon of jelly
1 slice of bread	1 glass of milk
1 pat of butter	

Menu 4	*Menu 5*
Baked apple	Fresh peaches and cream
Oatmeal and whole milk or thin cream	Griddle cakes (6 small), butter, and syrup
1 egg	2 slices of bacon
1 slice of buttered toast	1 glass of milk
1 cup of cocoa	

2. Plan a breakfast for yourself that you consider a good one. Bring the plan to class for evaluation.

Problem 8: HOW SHALL WE PREPARE AND SERVE RAW FRUIT?

Fruits which are often served raw are oranges, grapefruit, apples, pears, plums, grapes, berries, and peaches. The preparation of raw fruits is rather simple, so little equipment is needed. The articles usually needed are a crock or pan for washing the fruit; a paring knife or fruit knife to pare, core, and remove the decay; and a spoon to serve the fruit or sprinkle sugar on it.

Many fruits, including apples, pears, peaches, grapes, and oranges are eaten raw.

Regardless of the fruit, washing is the first step in its preparation. Washing is important and should always be done to remove dirt and injurious chemicals that may have been used in spraying. With the exception of berries, plunging the fruit into a bowl of water is the method used. Usually the excess of water is shaken gently from the washed fruit. However, the fruit may be wiped with a clean cloth or towel. Berries are delicate and should be washed by putting them in a wire sieve and pouring water over them, or by dipping the sieve lightly up and down in a crock of water until they are clean. Certain berries, such as strawberries and blackberries, require stemming. This is done either before or after washing.

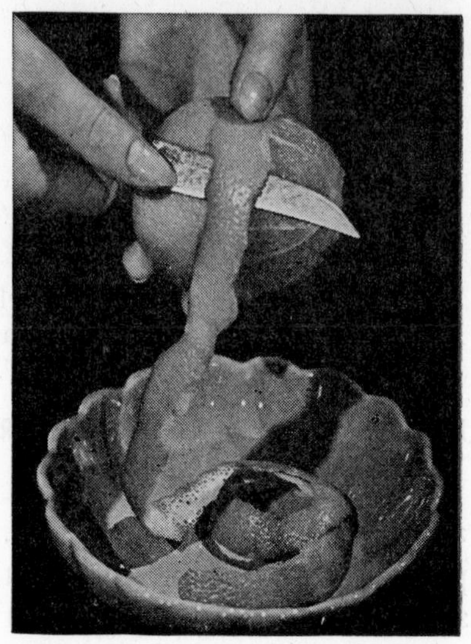

Peeling the breakfast orange is the first step in several ways of preparing it.

Oranges frequently are cut in halves, sprinkled with sugar if desired, and placed on a small individual plate. One or both halves are an individual serving. A spoon is used for eating.

Sliced oranges are prepared by first peeling the orange. Using a sharp knife, cut the orange into thin slices, crosswise of the fruit. The slices are arranged attractively on a small individual plate and sprinkled with sugar if desired. A whole or half a sliced orange is a serving. A fork is used in eating sliced oranges.

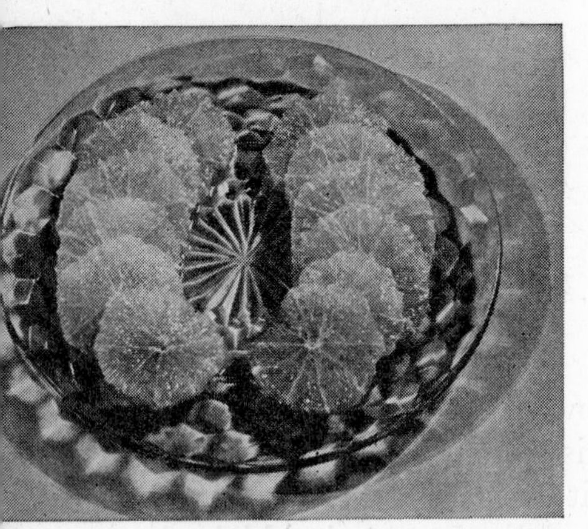

Some like orange slices for breakfast. They are served on a plate and eaten with a fork.

Orange juice is prepared by extracting the juice with a juicer. The juice is chilled and served in a small glass on the breakfast plate or a small individual plate. No sugar is added. The juice from one medium or large orange is considered one serving, unless more is desired.

A grapefruit is cut in half. If necessary, the seeds are removed and the tough membrane and

The sections of the orange are cut away from the membrane.

core are cut away at the center. Use a paring knife or a grapefruit knife. The sections are separated from the membrane surrounding them and at the same time are cut away from the rind, starting at the center to loosen each section. The fruit is sprinkled with sugar if desired. A red cherry placed in the center gives a colorful note. Grapefruit can be prepared several hours before serving. When this is done, it should be kept in a cool place. Grapefruit is served on a small individual plate, with a spoon. A half grapefruit is a serving.

Apples and pears are served whole or in sections, on a small individual plate with a fruit knife. Plums are served whole, three or four in number, in the same manner. Grapes are served in a bunch or part of a bunch on a small individual plate. Usually no silver is needed in serving plums and grapes.

Berries are served within a short time after washing. They are placed in a saucedish or sherbet dish and sprinkled with

Red raspberries served with orange juice are delicious.

granulated or powdered sugar. When served, the dish is placed upon the breakfast plate or upon a small individual plate. Milk or cream may be served with berries, and they are eaten with a teaspoon or dessert spoon. Orange juice gives a different but pleasing flavor to berries if served instead of milk or cream.

Peaches may be served whole, without paring, on a small individual plate with a fruit knife. They may also be pared and sliced, and placed in a saucedish or sherbet dish. They are served with sugar, or cream and sugar. The dish is placed on the breakfast or individual plate. Peaches are eaten with a teaspoon or dessert spoon.

Activities:

1. (*Class activity*) Prepare various raw fruits.
2. (*Class activity*) Serve the fruits prepared in the proper manner.
3. Decide what the raw fruits that have been prepared would add to the diet.
4. Estimate the cost per serving of raw fruits.
5. (*Class activity*) Judge various fruit products.
6. Suggest the foods that could be served with a given raw fruit to make a good breakfast.

Problem 9: HOW SHALL WE PREPARE AND SERVE STEWED FRUIT?

Fruits which are commonly stewed are apples, peaches, plums, pears, and berries. The method for all is much the same, except that hard fruits require more time to cook. Apples, pears, and peaches are usually pared before stewing and may be left whole or cut in sections.

The utensils

Cooking spoon	Measuring spoons
Crock or pan	Paring knife
Measuring cup	Kettle

The recipe for stewed fruit

Ingredients:

Fruit, 2 lbs. (Approximately 6 apples or pears; 8–10 peaches; 4–5 c. berries; 16–20 plums)

Sugar, ½ to 1 c. (according to fruit and to personal taste)
Water, 1 c. for apples and pears; ¼ to ⅓ c. for other fruit
Cinnamon, ¼ t. for apples, pears, and peaches, if desired
Nutmeg, ¼ t. for apples, pears, and peaches, if desired

Method:

Put the sugar and water in a kettle. Bring to the boiling point. Add the fruit and cook until tender. When done, sprinkle with spice if desired. If apples or pears are very hard, they should be cooked in water first to soften them. The sugar is then added and the cooking continued until the sugar is dissolved. If this method is used, 1½ cups of water will be needed instead of 1 cup.

Time required for the different fruits:

Apples		10 min.
Pears	soft	10–30 min.
	hard	1¼ hr.
Plums		10 min.
Berries		5–10 min.

Two girls—¼ recipe.

The serving

Stewed fruit is served either warm or chilled in a saucedish or sherbet dish placed either on an individual plate or directly on the table. A teaspoon is used for eating.

Activities:

Follow the general procedure as given in the Activities of Problem 8 (page 206).

Problem 10: HOW SHALL WE PREPARE AND SERVE DRIED FRUIT?

Dried fruits are much used because of their pleasing and different flavor, their high food value, and their reasonable cost. The most commonly used dried fruits are prunes, peaches, apricots, apples, raisins, and figs. In the process of drying, most of the water content which gives fresh fruit its juice has been removed, and the fruit becomes leathery and firm. Aside from soaking to restore some of the water, they are prepared and served similarly to stewed fruits.

The utensils

Cooking spoon	Measuring spoons
Crock or pan	Kettle
Measuring cup	

The recipe for dried fruit

Ingredients:

½ lb. (1–1¼ cups) dried fruit
2 c. warm water

Sugar—
- prunes, raisins, and figs: none to ⅛ to ¼ c.
- peaches and apples: ¼ to ⅓ c.
- apricots: ½ c.

Method:

Wash the fruit thoroughly in the crock or pan. Put the fruit in a kettle and pour warm water over it. Let it soak for an hour or until the fruit is plumped. Cover and place on the stove and cook slowly until tender. Add sugar. Boil until the sugar is thoroughly dissolved, then remove from the fire. Fifteen to 20 minutes is about the time required for cooking.

Two girls—⅓ recipe.

The serving

Dried fruit is served warm or chilled in a saucedish or sherbet dish placed either on an individual plate or directly on the table. A teaspoon is used for eating.

Activities:

Follow the general procedure as given in the Activities of Problem 8 (page 206).

Problem 11: HOW SHALL WE PREPARE AND SERVE COCOA AND CHOCOLATE?

Cocoa and chocolate are widely used beverages. They have a pleasing flavor that is liked by many. In the beverage form, they are so similar that few can tell the difference. Chocolate contains much more fat than does cocoa. Chocolate is sold in cakes, and cocoa in a powder form. They are especially good beverages because they are made with milk.

Cocoa

The utensils

Double boiler
Measuring cup
Measuring spoons
Cooking spoon
Dover egg beater

The recipe for cocoa

Ingredients:

2–4 T. cocoa
2–4 T. sugar
3 c. milk
1 c. hot water
speck salt
¼ t. vanilla
8 marshmallows *or*
½ c. whipped cream

Method:

Fill the bottom of double boiler ⅓ full of hot water and place on the fire. Put cocoa, sugar, and salt in the upper part of double boiler and mix. Add hot water and stir. Place over the fire and boil until smooth and glossy, stirring constantly. Add milk and place it in the upper part of the double boiler. Heat until scalding. Beat the mixture with a Dover egg beater for one or two minutes. Add vanilla just before serving.

One girl—¼ recipe.

Chocolate

The recipe for chocolate

Ingredients:

1 sq. unsweetened chocolate
2–4 T. sugar
1 c. boiling water
3 c. milk
dash salt
¼ t. vanilla
8 marshmallows *or*
½ c. whipped cream

Method:

Fill the bottom of the double boiler ⅓ full of hot water and place over the flame. Put chocolate in the upper part of the double boiler and place over the lower part. When melted, add sugar and salt. Add water gradually, stirring constantly. Remove the upper part of the double boiler from the lower part and cook over the fire four minutes or until smooth and glossy. Add milk and place back in the lower part of the double boiler. Heat until scalding. Beat the mixture with a Dover egg beater for one or two minutes. Add vanilla just before serving.

Note: If preferred, the vanilla can be omitted in both cocoa and chocolate.

One girl—¼ recipe. (One girl may prepare cocoa and one chocolate, and then compare the products.)

The serving

Cocoa and chocolate are both served hot in a teacup, filled to within ⅔ inch of the top, and placed on a saucer. If a marshmallow is used as a garnish, that is, a decoration, it is placed in the cup and the hot beverage poured over it, and the beverage stirred just before serving. If whipped cream is used as a garnish, a rounding teaspoon of whipped cream is added after the beverage is poured in the cup. On the saucer is placed a teaspoon which is used only to test the temperature of the beverage as it is drunk from the cup. Cocoa and chocolate are also served iced. In this case, a medium or tall tumbler is filled with the beverage to within ⅔ inch of the top and placed on a small individual plate with a teaspoon or iced-tea spoon. The spoon is used for stirring the beverage.

Activities:

Follow the general procedure as given in the Activities of Problem 8 (page 206).

Problem 12: HOW SHALL WE PREPARE AND SERVE COFFEE?

Coffee is one of our widely used beverages. It is not a beverage for children, but is very popular with grownups. Therefore it is well for us to know how to make coffee, even though we do not drink it. Coffee is made by several methods. Each method has its good points and poor ones.

Boiled Coffee

The utensils

Coffee pot
Measuring cup
Measuring spoons
Cooking spoon

The recipe for boiled coffee

Ingredients:

1 heaping T. medium-ground coffee
2 T. cold water
¾ t. egg white
1 c. boiling water

Method:

Mix coffee, one half of the cold water, and egg white in the clean coffee pot. Add boiling water. Place over the fire and bring to the boiling point *but do not boil the coffee.* Remove from the fire and let it stand in a warm place 3 or 5 minutes. Add 1 T. cold water to settle the coffee. Strain from the grounds through a wire sieve or cheesecloth to another heated pot. Some do not strain the coffee from the grounds, but in this case a bitter and less pleasing coffee usually results.

One girl—entire recipe.

Percolated Coffee

The utensils

Percolator
Measuring cup
Measuring spoons

The recipe for percolated coffee

Ingredients:

1 heaping T. of medium-ground coffee
1 c. cold water

Method:

Put water in the pot. Put coffee in the percolator basket and place in the pot. Cover and put over the fire and percolate gently for 5 to 7 minutes after the water has begun to boil up into the basket. Serve at once.

One girl—entire recipe.

Drip or Filtered Coffee

The utensils

Drip coffee pot
Measuring cup
Measuring spoons

The recipe for drip or filtered coffee

Ingredients:

1 heaping T. of medium or finely ground coffee
1 c. boiling water

Method:

Have the coffee pot hot. Put the coffee in the perforated section of the coffee pot. Pour the fresh boiling water over the coffee or into the section of the pot from which it will drip through the coffee. Cover and let it stand in a warm place until all the water has gone through the coffee once. Remove the upper part or parts of pot. Cover the pot and serve.

One girl—entire recipe.

The serving

Coffee is served hot in a teacup placed on a saucer. The cup is filled to within ⅔ inch of the top. Cream and sugar, or one of them, are often used in coffee. In many homes, when coffee is served the cream and sugar, if desired, are placed in the cup first and the hot coffee poured over them. In other homes, the coffee is poured and the cream and sugar are passed so that each may serve himself. A teaspoon is used in stirring and sipping coffee.

The following rules should be remembered in preparing and serving coffee:

Always use a clean pot.
Always use fresh water for making coffee.
Never allow coffee to boil.
Serve coffee hot and immediately.

Activities:

Follow the general procedure as given in the Activities of Problem 8 (page 206).

Ready-prepared cereal tastes good with fresh fruits, such as strawberries, added.

Problem 13: HOW SHALL WE PREPARE AND SERVE READY-PREPARED CEREALS?

A wide variety of ready-prepared cereals are found in the stores. The ease with which they can be served, and their attractive flavor and texture are among the reasons for their extensive use. Ready-prepared cereals include the puffed, shredded, and flaked grain products, as well as some others. Wheat, rice, and corn are the most common grains used for this purpose.

The ready-prepared cereals are more expensive than those that require cooking before serving. All the prepared cereals are commercial products and are sold under specific trade names.

The only preparation required for the ready-prepared cereals is crisping. Even this is not always necessary. The careful packaging of the cereals in boxes that are both lined and covered with waxed paper has lessened the possibility of their taking up moisture from the air. Directions are given on each package for the crisping of the contents.

Ready-prepared cereals that may be served in class either plain or with fruit are the following:

Bran flakes	Grapenuts
Grapenut flakes	Shredded Wheat
Corn flakes or Post Toasties	Puffed rice and wheat

Ready-prepared cereals are served either plain or with fruit. Bananas, fresh berries, peaches, and stewed fruit, either fresh or dried, are all used. These cereals alone or with fruit are served in a cereal dish placed on the breakfast plate. They are eaten with a teaspoon or cereal spoon. Cream or whole milk and sugar are served with them.

Activities:

Follow the general procedure as given in the Activities of Problem 8 (page 206).

Problem 14: HOW SHALL WE PREPARE AND SERVE ROLLED OATS?

Rolled oats are among the cereals that must be cooked before they are ready to eat. They are an especially good cereal because they contain the entire grain. Rolled oats have largely replaced oatmeal in the American diet. Those of us whose ancestors came from Scotland have heard much of the porridge made from oatmeal and of the long hours of cooking necessary in its making. Few, if any, of us would find oatmeal porridge as pleasing to our taste as the rolled oats which are the product of modern milling meth-

A bowl of rolled oats should be served steaming hot.

ods. In the preparation of this cereal the oat grain has been partly cooked and then rolled and dried. We like the flaky character that results far better than the pastiness of the porridge made from the ground oat grain. The modern product, too, has the further advantage of requiring a shorter cooking time.

The utensils

Double boiler
Measuring cup
Measuring spoons

The recipe for rolled oats

Ingredients:

1 c. rolled oats
1 t. salt
3 c. boiling water

Method:

Fill the lower part of the double boiler 1/3 full of boiling water. In the upper part of the double boiler put the 3 c. boiling water and salt. Place directly over the flame. Add the cereal slowly to the boiling water. Cook from 3 to 10 minutes. Place the upper part of double boiler over the lower part and set over the flame, and steam for 30 minutes.

Variations:

Use milk instead of water. Take great care when cooking over the flame, as milk scorches easily.

Add 1/2 to 1 c. of dried fruit, such as dates, raisins, or figs. Stir fruit into the cereal soon after the steaming begins.

One girl in each group—1/3 regular recipe or variation.

The serving

Rolled oats are served hot in a cereal dish placed upon the breakfast plate. Cream or whole milk and sugar are served with the cereal. It is eaten with a teaspoon or cereal spoon.

Activities:

Follow the general procedure as given in the Activities of Problem 8 (page 206).

Problem 15: HOW SHALL WE PREPARE AND SERVE GROUND CEREALS?

Favorite breakfast dishes are the ground cereals. Examples of these are the commercial products Wheatena and Farina, which contain the wheat heart and some of the bran and germ, and Cream of Wheat, a white cereal which contains none of the bran and germ. Ground cereals are cooked into a thick porridge not unlike the old-time corn-meal mush.

A bowl of cooked ground cereal should be free from lumps and not too stiff.

The utensils

Double boiler
Measuring cup
Measuring spoons

The recipe for ground cereals

Ingredients:

1 c. ground cereal
1¼–1½ t. salt
5 c. boiling water

Method:

Fill the lower part of the double boiler about ⅓ full of boiling water. In the upper part of double boiler, put the 5 c. boiling water and salt. Place directly over the flame. When boiling, add the ground cereal slowly, stirring constantly. Continue stirring and cook for 10 minutes. Place the upper part of the double boiler in the lower part and steam for 20 to 30 minutes.

Variations:

Use milk for part or all of the water. Take great care when cooking over the flame, as milk scorches easily.

Add ½ to 1 c. of dried fruit, such as raisins, dates, or figs. Stir the fruit into the cereal soon after the steaming begins.

One girl in each group—¼ regular recipe or variation.

The serving

Ground cereal is served in a cereal dish placed upon the breakfast plate. Cream or whole milk and sugar are commonly served with this cereal. Some prefer butter, or butter and sugar, instead of cream and sugar. It is eaten with a teaspoon or cereal spoon.

Activities:

Follow the general procedure as given in the Activities of Problem 8 (page 206).

Problem 16: HOW SHALL WE PREPARE AND SERVE EGGS COOKED IN WATER?

People in all lands have long used eggs for food. Although the kind of eggs has varied, chicken eggs have been the most favored. Enclosed within the shell of the hen's egg are all that is needed to build the blood, the muscle, the nervous system, the body structure, and the downy feathers of the young chick. From this we may know that the egg is rich in the grow foods and in certain of the regulating and protecting foods. In this country eggs are widely used as a regular food for breakfast. This is a fine custom, as it gives us one egg, which is what we need, each day. One of the simplest ways of preparing eggs is to cook them in water. As we shall see, there are several ways in which this may be done.

Soft-Cooked, Hard-Cooked, and Boiled Eggs

The utensils

Saucepan and cover
Cooking spoon
Tablespoon

The recipe for soft-cooked, hard-cooked, and boiled eggs

Ingredients:

Eggs
Boiling water sufficient to cover eggs

Method for soft- and hard-cooked eggs:

Put boiling water in a saucepan. Lower the eggs into the water, one at a time, using a tablespoon. Cover the pan and place where water and eggs will keep hot but will not boil. If soft-cooked eggs are desired, let them remain in the hot water for 5 minutes; for medium hard-cooked eggs allow 10 minutes; and for hard-cooked eggs allow 45 minutes.

Method for boiled eggs:

Boiled eggs are not as good as soft- and hard-cooked eggs, because the higher temperature of boiling water toughens them. When eggs are boiled, they are placed in the boiling water and boiled 3 to 5 minutes for soft eggs, and 15 minutes for hard eggs.

The shells are more easily removed from both hard-cooked and hard-boiled eggs if, upon removal from the hot water, the eggs are placed in cold water for a short time.

One girl—prepare 1 egg by one of the ways discussed above.

The serving

Eggs cooked in the shell, whether soft- or hard-cooked, or boiled, are served in an egg cup, saucedish, bowl, or on the breakfast plate. If served in an egg cup, the shell is cut from one end of the egg with the knife and the egg is eaten with a spoon. If served on a saucedish or plate, a knife and spoon are used to remove the egg from the shell. The egg is then seasoned and eaten with a spoon.

Poached Eggs

The utensils

Shallow pan or skillet
Lid for pan
Pancake turner or skimmer
Cup or saucer
Cooking spoon
Measuring spoon

The recipe for poached eggs

Ingredients:

Eggs
½ t. salt for each pint of water
Few grains of pepper

Method:

Oil a pan or skillet. Fill the pan ½ to ⅔ full of water to which salt has been added. Heat water to the boiling point. Break the eggs one at a time in a cup or saucer. Carefully slide each egg into the hot water, taking care not to break the yolk and to keep each egg separate. Cover and place where the water will keep hot, but do not boil. Occasionally, dip hot water from the pan over the eggs to cook the top part of the eggs. Let stand until the egg white is set, which will take about 5 minutes. Remove the egg with a pancake turner or skimmer. When placed on the serving dish, sprinkle with pepper.

One girl, or two girls—prepare 1 egg.

The serving

Poached eggs are served in a saucedish, in a serving dish, or on an individual breakfast plate. A favorite way is to serve them on toast, usually one egg to one slice of toast. They are eaten with a fork.

Activities:

Follow the general procedure as given in the Activities of Problem 8 (page 206).

Problem 17: HOW SHALL WE PREPARE AND SERVE FRIED AND SCRAMBLED EGGS?

Fried and scrambled eggs may be served at any of the day's meals. However, in many homes they are customary breakfast dishes. They are quickly and easily prepared, and combine well with other foods.

Fried Eggs

The utensils

Skillet or frying pan	Cooking spoon
Teacup or saucer	Pancake turner or skimmer

The recipe for fried eggs

Ingredients:

Fat (bacon or ham drippings, butter, lard, or other fat), 1 T. for 1 egg	Eggs
	Salt, 1/8 t. for 1 egg
	Pepper, few grains for 1 egg

Fried eggs and bacon make a hearty breakfast.

Method:

Heat fat in a skillet or frying pan until it is hot enough to set the egg but is not smoking hot. Break the egg carefully into a cup or saucer so as not to break the yolk. Slide the egg easily into the fat. Sprinkle with salt and pepper. Dip hot fat over the top of the egg to cook it. Remove with a pancake turner or skimmer.

Variations:

Sliced bacon and ham are often accompaniments of fried eggs. If these are used, they are fried first in the pan, and then the eggs are cooked in their drippings.

One girl—1 egg.

The serving

Fried eggs are served on a platter or on the individual breakfast plate. Bacon and ham, if used, are usually served on the same plate as the eggs. Fried eggs are eaten with a fork.

Scrambled Eggs

The utensils

Skillet or frying pan
Bowl
Measuring spoons
Cooking spoon
Wire whisk egg beater

The recipe for scrambled eggs

Ingredients:

5 eggs
½ c. milk
2 T. butter
½ t. salt
⅛ t. pepper

Method:

Beat eggs slightly, add salt and pepper and milk. Heat skillet or frying pan, but not smoking hot. Put in butter. When melted, add egg mixture, stir occasionally, lifting from the bottom, and cook slowly.

Variations:

The recipe for scrambled eggs given above may be varied by adding ½ c. chopped fresh tomato or canned tomato, minced beef, chopped ham, bacon, Vienna sausage, nuts, or chopped green peppers. Whichever of these is chosen for variation, it should be added to the beaten eggs before they are cooked.

One girl—1 egg.

The serving

Scrambled eggs are served on a platter, in a bowl, or directly on the individual breakfast plate. They are eaten with a fork.

Activities:

Follow the general procedure as given in the Activities of Problem 8 (page 206).

Problem 18: HOW SHALL WE PREPARE AND SERVE TOAST?

Toast in some form is a favorite breakfast bread in this country. No matter where you go, you find toast of some type served. All are made from yeast bread which is at least one day old, but not dry. Toast is made by exposing the surface of a slice of bread to heat, thus causing it to brown. This may be done by placing slices of bread in a wire frame and holding them over the flame to brown, by placing slices of bread in an oven or broiler to brown, or by using an electric toaster. A common custom is to make the toast at the table in the electric toaster.

The golden brown of nicely toasted bread is always tempting.

Dry Toast

Use sliced bread or cut bread in ½- to ¾-inch slices. Toast on both sides until the slice is an even, golden brown, but not burnt.

Buttered Toast

Prepare the same as for dry toast, except when done spread butter at once on one side of the toast. Keep near heat until the butter is melted into the bread.

Dry and buttered toast should be served at once on a covered plate or directly from the toaster. Jelly or honey may be served with it. Dry and buttered toast are eaten with the fingers.

Milk Toast

The utensils

Saucepan	Measuring spoons
Measuring cup	

The recipe for milk toast

Ingredients:

4 slices dry toast	2 T. butter
2 c. milk	½ t. salt

Method:

Put milk, butter, and salt in a saucepan and heat until hot, but do not boil. Pour over the toast and serve at once.

Two girls—½ recipe.

The serving

Milk toast is served in a large serving dish, individual soup or cereal bowl. It is eaten with a teaspoon or a cereal spoon. Syrup, jelly, or honey is often served with milk toast.

French Toast

The utensils

Skillet or frying pan	Pancake turner or wide spatula
Bowl	Measuring cup
Wire whisk egg beater	Measuring spoons

The recipe for French toast

Ingredients:

2 eggs	½ t. salt
1 c. milk	Fat for frying toast, ½ T. for each slice of bread
6 slices bread	

Method:

Beat eggs slightly, add milk and salt. Put a skillet or frying pan containing fat on the fire and heat until hot but not smoking. Dip bread quickly in milk and egg mixture, making sure both sides are covered with the mixture. Do not allow to stand in the mixture or the product will be soggy. Put it in the skillet and fry on both sides until a golden brown.

Two girls—⅓ recipe.

The serving

French toast is served on a heated plate or platter. Butter, syrup, jelly, or honey are often served with it. A knife is used to spread these on the toast. French toast is eaten with a fork.

Activities:

Follow the general procedure as given in the Activities of Problem 8 (page 206).

Problem 19: HOW SHALL WE PREPARE AND SERVE GRIDDLE CAKES?

Griddle cakes are a quick bread made from a pour batter. A quick bread is one made light by the use of baking powder, or by the use of soda and sour milk or some other acid. Griddle cakes, biscuits, and muffins are among the quick breads in common use. They are called quick breads because the time required to make them light is much less than the time required to make yeast breads light. A pour batter is one that contains one part of flour to one part of liquid. It is thin enough to pour from a pitcher or spoon.

Griddle cakes and sausages are a favorite breakfast on a winter morning.

The utensils

- Griddle iron or skillet
- Pancake turner or spatula
- 1 large mixing bowl
- 1 medium-size mixing bowl
- Dover egg beater
- Measuring cup
- Measuring spoons
- Mixing spoon
- Cooking spoon
- Sifter

The recipe for griddle cakes

Ingredients:

- 1¾ c. milk
- 2 t. fat
- 2 c. flour (sifted before measuring)
- 4 t. baking powder
- 2 eggs or 4 egg yolks
- 1 t. salt
- Fat for cooking (butter or butter substitute is not practical)

Method:

Sift the dry ingredients into a large mixing bowl. Make a well or small hole in the center. Beat the eggs or egg yolks in a medium-size mixing bowl, add the milk and then the melted fat. Pour the liquid ingredients into the hole or well in the dry ingredients and mix.

Heat the griddle or skillet hot but not smoking hot. Oil lightly but thoroughly. Drop the batter by tablespoonfuls on the hot iron, quickly smoothing to a thin, round cake. When upper surface appears well "bubbled" and the lower golden brown, turn cake over with pancake turner. When done, remove to a heated plate or platter, and serve at once.

Two girls—1/4 recipe.

The serving

Griddle cakes are served hot from a heated plate or platter to the individual breakfast plate. If the cakes are small in size, two or three are served at one time; if large, one is served. Butter and syrup, or honey or jelly are eaten with griddle cakes. A knife is used for spreading the butter and sweet. Griddle cakes are eaten with a fork.

Activities:

Follow the general procedure as given in the Activities of Problem 8 (page 206).

Problem 20: HOW SHALL WE PREPARE AND SERVE BISCUITS?

Biscuits are another quick bread, but they are made from soft dough. Like griddle cakes, they are made light by the use of baking powder. A soft dough contains three parts of flour to one of liquid, and is stiff enough to be taken in the hand and rolled or patted into shape. In this respect, it differs from griddle cakes.

The utensils

- Mixing bowl
- Measuring cup
- Measuring spoons
- 2 forks or 2 knives for working in the fat
- Breadboard
- Baking tin, pie pan, or muffin pan
- Biscuit cutter
- Sifter
- Mixing spoon

The recipe for biscuits

Ingredients:

2 c. flour (sifted before measuring)	¾ c. milk
	4 T. fat
4 t. baking powder	½ t. salt

Method:

To flour in the sifter add other dry ingredients and sift into the mixing bowl.

Work the fat into the dry ingredients with either two forks, two knives (held one in each hand), or with the tips of the fingers.

Nicely baked hot biscuits should "melt in your mouth."

Add liquid, a small quantity at a time, mixing by cutting in with forks or knives or working in with the tips of the fingers.

When the dough is the right consistency to take into the hands, roll or pat it out on a lightly floured board to ½ to 1 inch thickness. Cut out with a biscuit cutter. Put on an ungreased tin or pie pan, or in ungreased muffin pans. Bake in a quick oven (475° F.) about 20 minutes.

Good biscuits have an even, golden brown, crisp crust, no loose flour on them, and a pleasing flavor. Their inside is creamy-white in color, fine-grained, and flaky.

Two girls—¼ recipe.

The serving

Biscuits are served immediately upon removing from the oven, on a warm plate protected by a napkin or hot-roll cover. In eating, they are broken with the fingers, spread with a knife, and held in the fingers of the left hand. If served with gravy, they are eaten with a fork.

Activities:

Follow the general procedure as given in the Activities of Problem 8 (page 206).

Problem 21: HOW SHALL WE PLAN A BREAKFAST FOR OUR FAMILY?

We are now ready to plan a breakfast that we will prepare here in our school kitchen. It will be planned for a family but the "family" will be a group of us in the class. It is necessary for us to decide how many we shall have in each group, such as two, three, or four, so that the class can be divided into "families." After this is done each of the "families" will plan its breakfast.

In making our plans there are a number of things for us to do. We should recall the standards for a good breakfast (see page 199). We must decide upon the type of breakfast that our "family" should have, based on the food needs of the family members. We must plan so that a fair share of the essential foods for the day are included in this meal.

We must consider how much money we have to spend for the meal, whether ten cents or more or less per person. It is important to consider which foods are now in our markets or stores. In many localities we should not plan to have fresh strawberries in December. Also, we must think of whether or not we know how to prepare the foods. It might be well to choose foods and dishes that we have prepared in class.

The time we have for the preparation and serving of the meal must be carefully considered. Our class period is short, and all our work must be done within this time.

The likes and dislikes of the members of our "family" should enter into our planning, but not too much weight should be given to them. However, we want to plan a meal everyone will like if this is at all possible. The "family" members should work together in this, and no one person should hold out for or against any one food or dish that the others regard as desirable.

After the meal is planned, the plan should be given to

your teacher for approval. When she has approved this, a market order should be made out and given to whoever is responsible for purchasing the food. Plans for preparing the breakfast should be made in detail and each member of the "family" should know exactly what she is to do in the preparation of the meal.

Activities:

1. (*Class activity*) Divide into "family" groups and plan breakfasts for each "family" at a given cost.
2. (*Class activity*) Make out the market orders for the breakfasts.
3. (*Class activity*) Plan a breakfast menu for your own family.

Problem 22: HOW SHALL WE PLAN THE SERVICE OF OUR BREAKFAST?

Breakfast is an informal and simple meal. Its service should be simple and easy, though pleasing and attractive. The cloth, dishes, glasses, silverware, and napkins should be laid correctly. The table should have a fresh look as if it had been set just a few minutes before. The linen, china, glassware, and silverware should all be clean. Colored lunch cloths, dishes, and glassware add much in the way of brightness to the meal. If a flower or plant is used, it should be fresh and alive.

There are some general rules for setting the table and serving food that hold in nearly all types of table service. We should become familiar with them.

Setting the table. Have the table clean, then lay the silence cloth or board. Next lay the tablecloth, making sure it is on perfectly straight and even. If a breakfast cloth is used, no silence cloth is needed. Place chairs with the front edge even and in line with the edge of the table, and directly in front of the covers. Place the decoration in the center of the table.

The place set for each person is called a cover. The

napkin, glassware, china, and silverware for each person are included in the cover. Allow a space of 20 to 30 inches for each cover.

Place plates in the center of the cover, one inch from the edge of the table. Place the silver beside the plate, one inch from the edge and perpendicular to the edge. Lay close, but do not crowd. Place the knife, sharp edge in, to the right of the plate; the spoon, bowl up, to the right of the knife, and additional spoons to the right of the first spoon; the fork, tines up, to the left of the plate. Place additional forks to the left of the first fork. Place the main fork next to the plate, arranging others in order of their use. Salad forks are not necessary in a family meal, although some families like to use them.

Place the serving silver near and parallel to the dish on which it will be used. If one piece, place to the right of the dish; if two, place on both sides as in the individual cover. Be sure to provide serving silver for all serving dishes.

Place the napkin at the left of the fork in line with the silver. The napkin should be folded neatly with the loose corner at the lower right.

Place the water glass at the tip of the knife, slightly to the right. Place the milk at the right of the water glass.

Place the bread-and-butter plates, if used, at the tip of the fork, slightly to the left. Place the butter spreader across the top of the plate or at the side.

Place salts and peppers in convenient places, one set for every two persons.

Place the sugar bowl and creamer directly in front of the hostess or some other member of the family, sugar to the right, cream to the left, with handles parallel to the edge of the table.

Serving the food. Have chilled dishes for cold food, and warm dishes for hot food. Serve cold food *cold,* and hot

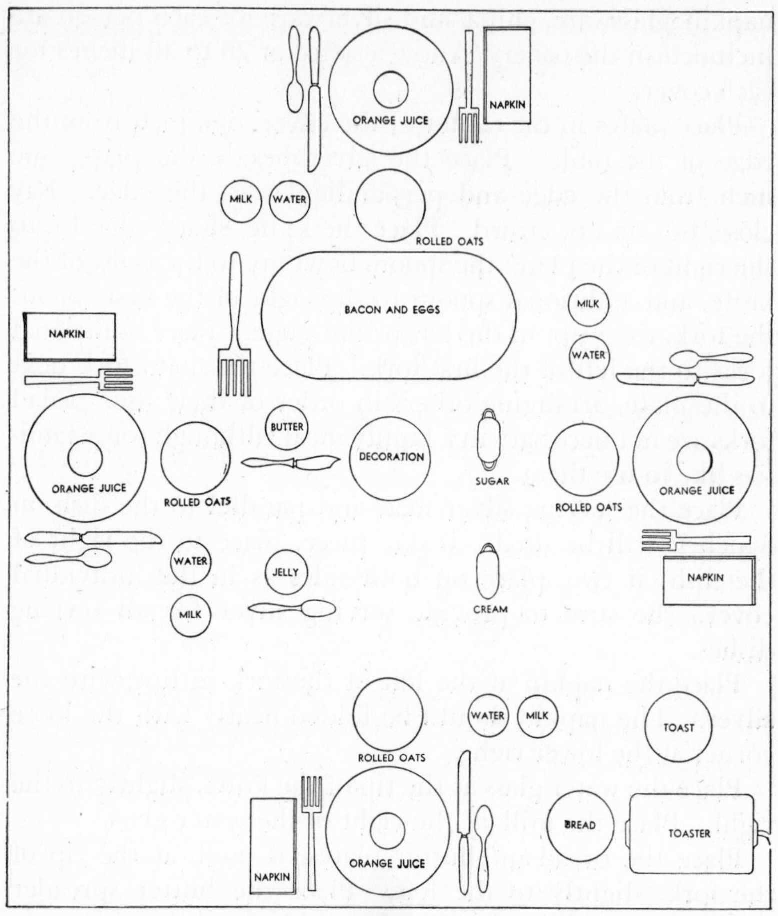

This diagram of the breakfast table shows the family style of service.

food *hot*. This is most important for a successful meal.

Fill the water glasses three-fourths full of cold water, just before the meal is ready. Place a filled pitcher near the person who is responsible for filling the glasses.

Cut bread in half slices, or less, and arrange on a plate. Place bread, butter, sweets, and other cold foods on the table just before the meal is served.

Place hot foods near the person who is responsible for the serving or passing.

The beverage may be served at the table or from the kitchen. Fill the beverage cups two-thirds full. If served at the table, the pot, cups and saucers, and cream and sugar are placed near the person responsible for the serving. At the individual cover, the beverage cup should be placed at the right of the spoons, with handles parallel to the edge of the table and with the center of the cup even with the center of the plate.

Pass the food to the right. When starting to pass a food, place the serving silver on the dish in a convenient position. Do not help yourself first unless it is customary in your family, or you are especially requested to do so.

The family style of service is the most suitable service for breakfast. All the food is placed on the table and passed by the people at the table. It requires less time than other types of service, and all family members share in carrying it out.

The details of the family style of service can best be explained by applying it to a particular breakfast.

Orange Juice
Rolled Oats
Bacon and Eggs
Toast Butter Jelly
Milk

Let us see what the serving procedure will be with this menu:

The cloth should be laid correctly; the decoration, if used, should be placed in the center of the table. However, a decoration is not necessary for a family breakfast.

The diagram on page 230 shows how the table should be

set, the table appointments that will be necessary, and how the food may be placed on the table.

After the orange juice is finished, remove the glass to the left of the cover, and place the dish of rolled oats on the breakfast plate.

The family member who is nearest the cream and sugar passes them to the right.

When the rolled oats are finished, return the dish and spoon to the top of the cover.

The "host" then places the tablespoon on the platter and passes the bacon and eggs.

The "hostess" meanwhile has been making the toast and keeping it covered on the plate. She passes the toast, and the other member passes the butter and jelly.

The "hostess" continues making toast as desired by the "family." Foods are passed and repassed as necessary.

A pitcher of water may be placed on the table if desired, and glasses will be passed for refilling to the person nearest the pitcher.

If one member finds it necessary to finish her breakfast and leave before the others are through, she asks permission of the "head of the table" to be excused and leaves quietly.

Each "family" in the class will plan the setting of the table and the family style of service for the breakfast planned. One person should be chosen as the host and one as the hostess. The duties should be divided equally among the family members. Assignments should be made so that everyone will know her duties and understand the order of tasks relating to the meal.

Activities:

1. (*Class activity*) Plan in detail the service of the meal planned for each group.
2. Practice setting the table for the meal planned.

Problem 23: WHAT SHALL WE ACCEPT AS GOOD TABLE MANNERS?

Table manners are the customs or forms of conduct relating to the eating of foods. Some deal with the position taken while eating, others with one's management of food and way of eating, and still others with the expressions of consideration and courtesy toward people who are together at the table.

Using the fork correctly is a necessary social grace.

Table manners vary in different countries, in different localities, and in different periods of time. The Romans reclined when dining; we are constantly reminded that we should sit erect in our dining chair. The natives of India prefer to eat alone and turn their backs to others during the meal; this is in great contrast to our making the mealtime one of shared mirth. The Burmese may eat daintily, rolling his rice and curry into a ball with his finger tips and conveying it to his mouth by the same means; much effort is spent on American children to teach them to keep their fingers out of their food

This girl is using her knife and fork correctly.

The knife and fork are placed on the plate when not in use.

and to use forks and spoons instead.

Strange as the customs of other people may seem to us, they are good manners to them. They enable the boys and girls of each land to manage their food and way of eating to the satisfaction of their families, and to express consideration and courtesy for others.

We do not need to know the rules for serving and eating food in faraway lands. We do need to know the customs relating to eating foods or the table manners of our own country. If we can master these, eating becomes dining and consideration of others at mealtime becomes a matter of course.

Table manners that we in America consider desirable are the following:

1. Sit erect in your chair at the table. Do not rest your arms on the table or crowd the person next to you. Reach for your napkin and spread your napkin, half unfolded, upon your knees as soon as the hostess does.

2. Talk in a low voice and avoid taking full control of the conversation.

Soup is eaten from the side of the spoon—and silently!

Bread is broken into small pieces and buttered. Some prefer holding the bread over the plate while buttering it.

Try to talk about pleasant things, and avoid topics that may lead to quarrels and arguments.

3. Wait until the hostess begins to eat, or until all are served, before eating.

4. In eating soup, dip the spoon away from you and eat from the side of the spoon.

5. Take small bites of food and do not talk while food is in your mouth. Eat quietly and slowly. Chew with your mouth closed.

6. Ask politely for a food to be passed; do not reach for it unless it is near you.

7. When passing food be sure that your fingers do not touch the food. Pass foods to the right.

8. Do not spread a whole slice of bread at one time. Break off small pieces and butter it as eaten.

9. Do not "sop" up gravy or sauce with a piece of bread in your fingers. Do not tip a dish to get the last bit in it.

10. Do not blow on your food to cool it, or pour it from one dish to another.

11. Use the knife for cutting food. Use the fork and spoon for eating. The proper way to hold the knife, fork, and soup spoon is shown on pages 233 and 234.

12. Do not put food and used silver on the tablecloth. Place them on the dishes to which they belong.

13. Place the used knife and fork, when not in use, parallel on the right side of the plate. Place the fork, tines up, to the left of the knife, and place the sharp side of the knife toward the fork.

14. Try to finish eating your meal at the same time the others at the table do.

15. At the end of the meal, if a family member, fold your napkin and place it to left of the cover. If a guest, place the napkin loosely in the same place.

16. At the table assume your responsibility for passing food near you, for helping in the conversation, and for making the meal a pleasant one.

Good table manners become our fixed habits and *our* table manners only through constant use and practice. We should observe them every day and at every meal, whether at home or away. The person who eats crudely at home is rarely able to eat correctly when away from home. Her bad practices have become a serious disadvantage.

Activities:

1. Decide the table manners that will apply to this meal.
2. Practice good table manners at a "play" or "pretend" meal.

Problem 24: HOW SHALL WE PREPARE AND SERVE OUR BREAKFAST?

With all plans made for the preparation and service of our breakfast, we should have little difficulty in carrying them out. Each of us should quickly check the whole plan to recall what is to be done and to see our own part in relation to the rest. We should begin our work at once so that we can have our meal ready, served, and finished on time. We should each strive to do our part to the best of our ability. When the meal is over, we should leave our kitchen and desks in good order.

Problem 25: HOW SUCCESSFUL WAS OUR BREAKFAST?

Now that our breakfast is over, we should discuss its success. We must consider the strong and the weak points in our plan and work so that we can prepare and serve a better meal the next time we try. Rating what we have done helps us to improve in our work the next time. We must be good sports and judge honestly. Unless this is done, our rating means nothing.

Listing the things that you regard as carried through successfully is one of the first steps in judging the meal. When this is done, write down those that were unsuccessful, together with a statement of what might have been the cause. Then make note of the difficulties met, and the suggestions for avoiding them another time.

Many find the use of a score card helpful in judging a meal. A person or class can make out a score card to use. One already made by someone else may be preferred. We give such a score card below. Try using it to judge your meal. It will be interesting to see if each one in your "family" gives the meal the same score.

Score Card for Judging Breakfast

Menu 15
Included milk, fruit, and cereal
Attractive, colorful, pleasing combinations
Adequate and suitable to the group
Kept within the money allowance

Table 10
Attractive
Set correctly

Preparation of food 15
Properly cooked
Well seasoned

Service of food 10
Correctly done
Easily done

Use of silverware 10
Correctly used
Easily used

Atmosphere at the table 10
Pleasing and comfortable

Organization of work 15
Good plans
Plans carried out well
Time well used

Cooperation 15
All worked well together
Each did her part

Activities:

1. Use the score card to judge the breakfasts.
2. Compare the scorings made of the meal in each group.
3. (*Class activity*) Make recommendations for different procedures and for improvements in another meal.
4. (*Class activity*) If time permits, repeat Problems 21, 22, 24 and 25 until several breakfasts have been served.

Problem 26: WHAT IS A GOOD LUNCHEON OR SUPPER?

Luncheon is a noon or evening meal, depending upon the time at which the main meal is served. The main meal is called dinner, whether it is served at noon or evening. When dinner is served in the evening, the noon meal is known as luncheon; when dinner is served at noon, the evening meal is called supper. Luncheons and suppers are practically identical meals.

Certain foods are characteristic of luncheon or supper. Among these are cream soups; scalloped dishes, such as vegetables, meat, and fish; meat substitute or "made dishes," such as Spanish rice, egg casserole, and macaroni and cheese; and vegetables, salads, and desserts, such as baked fruit, brown betty, and custards.

Like breakfast, there are three types of luncheons: light, medium, and heavy. The kind and amount of food included determines the type. Light luncheons are only for

This luncheon for a child includes creamed eggs, fresh carrots and beets, milk, bread and butter, and a gelatin dessert.

grownups who are very inactive, who have eaten a late heavy breakfast, or who will have an early heavy dinner. As most of us need a medium or heavy luncheon, we will consider only these. The following menus may be considered typical:

Medium Luncheons and Suppers

Scalloped Egg and Bacon
Cabbage and Carrot Salad
Bread Butter
Baked Apple
Milk

Cream of Tomato Soup
Crackers
Salmon Salad Potato Chips
Whole Wheat Muffins Butter
Honey
Canned Blackberries

Heavy Luncheons or Suppers

Baked Hash
Creamed Potatoes
Orange and Grapefruit Salad
Biscuits Butter
Cherry Preserves
Floating Island Cookies
Milk

Cream of Celery Soup
Crackers
Macaroni and Cheese
Head Lettuce and
French Dressing
Watermelon Pickle
Bread Butter
Ice Cream Vanilla Wafers

In deciding upon the type of meal needed, the following standard should be the guide. Luncheon or supper should contain one-third of the day's food. The more nearly we can make our three meals equal in amount and kind, the more likely we are to have a well-balanced and satisfactory day's diet.

All the essential foods (see page 35) should be represented in the luncheon or supper in generous amounts. A meal that is lacking in but one essential food is not a good one. Luncheon or supper is sometimes called the "make-up meal." This is because of the old rule that any food essentials omitted in the other two meals should be "made up" in this meal.

Leftover foods are more often used in luncheon or supper meals than in any other meal. No doubt the type of dishes served at these meals is largely responsible. Cream soups, scalloped dishes, salads, and "made dishes" are all foods in which leftovers can be used with successful "appetite appeal."

The luncheon or supper should be attractive, appealing to the appetite, well prepared, and well served. It should be planned as carefully as any meal in the day. Often it is a hurried meal, especially when the lunch period is short. Then a simple, easily digested meal that contains the essential foods is the most desirable.

Activities:

1. Judge the following luncheons or suppers for schoolgirls:

Menu 1	*Menu 2*	*Menu 3*
Baked rice and cheese	Vegetable soup	Mashed potatoes
Buttered carrots	Baked potato	Gravy
Stuffed tomato salad	1 slice bread	2 slices bread
Rolls and butter	Bread pudding	Ice cream
Rhubarb sauce		
Milk		

Menu 4	*Menu 5*
Scrambled eggs	Fried potatoes
Buttered sweet potatoes	Gooseberry pie
Cabbage slaw	Cheese
Whole wheat rolls	Coffee
Butter	
Honey	
Canned peaches	
Milk	

2. Plan a luncheon or supper menu for yourself which you consider good.

Problem 27: HOW SHALL WE PREPARE AND SERVE CREAM OF CORN SOUP?

Cream soups are made by adding cooked vegetables, fish, or meat to thin white sauce. They are excellent dishes to serve, because they contain milk as well as other valuable foods. If you have ever watched your mother make gravy, you know that she used flour to thicken the water or milk. To prevent the flour from lumping in the gravy, it was first stirred into melted fat. When the flour was so mixed with fat that every particle was coated with it, the water or milk was added, and the mixture stirred until it changed from its liquid form to a smooth, thick gravy. Just how thick the gravy was depended upon the amount of flour used for each cup of liquid. Cream soups are thin white sauces or thin gravies. Describing a white sauce as *thin* means that the proportion of the thickening agent, flour, to the liquid, milk, is 1 T. to 1 c.

The utensils

Double boiler	Measuring spoons
Saucepan	Wooden spoon
Measuring cup	Can opener

The recipe for cream of corn soup

Ingredients:

2 c. canned corn	2 T. butter or substitute
2 c. boiling water	2 T. flour
1 slice onion	1 t. salt
2 c. milk	Few grains pepper

Method:

Put onion in a saucepan and pour boiling water over it. Put the saucepan over the fire and let it come to a boil. Remove the onion, add corn directly from the can to the water. Simmer for 10 minutes.

Make a thin white sauce of the other ingredients in the following manner: Fill the lower part of double boiler ⅓ full of hot water and put butter in the upper part of the double boiler, place in the lower part, and place over the fire. When the butter is melted, add the flour, stirring until smooth, thoroughly mixed, and without lumps. Add milk and cook until slightly creamy, stirring occasionally. Add salt and pepper. Add corn and continue cooking 5 or 10 minutes.

Two girls—¼ recipe.

The serving

Cream of corn soup should be served hot in a soup dish or bowl. The soup dish is placed on a serving plate or on the luncheon plate. Crackers may be served with the soup. Crackers are passed on a plate at the table, or two or three are placed by the side of the soup dish. Popcorn is also pleasing to serve with the soup. It is sprinkled on the soup just before it is served. The soup is eaten with a soup spoon or dessert spoon. Three-fourths to 1 cup of soup is a serving.

In eating soup, dip the spoon away from you. Sip the soup from the side of the spoon, not from the tip. In America one should eat soup quietly. In certain Oriental countries, loud inhaling noises are accepted ways of saying the soup is good.

Activities:

1. (*Class activity*) Prepare cream of corn soup.
2. (*Class activity*) Serve the soup in the proper manner.

3. (*Class activity*) Judge the product.
4. Decide what cream of corn soup would add to the diet.
5. Estimate the cost per serving of the soup.
6. Suggest the foods that could be served with cream of corn soup to make a good luncheon or supper.

Problem 28: HOW SHALL WE PREPARE AND SERVE CREAM OF TOMATO SOUP?

Cream of tomato soup is also a thin white sauce to which another food has been added. Its attractive color and pleasing acid flavor make it one of the most popular soups. It is more difficult to make than cream of corn soup. We have an acid food to combine with the white sauce of which milk is the chief ingredient. Milk coagulates, or "curdles" as we usually say, when combined with acid foods, unless certain care is taken. Success in making tomato soup depends upon preventing this curdling. This may be done by combining the hot white sauce and the hot unsalted tomatoes just before serving. The soup should not be boiled or even heated after it is mixed. Soda is often used to prevent curdling. Soda neutralizes the acid in the tomatoes but it changes the flavor and destroys the vitamin C. If one follows the directions carefully, the use of soda will not be necessary.

Soup served with croutons or toast cubes is popular for luncheon.

The utensils

Double boiler	Saucepan
Wooden spoon	Sieve or coarse strainer
Measuring cup	Mixing bowl
Measuring spoons	Cooking spoon

The recipe for cream of tomato soup

Ingredients:

3 c. canned or stewed tomatoes	1/3 c. flour
	1/3 c. butter or substitute
1/8 t. soda (if you wish to use soda)	2 t. salt (added just before serving)
4 c. or 1 qt. milk	1/8 t. pepper

Method:

Put the tomatoes in a saucepan. Cover and simmer for 5 or 10 minutes. Press through a sieve or coarse strainer into a mixing bowl and then turn into the saucepan. If soda is used, add it to the tomatoes and mix thoroughly. Using a double boiler, make a thin white sauce of the other ingredients as you did in making cream of corn soup, except omit the salt.

Just before ready to serve, reheat tomato pulp, and add to the white sauce, stirring constantly. Add salt and serve at once. Do not reheat or boil after combining.

Two girls—1/6 recipe.

The serving

Cream of tomato soup is served in a soup dish or bowl, placed on the serving plate or luncheon plate. Crackers or toasted bread strips are served with the soup. It is eaten with a soup spoon or dessert spoon. Three-fourths to 1 cup is considered a serving.

Activities:

Follow the general procedure as given in the Activities of Problem 27 (page 242). In doing this you will 1) prepare cream of tomato soup, 2) serve the soup in the proper manner, 3) judge your soup, 4) decide what cream of tomato soup adds to the diet, 5) estimate the cost per serving of cream of tomato soup, and 6) suggest other foods that you might serve with cream of tomato soup to make a good luncheon or supper. Follow these same steps at the end of Problems 29 through 45 in this unit.

Problem 29: HOW SHALL WE PREPARE AND SERVE CREAMED DRIED BEEF?

Creamed dishes, like cream soups, are made by combining white sauce with other foods. They differ from cream soups, however, in that they are not so thin a product. Medium white sauce, which contains more flour than does thin white sauce and is thicker, is used in these recipes. Vegetables, meat, eggs, fish, and combinations of these are combined with medium white sauce to make creamed dishes. The proportions used for most creamed dishes are 1 cup of medium white sauce to 1 or 2 cups of one of these foods or a combination of them. Creamed dishes afford pleasing and different ways of including milk and butter in the diet.

The utensils

Double boiler
Wooden spoon
Measuring cup
Measuring spoons
Saucepan
Cooking spoon

The recipe for creamed dried beef

Ingredients:

1/8–1/4 lb. dried beef
1 1/2 c. milk
3 T. flour
3 T. butter
Few grains pepper
4 slices toast

Method:

Tear or cut the beef into pieces. Unless stated otherwise on the package, put in a saucepan, cover with hot water, and let it stand 10 minutes. Drain off the water. This is to freshen or to remove excess salt and to replace some of the water taken out in the drying of the beef.

Make a medium white sauce of the flour, butter, milk, and pepper in the double boiler as you made the thin white sauce. When the white sauce is done, add the cut, drained, dried beef, and continue cooking for 5 or 10 minutes.

Two girls—1/2 recipe.

The serving

Serve the creamed dried beef plain or on toast. If served plain, put it in a vegetable dish. If served on toast, use a platter or vegetable dish. Creamed dried beef is sometimes served directly on the luncheon plate. It is eaten with a fork, using a knife if necessary to separate the toast into smaller pieces.

Activities:

Follow the general procedure as given in the Activities of Problem 27 (page 242).

Problem 30: HOW SHALL WE PREPARE AND SERVE CREAMED GREEN BEANS?

Creamed green beans are another luncheon dish made by combining medium white sauce with another food. This time the other food is a vegetable. As the beans have not been preserved by means of salt, it is not necessary to freshen them as we did the dried beef. The water should be well drained from the beans if the white sauce is not to be watery.

The utensils

Double boiler
Wooden spoon
Measuring cup
Measuring spoons
Cooking spoon
Can opener (if canned beans are used)

The recipe for creamed green beans

Ingredients:

2 c. cooked or canned green beans, drained of their liquid
1 c. milk
2 T. butter
2 T. flour
½ t. salt
Few grains pepper

Method:

Make a medium white sauce of the milk, butter, flour, and salt and pepper in the double boiler. When done add the drained beans. Cook 7 to 10 minutes to heat the beans thoroughly and to blend the flavor. Take care when mixing beans and white sauce that the beans are not mashed or broken into too fine pieces.

Two girls—½ recipe.

The serving

Creamed green beans are served hot in a vegetable bowl and from this to the luncheon plates. From ⅓ to ½ cup is considered a serving. Creamed beans are eaten with a fork.

Activities:

Follow the general procedure as given in the Activities of Problem 27 (page 242).

Problem 31: HOW SHALL WE PREPARE AND SERVE SCALLOPED SALMON?

Scalloped dishes, too, are made by combining medium white sauce with other foods. Their preparation differs, though, from that of creamed dishes in an additional step. After the white sauce is mixed with the other food, the mixture is placed in a baking dish with alternate layers of crumbs, and is baked in the oven. Scalloped dishes in which fish, meat, eggs, or cheese are combined with white sauce are often the main dish of a luncheon or supper.

The utensils

Double boiler	Mixing bowl
Wooden spoon	Mixing spoon
Measuring cup	Baking dish
Measuring spoons	Can opener

The recipe for scalloped salmon

Ingredients:

2 c. salmon	¾ c. bread or cracker crumbs (made by rolling dry bread or crackers with rolling pin)
1 c. milk	1 T. butter (for oiling the dish and dotting the top of the crumbs)
2 T. butter or substitute	
2 T. flour	
½ t. salt	
Few grains pepper	

Method:

Make a medium white sauce of milk, flour, butter, salt, and pepper in the double boiler.

Put salmon in a mixing bowl, separate into pieces, and if desired, remove bones. Combine with the white sauce.

Oil a baking dish with butter and sprinkle the bottom lightly with crumbs. Pour in one-half of the salmon and white sauce mixture. Cover with a layer of crumbs. Pour on the remainder of the mixture. Cover with a layer of crumbs. Cut butter into small pieces and dot over the top.

Bake in a moderate oven (350°F.) 20 minutes.

2 girls—1/6 recipe.

The serving

Scalloped salmon is best served hot as soon as it is done. If the baking dish is suitable, the scalloped salmon is served directly from it. If not, the scalloped salmon is served on a hot platter or in a hot vegetable dish. A tablespoon is used for serving. If the serving dish is hot, it should be set on a hot dish pad or plate so as not to mar the table. Scalloped salmon is eaten with a fork.

Activities:

Follow the general procedure as given in the Activities of Problem 27 (page 242).

Problem 32: HOW SHALL WE PREPARE AND SERVE SCALLOPED CABBAGE?

The preparation of scalloped cabbage differs slightly from that of scalloped salmon. The cabbage must be cooked before combining with the white sauce. The cooking is only for a short time, not more than 7 minutes, so that the flavor and vitamins will not be destroyed. When the cabbage is cooked and drained, instead of mixing it with the white sauce, we will put alternate layers of crumbs, cabbage, and white sauce in the baking dish.

The utensils

Double boiler	Kettle
Wooden spoon	Cooking spoon
Measuring cup	Paring knife
Measuring spoons	Baking dish

The recipe for scalloped cabbage

Ingredients:

½ head cabbage (1½ lbs.)	Few grains pepper
1 c. milk	¾ c. bread or cracker crumbs
2 T. butter	1 T. butter for oiling dish and dotting the crumbs
2 T. flour	
½ t. salt	

Method:

Make a medium white sauce of milk, butter, flour, salt, and pepper, in a double boiler.

Wash the cabbage and remove any undesirable outer leaves, and pull the leaves apart from the cabbage head. If they are large, cut in halves or fourths. Cook the cabbage in a kettle, in boiling salted water that covers it well, from 5 to 7 minutes or until the thickest part of leaf feels tender to a fork. Do not cook too long. Drain the cabbage free from water. Oil the baking dish with butter. Sprinkle the bottom of the dish with crumbs. Put in a layer of cabbage, using half of the amount cooked. Cover with a layer of white sauce, using half the amount made. Cover this with a layer of crumbs. Put in a second layer, using the remainder of the cabbage that was cooked, and cover with the last half of the white sauce. Cover this with the crumbs. Cut butter in small bits and dot over the top.

Bake in a hot oven (400°F.) a few minutes until crumbs are browned.

Two girls—⅓ recipe.

The serving

Scalloped cabbage should be served hot at once, in the baking dish if suitable. If the baking dish is not suitable, the cabbage should be turned into a hot vegetable dish. The hot dish should be placed on a hot dish pad or plate. A tablespoon is used for serving. Scalloped cabbage is eaten with a fork.

Activities:

Follow the general procedure as given in the Activities of Problem 27 (page 242).

Problem 33: HOW SHALL WE PREPARE AND SERVE BUTTERED VEGETABLES?

The buttering of vegetables is a simple but a delicious way of preparing them. Beets, peas, corn, asparagus, beans, okra, spinach, and many other vegetables are commonly prepared by this method. Fresh or canned vegetables may be used. When fresh ones are used they must be cooked before they are buttered. Canned ones should be boiled for 3 minutes before being drained and buttered.

If fresh beets are used, they must be thoroughly washed. They are topped but not peeled before cooking, about one inch of the stem being left on. They are then cooked in briskly boiling salted water sufficient to cover. Young beets require 30 to 60 minutes for cooking; old ones, 2 to 3 hours. When done they are readily pierced by a fork.

If fresh peas are used, they are shelled, washed, and cooked for about 10 to 30 minutes in a small amount of briskly boiling salted water. Only enough water should be used to prevent scorching.

If fresh corn is used, it must be husked, silked, any damaged part cut away, and washed. The corn is then cut from the cob and cooked for about 10 to 15 minutes in briskly boiling water sufficient to cover.

The utensils

Double boiler	Measuring cup
Wooden spoon	Measuring spoons

The recipe for buttered vegetables

Ingredients:

2 c. cooked or canned vegetables	2 T. butter
½ c. water in which vegetable was cooked	Pepper as desired
	½ t. salt, if canned vegetables are used

Method:

Put butter, salt, pepper, and liquid in the upper part of the double boiler and place in the lower part, which is ⅓ full of hot water. Put over the fire. When hot, add vegetables, mix carefully, and steam 5 minutes. Just before ready to serve, remove the upper part of the double boiler and place directly over the fire. Allow its contents to boil up but not to continue cooking.

One girl—⅙ recipe. (Each girl in the group should prepare a different buttered vegetable.)

The serving

Turn the buttered vegetables into a hot vegetable dish and serve at once. A tablespoon or serving spoon is used. Buttered vegetables are eaten with a fork.

Activities:

Follow the general procedure as given in the Activities of Problem 27 (page 242).

Problem 34: HOW SHALL WE PREPARE AND SERVE COMBINATION VEGETABLE SALAD?

Combination vegetable salad takes its name, as you may have guessed, from the fact that a number of vegetables are combined with salad dressing to make it. Combination salad, made of raw, crisp vegetables, adds much food value and interest to the meal.

French Dressing

The utensils

Measuring cup	Mixing bowl or bottle
Measuring spoons	Dover egg beater

The recipe for French dressing

Ingredients:

2½ t. salt	2 T. sugar
5 T. vinegar	Few grains cayenne
½ t. paprika	1 c., less 1 T., salad oil

Method:

Add sugar, salt, paprika and cayenne to the vinegar and mix well. Add oil. Either beat with egg beater until thick and smooth, or put in a bottle and shake. Chill. Shake or beat always before using. (Makes 1⅓ cups.)

Two girls—¼ recipe.

Combination Salad

The utensils

Mixing bowl	Shears
Measuring cups	Fork
Measuring spoons	Plate
Paring knife	

The recipe for combination salad

Ingredients:

1 large head lettuce, or 2 small heads	½ large or 1 medium-size cucumber
2 tomatoes	Salt to taste, ½ t.
¼ green pepper	¼ or ⅓ c. French dressing

Method:

Wash all vegetables in cold water and pat dry with a clean dish towel or paper towels. Using knife, remove any damaged or undesirable part. Take off 6 leaves of lettuce for garnish. Those shaped like a cup are best.

Shred the remaining lettuce with shears or cut into small pieces with a knife. Put in a mixing bowl.

Cut tomatoes in pieces, either 1-inch cubes or small wedges. Cut pepper and cucumber into small pieces. Add all to the lettuce.

Add salt and mix the whole lightly with a fork.

Add French dressing and again mix lightly with a fork.

Two girls—¼ recipe.

The serving

Turn into a salad bowl lined with the six lettuce leaves saved for the garnish. In serving, a large salad spoon or a tablespoon and fork are used. If preferred, the lettuce leaves may be placed on individual salad plates and filled with the salad. The salad plate is then placed either at the left of the fork, or at the right of the knife just below the water glass, at each individual cover. Combination salad is eaten with a luncheon or salad fork.

Activities:

Follow the general procedure as given in the Activities of Problem 27 (page 242).

Problem 35: HOW SHALL WE PREPARE AND SERVE TUNA FISH SALAD?

Tuna fish salad may be used as the main dish in such meals as luncheon and supper. It is a heavier or more substantial salad than the vegetable combination salad. Both the tuna fish and the eggs are grow foods. Boiled salad dressing is used in this salad rather than French dressing. It binds or holds the salad mixture together in a better way.

Boiled Salad Dressing

The utensils

Double boiler
Measuring cup
Measuring spoons

This bowl of tuna fish salad looks good—and is good. It is a welcome luncheon or supper dish.

The recipe for boiled salad dressing

Ingredients:

2 t. sugar
1 t. salt
1 t. mustard
¾ c. water
2 T. flour
1 egg or 2 egg yolks, well beaten
2 T. melted butter
¼ c. vinegar
Few grains cayenne

Method:

Make a sauce of butter, flour, sugar, salt, mustard, cayenne, water, and vinegar and cook in a double boiler as in making medium white sauce. When the sauce is thick, remove the upper part of the double boiler from the lower part and from any source of heat. Beat the egg or egg yolks well, and add it to the mixture. Put away to cool. When ready to use, add ½ cup whipped cream or ¼ cup thick cream or evaporated milk.

Two girls—½ recipe.

Tuna Fish Salad

The utensils

Mixing bowl
Measuring cup
Measuring spoons
Knife
Shears or scissors
Mixing spoon
Fork
Can opener

The recipe for tuna fish salad

Ingredients:

½ c. shredded cabbage
1 c. tuna fish broken into pieces
2 hard-cooked eggs, chopped
½ c. chopped sweet pickles
½ c. chopped celery
Salt (1 t.) and pepper to taste
½ to 1 c. boiled salad dressing as needed
Lettuce leaves to garnish

Method:

Wash and drain the cabbage and celery. Prepare the fish, eggs, pickle, cabbage, and celery as stated in the recipe. Combine and add salt and pepper. Mix salad dressing with the ingredients lightly with a fork.

Two girls—¼ recipe.

The serving

Turn the tuna fish in a salad bowl lined with lettuce leaves, and serve with a large salad spoon or tablespoon and fork. The salad may be also served on individual salad plates as suggested for serving the combination salad. When this is done, garnishing the top of the salad with a teaspoon of salad dressing makes it attractive. Tuna fish salad is eaten with a luncheon or salad fork.

Activities:

Follow the general procedure as given in the Activities of Problem 27 (page 242).

Problem 36: HOW SHALL WE PREPARE AND SERVE BAKED HASH?

Hash is a meat dish made from cooked meat and vegetables. It furnishes a tasty way of using leftovers. Baked hash is cooked in the oven and may be made an attractive dish.

The utensils

Mixing bowl
Measuring cup
Measuring spoons
Mixing spoon
Baking dish

Baked hash and fruit salad are a good combination, and make a well-balanced meal.

The recipe for baked hash

Ingredients:

3 c. cooked meat, chopped (beef, veal, pork, ham, chicken, or combination of meats)
2 c. fresh bread crumbs
1 c. peas or mixed vegetables (cooked)
¾ c. vegetable liquor, soup stock, or water and 1 T. butter
½ t. salt
Dash pepper
½ t. fat for oiling baking dish

Method:

Mix all the ingredients and place the mixture in oiled baking dish. Bake in a moderate oven (400°F.) for about 20 minutes.

Two girls—⅙ recipe.

The serving

Baked hash is best served hot from the baking dish. If the baking dish is not suitable for serving, turn the hash into a hot vegetable dish. The hot dish is placed on a hot dish pad or plate. A serving spoon or tablespoon is used. Baked hash is eaten with a fork.

Activities:

Follow the general procedure as given in the Activities of Problem 27 (page 242).

Problem 37: HOW SHALL WE PREPARE AND SERVE LIVER AND GRAVY?

Liver is a valuable source of protein, iron, vitamin A, and vitamin C. It is a good-flavored food and can be prepared in a number of ways. It should be served often. Fried liver and gravy are especially good.

The utensils

Skillet or frying pan and cover
Pie pan or utility pan
Measuring cup
Measuring spoons
Fork
Cooking spoon

Liver can be tastily prepared and attractively served, and it deserves an important place in our diet.

The recipe for liver and gravy

Ingredients:

- 1 lb. liver cut in slices ¼–⅓ inch thick
- 1 t. salt
- ½ c. flour
- ⅛ t. pepper
- 4 T. lard or other cooking fat
- 2 c. milk

Method:

Sprinkle liver with salt and pepper. Place ¼ c. flour in utility pan. Roll liver slices in the flour until well covered. Put lard in a skillet and heat until hot but not smoking. Put floured liver in the hot fat. When brown, turn, and cover the skillet with a lid. Cook about 5 or 7 minutes, adjusting the fire so that the liver will not become hard or burned. When done, arrange slices of liver on a hot platter and keep them warm.

Use the fat in the skillet, ¼ c. flour, milk, salt, and pepper and make a gravy in the skillet as you would make a medium white sauce. If there is less than 4 T. of fat in the skillet, add enough fat to make that amount. Stir in the flour. When smooth, add the milk. Boil until thick, stirring constantly. Add salt and pepper.

Two girls—2 slices of liver and ½ cup gravy, or ¼ recipe.

The serving

The hot platter of liver is placed on a hot dish pad. The liver is served from the platter with a meat fork or a luncheon fork. The gravy is poured into a bowl and served with a gravy ladle or a tablespoon.

Meat balls served on buns, with slices of onion and tomato, are tempting.

Activities:

Follow the general procedure as given in the Activities of Problem 27 (page 242).

Problem 38: HOW SHALL WE PREPARE AND SERVE MEAT BALLS?

Meat balls are a popular luncheon or supper dish. They are an inexpensive meat dish, highly pleasing to the taste. Most meat-eating peoples have some kind of meat balls among their national dishes.

The utensils

Skillet or kettle
Measuring cup
Measuring spoons
Mixing bowl
Dover egg beater and bowl

The recipe for meat balls

Ingredients:

1¼ lb. hamburger, or 1 lb. hamburger and ¼ lb. sausage, ground fresh pork, or cured ham
2 T. finely minced onion (if desired)
1 c. soft bread cubes
Few grains cayenne and paprika
2 eggs, well beaten
4 c. tomato juice or strained tomatoes
¼ t. nutmeg
1 t. salt (more if necessary)
⅛ t. pepper
¼ c. flour for dredging balls

Method:

In the mixing bowl combine meat, seasoning, bread cubes, onion, and eggs. Mix thoroughly. Form into small balls and roll in flour. Salt tomato juice to taste and heat to boiling. Drop balls into boiling tomato juice. Cover and simmer 30 or 40 minutes. (If class period is too short to permit this, simmering for 20 minutes will cook the ball thoroughly enough to be served. However, the flavor may not be so good as with the longer cooking.)

Two girls—¼ recipe.

The serving

The meat balls and the sauce resulting from the simmering down of the tomato juice are served on a hot platter placed on a hot dish pad. They are served with a tablespoon. Meat balls are eaten with a fork.

Activities:

Follow the general procedure as given in the Activities of Problem 27 (page 242).

Problem 39: HOW SHALL WE PREPARE AND SERVE PLAIN MUFFINS?

Muffins are another quick bread. They differ from both griddle cakes and biscuits. Griddle cakes are made from a thin or pour batter. Biscuits are made from a soft dough. Muffins are made from a drop batter. This means that the amount of flour used is twice the amount of liquid. The resulting mixture is just right to drop from a spoon. Muffins are as commonly served as biscuits and they are one of our most pleasing quick breads.

The utensils

Mixing bowl
Mixing spoon
Measuring spoons
Measuring cup
Dover egg beater and bowl
Sifter
Muffin tins

The recipe for plain muffins

Ingredients:

2 c. flour (sifted before measuring)
4 t. baking powder
1 t. salt
2 T. sugar
1 c. milk
2 T. fat
1 egg or 2 egg yolks
1 T. fat for oiling muffin tins

Good muffins give the final touch of perfection to any well-prepared meal.

Method:

Combine the dry ingredients and mix thoroughly in a mixing bowl. Beat egg or yolks, add milk, and then melted fat. Make a well or small hole in the center of the dry ingredients. Add liquid ingredients to the dry by pouring them into this hole. Mix only enough to combine the ingredients. Drop the batter into oiled muffin tins, filling not more than ⅔ or ¾ full. Bake in a hot oven (425°F.) for about 25 minutes.

Good muffins are large for their weight, golden brown in color, and symmetrical in shape; the top is rough and free from knobs or peaks; the crust is crisp, but not hard and thick; the muffins are tender and of good flavor. The crumb is moist, and the air spaces are fine and evenly distributed with no long narrow tunnels.

Two girls—¼ recipe.

The serving

Muffins are served immediately upon removal from the oven. They are placed on a warm plate and are covered by either a napkin or a hot roll cover. Muffins are eaten with the fingers. They are broken into pieces and buttered with a knife.

Activities:

Follow the general procedure as given in the Activities of Problem 27 (page 242).

Problem 40: HOW SHALL WE PREPARE AND SERVE WHOLE WHEAT MUFFINS?

Whole wheat muffins, as the name suggests, are made from a flour containing the whole wheat grain. The whole wheat grain contains certain minerals and vitamins that are not retained in white flour. Whole wheat muffins are made by the same method used in making plain muffins.

The utensils

Mixing bowl	Dover egg beater and bowl
Mixing spoon	Sifter
Measuring cup	Muffin tins
Measuring spoons	

The recipe for whole wheat muffins

Ingredients:

1½ c. whole wheat flour	2 T. sugar
½ c. flour (sifted before measuring)	1 c. milk
	1 egg or 2 egg yolks
4 t. baking powder	2 T. fat
1 t. salt	1 T. fat for oiling muffin tins

Method:

The method of mixing and baking whole wheat muffins is the same as was used in making plain muffins in the preceding problem. The standards for whole wheat muffins are the same as those for plain muffins.

Two girls—¼ recipe.

The serving

Whole wheat muffins are served in the same manner as are plain muffins.

Activities:

Follow the general procedure as given in the Activities of Problem 27 (page 242).

Problem 41: HOW SHALL WE PREPARE AND SERVE FLOATING ISLAND?

Floating island has been a favorite dessert since before Colonial days. Its name comes from the "islands" of beaten egg white that garnish its surface. Floating island is one of the custards. That is, it is a mixture of egg, milk, sugar, and flavoring, cooked until thick. Floating island is a thin custard, never becoming stiff enough to mold. The egg white which, like the yolk, has thickening power is not added to the custard. It is saved, and when beaten stiff it is applied as a garnish.

The utensils

- Two mixing bowls
- Measuring cup
- Measuring spoons
- Wooden spoon
- Mixing spoon
- Double boiler
- Dover egg beater

The recipe for floating island

Ingredients:

- 2 c. milk
- 3 eggs
- 1/8 t. salt
- 1/2 c. sugar
- 1/2 t. vanilla

Thin custards pour easily, and are sometimes used as sauces for other desserts.

Method:

Break the eggs, separating the whites from the yolks and taking care not to break the yolks. Put yolks in one bowl and whites in another. Add salt to the yolks and beat slightly. Add sugar and mix thoroughly. Heat milk in the upper part of the double boiler until hot. Pour hot milk slowly on the mixture of eggs and sugar, stirring constantly. Return this mixture to the double boiler and cook over gently boiling water. Stir constantly until the mixture thickens and forms a thin coating on the spoon.

Remove at once to a cool place. When cooled, add vanilla.

To the egg whites add a pinch of salt and beat until stiff. Add the remainder of the sugar, folding in until the sugar is well mixed with the beaten egg whites. This is called a meringue. Pour the cold custard into individual sherbet or saucedishes or into a large serving dish. Drop the meringue with a tablespoon on top of the custard, forming floating islands of white.

Two girls—$\frac{1}{3}$ recipe.

The serving

The sherbet dish or saucedish containing floating island is placed on a dessert plate or salad plate or directly at the individual cover. If this dessert is served at the table from the serving dish, sherbet dishes or saucedishes are used. The serving is done with a tablespoon or large serving spoon. Floating island is eaten with a teaspoon or a dessert spoon.

Floating island has long been a favorite dessert.

Activities:

Follow the general procedure as given in the Activities of Problem 27 (page 242).

Problem 42: HOW SHALL WE PREPARE AND SERVE BAKED CUSTARD?

Baked custard contains the same ingredients as does floating island, but the method of preparation is different. The egg white, if used, is combined with the milk. The mixture is baked instead of steamed. The product is smooth and firm and may be molded.

The utensils

- Mixing bowl
- Dover egg beater
- Measuring cup
- Measuring spoons
- Mixing spoon
- Custard cups or baking dish
- Shallow baking pan

The recipe for baked custard

Ingredients:

2 c. milk	½ t. vanilla
2 eggs or 4 egg yolks	Few grains nutmeg
⅛ t. salt	1 T. fat for oiling custard cups or dish
¼ c. sugar	

Method:

Heat milk in the double boiler until hot. Break eggs or put yolks into a mixing bowl and add salt. Beat thoroughly with a Dover egg beater. Add sugar and mix well.

Pour hot milk slowly on the sugar and egg mixture, stirring constantly until thoroughly mixed.

Pour the mixture into oiled custard cups or a baking dish.

Place the cups or dish in a shallow baking pan. Pour a small amount of hot water in the pan around the cups or dish.

Bake in a moderately slow oven (350°F.) for 30 or 35 minutes, or until firm. When done, a knife inserted in the custard comes out clean.

Two girls—½ recipe.

The serving

Baked custard served in the custard cup is placed on a salad or dessert plate or directly on the table at the individual cover. When baked in a baking dish, the custard is served into individual sherbet dishes or saucedishes, which may be placed on a plate or at the individual cover. Baked custard is often topped with a small bit of jelly. It is eaten with a teaspoon or dessert spoon.

Activities:

Follow the general procedure as given in the Activities of Problem 27 (page 242).

Problem 43: HOW SHALL WE PREPARE AND SERVE BAKED APPLES?

Among the cooked fruits served for dessert, baked apples rank high in popularity. The unpared apple is baked. This is an advantage because the apple skin is included in the serving. Roughage is provided and the rich mineral content, much of which is in and near the skin, is largely retained. Baked apples make a tasty, colorful dish that is easily prepared.

This baked Delicious apple is attractively prepared.

The utensils

- Pan or bowl
- Paring knife
- Measuring cup
- Measuring spoons
- Baking dish or pan
- Cooking spoon

The recipe for baked apples

Ingredients:

- 6 tart, medium-size apples
- 6 T. brown sugar
- 1 T. butter
- ½ t. nutmeg
- ½ t. cinnamon
- ½ c. water
- 2 T. raisins, if desired

Method:

Wash apples. Remove stems, cores, and blossom ends. Place them in a baking dish or pan. Mix sugar, nutmeg, and cinnamon, and fill the cavities with the mixture. Sprinkle the top of the apples with the mixture. If desired, add raisins to this mixture. Dot the apples with butter. Pour water around the apples.

Bake in a slow oven (325°F.) until tender. This will take at least an hour and perhaps longer, depending upon the apples. Baste frequently during the baking.

Two girls—1 apple.

The serving

Baked apples are best served chilled. They are served at the table from a fruit dish with a tablespoon or serving spoon. They are served from the kitchen in saucedishes or sherbet dishes placed on salad or dessert plates, or placed directly at the individual cover. Baked apples are served plain, with thin or whole milk, or topped with whipped cream. They are eaten with a teaspoon or dessert spoon.

For variety, these cup cakes are topped with marshmallows instead of frosting.

Activities:

Follow the general procedure as given in the Activities of Problem 27 (page 242).

Problem 44: HOW SHALL WE PREPARE AND SERVE CUP CAKES?

Cup cakes are a drop batter mixture much like muffins. They contain more fat and sugar than muffins and therefore are a richer mixture. Their name comes from the type of utensil in which they are baked. Long ago they were baked in teacups. Now they are baked in cuplike pans or paper containers of various sizes. The size of the container determines the amount of batter used and the size of the cup cake. Tiny cup cakes are now widely used.

The utensils

- Mixing bowls
- Measuring cups
- Dover egg beater
- Wire cake rack
- Measuring spoons
- Mixing spoon
- Sifter
- Muffin tins or cup tins; or paper cups and muffin tins

The recipe for cup cakes

Ingredients:

1½ c. flour (sifted before measuring)	⅔ c. sugar
2 t. baking powder	1 egg
¼ t. salt	½ c. milk
¼ c. butter or substitute	1 t. vanilla or lemon extract
	1 T. fat for oiling pans

Method:

Add baking powder and salt to the flour and sift them together two times. Cream the butter thoroughly, add sugar gradually, and continue creaming until soft and light.

Add an unbeaten egg to the creamed mixture and mix. Add flour alternately with milk, a small amount of each at a time. Beat after each addition until smooth. Add flavoring.

Oil muffin tins or cup-cake pans. Pour these ⅓ full of batter. Bake in a moderate oven (350°F.) 20 or 25 minutes. When done, turn on a cake rack to cool. Use a spatula or thin-bladed knife to help remove cakes if they stick to the pans. When paper cups are used, they are not oiled but are filled with the batter and placed in muffin tins and baked. The paper cup is not removed until the cake is cold.

Two girls—½ recipe.

The serving

Cup cakes are served on a serving plate or on a dessert plate, alone or with another food. They are taken from the serving plate with the fingers and eaten with the fingers. If cakes are not tiny, they are broken into two or more pieces before eating.

Sometimes cup cakes are topped with whipped cream. When this is done, they are eaten with a fork.

Activities:

Follow the general procedure as given in the Activities of Problem 27 (page 242).

Problem 45: HOW SHALL WE PREPARE AND SERVE OATMEAL COOKIES?

Oatmeal cookies are another of the flour mixtures. They are called a drop cookie because the batter is dropped from

Oatmeal cookies with raisins in them are nourishing, as well as delicious.

a spoon onto the baking sheet. The batter is stiffer than that of muffins and cakes. However, it is not as stiff as the dough of the biscuits. Oatmeal cookies are a nutty, fruity kind of cookie that keeps well. Although they are ready to eat when first baked, their flavor is improved if they stand several days.

The utensils

- Mixing bowls
- Measuring cup
- Measuring spoons
- Dover egg beater and bowl
- Spatula
- Baking sheet or pie pans
- Cake rack
- Sifter

The recipe for oatmeal cookies

Ingredients:

- 3/4 c. flour (sifted before measuring)
- 1 1/2 t. baking powder
- 1/4 t. nutmeg
- 1/4 t. salt
- 1/2 c. butter or substitute
- 1/4 c. brown sugar, firmly packed
- 1 egg
- 1 c. raisins, chopped or well separated, and if sticky, floured slightly to keep apart
- 1 c. oatmeal
- 1/3 c. milk
- 1 T. fat for oiling baking sheet or pans

Method:

Sift together the flour, baking powder, nutmeg, and salt.

Cream the butter, add sugar gradually, and cream together until the mixture is soft and light. Beat the egg well. Add the beaten egg and raisins to the butter and sugar mixture. Add oatmeal and mix well. Add the flour mixture alternately with milk, a small amount of each at a time.

Oil a baking sheet or pie pans. Drop the mixture from a teaspoon on the baking sheet or pans, allowing some space between cookies.

Bake in a moderate oven (350°F.) 15 minutes. Remove the cookies with a spatula and place on a cake rack. When cold, put in a cookie jar or box.

Two girls—⅓ recipe.

The serving

Oatmeal cookies are served on a serving plate or on a salad or dessert plate. One large or two small or medium-size cookies are considered a serving. They are eaten with the fingers.

Activities:

Follow the general procedure as given in the Activities of Problem 27 (page 242).

Problem 46: HOW SHALL WE PLAN A LUNCHEON OR SUPPER FOR OUR FAMILY?

Our method in planning a luncheon or supper for our family will be much the same as it was for our breakfast. Our "family" again means the "family" group in our class to which we belong. We may decide this time to have a family of a different size, or we may have the same "family" that we had before. Whatever we do, our plans will be made in relation to our own "family" group.

The first matter to be settled in planning our meal is, of course, the menu. In doing this a number of decisions must be made. Shall we have a medium or a heavy luncheon? We should have one that is adequate and suitable for our "family" members and it should contain about one-third of our day's food. We should have all the essential foods represented in the menu and a generous amount of any that have been omitted in the other meals of the day.

We must choose our menu in relation to the amount of money we have for the meal, whether this be 15, 25, or 30 cents per person. The foods that are on the market, and the likes and dislikes of our family are important. We must not overlook the time we have for preparing the meal. We would do well to base our planning about some one of these dishes that are generally regarded as luncheon or supper dishes. We should do our best to have an attractive and pleasing menu.

We should have our menu checked, as we did before, and then prepare our market order. After this, we are ready to plan the preparation of the meal. All the tasks to be done should be listed in their proper order and divided evenly among the members of the "family." Each one should know exactly what she is to do. Each person should have different responsibilities than were hers for the breakfast meal, in order to get new experience. The time at which we will be ready to serve the meal and that at which we will be through eating should be agreed upon. Plans for the clearing away and cleaning up after the meal should be included also.

When our plans are completed they, too, should be checked with our teacher for her suggestions. In planning this meal, we should profit by our experience in planning and serving the breakfast. Any mistakes made at that time should be avoided in this meal. We should be able to do our work much better and more easily now than we did when we planned and served the breakfast.

Activities:

1. (*Class activity*) Divide into "family" groups. Plan a luncheon or supper for your "family" at a given cost.
2. (*Class activity*) Make out the market order for the luncheon or supper of your group.
3. Plan a luncheon or supper menu for your own family.

"LUNCHEON IS SERVED!"

Who would not welcome the call to an attractive table such as this? The fresh linen, the clean plates and glasses, the attractively prepared food—all contribute to the harmonious setting for this meal. The lovely view through the window also will add to the family's enjoyment.

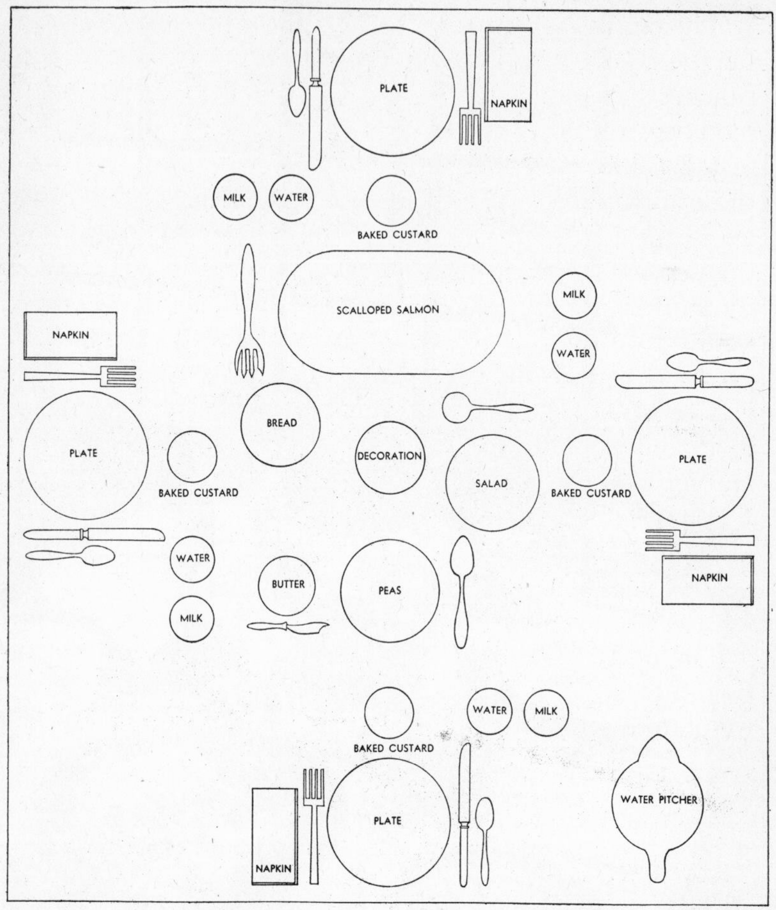

This is how a luncheon or supper table may be set for the family style of service.

Problem 47: HOW SHALL WE PLAN THE SERVICE OF OUR LUNCHEON OR SUPPER?

The service of a meal has much to do with the success of our luncheon or supper, just as it did in our breakfast. No matter how simple a meal, it should be well served. Well-prepared food loses much when poorly served.

The family style of service is the one most commonly used for the family luncheon or supper. We will use it for our luncheon or supper as we did for our breakfast. All the food, you recall, is placed on the table before the family is seated. The food then is passed as desired and needed by those at the table. When the mealtime is short, family service is especially satisfactory. Often variations are made in this service. For example, dessert is not always placed on the table with the other food, but is brought in when the family is ready for it to be served. When this is done, the used dishes from the first part of the meal are removed first.

The general rules for setting the table and serving the food, and the table manners given when we were planning and serving our breakfast hold for our luncheon or supper.

A tablecloth, luncheon cloth, or runners or doilies are used for a family luncheon. The silver, glassware, and china needed depends upon the menu. Some simple decoration, such as a bowl of flowers or a potted plant, adds to the meal.

The details of the service of the luncheon are best shown by indicating how a given menu would be served. Suppose we plan to serve this luncheon:

Scalloped Salmon
Buttered Peas
Combination Salad
Bread Butter
Baked Custard
Milk

All the food is placed on the table before the family is seated.

The host places the serving spoon or fork in the salmon and either serves himself or passes it to the person at his right, according to the custom of the family. If the person to his right is a guest, the host will pass the dish to the guest, always permitting the guest to be served first. In like manner, the hostess passes the peas. The other family members pass the salad, bread, and butter. Food is repassed as often as desired. Glasses are passed to the hostess for refilling. When the main part of the meal is finished, the luncheon plate is exchanged with the plate on which the custard stands. If preferred, the luncheon plate may be placed to the left of the cover and the custard service placed in its stead.

If there is time and the family so desires, the custard may be left in the kitchen and brought in after the luncheon plates and used silver have been removed. This is a variation of the family style of service which is liked by many.

Just as the details of service were worked out for this menu, the service for your luncheon menu should be planned in a similar way. Try to divide all the serving responsibilities as nearly equally as possible. Having one member of the group act as a guest will give a new experience in serving a meal.

When our plans are completed, they should be checked by our teacher and revised according to her suggestions.

Activities:

1. (*Class activity*) Plan in detail the service of the meal your group has planned.
2. Practice setting the table for the meal planned.
3. Decide upon the table manners that will apply to this meal.

Problem 48: HOW SHALL WE PREPARE AND SERVE OUR LUNCHEON OR SUPPER?

We are now ready to put into practice the plans that we have made during the past days. It will be fun to see how well they work, and the improvement we have made since we prepared and served our breakfast. We should each be familiar with what we are to do and know how we are going to do it. We should assume our responsibilities and start work at once. We should have our tasks done at the time agreed upon. We should work together in our "family" group and in every way try to do our part well.

If any difficulties or unexpected circumstances arise, we should try to meet them in an intelligent way, making changes as are necessary.

Activities:

1. (*Class activity*) Prepare and serve a luncheon or supper as planned.
2. Use correct table manners in eating the meal.

Problem 49: HOW SUCCESSFUL WAS OUR LUNCHEON OR SUPPER?

A consideration of the success of our meal is an interesting and valuable conclusion to the work of planning, preparing, and serving it. Through this we are able to improve and to do the job better the next time. One way to judge our work is to make a list of the strong points and the weak points, writing the strong ones in one column and the weak ones in another. The two are then compared and the success of our meal decided upon.

Another way of judging our work is to make a list of the things we would do again if we were repeating the meal, and another list of those we would not do. By comparing the two lists, we may know the success of the meal. A discussion of those we would do differently and how we would do them is also helpful. Difficulties met satisfactorily should also be discussed.

Such questions as these should be answered:

Were all the essential foods included?

Was the meal sufficient in quantity?

Was the meal attractive, pleasing, and appealing to the appetite?

Was the food well prepared?

Was the meal well served?

Was the cost of the meal within the money allowance made?

If we were to give ourselves a grade on our meal, would it be excellent, good, fair, or poor?

Activities:

1. Each group will list the strong points and the weak points of its meal.
2. Each group will list the things to be done differently another time.
3. Each group will list the difficulties that arose and how they were met.
4. Each group will decide upon the grade that should be given for the meal.
5. (*Class activity*) Make recommendations for the improvement of the meals.
6. (*Class activity*) If time permits, repeat Problems 46, 47, 48 and 49 several times.

Problem 50: HOW SHALL WE BUY FRESH FRUITS AND VEGETABLES?

Fresh fruits and vegetables are essential foods in our daily diet and are purchased frequently. Most of them spoil easily and are difficult to keep. Except in certain localities and at certain times of the year, fresh fruits and vegetables are rather expensive foods. If we are to obtain the best value possible for our money, we must make wise purchases.

The fresh fruits and vegetables bought depend upon the plans for our meals. We purchase those foods which we have included in our menus; these should have been planned according to the fresh fruits and vegetables available in the market. We must know not only what fruits and vegetables to buy but what quantity. It is always waste-

These girls are learning how to select fresh fruits and vegetables.

ful and expensive to buy more than is required. Many homemakers are good judges of quality but make poor estimates on quantity.

The money that one has to spend for fresh fruit and vegetables is an important consideration in their purchase. Some fresh fruits and vegetables are expensive and are no better in food value than many less expensive ones. Fancy fresh pears at 25 cents each, delicious though they may be, may have no more food value than an apple costing two to five cents. Some of the foods are expensive at one time of the year and not expensive at another. Strawberries may sell at 75 cents in December when they are not produced locally, and the same size basket may sell for ten or twelve cents in May.

We should observe the appearance and condition of fresh fruits and vegetables when buying. Wilted, mealy, and off-colored vegetables, and fruit that is extremely soft and withered or decayed in spots should not be purchased. If fruit is to be served raw and at once, green and immature products are not desirable. The purchase of fresh fruits and vegetables is better done in person. The standards and interests of the purchaser and the salesman are not always the same. Usually we are better satisfied if we can see what we are buying.

There are guides that help in judging the quality of vegetables and fruits. Some of these are given here:

Guides for Buying Vegetables

Asparagus: crisp-looking, unbroken tips; a freshly cut end that is not woody.

Cabbage: greenish-white, crisp leaves; leaves compact and solid; head heavy.

Carrots: fresh-looking, tender green leaves.

Celery: crisp leaves and stalk; no decayed and molded stalks and leaves; good odor.

Lettuce: fresh, crisp leaves; no mold or decay; if head lettuce, solid head.

Peas: pods crisp and green and well filled with peas, but not too full.

Potatoes: medium size; solid and smooth, not withered; no soft spots; shallow eyes.

Spinach: green, crisp, fresh leaves that are not too large; few or no roots; little or no sand.

String beans: crisp pods that snap when broken; no strings.

Sweet corn: well-developed kernels, filled with a milky juice.

Sweet potatoes: firm, not withered; without mold or soft spots.

Tomatoes: round, smooth, and solid; uniform color, red preferred.

Guides for Buying Fruits

Apples: firm; good color; shape characteristic of the variety; no rotten or moldy spots.

Bananas: firm and plump; bright yellow in color.

Berries: firm and plump; mature; no dirt, decay, or excess moisture.

Cherries: firm and plump; no decay, insects, or skin breaks.

Grapefruit: heavy for size; firm; thin-skinned.

Grapes: plump and fresh; firmly attached to stems; no mold or decay.

Oranges: heavy for size; firm; relatively smooth skin; no soft spots or mold.

The United States Government has determined grades for many of the fresh fruits and vegetables. In general, these grades are U. S. Fancy; U. S. No. 1; U. S. Commercial; U. S. No. 2; U. S. No. 3; and Unclassified. U. S. Fancy is the highest, and Unclassified is the lowest. If you see one of these classifications marked on a box or basket, you will know the quality of the fresh fruit or vegetable. However, in the retail market where most of us buy, grades are not indicated, so we have to buy by those qualities that we can recognize.

The cleanliness and condition of the market where fresh fruits and vegetables are sold is most important. The way they are cared for has much to do with their condition. A dirty and unsanitary market does not deserve our patronage.

Activities:

1. Judge various fresh fruits and vegetables as desirable purchases.
2. Try to decide what grade a product is.
3. (*Class activity*) Choose one fruit and one vegetable each and go to several stores or markets and see what you can learn about these foods there.
4. Compare the prices of various fresh fruits and vegetables.

Problem 51: HOW SHALL WE BUY CANNED FOODS?

Buying canned foods is quite different from buying fresh fruits and vegetables. We can inspect the latter and base our judgment on what we see. We cannot see the contents of the can so we must use other guides in our purchasing.

Many foods are canned, and more are being added all the time. Improved canning methods have improved the prod-

Read the labels on canned foods carefully. Often you will find information on them to aid you in shopping wisely.

ucts. Canned foods are used extensively today. An increasing amount of commercially canned foods is being consumed by the average American family. This makes the purchasing of canned foods an important responsibility.

Grades have been established for canned fruits and vegetables. These have been known as fancy, choice or extra standard, standard, and substandard. Recently, the terms A, B, C, and substandard or off-quality have come into use for grades. The best and most expensive is the fancy or A grade, and the lowest and least expensive is the substandard. The grade to purchase should be decided upon in relation to the intended use of the product. For many purposes the lower grades are satisfactory. Wise purchasing does not mean always knowing and buying the fancy grade.

If established grades were indicated on the can or label, it would be a simple matter to buy by grade. But this is not the case. The only grade required on the label by the government is the substandard. Manufacturers commonly indicate the grades by brand names. For example, "Starlight" may be the label for the A grade, "Moonlight," for B grade, "Sunlight" for C grade, and "Mialight" for substandard. Since each packer, and there are many of them, may even have several different sets of brand names, it is almost impossible to learn to identify grades by this means. Of course, if we use products of one or two packers only, we may find brand names helpful for our own use. Often we ask the dealer what grade a particular label stands for. Thus we do depend upon the reliability of our grocer. Recently a few packers have been indicating grades by the letters A, B, and C. This is helpful to the purchaser. It is hoped that more will follow this plan.

The appearance and condition of the can should be noted in buying canned foods. Cans that swell out at the ends or appear to have a leak should not be purchased. A rusted can or one of bad color should not be purchased without first examining it to see that only the surface of the can is affected.

The information on the label should be read. Some labels give much information, others practically none. The size of the can should be noted. Sometimes a can appears to be a certain size, but when the label is read the can is found to hold less than was expected. Acquaintance with the capacity of cans of common sizes will help greatly in the purchasing of canned foods.

Contents of the common sizes of cans used for fruits and vegetables are as follows:

Size of Can	*Average Net Weight*	*Average Volume in Cupfuls*
No. 1 tall	16 oz.	2
No. 2	20 oz.	2½
No. 2½	28 oz.	3½
No. 3	33 oz.	4
No. 10	6 lb. 10 oz.	13

One should buy canned foods in the size can that can best be used by the family. The quantity of canned foods to be purchased should be decided according to the family's needs, the storage space, and the amount of money that may wisely be spent for them at one time. Sometimes we are led by a special sale or price to purchase more than we should. Such practices are never thrifty.

Activities:

1. Examine labels on various cans of foods. Compare the information given.
2. How many of the cans indicate the grade?
3. Open cans of several grades of two or three given products. Compare them.
4. Note the differences in the sizes of cans of food. Is size of the can an important consideration? Why?

Problem 52: HOW SHALL WE BUY MEAT?

You may have seen someone buy meat this way: "I want fifteen cents worth of steak," or "Please cut me off a thirty-cent pork boil," or "I will take a sixty-cent lamb roast this time." If you follow this plan, you are certainly not an intelligent buyer of meat. Such purchasing leaves the responsibility up to the salesperson entirely. He may or may not make a selection to your advantage. You must know more than this about the buying of meats if you are to do the job well.

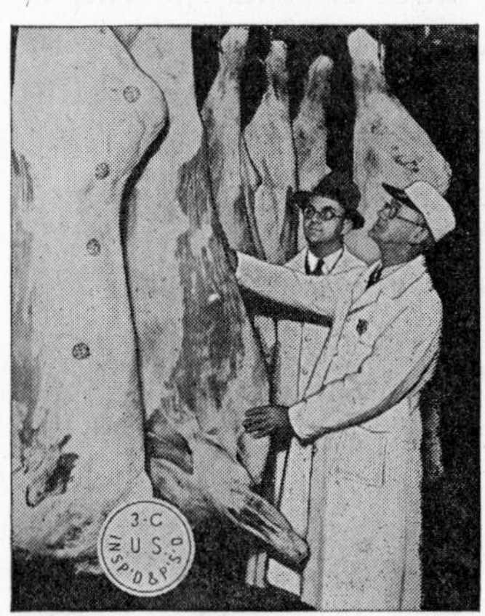

Meat is safe to eat if it bears the stamp (lower left) showing that it has been inspected and passed by the federal government.

The meats most commonly used are beef, pork, and lamb. One way of judging any of these meats is by the color of the flesh, and the amount and kind of fat. Good beef is a bright cherry-red, well marbled and coated with a white or cream-colored fat. Good lamb is reddish-pink and the fat is firm and white. Good pork is of a white or light pink color, and is well covered and marbled with a smooth, white fat. All three meats should be firm, fine-grained, and smooth.

The United States Government has set up certain standards for meat shipped from one state to another. These are based on the health and condition of the animals killed, and on the care given to the meat afterwards. No sick or diseased animals may be used for food. Our government has men to inspect all the meat shipped out of any state. A blue stamp is placed on all that is approved. Only meat so stamped may be shipped outside the state. This ruling does not apply to meat sold within a state. Wise shoppers, however, will not buy meat unless it has this stamp on it. Look for this stamp on the meat the next time you are in a meat market.

Our government has established grades for meat, but so far, only a small percentage of the meat on the market is stamped with the grade. Until grading is more commonly done, we shall have to depend upon other ways of judging meat.

When you go to the meat market to buy a roast, the salesman will want to know whether you want beef, pork, or lamb. Then he will ask, "What cut do you wish?" The meat that comes from the different parts of the animal is divided into cuts. There are two general classes of cuts, the tender and the less tender. Tender cuts come from the part of the animal that has little exercise, and require a short time to cook. The less tender cuts come from the other parts of the animal, and require a long time to cook.

The various loin cuts—sirloin, porterhouse, and T-bone steaks—and the prime rib roasts are tender cuts of beef. Round steak, and chuck, flank, and rump roasts are less tender ones. Corresponding cuts in pork and lamb, though

A meat market which is modern and sanitary should be selected when we shop for meat.

called by slightly different names, are similar in their degree of tenderness. Less tender cuts are just as nutritious as tender cuts. A different method of cooking, however, is required. If you wish to broil or fry your meat, you should buy as tender a cut as you can afford. If you wish to roast or stew your meat, a less tender cut will be quite as satisfactory. Tender cuts are always more expensive than those less tender. This simple chart shows the methods of cooking for the different cuts of meat:

Method	Cuts	Method	Cuts
Broiling or Frying	Beef: Tenderloin, Porterhouse, Sirloin, Hamburger Pork: Cured ham, Cured bacon, Chops Lamb: Chops	*Braising (Frying and Steaming)*	Beef: Round, Rump, Flank, Chuck Pork: Ham, Shoulder, Chops Lamb: Shoulder, Leg, Chops

Stewing
- Beef:
  - Round
  - Rump
  - Chuck
  - Neck
  - Shank
- Pork:
  - All cuts
- Lamb:
  - Shoulder
  - Breast
  - Neck

Roasting
- Beef:
  - Ribs
  - Loin
- Pork:
  - Loin
  - Ham
  - Shoulder
- Lamb:
  - Leg
  - Crown ribs

Our choice of meat should be made in relation to the money we have to spend and the time we have for its preparation. Planning meals some time ahead of their preparation helps us solve this time problem. One reason why so many people buy steak is that they wait until almost time for the meal to decide upon their meat. The use of the less tender cuts of meat helps reduce the meat bill.

The question of the quantity of meat to be purchased is an important one. A general rule is to allow one-fourth to one-half pound of meat per person. The amount varies some because of the quantity of bone and other waste that may be present in the meat.

The condition of the market should always be given consideration and only a strictly sanitary one should have our support.

Activities:

1. Identify pieces of beef, pork, and lamb.
2. Identify various cuts of meat.
3. What does the United States Government blue stamp tell us about the meat?
4. Compare the prices of various cuts of meat.

Problem 53: WHAT IS A GOOD DINNER?

Although few schoolgirls carry the full responsibility for the family dinner, many of them share in the work of planning, preparing, and serving this meal. This share may be small, such as filling the water glasses or removing the dishes after the main part of the meal has been eaten. Again, the responsibility may be broiling the steak and cooking the potatoes and vegetables for the main part of the meal. Whatever our responsibility, we should know the standards for a good dinner.

Dinner is usually considered the heaviest meal of the day. It contains one-third of the day's food, and sometimes more. It may be served at noon or in the evening; regardless of the time of serving, the character of the meal remains much the same.

We have three types of dinners: light, medium, and heavy. The following are examples of medium and heavy dinners:

Medium

Meat
2 Vegetables
Salad
Bread Butter
Sweet
Dessert

Heavy

Appetizer
Meat
Dressing Gravy
Potatoes
2 Green Vegetables
Bread Butter
Salad Crackers
Dessert
Beverage
Candy

For everyday meals, most of us have a medium dinner, unless our family members are doing heavy work or are very active. Then a heavy dinner is needed. The heavy dinner is usually served on special occasions, such as Thanksgiving, Christmas, or birthday anniversaries.

Dinner consists of at least a main part and a dessert.

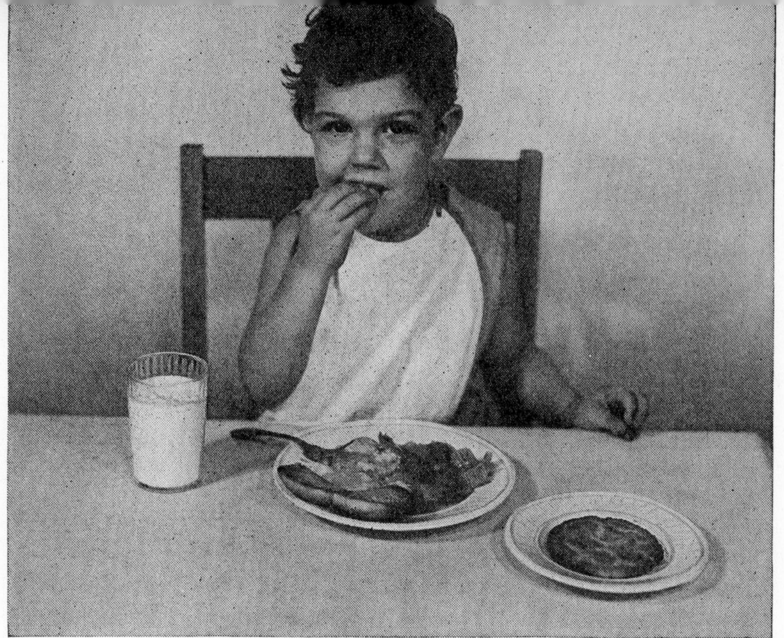

A meat ball, buttered celery, apple sauce, toast, milk, and an oatmeal cookie make a good dinner for a child.

Meat, one or more vegetables, bread, and a salad usually make up the main part of the meal. The heavier dinners include other foods, such as appetizers, additional vegetables, relishes, and sweets.

Care should be taken in planning the dinner menu that there is a balance between the rich and the light foods. A dinner that is light according to the number of foods can be made very heavy by the use of one or two rich foods.

The appetizer, which is served first, may be soup, fruit juice, a mixture of fruit, or even a tasty light salad. The beverage is served with the main part of the meal, with the dessert, or throughout the meal, as is the custom in many families. Coffee, tea, and milk are all suitable dinner beverages.

After the menu is planned, a final check should be made to see if all the essential foods are represented in the meal and that it meets the needs of all members of the family.

A good dinner, like a good breakfast and a good luncheon,

is well prepared, attractive, and pleasing. Its service is good and adds to the joy of the meal.

Activities:

1. Plan the three different types of dinners for yourself, according to the suggested form.
2. Decide upon what occasion you would wish each type of dinner.

Problem 54: HOW SHALL WE PLAN DINNER MENUS FOR OUR FAMILY?

So far we have planned menus for our school family. We will now plan dinner menus for our home family. In our school family, all the members were of the same sex and about the same age. In our home family, both sexes are represented and the ages of the family members vary. The time in school for preparing and serving our meal, and for clearing away and cleaning up afterwards was very short. At home there will be more time and it will be distributed throughout the day. Few of us have the same size of family at home as we did at school.

We must decide upon the type of dinner for which we will plan our menu. As in our school family, the needs of our home family, the money allowed for the meal, the likes and dislikes of the family members, the season of the year, and time to be had for food preparation and service—all are important considerations. After our menu plans are finished we should check to make sure that all the essential foods are represented, and that the cost of our menu comes within the money allowed for the meal.

Activities:

1. Plan a light dinner for your own family.
2. Plan a medium dinner for your own family.
3. Plan a heavy dinner for your own family.
4. How would you change your medium dinner to a light dinner for some family member who needed a light meal?

Problem 55: HOW SHALL WE PREPARE AND SERVE GELATIN FRUIT SALAD?

Gelatin is another means of thickening. It differs from flour and eggs in that the fruit juice or water which it thickens remains clear and transparent. Fruits set in gelatin appear in their original color. Because of this and the fact that the slices, dices, or pieces of fruit may be clearly seen, gelatin dishes are usually interesting and pleasing. Just as the amount of flour used for each cup of liquid determined the thickness of the sauce, so does the amount of gelatin used determine the thickness of the jelly. If too little is used, the jelly is thin, scarcely setting; if too much is used, the jelly is rubbery and tough. Many gelatin preparations, like the one we will use, have been sweetened, flavored, and colored before being packaged.

The utensils

Two bowls
Measuring cups
Measuring spoons
Mixing spoon
Paring knife
Large mold or individual molds
Spatula

The recipe for gelatin fruit salad

Ingredients:

1 package sweetened gelatin, lemon, orange, raspberry, or other fruit flavor
1 c. boiling water
1 c. cold water or fruit juice
Few grains salt
1 c. fruit, fresh or canned, cut into medium-size pieces—grapes, pineapple, cherries, bananas, oranges, etc. One kind of fruit or a combination of several may be used.

Method:

Put the gelatin in a bowl. Pour hot water on it, stirring until dissolved. Add cold water or fruit juice and salt. Mix thoroughly. Pour into a mold and set in a cold place to chill. If

An individual mold of fruit salad, served with sections of grapefruit, can be prepared for the meal in advance. It fits into a wide variety of menus and occasions.

time is limited, setting the mold in a pan of cracked ice will hasten the thickening process. When the liquid begins to thicken, add fruit to the gelatin. Continue chilling until the mixture is firm.

When individual molds are used, the salad is removed from the mold without breaking or destroying its shape. A very hot cloth wrapped around the outside of the mold for a minute or less releases the salad so that it can be taken out of the mold at once. If a large mold is used, the salad is cut in cubes or slices in the mold and removed with a spatula.

Two girls—¼ recipe.

The serving

Gelatin fruit salad is served as a salad on lettuce leaf with boiled dressing. It is placed on a salad plate and eaten with a salad or luncheon fork.

Gelatin fruit salad is served also as a dessert in a saucedish or sherbet dish. It is usually topped with whipped cream, though thin cream is sometimes used. The saucedish or sherbet dish is placed on a salad or dessert plate, or directly on the table. Gelatin fruit salad is eaten with a teaspoon or dessert spoon.

Activities:

1. (*Class activity*) Prepare gelatin fruit salad.
2. (*Class activity*) Serve the fruit salad in the proper manner.
3. (*Class activity*) Judge the products.
4. Decide what gelatin fruit salad would add to the diet.
5. Estimate the cost per serving.
6. Suggest the foods that could be served with gelatin fruit salad to make a good dinner.

Problem 56: HOW SHALL WE PREPARE AND SERVE MEAT PIE?

If all the kinds of meat pie that are made in various parts of the world were listed, the list would be long. There would be pasties from Cornwall, kidney pie from England, pork pie from Ireland, shepherd's pie from Scotland, hare or rabbit pie from France, goat pie from some of the countries of Central Europe, and cheese and beef pies from the United States. If you were to examine them closely, you would find they were made of various combinations of meat and vegetables, topped with or enclosed in a crust of biscuit dough, a layer of cereal, or a layer of mashed potatoes.

The utensils

Two mixing bowls
Measuring cup
Measuring spoons
Mixing spoons
Paring knife
Two forks or knives
Baking dish
Sifter

The recipe for meat pie

Ingredients for crust:

1 c. flour
2 t. baking powder
1/3 c. milk
1/4 t. salt
2 T. fat
2 t. fat for oiling dish

Mix as for biscuits (see page 226).

Meat pie served with peas makes a satisfying meal. The color contrast of green peas, light crust, and the brown of the meat adds to the appeal of the appetizing odor.

Ingredients for meat mixture:

- 1 c. cooked meat, cut in cubes
- 1 c. cooked potatoes, cut in cubes
- ½ c. cooked carrots, cut in cubes
- 1 c. of hot medium white sauce or gravy made with soup stock or water instead of milk (see pages 245, 246, and 257)
- ¼ c. diced onion, if desired
- Salt and pepper as desired

Method:

Mix meat, potatoes, carrots, onion, and white sauce. Season to taste. Pour into an oiled baking dish.

Pat or roll dough ⅜ inch thick into the same shape and size as the top of baking dish. Cover the mixture with the dough. Bake in a moderately hot oven (400°F.) for 18 or 20 minutes. If preferred, the dough may be cut into small squares or circles and placed on top of the mixture, instead of using the crust in one piece.

Two girls—¼ recipe.

The serving

Meat pie is served from the baking dish or from a platter with a serving spoon. The hot dish or platter should be placed on a dish pad. If baked in individual baking dishes, these are placed on the dinner plates. Meat pie is eaten with a fork.

Activities:

Follow the general procedure as given in the Activities of Problem 55 (page 291).

Problem 57: HOW SHALL WE PREPARE AND SERVE SPONGE CAKE?

Sponge cakes differ from cup cakes in that they contain no fat. There are two kinds of sponge cake: those made with the entire egg, and those made with the whites of eggs only. We will make a yellow sponge cake that contains the entire egg.

The utensils

Two or three mixing bowls
Measuring cup
Measuring spoons
Two egg beaters
Sifter
Spatula
Grater
Lemon juicer
Cake pan (stem or tube, loose bottom, is desirable)
Cake rack

The recipe for sponge cake

Ingredients:

1 c. flour (sifted before measuring)
4 eggs
1 c. sugar
½ t. salt
3 t. lemon juice
½ lemon rind, grated

Method:

Separate the egg yolks from the whites, using 2 different bowls.

Beat egg yolks well, add lemon juice and grated rind, salt, and sugar. Beat until well mixed. Sift in flour gradually, folding in until well mixed.

Unfrosted sponge cake is good eaten with milk or fruit. The texture of sponge cake is one indication of quality. This is a piece of a fine sponge cake.

Beat whites of egg well but not stiff. Fold into the mixture.

Pour cake batter into a smooth, unbuttered sponge-cake pan. Bake in a slow oven (275° to 325° F.) for 1 hour. If baked in small or individual pans, the time will be only about 30 to 40 minutes.

Sponge cake, when done, shrinks from the sides of the pan and the center crust springs back when touched lightly with the finger. When the cake is done, remove from the oven and turn the pan on a cake rack to cool. When the cake is thoroughly cold, loosen the edge with a sharp knife or thin spatula, then let the cake pull from the pan by its own weight.

Two girls—½ recipe.

The serving.

Sponge cake is cut in individual portions or served on a cake plate or on dessert plates. Sometimes it is topped with whipped cream or ice cream. When served plain, it may be eaten with the fingers or with a fork. When topped with cream, it is eaten with a fork. It may be served with stewed fruit or a fruit gelatin salad.

Activities:

Follow the general procedure as given in the Activities of Problem 55 (page 291).

Problem 58: HOW SHALL WE PREPARE AND SERVE PLAIN BUTTER CAKE?

The "plain butter cake" differs from the sponge cake in that it contains butter or a substitute. It is like the cup cake in ingredients, but differs from the cup cake in its method of mixing. Plain butter cake is not an expensive cake because it contains only simple ingredients. Sometimes the butter cake recipe given below is called the standard butter cake recipe, because many variations can be made from it. Even though the recipe for plain butter cake is followed, interesting variations can be made by the use of icings. Uncooked icing is a satisfactory one that can be easily and quickly made. We will use this icing on our cake.

An iced butter cake can be served with tea-party refreshments.

Plain Butter Cake

The utensils

Mixing bowls	Layer cake tins
Measuring cup	Spatula
Measuring spoons	Sifter
Mixing spoon	Cake rack
Egg beater	

The recipe for plain butter cake

Ingredients:

1/3 c. butter or substitute	2 1/2 t. baking powder
1 c. sugar	1/4 t. salt
2 eggs	1 t. vanilla or lemon extract
2/3 c. milk	1 t. fat for oiling cake pans
1 3/4 c. flour (sifted before measuring)	

Method:

Cream the butter and add sugar gradually, continuing creaming until the two are well blended and the mixture is soft and light.

Separate the eggs and beat each part until light.

Add beaten yolks to butter and sugar, and mix until well blended.

Sift flour, salt, and baking powder together. Add about one-fifth of flour mixture to the creamed mixture and mix for about 1/2 minute. Add 1/4 of the milk to the creamed mixture, stir slightly, then add 1/5 of the flour, stirring about 10 seconds, and so on until the milk and flour are all added and mixed. During this mixing, add the extract. Fold in the stiffly beaten whites, which should take no longer than 1/2 minute.

Turn into oiled cake tins, filling them 1/2 to 2/3 full. Bake in a moderate oven (350°F. to 375°F.) for 20 to 30 minutes.

When done, loosen the sides with a thin spatula or knife and turn on a cake rack.

A butter cake is done when an inserted toothpick comes out clean; when the cake begins to shrink and leave the sides of the pan; and when it springs back to its original shape when pressed lightly on top with the finger.

Two girls—1/2 recipe.

Uncooked Icing

The utensils

Mixing bowl
Measuring cup
Measuring spoons
Mixing spoon
Sifter

The recipe for uncooked icing

Ingredients:

5 T. milk
3 T. butter
3 c. powdered sugar, sifted
1 t. vanilla or lemon extract

Method:

Cream the butter, add sugar and milk gradually and alternately. Stir until soft and creamy. Add extract. Use at once. The icing should spread easily, cover the cake smoothly, and not run off. If too thick, add a little more milk; if too thin, add a little more sugar.

Place the bottom layer of the cake on a rack or plate. Spread a thick coat of icing over the cake with a spatula. Place the upper layer on top of this, making sure the sides are even. Spread icing over the top and sides so that cake is well covered. Set in a cool place for a few minutes for the icing to become firm.

Two girls—1/3 recipe.

The serving

Cake is cut into individual servings and placed on a cake plate or on dessert plates. Cake may be eaten with the fingers. However, an iced cake is usually eaten with a fork.

Activities:

Follow the general procedure as given in the Activities of Problem 55 (page 291).

Problem 59: HOW SHALL WE PREPARE AND SERVE BREAD PUDDING?

Bread pudding is an old-fashioned dish and has long been a favored dessert. Its recipe appears in many old cookbooks. The ingredients are not expensive. Leftover parts of loaves or slices of bread may be used. Lemon sauce is frequently served with bread pudding. In its preparation, cornstarch is used as the means of thickening. Cornstarch is more like flour than the other thickening agents we have used. A number of variations can be made in the pudding recipe. Chocolate or cocoa may be added to the milk. Brown sugar may be used and also brown bread.

Bread Pudding

The utensils

- Mixing bowl
- Measuring cups
- Measuring spoons
- Mixing spoons
- Baking dish
- Double boiler
- Wooden spoon
- Dover egg beater and bowl

Bread pudding is an old-fashioned dessert that finds favor with many people.

The recipe for bread pudding

Ingredients:

- 1 c. bread cubes or small pieces of bread
- 2 T. melted butter
- 1 egg
- ¼ c. sugar
- ¼ t. salt
- ½ t. vanilla extract
- ¼ t. cinnamon
- 2 c. milk
- ½ c. raisins, currants, or coconut
- ½ T. fat for oiling baking dish

Method:

Beat the eggs slightly and mix with sugar, salt, vanilla, butter, and cinnamon in a mixing bowl. Scald the milk in a double boiler and add slowly to the egg mixture, stirring constantly. Add bread and raisins, currants, or coconut. Mix thoroughly. Pour into an oiled baking dish. Set in a pan of warm water as in preparing baked custard. Bake in a moderate oven (350° F.) about 1 hour, or until a knife inserted in the center comes out clean. Remove from the oven and cool.

Two girls—½ recipe.

Lemon Sauce

The utensils

Double boiler	Grater
Mixing bowl	Lemon juicer
Measuring cup	Mixing spoon
Measuring spoons	Wooden spoon

The recipe for lemon sauce

Ingredients:

1½ c. hot water	¼ c. sugar
1½ T. cornstarch	¼ t. salt
2 T. lemon juice	1½ T. butter or substitute
Grated rind of ¼ lemon	

Method:

Mix cornstarch, sugar, and salt. Add hot water gradually, stirring constantly. Add grated lemon rind. Put in a double boiler and cook until the mixture thickens, stirring constantly. Then add lemon juice and butter or a substitute. Remove from the fire and cool. If the lemon juice is added earlier, it tends to lessen the thickening power of the cornstarch.

Two girls—⅓ recipe.

The serving

Serve bread pudding cold with lemon sauce poured over it. Whole milk or thin cream can be used instead of the sauce if preferred. A saucedish or sherbet dish is used and is placed on a dessert or salad plate or directly on the table. Bread pudding is eaten with a teaspoon or a dessert spoon.

Activities:

Follow the general procedure as given in the Activities of Problem 55 (page 291).

Problem 60: HOW SHALL WE SET THE TABLE FOR DINNER?

Setting the table for dinner is a common responsibility of many schoolgirls. It is a pleasant task, for it has much to do with the appearance and success of a meal, and gives us

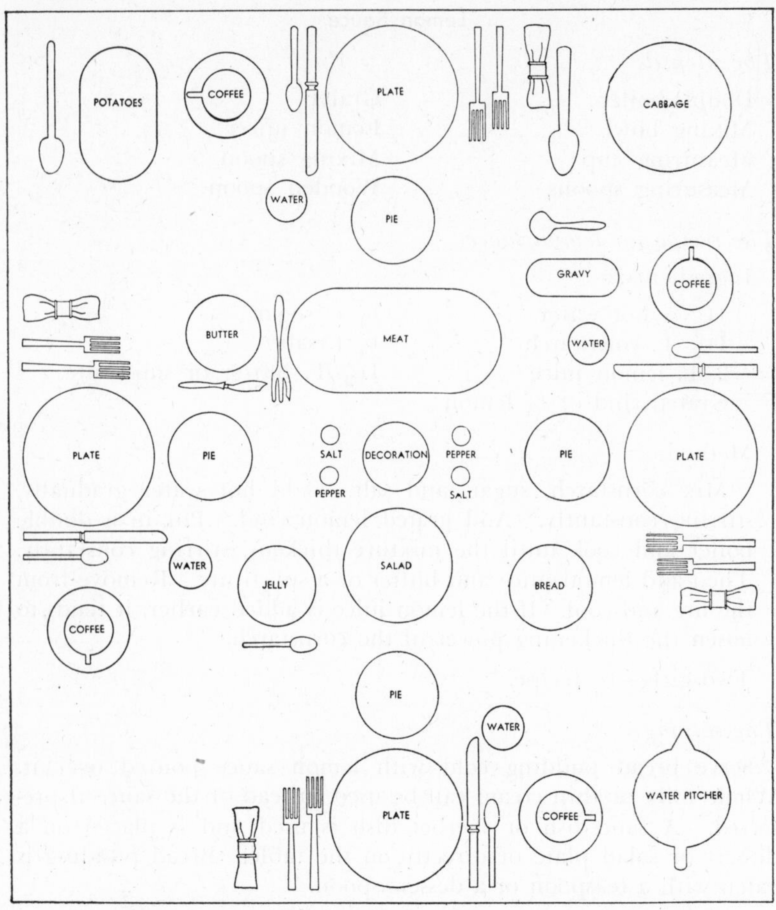

This is a dinner table set for the family style of service.

opportunity to express ourselves in the creation of order and beauty.

There are a few things that always go on the table, such as the tablecloth, napkins, plates, and water glasses. Beyond this, there are choices to be made according to the plans for the meal. Therefore, we need to know the menu for the dinner before we set the table and the way in which the

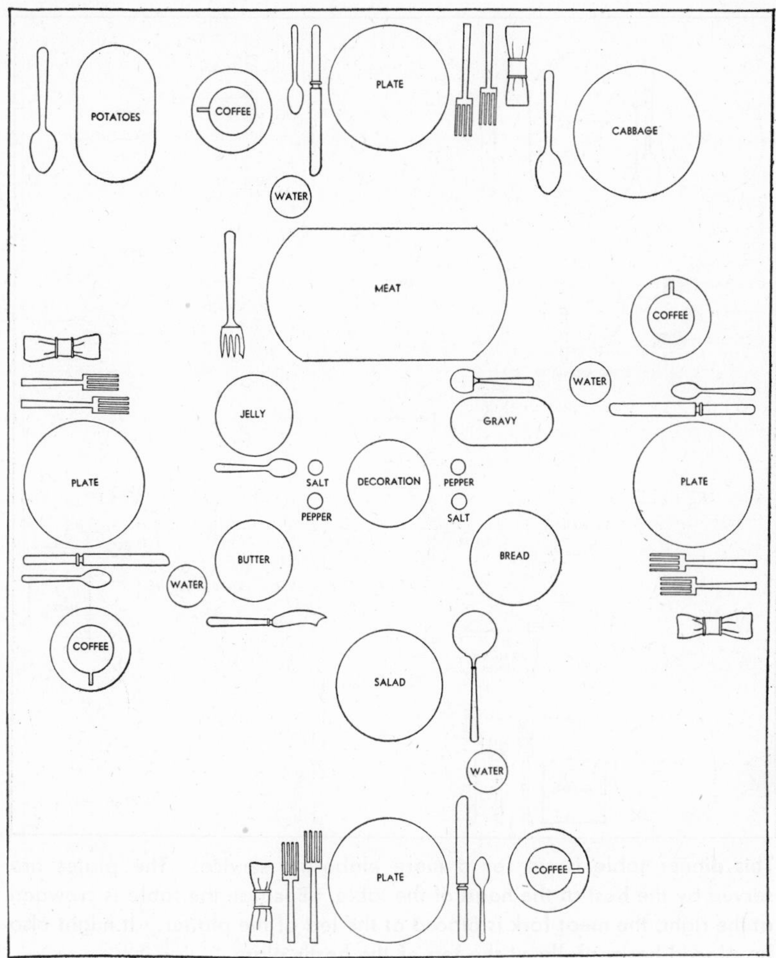

This dinner table is set for modified family style of service.

meal will be served. If strictly family style is used, all the table appointments and food will be on the table before the family is seated. If modified family style is used, we must decide what foods will be placed on the table and what foods will be served later. Many families like to

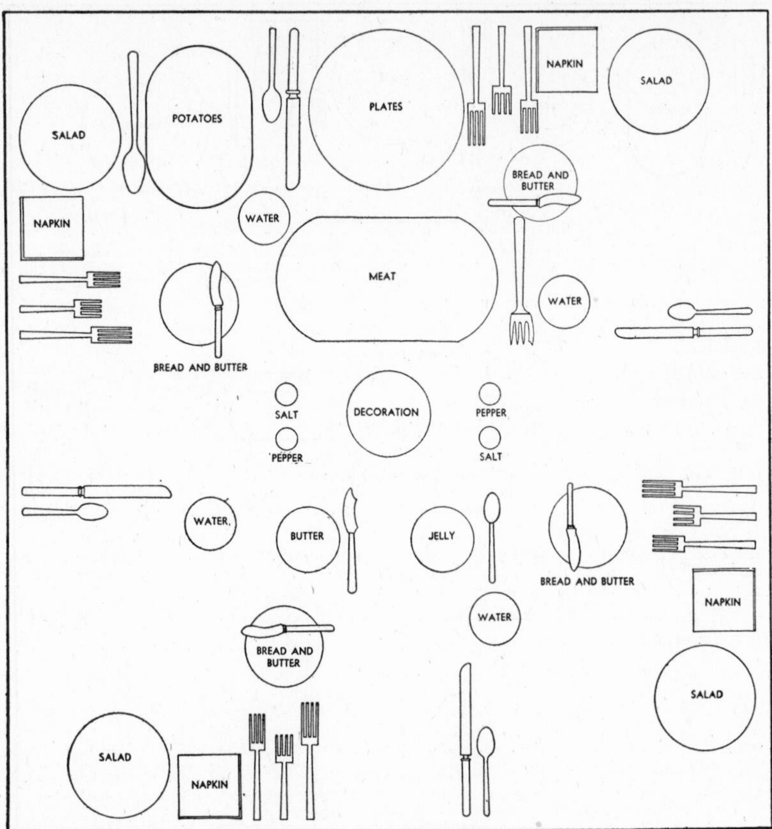

This dinner table is set for a more elaborate service. The plates are served by the host at the head of the table. Because the table is crowded at the right, the meat fork is placed at the left of the platter. It might also be placed horizontally at the top of the host's plate.

use the family style for everything except the soup or appetizer and the dessert. Some families like to have a more elaborate service for the dinner meal than for the other meals. Instead of the food being served and passed by all the people at the table, the father or host serves the plates with the meat, gravy, and vegetables, and passes them to the other family members at the table.

Along with the type of service, the dishes and silver to be used must be considered. Shall we have bread-and-butter plates and butter spreaders? Shall we serve our salad on individual plates? Shall we use salad forks? Many times the answer to such questions can be made only after a consideration of the time and the help that those preparing and serving the meal have. The more elaborate our service is, the more dishes and silver are required. Elaborate service always means more time and work for someone. We must decide what is best for us.

Suppose we take a dinner menu and see how we would set the table for different styles of service. The preceding diagrams show how the type of service used affects the setting of the table. We will use the following menu as an example:

Roast Beef
Browned Potatoes Buttered Cabbage
Orange-Pineapple Salad
Bread Butter Jelly
Cherry Tarts
Coffee

Activities:

1. Select one dinner for each "family" of the dinners previously planned (page 288) and decide the general plan of service that will be used.
2. Set the table for this meal.

Problem 61: HOW SHALL WE HELP WITH THE SERVICE OF THE DINNER?

Family style of service, or some variation of it, is used largely for the family dinner. Only a very small percentage of families have maids, and in most families the members serve their meals themselves. It is much better for every member to have a share in the responsibility than to detail some one member to act as maid and wait on the others. Family style of service gives everyone a part to do.

The details of the service of the meal should be carefully planned. Some of these details must be decided upon before the table is set. Many of them must be planned after this job is done. When everything has been agreed upon, a division of the duties must be made. They should be distributed as evenly as possible, so that no one has too much work during the meal. Each one should know what he is expected to do. Each family member should find out how the task is to be done if he is not certain, so that he can do his part easily and properly. In assigning tasks, the clearing away of the meal and the cleaning up of the dining room and kitchen should be included. These jobs are a part of the preparation and service of the meal.

The details of the strictly family style of service are fairly simple. They consist chiefly of the passing and repassing of food, the refilling of service dishes with food, and the refilling of the water pitcher and glasses, or the serving of other beverages. The modified family style of service adds the details of serving the appetizer and dessert and of removing used dishes during the meal.

In the more elaborate style of service mentioned in Problem 60, still more details are added and the service becomes more difficult. Often some member seated at the right of the host assists in serving the plates. Thus the host carves the meat, places the meat and potatoes on the plate, and passes the filled plate to his assistant, who serves the cabbage and gravy and then passes the plate to the person for whom it is intended.

If there is a guest for dinner and she is seated at the right of the host, the hostess or a family member at the left of the host often assists in the serving. The plates are then passed to the left instead of the right so that the guest's plate is served first.

Plans should provide for second servings. They should also care for the removal of the food, dishes, and silver of the first part of the meal, and for the serving of the dessert and beverage. Details concerning these steps will be slightly different in the various styles of serving the meal.

The placing and removal of dishes and foods is from the left side with the left hand, except for those dishes and foods which belong on the right side; these are placed and removed from the right side with the right hand. Service dishes and their silver are removed, beginning with those used by the host. If a tea cart or serving table is used, the individual dishes may be passed to the hostess to be placed on it, being exchanged for the dessert which is on the cart or serving table. This will save many steps in serving.

Activities:

1. Plan the service of the meal in detail.
2. Plan the distribution of the responsibilities of the service, using your school "family."
3. Plan the distribution of the responsibilities of the service, using your home family.

REFERENCES FOR THE UNIT

Calvert, Maude Richman, *The New First Course in Homemaking.* Atlanta: Turner Smith Co., 1932.

Friend, Mata Roman, and Shultz, Hazel, *Junior Home Economics: Food.* New York: D. Appleton-Century Co., 1933.

Jensen, Milton B., Jensen, Mildred R., and Ziller, M. Louisa, *Fundamentals of Home Economics.* New York: The Macmillan Co., 1935.

Kinyon, Kate W., and Hopkins, L. Thomas, *Junior Foods,* Revised Edition. New York: Benj. H. Sanborn and Co., 1938.

Matthews, Mary Lockwood, *The New Elementary Home Economics.* Boston: Little, Brown and Co., 1937.

Talbot, Nora, and Others, *Practical Problems in Home Life for Boys and Girls.* New York: American Book Co., 1936.

Trilling, Mabel, Williams, Florence, and Reeves, Grace G., *Problems in Home Economics.* Chicago: J. B. Lippincott Co., 1939.

SUGGESTED HOME EXPERIENCES

1. Assume certain responsibilities for washing the dishes and utensils.
2. Prepare the various recipes and dishes made at school.
3. Prepare recipes and dishes similar to those made at school, such as cream of celery soup, creamed potatoes, and scalloped tomatoes.
4. Assume responsibility for setting the table for certain meals.
5. Plan, prepare, and serve family meals at home.
6. Help with the planning, preparing, and serving of family meals at home.
7. Assume the responsibility for serving meals at home, both for the family and for company.
8. Purchase fresh fruits and vegetables, canned foods, and meats for your family at various times.
9. Conduct table etiquette drills or games in your home.

UNIT

9

HOW TO LOOK OUR BEST

WHEN WE WERE LITTLE GIRLS AND played at "keeping house" we tried to look like settled married women caring for children, making calls, and taking care of a house. Perhaps an old eye-glass frame perched on our nose and the long skirts firmly pinned under our arms with safety pins helped us to feel and look the part of Mrs. Jones. That was all make-believe, played as a game. Now as we grow older we want to look not like Mrs. Jones, nor like our favorite moving-picture star, but like our own selves. We want to understand ourselves far better than we did the grownup whom we copied in our childish play. If we can do that, we will be better able to look our best and become our best. Becoming our best selves is something that will take all our lives. Looking our best selves may be done here and now. First, we must know what we want to look like, and then we must work to reach our goal.

There is an old rhyme that goes:

> Good, better, best:
> Never let it rest
> Till your good is better,
> And your better, best!

This may serve as a rule for improving ourselves, whether we are trying to build lovely bodies or well-trained minds.

Feeling fit matters above everything else in looking our best. Swimming, indoors or out-of-doors, is a sport which is of great help in keeping healthy.

Problem 1: WHAT DOES LOOKING OUR BEST REQUIRE?

First in the list of requirements for looking our best is the acceptance of ourselves as interesting persons, able to grow into even more interesting ones. As we do this, we will develop poise, assurance, and graciousness. Simply by being ourselves day after day, we will help our appearance far more than we could by aping a different movie star each week.

We cannot truly look our best unless we are building an honest, unselfish, and interesting personality for ourselves. From these efforts will naturally follow the quality of charm, which is a part of beauty. Next, we want to have physical loveliness. We know—or we soon will find out—that very little of this comes from the jars and bottles that fill the shelves of the drugstore. Physical loveliness comes from having a shapely body in good health, held in good posture, and kept in fine condition through bathing, exercise, rest and sleep, and proper food. Good grooming of hair and nails contributes largely to good looks. Tousled hair, grimy hands with nails encircled in black, unbrushed teeth, and a careless walk are to be avoided by those who would look their best.

Our clothing should be suitable and becoming; it should be clean, well pressed, and in good repair. If in the theater a character must be shown in a bad light, the actor comes into the play overdressed in some absurd way, or with clothes badly fitted, in need of patches, or in need of cleaning and pressing. The silly girl in the play appears having a ruffled dress with many bows tacked on in the wrong places, and a funny veil falling from an unbecoming hat. She minces along on uncomfortable high-heeled shoes. The man who is shown as a failure has baggy, unpressed trousers, shoes sadly in need of repairs and polish, and a coat either much too large or too small. Thus, dress is used to make the characters look much less than their best.

Sometimes on the streets in our town or city, we see girls whose manner of dress takes away from, rather than adds to, their looks. High heels, such as would be suitable only for evening wear, coats that clash with the color of the hat or dress, and an overloading of neck and wrists with costume jewelry are common faults. If we want to look our best, there is much that we must know before we can tackle our problem wisely.

Activities:

1. What habits could you change that would improve your appearance?
2. Describe a friend of yours who spends a great deal on clothes but who does not seem well dressed. Why is this true?
3. What is a suitable costume for street wear?

Problem 2: WHAT IS GOOD POSTURE?

You may have heard someone say to you or to someone you know, "Oh, do straighten up—slouching and stooping

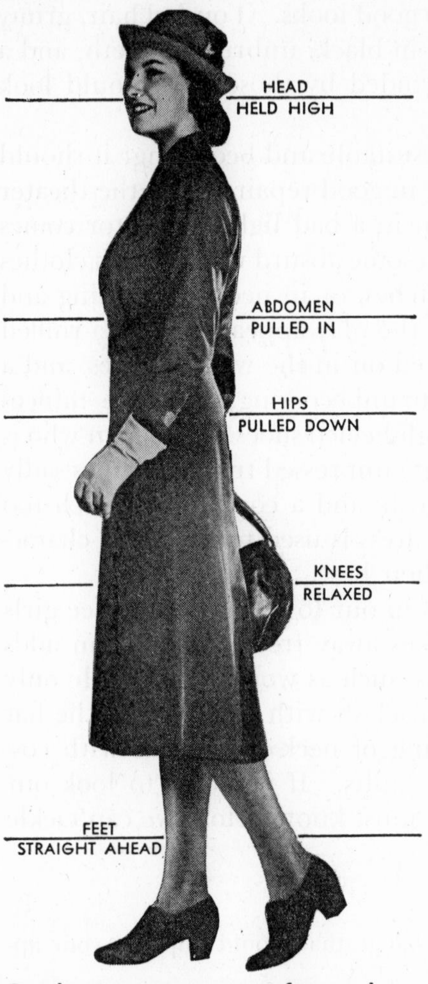

Good posture is necessary for good appearance. Notice how this girl puts into practice the necessary rules of good posture.

will just ruin your figure!" Perhaps, for a moment, the person spoken to pulled herself up, and then, like a string released from being pulled straight and tight, sank back into all sorts of loops and curves. Then perhaps the criticism continued: "Oh, such awful posture!" Posture refers to the position in which the body is held. In a correct standing position the ear, the shoulder, the hip, and the instep are all in a straight line. Both the abdomen and the back are flat, the head is erect, and the chin in. Shoulders and knees are relaxed. In Colonial days, girls were required to walk for hours with books on their heads to develop the habits of good posture. They prided themselves on being erect and well poised. They had lessons in sitting, too, so that they might be trained in seating themselves and rising from the chair gracefully. They tried to keep their posture erect when seated. Good sitting posture requires that the hips be well back in the chair, the abdomen flat, the head and the chest up, and the shoulders relaxed.

Let us look around the schoolroom and see how many of us have good sitting posture. Then when the bell rings for classes to change, let us observe the standing and walking posture of our group. It will be interesting to list the mistakes in posture which we see in both cases. Slouching, humping the shoulders, ducking the head, and lolling in the chair are perhaps the most common faults.

Shall we look at our walking posture? If our standing posture is good, we should be able to keep it even if our body is in motion. However, much will depend upon the condition of our feet and the sort of shoes we have on. As we have learned in our hygiene class, the foot is elastic and arched, being made up of many small bones. The foot rests on the ground along its outer borders as it carries the body weight. When we walk, the weight shifts from the heel to the outer border and the ball of the foot. The feet should toe out rather than in, but, ideally, the feet should be parallel or nearly so when we stand to walk.

The shoes we wear should fit the feet. Many shoes are too narrow and too pointed. Many have high heels that throw the body into a strained and awkward position in its effort to keep in balance. Healthy, well-shod feet make possible graceful walking and standing postures.

If our posture is not as good as we desire, let us remember again and act on the old rhyme:

> Good, better, best:
> Never let it rest
> Till your good is better,
> And your better, best!

Activities:

1. Describe the posture and appearance of someone who has good posture.

2. How was this good posture obtained?
3. How can you improve *your* posture?
4. What kind of shoes should you wear? Do you wear proper shoes?

Problem 3: WHAT DAILY CARE SHALL WE GIVE OUR BODIES?

We all remember an old saying, "Cleanliness is next to godliness." This adage is true in the matter of caring for our bodies and keeping them well. Personal cleanliness comes next to thinking right thoughts and seeking to find good in everyday living. Planning to give our bodies the care that will keep them clean is a part of growing up. When we were little, our mothers said, "Did you wash your hands?" "Did you get your neck clean behind your ears?" They decided when we should wash our hair; they helped us keep our nails tidy; and they called us to our evening bath. Now that we have grown older, caring for our bodies becomes our own responsibility. We should keep ourselves clean without the reminders which little children require. Included in the necessary daily care of your body is the care of the teeth, the care of the skin, the care of the hair, and the care of the hands. Shampooing the hair and manicuring the nails will be considered in the next problems.

Keeping the *teeth* in good condition requires that they be scrubbed, morning and night, with a good toothbrush. Use either table salt or a good dentifrice with water to help the brush do a good job of cleaning. Brushing is done with a circular motion. If it is possible, you will find that it helps keep teeth shining and bright to brush them after the noon meal, too. The use of a mild mouthwash each morning helps keep the mouth and teeth in good condition.

The bath is important in the daily care of the *skin*. The bath frees the skin of the dirt and grime which it has gathered from contact with the air; perspiration and oil given off by glands in the skin are removed. Cleansing the skin is best done in a bath of warm water with suds created by the use of a mild soap. The lather should be rubbed briskly on the body with a clean washcloth. After the cleansing, sudsy warm bath, a shower or quick rinse in cool water is desirable to close the pores of the skin and give the body a "toning up." Vigorous rubbing with a clean, coarse towel adds to the sense of well-being.

If the convenience of the home makes it possible, a daily tub bath is desirable. If this is not possible, one can keep fresh and dainty by taking a daily sponge bath and as many tub baths as can be arranged.

A daily tubbing and rubbing is a good health habit.

In addition to the all-over bath, it is necessary to wash the face and hands several times daily. Use warm water with a mild soap for cleansing, and follow this with a cool rinse. If the skin is dry or chafed, a cold cream or lotion may be used to soften and soothe it.

The *hair* should be brushed daily to keep it glossy and healthy. If it is worn in curls, it must be kept in curl; untidy, straggling ends make hair anything but "a crown of glory." If the hair is worn short, it should be cut frequently enough to keep the effect right.

The daily care of the *hands* is given by washing them thoroughly several times a day. A thorough handwashing includes wetting the hands thoroughly, using enough soap to work up a good lather, and rubbing the two hands against each other on all sides. Rinse them in clean water and dry them with a clean towel. A few drops of hand lotion may be rubbed into the skin to keep the hands soft.

Daily care of the nails is given by keeping them neatly

filed and scrubbing them with a well-soaped nail brush. This is done when the hands are being washed. After this scrubbing, run the end of a file or an orangewood stick under the nail ends to free them of any dirt. If the orangewood stick is used, the pointed end is wrapped with a thin coating of absorbent cotton. This is dipped in clean suds and used to clean under the nails, care being taken to clean the corners. The cleaning is finished by scrubbing the nails again with the soaped nail brush, and then rinsing the hands and drying them thoroughly with a clean towel.

If we follow such a program of daily care as we have just considered, we will need little make-up. Our skin will be fresh and clear, and we will appear well groomed. If rouge is used, it should be carefully applied, so that the effect will be natural rather than startling.

Activities:

1. Care for your hands by the method given. Report the results to the class.
2. What procedure should you follow to take good care of your body?
3. Why do we desire well-cared-for bodies?

Problem 4: HOW SHALL WE MANICURE OUR NAILS?

Even if our hands receive the best of daily care, once each week they will need a thorough manicure. Although the giving of manicures is one of the major activities in the beauty shops, it is something we may learn to do satisfactorily ourselves in our own home.

For the home manicure, the following equipment will be necessary: A small bowl for soapy water, a ten-cent nail brush, a five-cent orangewood stick, a ten-cent nail file, a pair of manicure scissors or clippers (or a small pair of sewing scissors), a buffer, polish remover, cuticle remover, and nail polish.

The manicure is begun by washing the hands. Remove

the old polish, if necessary, and file the nails of both hands. Then soak the finger tips of each hand in a bowl of soapy water. The soaking loosens the cuticle and makes it easier to push it back and reveal the moons. The blunt end of an orangewood stick covered with cotton dipped in water is used to push back the cuticle. If a little vaseline, oil, or cold cream is rubbed along the cuticle first, it will be easier to remove. If needed, cuticle remover is then applied, using the cotton-wrapped tip of the orangewood stick. After this process has been done, pass the soapy brush over the finger tips, and dry the hands. Hangnails and loosened cuticle are removed with clippers or scissors, with care being taken not to cut into the skin. After the last rinsing, dry the hands thoroughly. A small amount of hand lotion may be applied to keep the skin soft.

Many girls follow this operation by using a buffer on the nails to give them a glow. Others apply a liquid polish. If the latter is done, the schoolgirl should limit herself to a light polish that gives merely a faint tinge of color. Polish of brilliant red or other colors lacks both attractiveness and suitability as a finish for our nails.

Activities:

1. Examine your nails and decide how you can improve their appearance.
2. Manicure the nails of your partner.

Problem 5: HOW SHALL WE SHAMPOO OUR HAIR?

Even well-brushed hair needs shampooing once each week, or once in two weeks, depending upon its condition. Oily hair requires more frequent shampooing. If one has patience, one may easily learn to give a shampoo at home. Soap jelly or liquid shampoo should be made before starting to wash the hair. Enough for several shampoos may be made by shaving half a bar of a mild soap into a pan or porcelain bowl, covering the shavings with three cups of warm water, and cooking slowly until the soap has fully dissolved.

In beginning the shampoo, the hair should be dipped in clear, warm water, and then the liquid shampoo should be applied to the wet scalp in small amounts as needed to make a heavy suds on the hair and scalp. The scalp should be rubbed with firmness so as to loosen any dirt present so that it can be washed away. It may be necessary to apply the liquid shampoo a second time, or to follow the first application with a wash in soapy water.

Hair must be washed regularly to keep it soft and shining.

When the hair and scalp are clean, they should be rinsed thoroughly through several waters to remove every trace of soap. Each rinse water may be somewhat cooler than the preceding one. The last should be fairly cool, and should remain clean and free from soap after the hair has been rinsed in it; if any trace of soap shows, another rinsing is needed. The hair is then rubbed dry with a bath towel, in the sunlight and fresh air if conditions permit. Sometimes a wave set is desired; in such case, the hair is combed while wet, then pushed into place and held there by a net while it drys.

Activities:

1. Make a jar of liquid shampoo. Figure the cost and see if it is cheaper to make it or to buy one which is already prepared.
2. Wash your hair by the method given. What changes would you suggest in the method?
3. When is a good time to wash the hair?

Problem 6: HOW CAN OUR CLOTHES HELP US TO LOOK OUR BEST?

First we must consider what is *our best.* It is not our little sister's best, nor is it our mother's best. We are not children, nor yet women, but schoolgirls with bodies which are growing. Not always does this growth come in an all-around, balanced way as we would wish, and yet there is nothing to do but to take it as it comes.

If we look around the classroom, we will find that some of our classmates have shot up like bean poles, the chief part of their growth seeming to be in length. There are others who are chubby and tubby, with wide shoulders,

Poorly selected clothes, such as those shown here, emphasize figure difficulties and lessen the self-confidence of the wearer.

Boleros are becoming both to the stocky figure and to the more slender figure.

deep chests, and broad hips. These girls seem chunky rather than lengthy. There are others whose busts have developed to a much greater degree than the rest of their figures, giving them a problem of figure control which they must get used to. Finally, there is the girl who is neither fat nor lean, but whose figure and posture seem awkward and gangly.

Now let us look at each of them in their turn. The thin girl finds that a hair dress which is short, yet softly curled, adds to the interest and charm of her face. Dresses in bright, becoming colors in fairly stiff materials, which have square shoulders, wide belts with striking buckles or bows in front, and fullness at the waist are very good. Bright socks dropped just below the knee seem to lessen the leg length and to fill out legs which are too thin. Shoes may be blunt-toed, and made of contrasting leathers or cloth.

The chubby girl who has grown *out* instead of *up* may need a straight hair style of becoming length, to make her face seem more slender. She may need a well-fitted girdle to control her hips and waistline. She should avoid the separate waists and skirts that seem to divide her height in half. Better for her are dresses cut on long lines with flat pleats. Her skirts should be wide enough so that they will not cup at the back of the hips. Because her legs are chubby, she should have her skirt flared and at a length short enough so as not to strike the fattest part of her calf. She may wear

Four little maids from school are poised and happy because they are well groomed and know that their clothes are becoming to them.

stockings. If she chooses socks, they should be short and quiet in color. Her shoes should be long and well fitted to make her legs look slimmer and longer.

The girl with the heavy bust line will need wide-shouldered dresses with fullness in the waist, and boleros or short jackets, to add to the grace of her figure. A dress all one color is found to be more becoming than the contrasting waist and skirt. Well-fitted shoes that are comfortable for walking help greatly in improving posture.

The awkward girl whose figure has not yet become definite needs to have a hair dress that is becoming, easily kept in condition, and suited to her age. She may need a girdle to help establish a waistline. Tailored clothes that will add to her dignity and poise are good for her. She should avoid the ruffled, babyish sort of dresses—these only emphasize her feeling of being a misfit.

If we can plan and choose our clothes wisely, we can make them help us look right for what we are—growing girls.

Then we will be happier, gayer, and more cheerful, and this will go far toward making us look our best.

Activities:

1. What will you consider first when buying your clothes?
2. How will your partner's choice of style of clothes differ from yours?
3. What can you do to emphasize the best lines of your body?

REFERENCES FOR THE UNIT

Friend, Mata Roman, and Shultz, Hazel, *Junior Home Economics: Clothing*. New York: D. Appleton-Century Co., 1933.

Jensen, Milton B., Jensen, Mildred R., and Ziller, M. Louisa, *Fundamentals of Home Economics*. New York: The Macmillan Co., 1935.

Kinyon, Kate W., and Hopkins, L. Thomas, *Junior Clothing,* Revised Edition. New York: Benj. H. Sanborn and Co., 1938.

Matthews, Mary Lockwood, *The New Elementary Home Economics.* Boston: Little, Brown and Co., 1937.

Todd, Elizabeth, *Clothes for Girls*. Boston: Little, Brown and Co., 1935.

SUGGESTED HOME EXPERIENCES

1. Wash your hair according to the method you outlined. How much money can you save by washing your own hair?
2. Manicure the nails of some member of your family?
3. Check yourself for one week and see how much time you spend on the care of your body? Would it help to use more time?
4. If you have younger sisters or brothers, help them to learn how to care for their skin, nails, and hair.

UNIT 10

CARING FOR OUR CLOTHING

IF EACH GIRL IN THE CLASS WERE TO make a list of the clothing she owns at the present moment, there would be a wide variety of articles listed. Shoes, hose, panties, slips, dresses, coats, hats, kerchiefs, raincoat, rubbers, and so on, the list of wearables would go. A comparison of several of these lists doubtless would show that some girls had more of certain items than others had, certain articles being entirely lacking from some wardrobes. Yet there would surely be enough similarity so that we would know that these girls all shared the common problem of the care of clothes.

This problem is a very real one to anyone who wishes, as we all should, to get the most service from her wardrobe. "Care lengthens wear" is a saying that girls of another generation heard frequently. It applies to every article of clothing. If we wish to get the most satisfaction in service from the investment we have made in our clothing, we must do as the wise home-owner does with his property—he keeps it appearing as nearly like new as possible.

In addition to safeguarding the investment we have made in our garments, care of our clothing brings good returns in the improvement of our personal appearance and our sense of well-being. Few people can carry themselves with a queenly air if the heels of their hose or the elbows of their coats are in holes. From the standpoint of thrift, satisfaction, and personal well-being, the time and effort used to keep our clothing in good condition may be regarded as time and effort well spent.

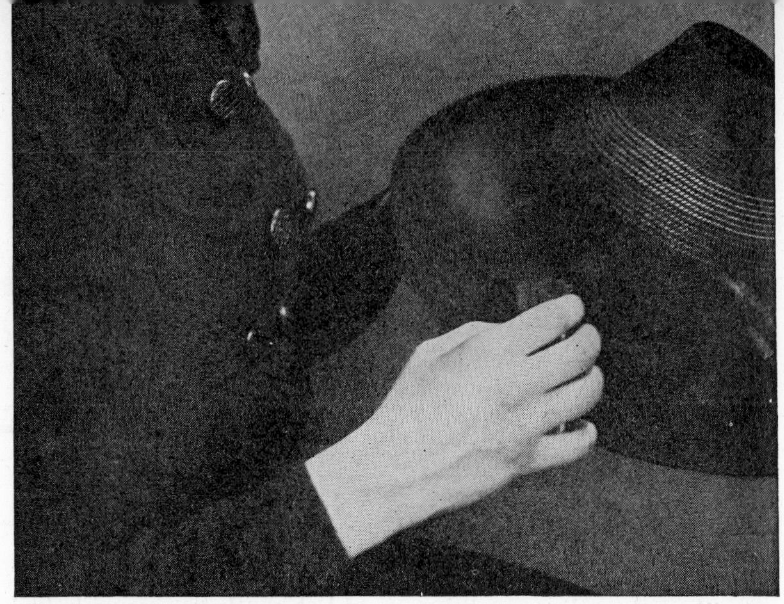

Frequent brushing keeps our clothes looking well and adds to the wear they give us.

Problem 1: WHAT DAILY CARE SHALL WE GIVE OUR CLOTHING?

The clothing we own may be roughly classified as that which we are using, and that which is not in use. When you are in bed, sound asleep for the night, your dress, coat, hat, and shoes are not in use. When you are out on the tennis court, stretching your arms to return high balls, your sports costume is in use, and your pajamas and bathrobe are not. If you are to give your clothing good care you must provide satisfactory storage for frequently used garments when they are not being worn.

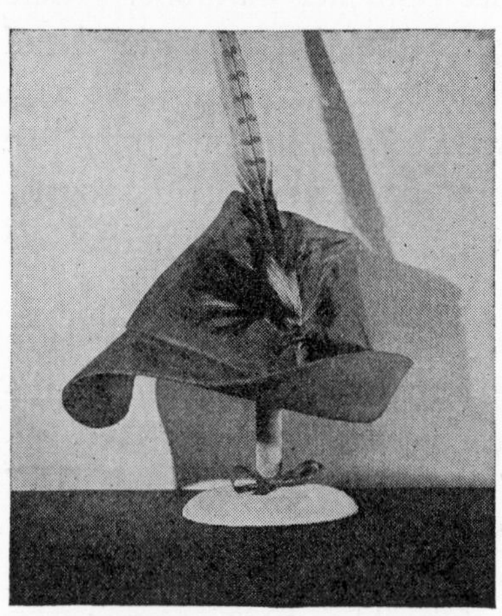

A hat stand is useful to keep the hat brim in proper line.

Good care includes two steps of primary importance:

putting the garments away in an orderly manner, and keeping them clean. A clothes closet of some type is essential for hanging clothes in order. It should provide enough space so that such things as coats, dresses, and blouses may be hung on hangers; it should provide a place for hats, rubbers, and shoes. Space for hanging garments is best provided by a rod placed lengthwise of the closet, on which hangers are hung, or by extension hooks that may be pulled out to permit placing of the hangers. Hats may be put on hat stands, in boxes on the closet shelf, or in boxes hung on hooks. A shelf built about six inches above the floor gives adequate storage for shoes. Some may prefer for this purpose a shoebag hung on the closet door.

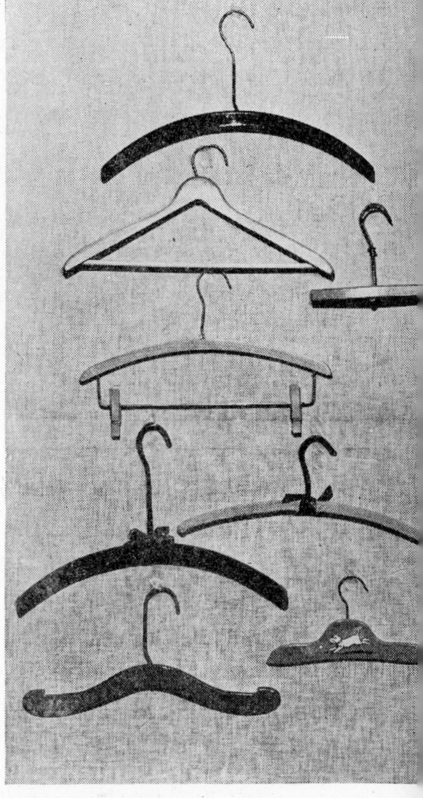

There are hangers for every need, from hanging the heavy coat to hanging evening dresses and children's clothes. Can you name the use of each of these hangers?

If a room does not have a closet, a temporary one may be made by curtaining off a small corner of the room with a plain fabric. Sometimes a rectangular closet is built in a corner of the room, from some light-weight building material. A curtain usually serves as a door in such closets. In modern homes, closets provide not only adequate space for hanging garments, but also carefully planned drawer and shelf space for all wardrobe needs.

In the caring for coats, hats, and wool and silk dresses, it is well to brush them after each wearing, before putting

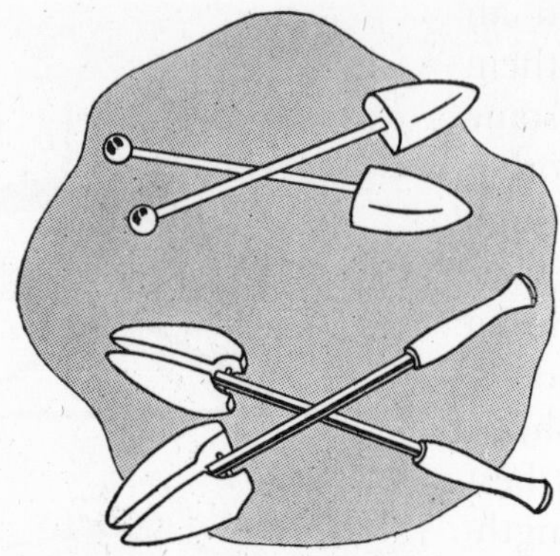

Shoetrees help keep our shoes in shape.

them away. A small whisk broom serves best for brushing hats, and a large one for dresses and coats. Shoes should be cleaned and wiped daily and polished when necessary. All material for polishing and wiping can be kept in a box on the shelf in the closet. When putting shoes away, it is a good practice to put shoetrees in the shoes. Rubbers should be wiped or washed if necessary. Rubbers may be stuffed with tissue paper and placed on the shoe shelf or in a drawer set aside for their storage.

Hose and all clothing that is worn next to the body should be washed daily. If any mending is needed on these garments, it should be done before they are put away. Hose and underwear are usually kept in a drawer where they may be protected from snagging.

Cotton and linen dresses may require pressing after each wearing. In summer it is usually necessary to launder them after a day's wearing. Any garment that has been worn should be checked for rips, tears, or worn places. If such are found they should be mended as soon as possible, at least before the garment is worn again. Fasteners of any kind should be checked for secureness and kept ready for wear at all times. Stains and soiled places should be removed before the garment is to be worn again, or before the garment is laundered.

If you have ever entered a bedroom that was in complete disorder, you have doubtless felt the sense of unrest that it gave. Dresses and slips tumbled on the floor where the owner stepped out of them, shoes and slippers tossed this way and that, and the litter of handkerchiefs and hose on the floor—they all seemed to be protesting their abuse. If they could speak surely they would have said in reproach to their owner, "You may deserve this, but do we?" Good care lengthens wear.

Activities:

1. What daily care do you give your clothing?
2. What additional daily care should you give your clothing?
3. How does good care of clothing help one to save money?
4. Make a plan for giving your clothing the needed daily care.

Problem 2: HOW SHALL WE CARE FOR OUR UNDERGARMENTS AND HOSE?

Undergarments include girdles, panties, brassieres, and slips. Of this group panties and brassieres should be laundered after each wearing. Repair any rips, tears, or worn places before laundering.

While girdles are often worn next to the body, laundering them once or twice a week has been found sufficient, except in hot weather, when daily laundry may be needed. Slips that are in constant use should be laundered at least twice a week.

The following procedure is suggested for laundering:

1. Use lukewarm water and a neutral soap for suds.
2. Wash the garment in the lukewarm suds until clean, rubbing gently between the hands.
3. Give special attention to straps and unusually soiled places.
4. Rinse twice in clear, warm water.
5. Squeeze out excess water and roll the garment in a turkish towel.
6. When the garment is partially dry, press it with a moderately warm iron until it is dry, except in the case of the

Every day should be wash day for stockings and undergarments.

girdle or garments made of knit material—these may be placed in the open air to dry, and need no ironing.

The neat, well-dressed person keeps her undergarments in just as good condition as her outer garments.

Care in putting on and taking off hose adds much to the length of their wear. Open the hose at the top and grasp the top between the two hands so that the seam is at the back. With the hands, gather up the hose the entire length to the toe. Place the toe of the hose over the corresponding part of the foot, and as you release the hose bring it over the foot and on over the leg. Always keep the back seam straight.

It is advisable to wash new hose before wearing and after each wearing. A good method for washing hose is as follows:

1. Use lukewarm water and a neutral soap for suds.
2. Squeeze the hose gently in the suds to remove soil and perspiration.
3. Rinse them twice in clear, lukewarm water.
4. Squeeze them gently in the hands to remove water.
5. Hang them up carefully.

It is best to dry hose in the open air if the temperature is above freezing and only a gentle breeze is blowing.

Hose should be mended at the first sign of wear. Runs are mended by hand stitching or by machine stitching. Mending is done on the wrong side. Holes in the foot of hose are repaired by darning. When not in use, hose should be stored in a drawer or box where there is no danger of snagging.

Activities:

1. Where do you keep your hose and underwear? Is this a good place? Why?
2. Wash some piece of underwear by the method given.
3. Wash hose by the method given.
4. What changes in the methods would you recommend? Why?

Problem 3: HOW SHALL WE DARN OUR CLOTHING?

Darning is a method used to mend small holes, tears, and slightly worn places in hose, knitted underwear, and woolen and silk material. It is also used in the mending of table linen. Darning is the interlacing of new threads to replace worn or broken threads of the fabric. The thread that we use in darning should match as nearly as possible the thread of the material being darned. The threads of the darn should be placed parallel to the threads of the material. As the threads are interlaced, the crosswise and lengthwise threads should alternate over and under at the edge of the darn. This tends to make a smooth and secure mending job.

A stitch in time saves nine—particularly with a stocking.

A good method of making a darn in a stocking is as follows:

1. With the stocking right side out, place the darning egg in it so that the place to be mended is over a flat surface.

2. Trim all ravelings on the edge of the hole.

3. Bring the thread up from the wrong side and make a row of small stitches far enough from the hole to reinforce the broken threads.

4. Repeat the rows of running stitches $1/16$ of an inch apart until the hole is reached.

5. Continue running stitches at the side of the hole until the hole is reached, then take a long stitch across each time you reach the edge of the hole and repeat running stitches at the opposite side.

6. Continue until the hole is covered, and make rows of small stitches as was done in the beginning.

7. Make running stitches out from the hole at right angles to the first stitches made.

8. As the hole is reached, cross the threads over one thread and under one thread across the length of the thread over the hole.

9. Continue until the hole is covered and out the same distance from the hole as in the beginning.

10. Interlace the thread through to the opposite side, and cut.

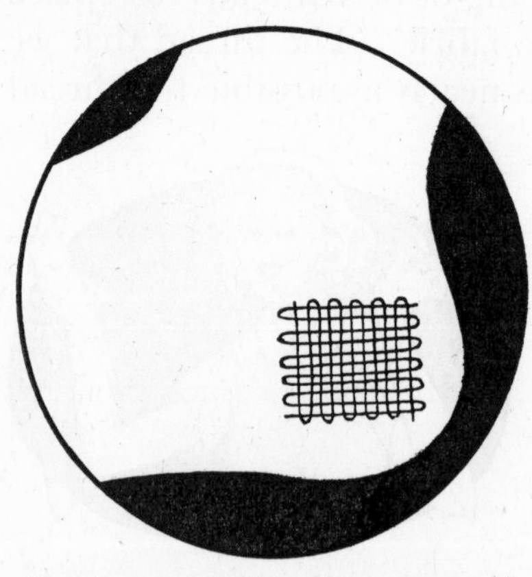

Darning must be done smoothly with an over-and-under stitch.

A good darn is smooth and free from knots, and the stitches in the weave are placed close together.

Tears in a dress or a coat may be one of three kinds:

straight, diagonal, or three-cornered. The straight tear is darned by fitting the edges of the tear together and taking small running stitches one-half inch from the tear, across the tear, and one-half inch on the opposite side. Make these rows of running stitches at right angles to the tear and one inch from either end of the tear. As the tear is reached from either side, the stitches alternate, one over and the next one under the edge.

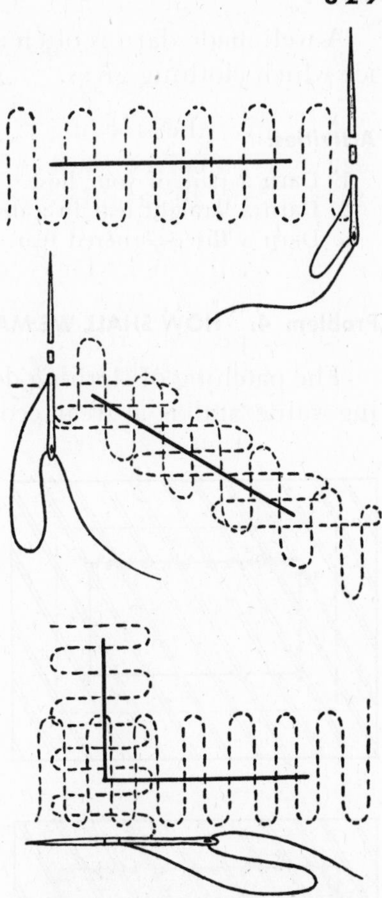

A tear can be neatly darned whether it is straight (top), diagonal (center), or three-cornered (bottom).

A three-cornered tear is darned as a straight tear, with the stitches placed at right angles to the tear. Begin at one end and complete one side of the tear. Then begin at other end and darn that side. This makes a very strong corner, as the stitches will overlap.

A diagonal tear is one in which both the up-and-down and crosswise threads are torn on the bias. This makes it necessary to place running stitches parallel to both sets of threads. The first stitches are made as for the straight or three-cornered tear, except that they are not at right angles to the tear. The second set is worked at right angles to the first.

A well-made darn is often a means of extending the service which clothing gives.

Activities:

1. Darn a pair of your hose.
2. Darn a straight tear in a dress.
3. Darn a three-cornered tear.

Problem 4: HOW SHALL WE MAKE A PATCH?

The patching of clothing does much to lengthen its wearing value and is a great economy for most families. To patch means to mend by setting a piece of material over the hole or worn place. A hemmed patch is the one most commonly used and is a very good one where strength is required. A satisfactory method for making a hemmed patch is as follows:

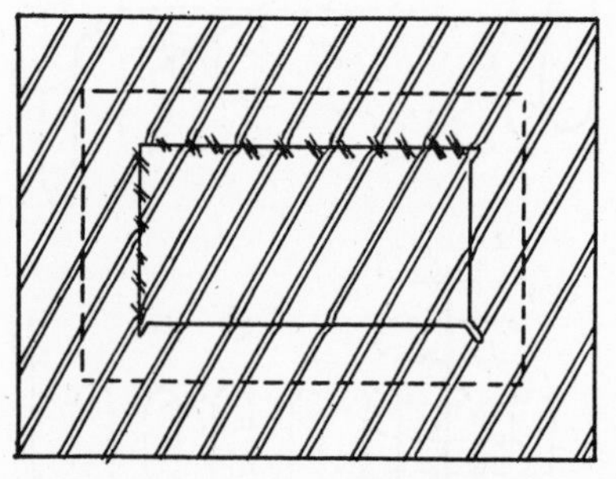

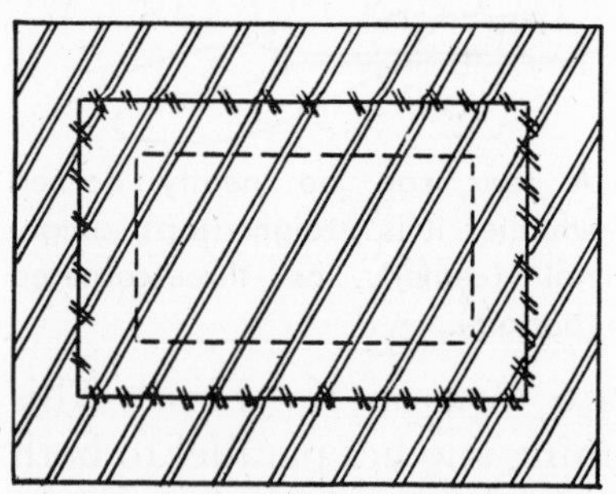

In a well-made patch, the design and texture of the added piece should match the original. Both sides should be neatly finished.

1. Trim the worn parts, leaving the hole in the shape of a square or rectangle.

2. Cut carefully diagonals ¼ inch deep at each corner and turn back the raw edges ¼ inch, leaving straight sides and square corners.

3. Select a patch piece the same weight and color as the garment.

4. Match lengthwise and

crosswise threads, plaids, or figures to the nap of the material.

5. Baste the patch piece carefully in place under the hole, its right side to the wrong side of the garment, and hem or stitch on the right side, taking care that the stitches do not show.

6. Trim and turn under the outer edge of the patch, and baste on the wrong side of the material, avoiding fullness on the right side.

7. Stitch or hem the outer edge by hand, using stitches that do not show.

8. Press the patch, making a final pressing on the right side.

Activities:

1. Make a hemmed patch.
2. List the places where you think a hemmed patch would be good to use.

Problem 5: WHAT OTHER REGULAR CARE SHALL WE GIVE OUR CLOTHING?

In addition to the daily care already discussed, clothing requires other attention to keep it in good condition. Many people forget or fail to include the airing of garments in the plans for their care. If you have ever been to a moving-picture show or a crowded arena where smoking was allowed, you know all too well the offensive and persistent odor that your winter coat acquired. Hung in the closet in this condition, this odor would not only persist but it would spread to the other garments in the closet. The desired freshness can be restored to the coat only by a thorough airing in fresh air. It takes much longer to air away unpleasant odors than it takes the coat to absorb them.

To air coats and dresses, place the garments on hangers

and hang them on a clothesline where they will be free from dust but where there is a circulation of air.

Often dresses require pressing as well as airing to bring them into good condition. Damp, foggy days very often make pressing necessary. Some fabrics, of course, require more frequent pressing than others, regardless of the weather. The procedure to be followed in pressing dresses depends somewhat upon the cut of the garment and upon the fabric. In previous problems, good procedures for pressing simple dresses have been given.

If dresses have detachable collars or scarfs, inspect them frequently and keep them fresh. Soiled collar and cuffs should be removed, washed, and pressed, and any repairs should be made as needed. They should then be replaced, before the next wearing.

From time to time the wardrobe should be checked to see what articles, if any, require cleaning that cannot be given with soap and water. Such garments should be sent to the dry-cleaner's, where experienced workmen, familiar with the various cleaning agents, skillfully handle a task which is dangerous as a home practice.

A half a century ago the schoolgirl examined her shoes, as you should do yours, to make sure that the heels were straight, the soles in good repair, and the toes were not in need of taps. If she found repair necessary, she would take the shoes to her father, who would undertake their repair on the cobbler's last. But with the present-day shoe, a more finished task is insisted upon than was thought necessary years ago. So shoe repairing, too, must be taken from the home. Wise is the girl who sees that her shoes receive attention as it is needed. She receives good dividends in comfort, appearance, and lengthened service from the shoes. The threading in of new shoelaces to replace those that have broken can be done at home. It is desirable to keep an extra pair of laces on hand so as to prevent delay and pro-

Carefully cleaned wool dresses and coats may be safely stored in a tightly closed trunk if they are well sprinkled with a reliable moth preventive.

longed annoyance. Shoe buttons can be temporarily replaced by hand sewing with a thread, but it is difficult to do and the thread wears but a short time. It is desirable to have buttons sewed on with a machine at the shoe-repair shop.

Hats of felt, velvet, or velour need special attention, such as brushing and steaming. Brush the hat well to remove all dust, remove the lining, and then hold or place the hat over a pan of boiling water. Let the steam pass all around the hat, both inside the crown and out, as well as over the brim. Sometimes it may be necessary to remove certain trimmings before the steaming is done. When the job is finished they can be readily replaced. When a hat has been steamed, it should be put in shape, put on a hat stand, and left in the open air until thoroughly dry. Any trimming or lining should not be replaced until the hat is dry. Linings should be kept in good condition. Sometimes it is necessary to launder the lining. In putting hats away, if the crown is stuffed with tissue paper the hat will keep in good shape.

Activities:

1. Press one of your school dresses.
2. Remove a hat lining, wash, press, and replace it in the hat.
3. Check your shoes and note if any of them need repair.

Problem 6: HOW SHALL WE PUT CLOTHES AWAY FOR THE SEASON?

When the warm days of spring come, we no longer need heavy winter coats, wool gloves, and galoshes. When summer yields to fall and then to winter, we no longer wear the tennis shorts, straw hats, and organdy dresses. In most homes such garments are not discarded when no longer in immediate use, but are stored until their season again returns. Whether a wardrobe is extensive or limited, it will have clothes suitable for each season. Thus we all have the problem of knowing how to put away clothes safely from one season until its return.

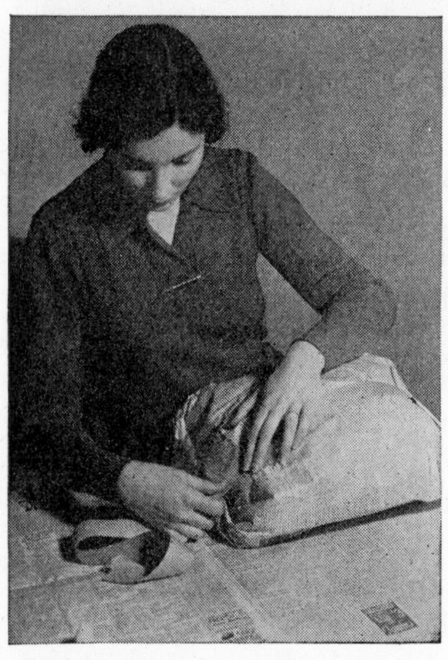

Hats and other clothes will look well and wear longer if they are carefully wrapped for storage during the season when they are not in use.

At the end of the season we put away clothes worn during the past months. These include dresses, hats, coats, shoes, gloves, and other articles of clothing.

The dresses worn in the late spring, summer, and early fall are commonly made from cotton, linen, rayon, and summer silk. Most of these garments are usually cleaned by washing. When their season ends, they are washed, mended, and stored in drawers or boxes provided for this purpose. Anything put in storage should be kept in darkness, as sunlight tends to weaken the fabric. One should also be sure that garments are stored free from starch, which has a tendency to weaken the fibers. Some silks and rayons may need to be dry-cleaned before being stored.

A cedar box that can be tightly closed is desirable for the summer storage of winter clothes.

The successful storage of wool dresses is made difficult by the fact that the larva or worm of the clothes moth feeds on the wool fiber. It eats many times its weight daily, and causes great loss. The larva flourishes in warm, dark places, and is particularly likely to invade clothing soiled with food spots. Clothes moths dislike sunlight, freezing, and moth repellents. These dislikes are important in helping us plan wisely for the storage of winter dresses.

Wool dresses should be brushed, sunned, dry-cleaned if necessary, and stored in a cool, dark, and protected place. If the garment does not need an entire cleaning, it may have to have a spot or spots removed before storing. Paradichlorobenzene, or moth balls, placed in the storage place, will prevent the growth or development of clothes moths.

Closets lined with cedar, chests made of cedar, and moth-

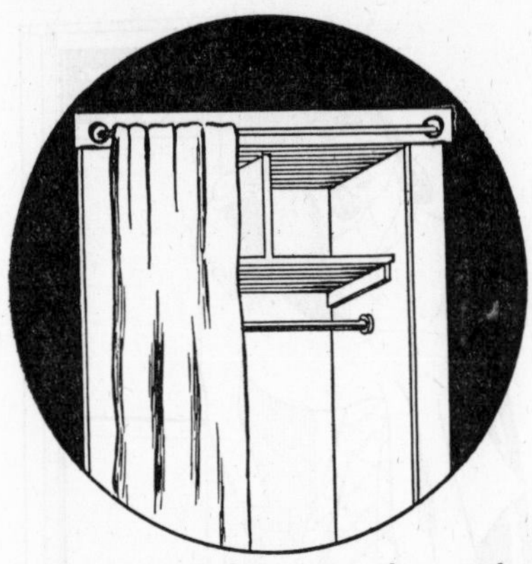

A temporary closet may be made from a refrigerator crate faced with heavy cardboard. Plain, heavy cotton material may be used for the curtain.

proof bags are often provided for the storage of wool garments. Such provision is satisfactory when the clothes being stored are free from moths or moth eggs at the time of storage. Cedar does not kill moths, but moths will not go to a garment surrounded by cedar. The same is true for the so-called mothproof bags. Whenever these are used, they must be kept tightly sealed. Ample moth repellent should be used at all times.

Wool coats present the same storage problem as wool dresses. Those that are trimmed with fur seem particularly likely to attract the moth. So special care should be given plans for their storage.

Hats should be brushed, dry-cleaned if necessary, and their crowns stuffed with tissue paper. Hats should be stored in a box that closes tightly. Felt hats and hats of any other woolen material should be stored with the use of paradichlorobenzene.

The storage for shoes and galoshes is the same, regardless of the season. Shoes and galoshes are thoroughly cleaned, stuffed with paper, wrapped, and stored

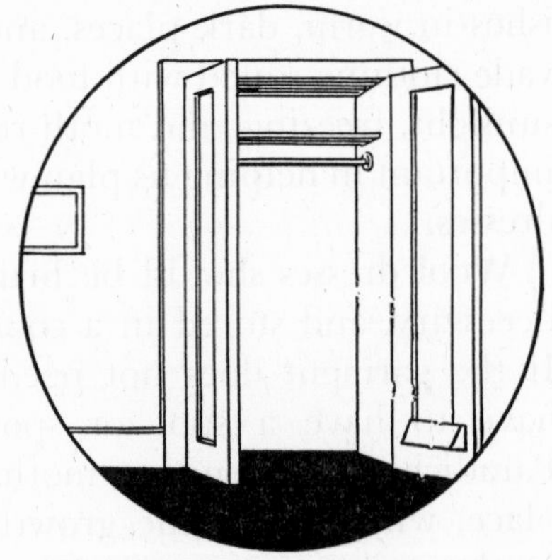

A closet with a double door is convenient and is easily kept in order.

in a cool, dry place. Leather molds and spoils if left in damp air.

Gloves should be mended, washed or dry-cleaned, and stored flat in a drawer or box.

Some homes are fortunate in having a large storage closet for storing clothing. In such case, bags or perforated cans of moth repellent may be hung in the closet. If such space is not available, it may be best to put the clothing in boxes or drawers to keep it dark and free from dust. A moth preventive should be used in the storage of wool and silk. Careful storage of clothing is necessary to obtain full benefit from the investment made and to give satisfaction to the owners.

Activities:

1. What clothes do you have to be put away at the present time?
2. How will you put these clothes away?
3. What special place do you have for clothes storage in your home? Is it adequate? Why?

Problem 7: HOW CAN WE OBTAIN MORE SERVICE FROM OUR USED GARMENTS?

In almost every person's wardrobe there are garments which are not giving full service to their owner. Sometimes the garment has been outgrown. Sometimes its style needs some slight change. Whatever the situation may be, the owner should analyze the garment to see what can be done.

Dresses owned by the growing girl frequently need the hem lines changed to prolong their wearability. Sleeves may have to be lengthened. This may be done by adding cuffs or bands. The addition of new collars or scarfs, and cuffs may help lengthen the service. Such slight remodeling may change the dress in appearance, adding to its attractiveness and giving the wearer more personal satisfaction in return.

Frequently an old garment is combined with some new material to make a more satisfactory garment.

A wider belt than that previously used may hide the too-short waistline, as well as the mended place at the side seam. Different belts may be used to give variation and show individuality.

The dress which we have outgrown may be made smaller for the younger sister or for some needy child. A jacket added to last year's dress often adds newness and covers the worn place at the armscye or the underarm seam.

The hat carefully stored from a past season may be renovated or changed by the addition of new trimmings. These may sometimes be replaced at home, but often it is wise to have a trained milliner do such work.

Upon careful examination, shoes about to be discarded may be found to be worth new heels and new soles.

More service may be obtained from our used garments by proper care. Provision for such care is an excellent way of extending our clothing allowance.

Activities:

1. What garments do you have that are not giving service now that could be fixed to give more service?
2. How can you help fix these garments?
3. What will the cost be to do such repair?
4. Bring some worn garments to school. Plan in detail what should be done to them to make them more satisfactory for wearing. Estimate the cost in time and money of carrying out these plans.

REFERENCES FOR THE UNIT

Friend, Mata Roman, and Shultz, Hazel, *Junior Home Economics: Clothing*. New York: D. Appleton-Century Co., 1933.

Jensen, Milton B., Jensen, Mildred R., and Ziller, M. Louisa, *Fundamentals of Home Economics*. New York: The Macmillan Co., 1935.

Matthews, Mary Lockwood, *The New Elementary Home Economics*. Boston: Little, Brown and Co., 1937.

SUGGESTED HOME EXPERIENCES

1. Go through the clothes in your closet, and care for them in a suitable way.
2. Wash and keep in repair the underwear and hose you wear during one week.
3. Do the darning for your mother for one week.
4. Help your mother to store clothing for a season.

UNIT 11

IF WE HAVE GUESTS

EXTENDING HOSPITALITY TO PERSONS not of the family group is an old, old custom, so old that we do not know when the practice first began. In your own life you perhaps cannot remember a time when you did not have the privilege of inviting guests to your home. "Mother, can Jane come over this afternoon?" or "Mother, I want Sue to stay for dinner" were some of the ways you expressed your concern with guests. In those early days, you planned no special entertainment, for you spent the time playing "house" or "school." You assumed no responsibility for the afternoon's treat or the dinner, for you knew your mother would attend to that. Always there would be some surprise for you and your guest.

Now that you are older, you know that extending hospitality is a way of honoring others. In inviting a person to be your guest in your home or elsewhere, you have offered him an opportunity to share in the best you have. In order that you may give him the best, you must plan for his coming. No longer can you expect others to do this for you. It has now become your own personal responsibility. To carry out this responsibility will require knowledge of the accepted rules of hospitality which have governed social life through many years.

Problem 1: WHY DO WE HAVE GUESTS?

"Why do we have guests?" a small boy asked his father as much preparation was being made for some guests in his home. The father paused a moment and then made this reply: "This is our home, the place where we enjoy each other and are very happy. We have many friends and we want them to come and be happy with us. Because of this, we invite our friends from time to time to be our guests." If the boy had been older, the father might have given other reasons, for there are many of them.

By having guests we learn to share with others. No matter how little or how much we may have to share, it is good for us to do it. The sharing of our hospitality is one of the finest things that we can do for our friends. The guest who comes into our home immediately receives a part of our family spirit, our friendship, our food, and our house. He will always have a different relation to us than if we had only bowed and passed each other on the street. This sharing goes far in making us finer persons as well as better family members.

All families need social relations with others outside the family group. If this is not done, the family members are likely to become narrow and selfish. As we live in our homes, we often tend to become so interested in what we are doing—our record at school, our dog, and our garden—that we may give little thought to the record of other people, the size and smartness of their dogs, and the beauty of their gardens. Guests in the home broaden our interests and aid us in making the social contacts which we need. Even the caller who stays for only a few minutes may bring in something of value from the outside world and, of course, the visitor who stays for a longer time may bring more.

There was a time when visitors to the home were the chief means of news from the outside world. The pioneer homemaker in a faraway place or the farm homemaker living in isolation welcomed even the peddler with his news of the outside world. Today, with newspapers, telephones, and radios, we desire visitors not so much for the news of world events, as for the sharing of their interest and response to the news with us. The visitor may help us to a better understanding of events outside our home.

All education is not gained in books. Often information and advice which we receive from other persons is most valuable, and many times guests are an important means of educating us. They may make us see, as with our own eyes, the life and customs of other peoples in other lands; they may make the inside story of a new variety of wheat seem so amazing that wheat, and wheat products, can never again be a dull subject; they may share with us small bits of fun that cause us to smile long after they are gone; they may recite poems or sing songs which awaken our interest in poetry and music.

Guests may aid us in the development of many desirable personal qualities. Often the closeness of the family circle makes us so used to each other that we forget about showing each other common, everyday courtesies. Guests cause us to act our best and to be courteous through practice in thoughtful ways.

Having guests may help strengthen family ties. The presence of a guest may encourage some member to forget herself and talk freely. The other family members may see her in a new light. A guest may praise the special ability of some member. This may encourage her and also cause other members of the family to take pride in what she can do.

Activities:

1. Recall four or five guests you have had in your home recently. What did each do for you and your family?
2. Think of yourself as a guest in someone's home. What do you contribute to those whose guest you are?

Problem 2: WHAT SHALL BE OUR ATTITUDE TOWARD GUESTS?

The guest who comes to our home at our invitation has a right to expect that we will find pleasure in her company, enjoy her, and accept her as a friend. An assurance of welcome can be easily given. A few honest and cordial words and a thoroughly friendly manner do more to establish this feeling than much lavish and expensive entertaining.

When any one member of the family has a guest, all other members should be courteous and polite to her. They may even assist in the entertaining. A visit has often been spoiled because some family member was not helpful and friendly to the guest. This rudeness reflects upon the family as a whole, as well as upon the offending person.

The family as a group may have guests. When this is the case, all members should share in the responsibility and do their best to make it a happy time. Some families plan as a group for these guests, and each member has in mind what her responsibilities are. A person always remembers her experience as a guest of such a family in a most favorable way. Having guests in the home should be considered as a regular part of family life. The family should know in what form the hospitality will be extended and how much expenditure can be afforded. Whatever is decided upon, it should be such that the life of the family is not upset or disturbed.

The guests of children should be regarded as important and should be given special consideration. A chaperon or older person should be in charge or at home while the guests are there. Children and their guests should not be left alone to their own devices, and if supervision cannot be arranged at the particular time, another date should be set for the guests.

The family should recognize that guests are desirable for the best development of the family and should be interested in having them. We should keep in mind the many reasons for having guests when we form our attitudes toward them. Though we may think first of the many things we can do for our guests, we should not forget that this doing for others makes us better persons.

Guests should be considered a pleasure, and even a privilege, rather than a duty. Such feelings as "I just must invite Mary Jane to my home" or "I have to give a party to pay back everybody" do not express the right attitudes toward guests. If guests are a burden to us and give us no pleasure, there is either something wrong with us or with the situation.

Important in our attitude toward guests is our desire for company. Some families keep "open house," with guests constantly coming and going. There is always gay laughter, pleasant conversation, and something going on. It may be difficult to have time for the give-and-take of intimate family living under such conditions. It may be difficult to stretch the family's money to provide for so much hospitality without neglecting other needs of the family. In contrast to this, some homes refuse to spend any time, money, and effort in entertaining guests at all. These homes are likely to lack an interest and sparkle which they need. Perhaps a middle course in plans for our hospitality is best, just as it is in nearly all other matters.

Activities:

1. What are your responsibilities to the guests of other family members? What are the other members' responsibilities to your guests?
2. When would you say a family had too few guests? Too many guests?

Problem 3: IN WHAT WAYS CAN WE ENTERTAIN GUESTS?

There are many ways in which we can entertain guests. Some are intimate and others are not; some are expensive

Both boys and girls enjoy a tea party with festive decorations and good things to eat. Then, too, they find the experience is good for them. Through it they develop poise and ease in their social conduct.

and others are not; some require much time and thought and others but little. Making the right choice is an important responsibility in entertaining.

Among the first things to consider are our income and our standard of living. Our entertaining should always be in keeping with these. Next in importance are the size of our house and the amount of help and free time we have. These things limit the type and extent of our entertaining. The interests of our guests must be given thought. We should plan for our guests the type of events which they like. It would be a mistake to ask a girl to a "slumber" or overnight party if we knew she would not enjoy it, or to ask her to go to the movies if they bore her. Bringing together people who like to do the same things is a good basis for successful hospitality.

The type of entertainment common in our community influences our choice. In certain mountain towns the usual entertainment is a "coffee pot." This is a hike up the mountain, ending in a bonfire on which the coffee pot bubbles and boils. Good fellowship prevails; the fun is entirely informal. In the large city, musical matinees and parties at the dancing school may be popular ways of entertaining. At both of these, one's manners and dress are more formal

Picnics are always fun, whether for two or for twenty. Fresh air and gay spirits add zest to the picnic luncheon.

than at the "coffee pot." Any way of entertaining will be successful in its right place, but it will be a failure if attempted elsewhere.

Guests may be entertained by an informal, chatty "at home," where one or more persons stop to visit for a few minutes or longer. Food may or may not be served. Often women and girls take their work along and mend, knit, or sew. Guests also may be entertained at tea. This may be informal or semiformal, as desired. The guests visit awhile or listen to a planned program. Then they are served with tea and accompanying foods, and take leave.

Guests may be entertained at the theater or movies. If there are several guests this is called a theater or line party. After the show is over, refreshments may be served either at home or at a snack shop, if you wish, although this is not necessary. Picnics and hikes are other informal ways of entertaining. They are very popular with people who enjoy being out-of-doors. The food always contributes largely to the success of picnics and hikes. It may be simple and cost little, but if it is well prepared the "sauce" of fresh air and exercise makes the meal fit for a king. Both small and large groups can be entertained at picnics. Fortunately, almost everyone enjoys this type of hospitality.

Parties are a favorite way of entertaining. Usually they are held at home, but school and church parties are common. Old and young alike enjoy them. At a party some of the time may be spent in games and some in chatter. Light refreshments are served. Parties are usually given in the afternoon or evening.

Guests may be entertained at meals. This is a favorite way of extending hospitality. It gives an opportunity for more intimate contact than is possible through some of the other ways. Guests may be invited for breakfast, luncheon, or dinner. The meal may be a family one which requires only setting on another plate. It may be a company meal, for which special dishes are planned and served. An invitation to "break bread" with a family is a real honor and has long been so considered.

Guests are sometimes invited for a week end or for an extended visit in our homes. Relatives and close friends are those most commonly entertained in this way. Such visits should be made only on invitation, and require special planning to make them highly successful.

Activities:

1. Make a list of ways which would be suitable for entertaining your guests.
2. State for whom you would use each different method of entertainment.

3. What are some inexpensive ways of entertaining guests?
4. To which would you feel more honored to be invited: a family meal or an elaborate company meal? Why?

Problem 4: WHAT ARE OUR RESPONSIBILITIES AS HOSTESSES?

The hostess is the girl or woman who extends the invitation and plans for the entertainment of guests. The host is the boy or man who does the same. There are certain responsibilities which are accepted by hostesses and hosts. How well we carry them determines much of the success and pleasure of our entertaining. Because these duties of hostess and host are much the same, we are considering here only the duties of the hostess.

The hostess must first decide upon the guests she will invite, upon the way that she will entertain them, and upon the date. She may need to discuss the matter with other members of her family and reach a decision satisfactory to all. She must know that her mother will be at home, that no other members of the family have made plans for use of the home, and that there is no other reason why the date would not be convenient. Failure to check on this has led to many an embarrassing situation. One girl found that paper hangers were in control of the kitchen on the day when she had guests coming for luncheon. Another discovered that all the upholstered furniture had been sent to be cleaned on the date of her tea party.

The hostess's responsibilities vary with the type of function that is being given. An informal afternoon "at home" for neighborhood friends brings only a few responsibilities, while a dinner party brings many. The hostess should plan all the details of decorations, entertainment, and food to be served well in advance of the event. She should have everything well in hand before the guests arrive. The hostess who is still preparing for the party when the guests come can give little attention to them. She falls far short of carrying her responsibilities properly.

The hostess should dress in keeping with the event. She should be well groomed and look her best. However, she should dress so that no guest will feel embarrassed. It is poor taste to try to outdress one's guests and thereby make them feel ill at ease. The hostess should allow ample time for dressing so that she may be ready before her guests arrive without too much hurry. She should be well poised and at ease. The fluttering hostess rushing here and there takes from the pleasure of her guests.

The hostess should greet her guests in a cordial manner and make them feel welcome. This assures the guest that she is wanted and brings about a friendly atmosphere in the group. The hostess should make sure that her guests know each other, and those who do not should be introduced. The following are examples of gracious and informal ways of doing this: "Mary, I should like you to know Alice." "Ruth, may I present my cousin George?" If an older person is being introduced, the form would be something like this: "Mother, this is Beulah, my partner in the Home Economics class" or "Miss Black, I wish to present my father. Miss Black, you know, is my history teacher." If introductions have been overlooked, guests should introduce themselves. This is much better than standing around aloof and alone. One way to introduce oneself is to extend the right hand and say, "I am Louise Hill." The reply should be a grasping of the hand, with the statement, "I am Frances Martin."

The hostess should visit with her guests, seeing that all have a happy time. If the function is a large one, she should ask a friend or two to help her, so that attention can be given to all the guests. These friends are really assistant hostesses and share in making the event a pleasant one for the guests.

Any necessary changes in plans should be made quietly and smoothly so that the guests are unaware of them. The well-poised hostess is able to do this. Unusual occurrences or accidents, such as the spilling of a cup of tea or the dropping of a spoon, should be paid no attention. The guest who has been thus embarrassed should be set at ease. Any lack of courtesy or any bad manners on the part of the hostess reflects adversely upon her, whether it comes from ignorance or from rudeness.

The hostess should be in a convenient place for the guests to take their leave of her. She should be ready to tell them good-bye and to receive graciously any words of appreciation.

Activities:

1. Practice greeting and taking leave of a hostess; practice greeting guests and saying good-bye to them.
2. Practice visiting with guests.
3. Decide how a hostess should dress for functions such as an informal tea; a party; a school dinner; a theater or line party.

Problem 5: HOW SHALL WE INVITE GUESTS?

If we could go far back into the history of man, we would find that invitations were first given by pounding on a stretched skin or by making loud calls to indicate that a kill had been made and that there was food for all. Later, when spoken words came into use, runners or messengers carried by word of mouth to people far away the invitation to the feast. After the development of writing, written invitations became possible.

Today invitations are still by word of mouth, or oral, and by note, or written, as they were long ago. However, we make much use of the telephone and the post or mail in inviting guests. Though the oral invitation is thought by many the easiest to give, there are may difficulties that result from this method. The guest may not understand the date, the time, or the place. The hostess may not have a record of the invited guests and may not know just who is coming. The invitation given orally to someone to pass on to another is even less satisfactory. The invitation may not reach the intended guest. The hostess may not be sure whether or not the invitation was received until the guest arrives or fails to do so. The written invitation prevents these difficulties.

The type of invitation depends upon the kind of hospitality extended. An informal function requires an informal invitation. It may be given orally or written, as desired. Sometimes the hostess speaks directly with the persons and knows immediately whether or not they will accept the invitation. Sometimes she finds it more convenient to write the invitation. Functions for which informal invitations are extended include parties, teas, family meals, company meals, picnics, house parties, and theater parties.

A semiformal function requires a semiformal invitation, which is written or, occasionally, printed. Semiformal functions include school dinners and banquets, parties, dances, and teas.

Most of us, however, entertain informally more than we do semiformally and are more interested in the invitation for informal events. Informal invitations given orally should be correctly worded and in an interesting way. They should be cordial and should indicate a sincere desire for acceptance. Whether given in person or over the telephone, the form and expressions used are much the same. Examples of such invitations follow:

"I am having a fireside tea Sunday from 5 to 7. Will you come?"

"Elise and I are having a kitchen shower for Miss Roper Tuesday evening at eight and we hope you will join us.

The colors for her kitchen are green and white. Do write one of your clever little verses to add to the fun."

"I am planning a surprise birthday party for Mother Thursday evening at 7:30. Will you come? If you meet at our east door about 7:25, I believe we can make it a real surprise."

Written informal invitations are sent by mail or special messenger. They are written neatly and carefully on regular correspondence stationery. The words should be spelled correctly, and commas and periods should be where they belong. Often one's personality can be shown in an invitation and so add interest to the event.

Four examples of written informal invitations are given below. Notice that the second example is in the form of a rhyme; this device often adds interest to the event:

Dear Faye,

Several of the girls are coming over Wednesday afternoon at 2:30 for a talk-fest and knitting. Will you join us?

Sincerely yours,
Beth Foster

Next Friday night is Halloween,
The time when witches and ghosts are seen.
Come to my house at a quarter to eight;
Remember the time and don't be late.
We are going to have a heap of fun
And put all sour faces on the run.
Grace Elizabeth Martin

Dear Alice,

Marion Hiller is spending the week end with me. You will remember that she visited me in camp last summer. Will you have dinner with us Saturday evening at 6:30? Later we plan to go to the movies.

Sincerely yours,
Opal Gardner

Dear Mabel,

Mother and I hope that you will spend your spring vacation with us. It has been a long time since you were here. If you do not come soon, we will have to become acquainted all over again.

You will need some hiking clothes for a trip to the Dells, and a formal for the DeMolay dance at the Country Club.

We can meet you at Bates Junction, so you will not have that long tiresome wait there. Do let us know when we may expect you.

Sincerely yours,
Mary Jo Cline

Semiformal invitations are written or printed, usually written. They are written in the third person (that is, names are used in the wording instead of "I" or "we") and sent by messenger or by mail. Plain white or cream stationery or cards are used, with black ink. They are issued one or two weeks before the date of the event. If the function is one for which the exact number accepting must be known, a request for reply such as "Please reply" or "R. S. V. P." is often included. The letters are abbreviations of the French words meaning "please reply." Three examples follow:

The Home Economics Class of
Woodson High School
Friday, March the first
Tea and Exhibit
Three to five o'clock
Home Economics Room

Miss June Delaney
Bunco
Friday, January 6
8 P.M. 603 Burke Street

The Girl Reserves of Lincoln Junior High School
desire your presence at their
Mother-Daughter dinner
Tuesday, March 10, 6:30 P.M.
Gymnasium Please reply

Replying to invitations has been discussed on page 80.

Activities:

1. Give an invitation to a theater party orally, in person.
2. Give an invitation to a picnic over the telephone.
3. Write an informal invitation to a Sunday evening supper.
4. Write an invitation in rhyme to a party.
5. Write a semiformal invitation to an evening party.

Problem 6: HOW SHALL WE ENTERTAIN A WEEK-END GUEST?

An invitation to be a week-end guest always brings a thrill. For the guest, it means a few days away from home and all sorts of interesting experiences. Often new and delightful friendships are formed. For the hostess, it means a chance to share her home with her friend and enjoy a visit with her. Entertaining the week-end guest is somewhat different from entertaining one for a short time, such as at a party, a movie, or a dinner. The week-end guest is with the hostess and her family twenty-four hours a day for several days. She becomes more or less a part of the family and enters into many of its activities.

The regular way of doing things in the household should be explained to the guest soon after her arrival, if she is expected to follow it. The hours of the meals, the bath hours of family members, any special family customs to be observed, and the general plans for her visit should be discussed with her. Such measures will help her to fit into the family easily and happily.

Opportunity should be given for the guest to meet those friends and relatives of the family in whom she is particularly interested and those who would like to meet her. Most guests enjoy seeing the town and the surrounding country. If possible, a drive should be arranged. A trip to town and a visit to the favorite snack shop might well be included in the fun.

Some special entertainment is often planned. Whatever is decided upon, the event should be one that the guest would especially enjoy. It should be in keeping with the usual habits of living and spending in the hostess's family. It should be carefully planned and carried out in the nicest way possible. A tea, a party, a dance, a dinner, or a picnic would be suitable.

Often friends of the hostess or guest assist in entertaining the guest. This is a pleasant expression of friendship which the hostess should remember to return. Such plans of friends may affect those that the hostess makes for her guest.

Frequently week-end guests are invited when some special event is scheduled, such as the Junior-Senior dance, the high school play, or the winter sports carnival. Such attractions add to the pleasure of the guest and make the entertaining easier.

The guest should have some free time for herself. She will need some time for rest and she may need some time for care of her clothes. This free time should be so planned that she will not be embarrassed by the arrangement.

Throughout the time of her visit the guest should be made to feel welcome. Every member of the family should help in entertaining the guest in the home. They should be on their good behavior. Quarreling, fussing, or failing to do one's part may lead to hurt and misunderstanding. Members within the family may understand and forgive such actions, but others may not. The pleasure of the visit may be spoiled, and a promising friendship ended for the hostess, unless the family shares pleasantly in the entertainment.

Activities:

1. What are some customs in your home that would affect the plans for entertaining a week-end guest?
2. Plan in detail the entertaining of a week-end guest in your home.
3. Make a list of the ways in which you could help a friend entertain a week-end guest.

Problem 7: HOW SHALL WE PLAN A PARTY?

A party is a social event that everyone likes. It may be given at almost any hour of the day, and includes some form of entertainment, often games, for the pleasure of the guests, followed by refreshments.

When one hostess gives the party, all the planning is done by her. When several hostesses give the party, the planning is done together and the results include the ideas of all. Whether one person or several are giving the party, the steps in planning are much the same.

The *type of party* to be given must first be decided. The choice may be made in favor of the easiest party to give, the most unusual one, or the one that is in keeping with the spirit of the particular season.

The *time and place* are next to be considered. Scheduled events, as well as the convenience of the hostesses, affect the choice of the date. The decision as to the place will depend upon the type of party and the number of guests invited.

The *amount of money* to be had for the party is important in the planning. It often determines the type of party as well as the number invited. However, there is little relation between the money spent and the good times to be had at a party. It is surprising how far a little money will go when the right kind of planning is done. Cleverness and originality are much more important. The money, even though spent for a party, should be in keeping with what one can afford and with the standards of the community. Extravagant parties are never in good taste.

Making the guest list is next in order. This is always a problem, but an especially difficult one when there are several hostesses. Some basis for selecting those to be invited is necessary. No matter how large or how small the party, some limits must be made. The invitations must be planned and given. If there are several hostesses, this responsibility

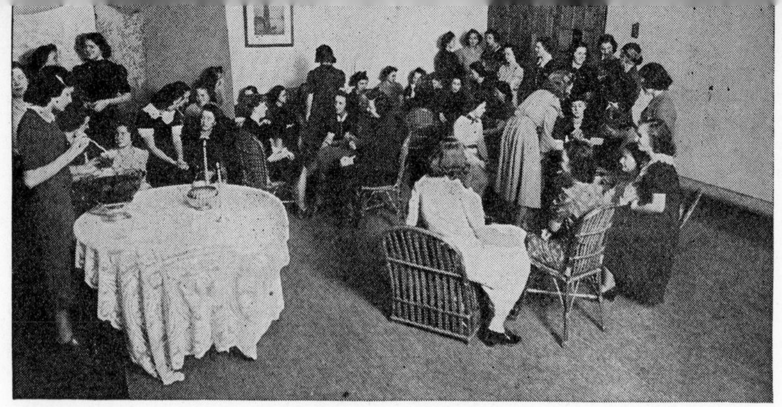

Careful planning makes the school party a success. A gathering such as this gives excellent training in meeting people with ease and enjoyment.

must be definitely assigned. The type and form that will be used and how and when the invitations will be given must all be decided.

The *choice of the food* to be served must be made. In this, the type of party and the time of year have much to do with the plans. For example, doughnuts and cider, cherry pie with whipped cream, watermelon, and mincemeat sundae all have their season. Sometimes a special idea or color scheme influences the choice of food, just as it does our plans for the decorations. For example, a Valentine party may have as refreshments cherry ice and white cake, and the table decorations may be a bowl of red carnations and red paper hearts on a white cloth.

Plans for the *entertainment* of the guests are most important. Plenty of time should be given for their perfection. The entertainment is really what makes the party. The fun is remembered long after the other things are forgotten. The games to be played should be chosen and the necessary equipment assembled for them. If contests are to be held, similar preparation should be made. If the choice is stunts, group singing, or dancing, plans must be made ahead of time so that the necessary things will be on hand. It is well to have more entertainment planned than may be used, in case it becomes necessary to make changes. The entertainment should never be left to chance or for guests to plan after they arrive.

When there are several hostesses, the responsibilities should be divided as fairly and equally as possible. The time at which all the duties are to be done should be thoroughly understood. A good procedure is to have one hostess be the chairman who is in charge and to whom the others report.

Activities:

1. (*Class activity*) Make general plans for a party to be given in a home.
2. (*Class activity*) Make general plans for a class or all-school party.
3. Make general plans for a party to be given by you in your home.

Problem 8: WHAT SHALL WE DO AT OUR PARTY?

It is most important to decide what we will do for fun at our party. Upon our choice depends much of the success of the party. The entertainment should be such that the guests will enjoy it. It should also be suited to the type of party being given. Suggestions for things to do at various kinds of parties follow:

Get-Acquainted Games

1. Pin on each guest a piece of paper with his name written on it. Give each guest a piece of paper and a pencil. Then see who can meet the most persons and write down their names in a given length of time.
2. Have each guest introduce two people to two others.
3. Cut out well-known advertisements from magazines. Remove or cover the names of the products and pin the pictures around on the walls. Working singly or in groups of two or three, have the guests try to name the products advertised.

Outdoor Games

Drop-the-handkerchief. All but one who is "It" form a circle. The "It" has the handkerchief and runs around the outside of the circle several times, dropping the handkerchief behind someone. She tries to do it when the person is not looking. The "It" tries to get around to the person's place without being touched by her. As soon as the person sees the handkerchief is behind her, she picks it up and tries to catch the "It." If unsuccessful, this new person then becomes the "It" and so it goes. Sometimes the game is made more difficult by putting those "Its" who are caught in the center of the circle. The only way they can get themselves out is to steal the dropped handkerchief and catch the "It."

Relays. Players are divided into a number of equal teams with a captain for each. Each team does the same things. Players are lined up equally and at a given signal all of the teams start. The team finishing first wins. The captain of each team starts first. Each player must wait until the one ahead of her finishes before she starts, going to the end of the line when she has completed her run.

1. Carry a potato on a teaspoon a given distance and back without dropping it.
2. Carry navy beans on a knife.
3. Run to a chair, untie the shoestrings of one shoe, take the shoe off, put it on, tie the strings, and run back to the starting place.
4. Run to a designated place, remove the pillowcase from a pillow, put it back on, and return to starting place.

Informal Indoor Games

Fruit basket upsets. The players sit in a circle around the room. One player is named as "It" and stands in the center. Another player whispers to each one the name of a fruit. The "It" calls for two or more fruits to exchange places. As they do this, she tries to obtain a chair. If she is successful, the player who lost her chair becomes "It." Whenever she desires, the "It" can call, "Fruit basket upsets!" and every player changes places. The "It" tries to obtain a chair, and the loser then becomes "It."

Malaga grapes. The players sit in a circle. The player who is "It" takes a parasol or cane and, looking at it all the time, lifts it back and forth in front of herself as she says, "Malaga grapes are very fine grapes but the grapes of the North are better." Then she hands the parasol or cane to the player at her right for her to do the same. This continues until the players have caught on to the trick. The trick consists of the player clearing her throat slightly before beginning the lines.

Hot or cold. The "It" goes out of the room. The players decide on some object in the room. The "It" comes in and discovers the object by the players calling "hot" as she nears it and "cold" as she goes away. When she guesses correctly, she chooses the next "It."

Card games and similar games. Dominoes, authors, old maid, checkers, chess, sticks, Chinese checkers, lotto, bingo, pollyanna, and parchesi can be played by a small group, each player trying to get the highest score, working independently.

Progressive games. In the above games, and in many other card games, the guests play seated at tables. To play progressively, usually four are at a table, opposite players being partners. At the end of a certain period of playing, often fifteen minutes, a signal is given. Then the winning partners at each table progress to the next higher table and change partners. This is done all evening, and at its close those having the highest scores receive prizes. Tally cards on which to record scores are necessary for the players. Many games are suitable to progressive playing. The games mentioned above follow the rules that accompany them. The game of Hearts is an enjoyable one. It is played as follows:

Wooden cubes of ½ to ⅝ inch have the letters H E A R T S printed on them, one on each side. Six cubes are necessary for each game. Each player shakes the "dice" a few times and throws them on the table. The count is:

HE	5 points
HEA	10 points
HEAR	15 points
HEART . . .	20 points
HEARTS . . .	25 points

4 H's cancel the score.

When it is time to progress, partners add the score and put the total on the tally card and change places.

Contests. Contests add to party fun, but should not be too difficult for the guests to answer easily and quickly. They must be prepared before the party, and pencils should be supplied. Hostesses often enjoy planning original ones themselves.

"Number, please" is one of these games. Fill in the blanks with a number that correctly completes the statement. The answers are numbers that are most often associated with the rest of the phrase.

1. The house of .... gables.
2. The spirit of ....
3. Friday the ....
4. He ran like ....
5. She is one of the .... in society.
6. Everything was at ....s and ....s.
7. The .... musketeers.
8. She is a perfect ....
9. The .... horsemen of the apocalypse.
10. A .... by .... person.
11. Over the top at the .... hour.
12. He arrived at the .... hour.
13. The .... nighter.
14. .... nights in a barroom.
15. The animals went in .... by ....
16. .... is company; .... is a crowd.
17. ...., ..., buckle my shoe.
18. ...., ..., shut the door.
19. Possession is .... points of the law.
20. The .... ages of man.

Answers:

1. 7	6. 6; 7	11. 0	16. 2; 3
2. 76	7. 3	12. 11th	17. 1; 2
3. 13th	8. 36	13. 1st	18. 3; 4
4. 60	9. 4	14. 10	19. 9
5. 400	10. 2; 4	15. 2; 2	20. 7

In "What shall *he* wear?", the answers are names of fabrics and should be written in across from each character.

The Fisherman (*net*)
The Salesman (*canvas*)
The Banker (*checks*)
The Scotchman (*plaid*)
The Sunshine Enthusiast (*rayon*)
The Editor (*prints*)
The Osteopath (*rubber*)
The Pipe Smoker (*velvet*)
The Unfortunate Flyer (*crash*)
The Tourist (*outing flannel*)
The Farmer (*gros grain*)
The Broker (*tape*)
The Blindman (*felt*)
The Chairmaker (*satin*)
The Swindler (*slicker*)
The Friar (*monk's cloth*)

Another way is to have tiny samples of the materials listed above to be pinned in the proper space instead of written. A contest can be made of well-known advertisements. Another contest called "Prominent People in Our Community" is a good one. The names of people well-known locally are used, such as *a craftsman* (Smith); *a metal man of great worth* (Goldman); *a cereal* (Rice).

Stunts and charades. Games in which the group is divided into actors and audience are popular. Stunts and charades are the commonest of these. In both of these the guests are divided into two groups and each group entertains the other with a stunt or charade. In the charade, the acting presents a word, phrase, or statement to be guessed by the audience. The stunt is usually amusing and entertaining and requires nothing but the attention of the audience.

Group singing. For group singing a leader is needed, and a pianist helps. Songs should be planned ahead of time and song sheets provided if needed. Old and new popular songs, folk songs, and even church songs are used.

Folk games and dancing. Folk dancing is enjoyable if there is sufficient room for the guests to take part. Folk games are played as the group sings. "The Miller Boy," "Boys and Girls Come Out to Play," and "Make a Cake for Charley" are examples of these.

"The Miller Boy" is played in this way: Players arrange themselves in couples and then form a circle, the boys on the outside and the girls on the inside. Each girl takes her partner's arm, and they all start marching around, singing:

"Happy is the miller boy
Who lives by the mill.
The wheel turns round
With a very good will.
One hand in the hopper,
And the other in the sack;
The ladies step forward,
And the men step back."

The players do as the last lines suggest and each has a new partner. This is repeated again and again until the players wish to end the game.

In certain localities these games are very popular. It is unfortunate that they are no longer known in many communities. Dancing can only be done if music can be had. Phonograph, radio, and kind friends or members of the family who can play instruments usually furnish music for dancing, except for semiformal occasions, such as a school or club party, when an orchestra may be hired.

Activities:

1. (*Class activity*) Plan the entertainment for a party to be given in a home.
2. (*Class activity*) Plan entertainment for a class or school party.
3. Plan the entertainment for your own party in your home.
4. Plan some original games for a party.

Problem 9: WHAT SHALL WE SERVE AT OUR PARTY?

Refreshments are an important part of a party, even though no great amount of food is served. The food served at a party is much lighter than at a meal. Two, three, or four foods may be included. These may vary from the simplest and plainest of food to that which is rich and more elaborate. Punch and wafers are familiar refreshments, as are ice cream, cake, and salted nuts. Often the hostess tries to serve something different and unusual. In party menus, perhaps more than in any other, we want to be original. If time and thought are given to the planning, interesting and different menus may result.

Refreshments should be planned in relation to the kind of party. For outdoor parties, such foods as hamburgers, "hot dog" sandwiches, potato chips, lemonade or coffee, and ice cream cones are often served. At an afternoon card party in winter, a salad, tea, hot rolls, and jelly are suitable. At an all-school party, hot spiced cider and doughnuts are always well received.

Certain foods have come to be served at certain seasons and times. Pumpkin pie, apples, doughnuts, and cider seem to belong to Halloween time; plum pudding and fruit cake to Christmas; cherry pie and cherry puddings to Washington's Birthday; green-colored foods to St. Patrick's Day;

An attractive plate of sandwiches served with lemonade makes nice party refreshments.

and eggs to Easter. These associations, as well as many others, influence us in planning our party menus.

Sometimes the hostess wishes to carry out a color scheme in her food. She uses either pink, red, orange, brown, green, or perhaps two or more colors together. The use of a color scheme may make attractive refreshments, but it requires detailed planning. For a color scheme one should rely upon the natural color of the food and not use artificially colored food which may give queer and unpleasant effects.

The hostess planning party refreshments should always consider the money to be had; the time required for food preparation and service; the utensils, dishes, and silverware needed; and the ease with which the food can be eaten from a plate held on the lap or in the left hand.

The following party menus have been well received:

Spiced fruit punch
Date cookies

Hot chocolate
Gingerbread

Lemonade
Assorted sandwiches

Orange sherbet
Vanilla wafers

Jellied fruit, whipped cream
Sponge cake
Iced tea

Chicken salad
Olives and pickles
Hot rolls
Tea

Ice cream and cake are always pleasing refreshments. Both can be varied to fit color schemes and the requirements of special seasons and days.

Activities:

1. (*Class activity*) Plan the refreshments for a party to be given in the home.
2. (*Class activity*) Plan the refreshments for a class or all-school party.
3. Plan the refreshments for your own party.

Problem 10: HOW SHALL WE PREPARE AND SERVE DEVIL'S FOOD CAKE?

Devil's food cake is a butter cake like the standard cake or plain butter cake which we have already made (see page 295). It differs from the standard cake in its ingredients and way of mixing. It is a well-liked cake and one that does not dry out quickly.

The utensils

Mixing bowls
Measuring cup
Measuring spoons
Sifter
Mixing spoon
Pan
Dover egg beater
Spatula
Knife
Cake pans
Cake rack

The recipe for devil's food cake

Ingredients:

Part 1

2½ sq. chocolate cut in pieces, *or*
½ c. cocoa
½ c. sugar
½ c. sweet milk
2 t. vanilla

This is the way we put icing on a cake. Each layer is spread with frosting. The layers are then carefully placed one upon the other. The sides are frosted after the top layer has been put on.

Part 2

1 c. sugar	2 c. flour, sifted before measuring
½ c. butter or substitute	1 t. soda
2 eggs, beaten separately	½ t. salt
1 c. sour milk	1 t. fat for oiling pans

Method:

Part 1

Put the chocolate, sugar, and sweet milk in a pan and cook 5 minutes, or until thick, over a low flame, stirring constantly. Remove from the fire. When the mixture is cool, add the vanilla flavoring.

Part 2

Cream the butter, add sugar, and continue creaming until it is well mixed. Add beaten yolks of eggs. Sift the soda and salt with the flour. Add in small amounts alternately the sour milk and the sifted flour to the creamed mixture.

Add Part 1 mixture to Part 2 mixture. Fold in stiffly beaten whites of egg.

Turn into oiled cake pans and bake in a moderate oven (375°F.) about 20 minutes.

Two girls—1/4 recipe.

If an icing is desired, the "seven-minute" icing is one that is easily made. The recipe for this icing is given below:

The finished cake has icing on the sides, the top, and between each layer.

The utensils

Double boiler
Dover egg beater
Measuring cup
Measuring spoons
Spatula

The recipe for seven-minute icing

Ingredients:

1 egg white
1/8 t. cream of tartar
1/3 c. boiling water
1 c. sugar
Few grains salt
1/2 t. vanilla

Method:

Combine sugar, salt, cream of tartar, and water. Put these ingredients in the top part of the double boiler.

Place it over the lower part of the double boiler containing boiling water and place it on the flame.

Add unbeaten white of egg. Begin beating with an egg beater and continue about 7 minutes. Remove from the fire and continue beating until the icing is thick enough to spread.

Spread with a spatula between the layers of cake and on the top and sides.

Two girls—entire recipe.

The serving

Devil's food cake is cut in individual pieces and served on a large cake platter or on individual plates. It is eaten with the fingers or with a fork.

Activities:

1. (*Class activity*) Prepare devil's food cake.
2. (*Class activity*) Serve the cake in the proper manner.
3. (*Class activity*) Judge the cakes.
4. Estimate the cost per serving of the cake.
5. Suggest foods that might be served with devil's food cake.

Problem 11: HOW SHALL WE PREPARE AND SERVE VANILLA ICE CREAM?

Vanilla ice cream is a favorite. It is made of cream, sugar, and vanilla, and is usually frozen in a crank freezer.

The utensils

Double boiler
Measuring cup
Measuring spoons
Mixing spoon
Ice cream freezer

What is a party without ice cream to young children?

The recipe for vanilla ice cream

Ingredients:

4 c. thin cream (coffee cream)
1 c. sugar
3 t. vanilla
Few grains salt

Method:

Heat ⅓ of the cream in a double boiler and add sugar. Stir and keep warm until the sugar is thoroughly dissolved. Remove from the hot water, add the remainder of the cream. When entirely cold, add vanilla, then freeze.

Two girls—¼ recipe.

Freezing:

Put all parts of the freezer together and test it. Scald the freezer and cool it thoroughly. Fill it ⅔ full with ice cream mixture, and place in position ready for freezing.

Crush the ice evenly into small enough pieces to fit in well around the freezer. Use rock salt. Mix the ice and salt in the proportion of 6 or 8 parts of ice to 1 part of salt. Pack the ice and salt mixture in around the can. Turn the crank slowly at first until the mixture begins to stiffen. Then turn rapidly until the mixture is firm.

If the ice cream is to stand some time before serving, the water from the melted ice should be drained off. The top of the can should be wiped carefully and the cover removed. The dasher is then taken out and the cream packed down. The ice cream is covered with waxed paper, and the opening in the cover of the freezer can is plugged with a cork stopper and replaced on the can. Ice and salt in the proportion of 4 parts of ice to 1 part of salt are packed firmly around the can and well over the top. The freezer should be covered with burlap or other heavy covering.

The serving

Ice cream is served in a saucedish or sherbet dish placed on a salad or dessert plate. It is eaten with a spoon. Ice cream is sometimes served on or with cake on an individual salad or dessert plate. When served in this manner, it is eaten with a fork.

Activities:

Follow the general procedure as given in the Activities of Problem 10 (page 369).

Problem 12: HOW SHALL WE PLAN A TEA?

The steps in planning a tea are much the same as those in planning a party, although the actual plans are different. If one person is giving the tea, the plans must all be made by her. If several are giving the tea together, the plans are made by the group and the responsibilities and expenses are divided among them.

The *type* of tea that is to be given must be decided upon first, since all plans depend upon this. A semiformal tea requires semiformal invitations, decorations, food, service,

These girls are making plans for their Home Economics Club tea, discussing expenses, menus, decorations, and how the tea will be conducted.

and even entertainment. An informal tea requires the opposite.

Next for consideration are the *time and place*. An hour and day convenient for all and a place suitable for the tea must be found. Some homes are just right for an informal tea. Other homes provide nicely for a semiformal tea.

The *amount of money* that one has to spend for the tea is important. A tea may cost much or little. Decorations and entertainment may increase the expense, even though the food costs are small.

The *guest list* should be made early in the planning. For an informal tea, sometimes only a small number are invited. This makes a chatty, homey sort of party, usually simple and not expensive. For a semiformal tea, a large number of people may be invited. In such case, the guest list will be rather long, and may include many who are mere acquaintances.

The *invitations* may be given orally, written, or printed, according to the type of the tea. Whatever method is used, the invitation should be given in the correct manner. An invitation poorly given makes a bad impression upon the guest before attending the tea.

The *decorations* should be carefully planned. These are

Tall, slender candles, flowers, and a lace cloth are the keynotes of decoration for this simply arranged tea table.

frequently much more elaborate than at a party or a company meal. The tea table is the center of the decorations and should be arranged attractively. Other surfaces, such as the buffet, bookcases, and table tops hold decorations also. Flowers, winter greens, plants, and candles are the chief decorations used. Lace and other beautiful tablecloths and doilies are used to add to the charm of the occasion. Silverware, chinaware, and glassware are also a part of the decorations.

The *food* to be served should be in keeping with the type of tea. It should be well prepared and should be in harmony with the decorations.

Plans must be made for the *entertainment*. At a small informal tea the entertainment consists merely of friendly visiting in a comfortable room. At a large tea, if visiting is to be the means of entertainment, several friends should be asked to help see that guests meet old friends and make new acquaintances. Sometimes a short program is given at a tea. Frequently music is provided all through the tea hour. The semiformal tea is apt to be stiff unless definite plans are made to prevent this.

Someone should be responsible for *meeting the guests* at the door. Except at a very small tea, the hostess will not have time to do this. Sometimes at a semiformal tea there is a receiving line in which the hostess and one or two friends stand to meet the guests as they come.

The hostess or hostesses and those assisting should dress in keeping with the type of tea. This is one function where the hostess or hostesses may dress up a little more than the guests and still be in good taste.

Activities:

1. (*Class activity*) Plan a tea to be given at school.
2. (*Class activity*) Plan an informal home tea.

Problem 13: WHAT SHALL WE SERVE AT OUR TEA?

The food served at a tea should be dainty and attractive. Small sandwiches, closed or open face, tiny cookies and cakes, little cream puffs, small crackers, candies, nuts, ices, and a beverage make up the list of foods from which the tea menu is chosen. The food served at an informal tea is plainer and simpler than that served at a semiformal one.

Except in a very small informal tea, a color scheme is usually carried out in the food and the decorations of the tea table. Often these are in keeping with the season or with some special event. Pale colors, such as lavender, pink, green, and yellow, are the ones most used. Orange and brown are suitable for a fall tea; red and green for a Christmas tea; and red and white for a February tea on Valentine's Day or Washington's Birthday.

Both hot and cold beverages are served at teas. The most common ones are tea, Russian tea, fruit punch, cider, grape juice, coffee, chocolate, and fruit juice "freezes." Whether a hot or iced beverage will be served depends upon the season, a hot one being preferred in the winter and an iced one in the summer. The other foods are selected in relation to how well they go with the beverage. Often this is

Dainty cakes and sandwiches are set out for a tea party on a table artistically arranged and decorated.

a matter of personal taste. An informal tea may include only one other food besides the beverage. For a semiformal tea, several foods other than the beverage are served.

As a rule, the food is served from a central table which is made as attractive as possible. The food, dishes, silverware, and other things are arranged in a convenient and artistic manner on the table. If the beverage is to be served by someone seated at the table, one end of the table should be prepared for this.

At a small tea the hostess may serve the beverage herself. At larger teas one or more friends are asked to serve. Help is needed to keep the dishes filled with food and to replace plates, cups, and silver. Sometimes the daughter in the family takes care of this, or a friend may do it.

Guests may pass around the table and, after the beverage is poured, take their cups and plates and help themselves to the other foods. Some hostesses prefer to have friends or waitresses assist with the serving and bring the served plate from the table to the guest. Guests may be seated in the dining room or living room, or they may stand while eating. A tea should appear to be deliberate and not hurried. A few minutes should pass after the guests' arrival before they are served. Examples of some menus for teas are suggested:

Informal Tea

Winter	*Summer*
Hot cider	Raspberry and lime freeze
Doughnuts	Sugar cookies

Semiformal Tea

Winter	*Summer*
Russian tea	Iced tea, orange and lemon slices
Open-face sandwiches	Assorted ices
Cookies	Individual cakes
Nuts	Candies Nuts

Tea, orange and lemon slices
Cream puffs
Tea cakes Nuts

Activities:

1. (*Class activity*) Plan the refreshments for a school tea.
2. Estimate the cost of these refreshments.

Problem 14: HOW SHALL WE PREPARE AND SERVE SANDWICHES FOR OUR TEA?

Sandwiches served at a tea should be small and dainty. They should add to the beauty of the tea table. In making sandwiches for tea, the bread is sliced very thin and is sometimes cut in fancy shapes. Both open-face and closed sandwiches are served. Some suggestions are given in this Problem.

The utensils

Sharp bread or butcher knives
Measuring cup
Measuring spoons
Mixing bowls
Paring knife
Food chopper
Tablespoon
Mixing spoon
Spatula
Waxed paper
Towel for covering

Variety of both flavor and shape makes this tray of sandwiches a tempting sight to the tea-party guest.

The recipes

Method for *open-face tea sandwiches:*

Cut bread in ⅓-inch slices. Cut in various shapes—rounds, diamonds, squares, rectangles, or triangles. Cream butter and spread it on the bread. Spread thinly with various sandwich spreads, such as cream cheese and salad dressing, chopped nuts and salad dressing, ground meat and salad dressing, or a fruit and nut mixture. Decorate with thinly sliced olives, pieces of tomato, pimento, or a candied cherry.

Method for *closed tea sandwiches:*

Cut bread in ⅓-inch slices. Cut off the crusts. Butter one slice and spread the other thinly with a sandwich spread. Put the slices together and cut in small fancy shapes. Spread mixtures used in making open-face sandwiches are satisfactory spreads. A colorful spread makes attractive sandwiches. Sometimes these sandwiches are made of several layers.

Each girl—3 or 4 sandwiches.

The serving

Tea sandwiches are arranged in a pleasing manner on a sandwich plate, from which guests serve themselves. Tea sandwiches are eaten with the fingers, being held by the tips of the thumb and forefinger.

Activities:

Follow the general procedure as given in the Activities of Problem 10 (page 369).

Problem 15: HOW SHALL WE PREPARE AND SERVE BEVERAGES FOR OUR TEA?

Tea, or some variation, is the beverage most often served at teas, although fruit beverages are preferred by many. If hot tea is served, it should be made fresh, hot, and of the strength generally preferred by one's guests. If iced tea is served, it should be thoroughly chilled. The same is true of fruit beverages. Lukewarm beverages are never pleasing. Tea combinations are made by adding different fruit juices to tea.

The utensils

Teapot
Measuring cup
Measuring spoons
Fruit juicer
Paring knife

The recipes

Ingredients for *hot tea:*

4 t. tea
4 c. boiling water

Method:

Scald the pot to freshen. Put tea into a tea ball and place in the pot. Pour boiling water over the tea and cover it. Allow to steep 2 or 3 minutes. Remove the tea ball and serve at once. The tea can be put directly in the pot, but then the beverage should be poured at once into another pot when it has steeped the required time.

Ingredients for *iced tea:*

8 t. tea
4 c. boiling water

Method:

The tea is allowed to steep 3 or 4 minutes. The tea ball is then removed and the hot tea poured into tall glasses half filled or more with ice cubes. Slices of lemon or orange or mint leaves are often placed in the glass.

Ingredients for *Russian tea:*

1 pt. tea	3/8 c. sugar
1 pt. water	1½ lemons

Method:

Make a syrup by boiling sugar, ¼ c. water and a slice of lemon. Cool. Add the juice of the lemons and the remainder of the water. Combine with the tea. Serve either hot or iced.

Tea combination beverages:

Equal parts of tea and fruit juices make a good beverage. Tea and cider, tea and grape juice, and tea and pineapple juice are pleasing combinations. If the fruit juice is strong, it may have to be diluted with water before adding it to the tea.

Ingredients for *fruit punch:*

6 oranges	2½ qts. water
4 lemons	1 pt. ginger ale, if punch is to be served iced
2 grapefruit	
2⅔ c. sugar	

Method:

Boil sugar and 1 quart of the water until the sugar is dissolved. Set it aside to cool. Extract juice from the fruit and add it to the syrup. Stir thoroughly and add it to the rest of the water.

If iced punch is desired, add ice and ginger ale just before serving.

If hot punch is desired, heat just before serving and omit the ginger ale.

The recipe makes one gallon of punch.

Two girls—½ pt. or 1 pt. of a beverage.

The serving

Hot tea and hot fruit beverages are served in teacups with a teaspoon. Iced beverages are served in tumblers or iced-tea glasses.

A teaspoon or iced-tea spoon is used. Cups and glasses are placed on plates for serving.

Activities:

Follow the general procedure as given in the Activities of Problem 10 (page 369).

Problem 16: HOW SHALL WE ARRANGE OUR TABLE FOR TEA?

The laying of the cloth is the first step in the table arrangement. If a damask cloth is to be used, it will be spread over a silence cloth, following the steps outlined for preparing the table for a family meal. (See page 228.) If a lace or embroidered cloth is used, it is spread directly over the gleaming wood of the freshly dusted table.

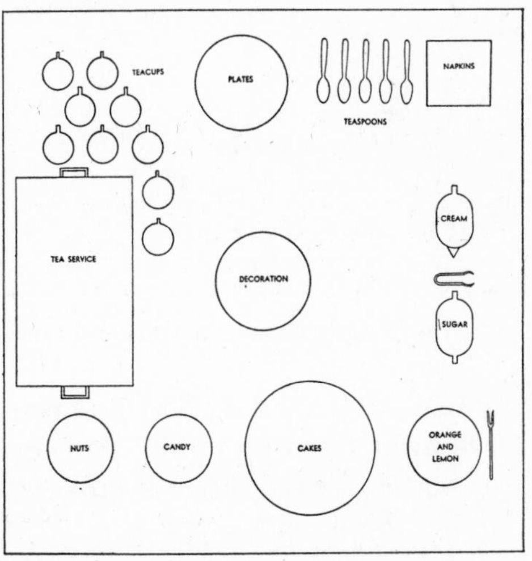

This diagram shows a tea table set for one person to serve.

The arrangement of the centerpiece comes next. The bouquet should be of a size in keeping with the tea table. A huge bouquet seems to overwhelm everything else. A tiny one seems lost and not enough. The flower arrangement should be pleasing; usually a low one that does not hide part of the tea table from the person who is serving is most desirable. Various bowls or vases for the bouquet may be tried on the table with the candlesticks or decorations before they are arranged. When the bowl or vase most satisfactory for both

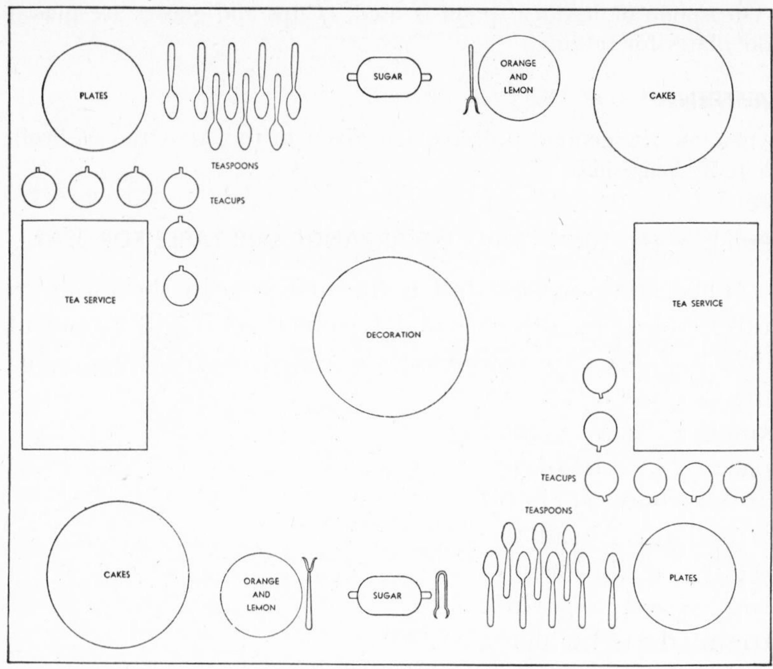

This diagram shows a tea table set for two persons to serve.

the bouquet and the table has been decided upon, it is then filled away from the table, preventing the possible litter of leaves and petals on the tea table.

The menu will show what silver, china, and glassware will be needed for the tea. These, of course, should be in perfect condition and should be as dainty and attractive as possible. Their placement on the table should be orderly and in a convenient position for serving.

Diagrams are a helpful means of checking our plans for table arrangement. Study those above and on page 379.

Activities:

1. (*Class activity*) Plan the arrangement of the tea table for a school tea.

2. (*Class activity*) Arrange the tea table for this tea.
3. (*Class activity*) Give the tea.

REFERENCES FOR THE UNIT

Allen, Betty, and Briggs, Mitchell Pirie, *Behave Yourself!* Chicago: J. B. Lippincott Co., 1937.

Calvert, Maude Richman, *The New First Course in Homemaking.* Atlanta: Turner Smith Co., 1932.

Friend, Mata Roman, and Shultz, Hazel, *Junior Home Economics: Living in Our Homes.* New York: D. Appleton-Century Co., 1933.

Jensen, Milton B., Jensen, Mildred R., and Ziller, M. Louisa, *Fundamentals of Home Economics.* New York: The Macmillan Co., 1935.

Matthews, Mary Lockwood, *The New Elementary Home Economics.* Boston: Little, Brown and Co., 1937.

Talbot, Nora, and Others, *Practical Problems in Home Life for Boys and Girls.* New York: American Book Co., 1936.

Young, William P., and Gardner, Horace J., *The Year Round Party Book.* Philadelphia: J. B. Lippincott Co., 1938.

SUGGESTED HOME EXPERIENCES

1. Help with the entertaining of guests in your home.
2. Entertain a guest of your own in some way.
3. Entertain your friends with a party.
4. Help another family member or a friend give a tea.
5. Entertain your friends at a tea.

UNIT

12

HELPING TO CARE FOR THE HOUSE

CARING FOR THE HOUSE IS AN IMPORtant part of homemaking. It requires so much of the homemaker's time that homemaking is sometimes called "keeping house."

Caring for the house is not just a single job in itself. It consists of many jobs, all done for the purpose of keeping the house clean and in order. Most of these must be done over and over again, often several times each day. The old rhyme whose lines say, "Woman's work is never done" might easily be referring to the care of the house. The many jobs necessary for a well-cared-for home usually should be shared by the various family members. Because the house is "our house," the work of keeping it in order becomes our concern. Additional evidence of the importance placed upon the care of the house is given by the frequent comments showing that homemakers and families are judged by the way they "keep their house."

Caring for the house is important not only because of the time and effort it requires but also for what good care contributes to the success of the family life.

A well-cared-for house adds much to the pleasure and enjoyment of the whole family. It helps us take pride and satisfaction in our home. It helps make the house a desirable place to live. Helping in the care of the house is a responsibility in the lives of most high school girls. If this is to be our work, we should know how to do it in a satisfactory manner.

Problem 1: WHAT SHALL BE OUR STANDARD FOR THE CARE OF OUR HOUSE?

In many homes there hangs on the wall this old fireside motto:

> The Beauty of the house is Order;
> The Blessing of the house is Contentment;
> The Glory of the house is Hospitality;
> The Crown of the house is Godliness.

We all want this beauty of order in our home. We know that having it depends much upon the way the house is kept. How well or how poorly our house will be kept is influenced much by our standard for its care. If our standard requires a clean, orderly, and well-kept house, we are likely to have that kind of a house. If our standard does not require cleanliness and order, our house will very likely be dirty, without order, and poorly kept. We seldom go much higher than the standard we hold, and often not as high.

Sometimes not all the members within the family have a high standard for the care of the house. Keeping the house in good condition is difficult if all are not working toward the same end. It is most important that the family members have the same standard if the house is to be well cared for.

The family's standard for the care of the house is influenced by a number of things. A family with several growing children will have a different standard from one that has only grownups. Whether the children are babies or school boys and girls makes a difference. A toddler will have to leave his playthings on the floor. He will have to clutch chairs and pieces of furniture to keep from falling, so his fingerprints are everywhere. He is interested in the baby in the mirror and will pat it with his sticky hands. Later his playing with paper dolls cut from newspapers and maga-

Orderliness adds to the beauty and restfulness of this room. Can you name the arrangements which seem to do most to make this an attractive room?

zines keeps the house in a constant litter. By the time a child reaches the fifth or sixth grade in school, he no longer makes this kind of disorder. However, there are few school children who do not dump books here, toss coat and cap there, and leave jack stones and bits of jigsaw puzzle everywhere. Though high school pupils are through with such games as these, sometimes even they forget to put their books and clothes away. Sometimes they strew handkerchiefs, combs, and compacts about, creating a disorder which perhaps they already are beginning to dislike. Thus, the age of the family members and their habits affect the standard of order and cleanliness for their home.

If one or more of the family members is not in good health, the standard may of necessity be lowered. The

Keeping the house in good condition becomes a habit as a result of having a good standard, making a plan of work, and then following it.

house may be located far from the water supply and in such a place that dirt is easily carried in. It may be located where dust storms are frequent or where coal smoke is thick and heavy the year around. All of these conditions tend to make the standard of caring for the house difficult to maintain.

The house should be as clean, orderly, and attractive as it is possible for it to be without making too much work for the mother or any other family member. However, there is no limit to the standard that can be kept if everyone in the family does his part.

The house should receive such care as will make it a livable home. A house may be kept so well that there is no place to live, or it may be kept so poorly that the same situation holds true. The house is where we make our home. It should be kept so that we want to live there and can live there happily and with satisfaction. Our standard should be such that good family life is possible.

A good standard for care of the house requires that the right kind of care be given regularly. Many homemakers have found that making a plan for the work to be done and following it is a great help. Though changes in the plan may be necessary from time to time, planning makes the care of the house much easier.

Activities:

1. Consider your own family. Do all the members have the same standard for the care of the house? How do their standards differ?
2. Write a paragraph describing the standard that your family should have and could have for the care of the house.
3. Give an example of a standard that is too high for a family; of one that is too low.

Problem 2: WHAT IS OUR RESPONSIBILITY IN CARING FOR THE HOUSE?

"Who shall care for the house?" is a question that must be decided in every family. In some homes one person takes the job and the rest of the family forget all about it. Easy as it may seem, this is not desirable. Caring for the house is a heavy and difficult task for one person to manage alone, even though the family is small. Every family member should share in so large a responsibility.

Although the responsibilities in caring for the house vary somewhat, they are much the same in all households. The rooms must be cleaned and kept in order. The furniture and equipment must be cared for. Clothing and household linens must be laundered. Pantries, closets, and dresser drawers must be given regular attention. Dishes, glassware, and silverware must be washed and polished when necessary. Equipment and furnishings must be kept in repair. Last season's things must be put away and this season's brought out for use.

This little girl is learning early to share in the care of the house. Orderly shelves have a charm for her, even though she is only beginning her school days.

In most families, the major responsibility for the care of the house belongs to the mother. This does not mean that she does all the work herself, but that she is in charge of the whole job. She either does the planning or directs the planning. She sees that the tasks are divided fairly. She gives the proper help to those members who need it. If caring for the house is regarded as a family responsibility, every member has a definite part to do.

Sometimes part of the care of the house, such as the weekly cleaning and laundry, is done by paid helpers. Even when this is the case, family members still must share in the work if the house is to be well kept. Their share will be chiefly keeping the house in order after the thorough cleaning is done. Hanging up one's clothing, putting games and books away, straightening up the newspapers and magazines, and dusting—all these are necessary tasks each day.

Schoolgirls seldom have the full responsibility of caring for the house. Their part is usually that of helpers. The jobs that they are most often called upon to do rarely include more than some part of the thorough cleaning of the house. Tasks commonly given to them include sweeping and dusting, taking care of cupboards and closets, caring for the bathroom, cleaning and polishing the silverware and other metals, keeping tables and desks in order, and washing dishes and utensils. In addition to these jobs, most high school girls are responsible for the care of their own room.

Whatever our part happens to be, we should assume it cheerfully and willingly. We should do the tasks regularly, as well as we can, and without being reminded. Many families follow the plan of changing the assignment of tasks frequently. This gives each person a turn at both the pleasant and the disagreeable tasks. It also gives opportunity for everyone in the family to learn the many skills of housekeeping and homemaking.

> The house is the home of the family and we should all be willing to do a little more than our assigned tasks so that we may have a well-kept house.

The right way to sweep a rug is to brush with the nap, toward you.

We should each do our best to keep the house in order. If we have been using the library table we should leave everything on it in order when we are through, even though our special task for the week is the care of the pantry. If we go to the pantry for a sandwich we should return the peanut butter to the refrigerator, put away the bread, clear away the crumbs, and wash the utensils used, even though our special task for the week is the care of the living room. We should not "dirty things up" for someone else to clean after us. If we see some little thing in disorder, such as a picture crooked on the wall or magazines tumbled about, we should put this in order no matter what our particular responsibility happens to be.

Activities:

1. Make a list of the responsibilities that you should and could assume in the care of your house.
2. Which of these are you already assuming?
3. Make a plan of your time for one week which includes all these responsibilities.

Problem 3: HOW SHALL WE SWEEP AND DUST?

Sweeping and dusting must be done regularly and often in caring for the house. These are common responsibilities of schoolgirls. The general methods used are much the same, regardless of the rooms and furnishings to be swept and dusted.

On page 163 the steps for sweeping a wood floor were given. Let us review these. They are as follows:

1. Use a good, firm broom that is not too stiff and scratchy.
2. Sweep with the length of the flooring as much as possible.
3. Lap the broom strokes over each other and sweep the dirt and waste to one place, going back to get any left wastes.
4. Give special sweeping to the corners.
5. Take up all dirt and waste on a dust pan.

The steps in sweeping carpets with a vacuum cleaner or sweeper are as follows:

1. Run the sweeper slowly lengthwise and then crosswise of the rug.
2. Repeat this again and again until the dirt is removed.
3. Empty the bag of the vacuum cleaner or the bin of the sweeper after a thorough or weekly cleaning.

The steps in sweeping carpets with a broom are as follows:

1. Sweep evenly, going across the width of the carpet.
2. Overlap the broom strokes.
3. Sweep the ends and edges well.
4. Keep the broom on the carpet while sweeping.
5. Sweep the dirt to one place, going back to get any left wastes.
6. Take up all dirt and waste on a dust pan.
7. Do not sweep dirt from one room to another.
8. Use bits of moistened paper to reduce dust and brighten the carpet.

Often when thorough sweeping is done, the furniture and ornaments are covered or removed from the room.

The steps in dusting are as follows:

1. Use soft cloths or brushes that do not shed lint.

2. Use only a small amount of oil on the dustcloths or brushes. Many of the dustbrushes are treated and require no oil.

3. Wipe the dust off surfaces with care, taking up the dust into the cloth.

4. Dust the high things first and then the low ones.

5. Use a dustmop for floors that are not carpeted, wiping well the corners and the surfaces under the large pieces of furniture.

Some prefer to dust furniture with a hand mop designed for this purpose. Others use a cloth.

Sometimes it is desirable to use a sweeper on carpets after the dusting.

Activities:

1. Sweep a wood floor and a carpet, following the method given in this Problem.

2. Dust a room or several pieces of furniture, following the method given in this Problem.

3. Report your experiences and results to the class.

Problem 4: HOW SHALL WE CARE FOR MAGAZINES, BOOKS, AND ORNAMENTS?

Magazines, books, and such ornaments as vases and candlesticks are among the things that make a house at-

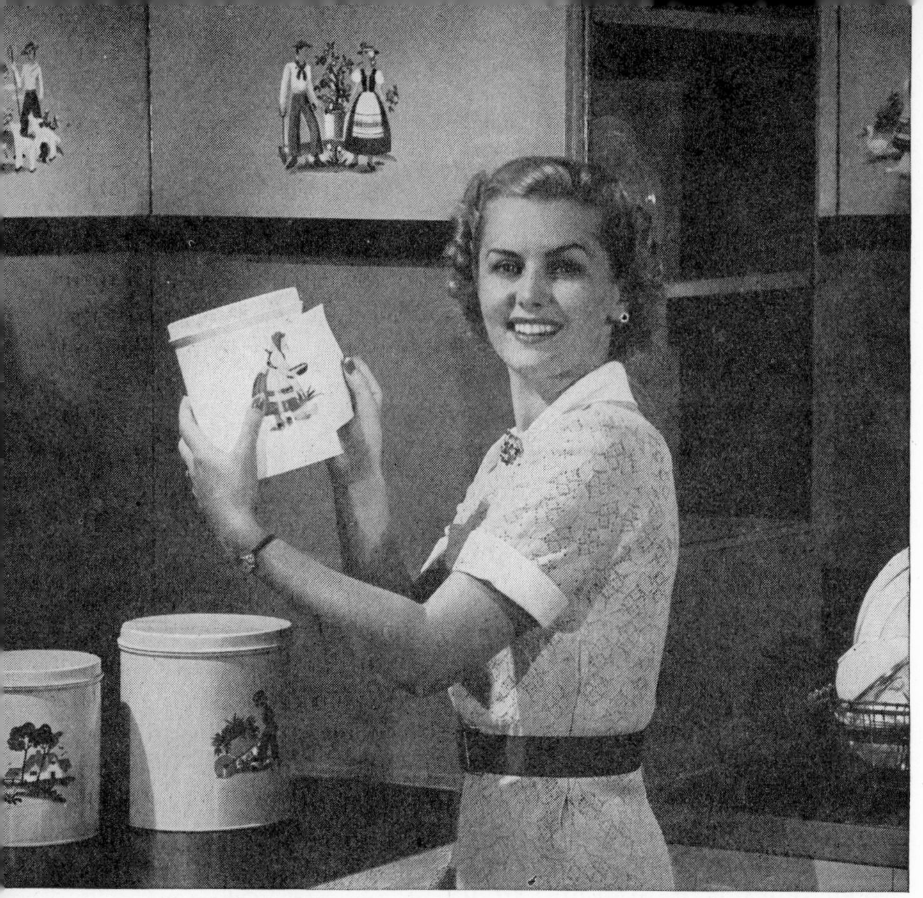

The decorating of cans and containers is not difficult to do, and the gay colors add greatly to the appearance of the kitchen. These designs are being transferred directly from paper to the cans.

tractive and give it the appearance of home. Because of their very nature, they require care. They must be dusted often, cleaned, and put in the right place. Magazines, books, and ornaments that are dirty and in disorder are anything but pleasing. They give a poor impression of the family and destroy the feeling of rest that the home can give.

Books should be wiped with a soft, clean cloth at least every two weeks. Some vacuum cleaners have a special attachment for cleaning books, which may be used in preference to wiping with a cloth. Several times a year the books should be opened and the dust brushed out. When this is done, the shelves should be thoroughly dusted and wiped before replacing the books.

Magazines are cared for in the same manner as are books. Frequent, if not continual, attention needs to be given the magazines and books which are lying on tables or are in racks, if they are to be kept in order. Every family member should feel responsible for keeping the magazines and books in order.

Ornaments should be dusted and wiped just as frequently as the furniture. If we have a collection of a hundred or more tiny dogs, elephants, or pitchers, this is no small task. Vases, china, and glassware should be washed once in a while if they can be washed safely. Pictures should be dusted daily. In the thorough cleaning of the house the pictures are taken down and thoroughly wiped, both front and back.

Textiles used for decoration, cushions, and table covers should be brushed and dusted often. Once in a while they should be dry-cleaned or laundered, depending upon the nature of the material.

Lamp shades should be dusted frequently. Paper or parchment shades are wiped with a dust cloth. Silk or rayon shades, whether pleated or plain, are best cleaned by brushing with a soft brush.

Activities:

1. Care for magazines, books, or accessories, following the methods given in this Problem.
2. Report any difficulties or unusual experiences and how these were met.

Problem 5: HOW SHALL WE CARE FOR THE BATHROOM?

The bathroom requires thorough cleaning twice each week as well as some care each day. Thorough cleaning consists of wiping down the walls, mopping or scrubbing the

Caring for the tub should be done frequently. Using a good cleanser will keep it white and sparkling.

floor, washing the woodwork, and cleaning the mirrors, cabinets, tub, stool, and lavatory. The tub and lavatory should be cleaned after each using. The stool should be cleaned daily. Daily care is often the responsibility of high school girls. This includes care of the tub and lavatory, the stool, the mirror, and the floor.

The steps in cleaning the tub and lavatory are as follows:

1. Scrub with a soft mesh or cloth, moistened with water, and a fine cleanser, thus removing soil and any scum left by hard water.
2. Rinse thoroughly with water.
3. Wash the faucets with soap and hot water.
4. Wipe them dry.

The steps in cleaning the stool are as follows:

1. Use a stool brush or one made from a string dish mop with the strings cut short.
2. Use soapy hot water and clean thoroughly.
3. Disinfect and cleanse once or twice each week with chloride of lime or a commercial cleanser prepared especially for stools.

The steps in the cleaning of a mirror are as follows:

1. Use soft cloths that are nonlinting.
2. Moisten the cloth in clear, warm water, and wring moderately dry.
3. Wipe the mirror, taking care that water does not seep under the frame or backing.
4. Dry with a clean, dry, soft cloth.

The steps in cleaning the bathroom floor, whether linoleum or tile, are as follows:

1. Sweep up all dust, lint, and other dirt, and remove in a dustpan.
2. Make a suds of mild soap and warm water in a pail.
3. Dip a clean mop in the suds and wring it moderately dry.
4. Wipe the floor in parts, dipping and wringing the mop as each part is finished.
5. Dip the mop and wring it dry, and go over the floor to remove any excess water.

Activities:

1. Clean a bathroom and its equipment.
2. Report any difficulties and the ways they were met.

Problem 6: HOW SHALL WE CARE FOR THE PANTRY AND CUPBOARDS?

The pantry and cupboards need frequent and regular cleaning. How often this should be done depends upon where we live and the type of the pantry and cupboards. If our home is in a dry, dusty region where the wind blows and carries dust with it, or if it is where there is much coal smoke in the air, frequent cleanings will be necessary. If the air is cleaner, or if our pantry and cupboards are somewhat protected and fitted with doors, less frequent cleaning may be needed. A regular time should be set for the cleaning of the pantry and cupboards and a plan made for their general care.

The shelves should be washed in warm, soapy water, and dried. This should be done as often as is needed, in many homes once each week. The cans and jars should be wiped or washed daily if needed, but at least once each week. A cloth wrung out of soapy water should be used for the wiping. If washed, they should be washed in warm, soapy water, rinsed in hot water, and dried thoroughly.

Drawers should be dusted every few days, and washed with a cloth wrung from warm, soapy water once or twice each month. Once or twice each year a more thorough washing may be done. After this cleaning, drying in the sunshine is good. Shelves and drawers both may be covered or lined with paper folded to size and held in place by thumbtacks. Wrapping paper, shelf paper, heavy waxed paper, and newspapers are all used for this purpose.

Dishes and glassware should be kept clean. Those that are used only once in a while should be taken off the shelves and washed as necessary. In most homes this will be two or three times a year. When this is done, the regular method for washing dishes and glassware should be followed. The utensils should be kept clean. Those not in regular use should be cleaned now and then. Once or twice a year, or even more often, a special cleaning of utensils should be done to remove stains not attended to in their regular care.

All articles in the pantry and cupboards should be kept in the proper place all the time. There should be a place for everything and it should be put there after each using. If this is done, the pantry and cupboard will always be in fairly good order.

The pantry and cupboards can be made to be attractive as well as useful places in the house. Pleasing arrangements and attractive color schemes can be worked out with the dishes, jars, cans, and utensils. The present use of gayly colored pottery and enameled ware makes this possible.

Activities:

1. Clean the pantry and cupboards in the school laboratory.
2. Clean the pantry or cupboard at home or in a friend's home.
3. Plan an attractive arrangement for pantry or cupboard shelves in the school laboratory. Plan an arrangement for the shelves at home.
4. Suggest ways of building and altering cupboards to exclude dust and reduce the amount of cleaning necessary.

Problem 7: HOW SHALL WE CARE FOR THE SILVERWARE?

Silverware tarnishes very easily and turns an ugly color. Frequent and regular care are required to keep silverware attractive and in good condition. There are two methods of cleaning silverware that are commonly used. One is by the use of silverware polish and the other is by the aluminum pan method. The last method should not be used on silver with a dark design.

The steps in cleaning silverware with polish are as follows:

1. Use a good silver polish or cream.
2. Apply this polish with soft cloths and brushes, rubbing gently until the tarnish disappears.
3. Rinse in hot water and wipe dry at once.
4. Polish with a clean, dry, soft cloth.

The steps in cleaning silverware by the aluminum pan method are as follows:

1. Put one quart of boiling water in an aluminum kettle or pan and set it on the stove.
2. Put the silver in the water, being sure that the water covers the silver.

3. Add one tablespoon of salt and one teaspoon of baking soda to the water, stirring well.
4. Allow the silver to stand in hot water until it becomes bright.
5. Remove the silver and wash it in hot, soapy water.
6. Rinse it in clean, hot water.
7. Polish it with a clean, dry, soft cloth.

Activities:

1. (*Class activity*) Clean the school silverware, part of the class using one method and part the other.
2. Compare the methods and results. Decide the advantages and disadvantages of each method.

Problem 8: HOW SHALL WE HELP WITH THE ODD CLEANING JOBS ABOUT THE HOUSE?

Some of the odd jobs of cleaning that must be done frequently in the house are cleaning mirrors, piano keys, pictures, combs and brushes, and windows; oiling squeaking hinges; and caring for the garbage can. Most of these are definite home responsibilities of schoolgirls.

The steps in cleaning drawers are as follows:

1. Remove the drawers.
2. Empty them of their contents.
3. Take a stiff brush and clean out the corners.
4. Shake out all dirt.
5. Wipe on the inside and the outside with a dry cloth, or, if necessary, wash with a cloth wrung from warm, soapy water.
6. When dry, place the contents back in the drawers and put the drawers in place in the dresser or cabinet. Sometimes the drawers are lined to help keep them clean. If paper lining is used, it is folded to fit the drawer and fastened in place with thumbtacks.

The steps in cleaning piano keys are as follows:

1. Use a soft cloth.
2. Wring the cloth dry from clean, warm water or moisten with denatured alcohol.
3. Wipe each key with the cloth.
4. If necessary, dry with a dry cloth.

The steps in cleaning pictures are as follows:

1. Pictures not covered with glass are wiped with a dry, soft cloth on both the front and back sides, as well as the frame.
2. Pictures covered with glass are wiped as are the other pictures.
3. The glass is cleaned as are mirrors.

The steps in cleaning combs and brushes are as follows:

1. Put a few drops of ammonia or two or three teaspoons of borax in a bowl of warm water.
2. Dip the brush up and down in the solution.
3. When it is clean, dip it in clear, warm water in order to rinse it thoroughly.
4. Shake out the water and put it on a flat, warm place to dry.
5. Soak the combs in warm ammonia or borax solution. Rub water on each comb with a soft cloth or a stiff cleaning brush.
6. When clean, rinse in clear, cold water.

The steps in cleaning windows are as follows:

1. Use soft, nonlinting cloths and warm, soapy water, or warm water containing a few drops of ammonia.
2. Wipe or brush off all the dust with a soft brush.
3. Wring the cloth from the water.

4. Wash the panes until they are clean.
5. Wipe them dry with a dry cloth.

Whiting made into a paste by adding water is often used to clean windows. Put it on the glass, allowing it to dry. Wipe with a dry cloth. This method requires a special dusting and sometimes washing of the window casings and woodwork.

The steps in oiling hinges are as follows:

1. Use a can of sewing-machine oil or another similar oil.
2. Drop a few drops of oil on the top of the hinge.
3. Work the hinge back and forth to allow the oil to run down in.
4. Wipe away any excess oil.
5. Repeat as many times as is needed to take away the squeaking.

The steps in caring for the kitchen garbage can are as follows:

1. Place a paper bag, or a newspaper folded in the shape of a bag, in the can.
2. Place in it garbage from which the water has been drained.
3. Empty the can every day.
4. Wash off the outside of the can as often as is needed with a cloth wrung from hot, soapy water.
5. Wash the inside of the can with hot, soapy water, using a long-handled brush, frequently. This should be done at least once each week.
6. If necessary, let a strong solution of washing soda or lye stand in the can for an hour or more.
7. Rinse the can.
8. Sun and air the garbage can.

Activities:

1. Do some odd cleaning job at school. Report any difficulties or problems to the class. Tell how you met these.
2. Do one or more odd cleaning jobs at home. Report experiences to the class.
3. Choose some odd cleaning job not included here and list in steps the procedure you would follow.

Problem 9: HOW MAY CARE PREVENT ACCIDENTS IN THE HOME?

We commonly think of home as being the safest place in the world for us. However, when we look at the reports of accidents for the past few years, we find that such is not the case. Home accidents are reported as the most numerous, being even greater in number than traffic accidents. Many of, if not all, these accidents might have been prevented. No one wishes his house to be a place for accidents. It would be well to give some thought to the matter.

Smoke curling up from this ironing board is a serious warning that someone has been very careless.

Fire is one of the chief causes of accidents in the home. Defective heating plants are often responsible for fire. These defects include dirty chimneys, rusted or broken smoke pipes or those poorly insulated, stoves and furnaces out of order, and lack of protection of wooden floors under stoves. Oil-soaked dusting rags, sweeping compound, and paint-stained rags left in the attic, closet, pantry, or cellar often cause fires. Faulty electrical equipment or cords, and poor electrical wiring are other causes. Home cleaning of clothes with gasoline, benzine, or naphtha is a frequent cause of fire. A spark will set on fire the fumes from these fluids. Gas connections which are not firm and tight are dangerous. Many accidents are reported from the throwing of kerosene on smoldering fires, and the filling of kerosene lamps and stoves while they are lighted.

The following are some "don'ts" which we should observe to prevent fires:

1. Don't permit rubbish or wastepaper to collect; burn it, but not near any building.

2. Don't keep matches where young children can get at them.

3. Don't be careless with matches.

4. Don't leave oily rags or mops in corners where they may start a fire. Keep them in closed metal cans or boxes, or wash them and hang them out to dry.

5. Don't use worn electric cord, or leave electrical equipment connected when you are through using it.

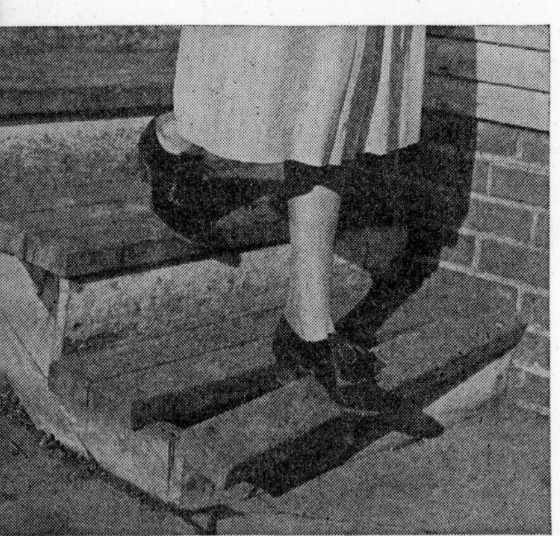

A broken step may cause a serious accident. It takes only a few minutes to fix the step.

6. Don't store gasoline in your house or use it there for cleaning.

7. Don't use kerosene to start fires.

8. Don't allow leaky gas connections to go unrepaired.

9. Don't build a fire in a stove unless the floor beneath it is protected with a metal sheet.

10. Don't put ashes into wooden boxes or paper cartons. Keep ashes in metal cans.

11. Don't fail to screen open fireplaces.

12. Don't look into clothes closets with lighted matches.

13. Don't permit curtains to be blown near or over flames.

14. Don't fill a coal furnace or stove without "burning off the gas" by opening the dampers and possibly the door to create a strong draft.

15. Don't investigate escaping gas with a lighted match or open-flame lamp; turn on an electric light or use a flashlight.

Slipping and falling are common and serious accidents in the home. People fall downstairs, stumble over toys, and slip on slippery floors and in the bathtub. Their injuries extend from a "barked shin" to a broken back. Such accidents can be avoided to a large extent by the following measures:

1. Make the rugs and carpets secure on the floor.
2. Put furniture in place before going to bed at night.
3. Remove all toys and small objects from the floor.
4. Use solid stepladders when reaching up to high places.
5. Use handrails on old stairs and keep stairsteps clear.
6. Turn on lights or use a flashlight for dark stairways.
7. Use a rubber mat in the bathtub, and get out of the tub carefully.
8. Close all bureau drawers and closet doors after use.
9. Use soap dishes for soap, never permitting soap, soap powder, or suds to be on the floor.
10. Have a flashlight within reaching distance of the bed if the light switch is not so placed.

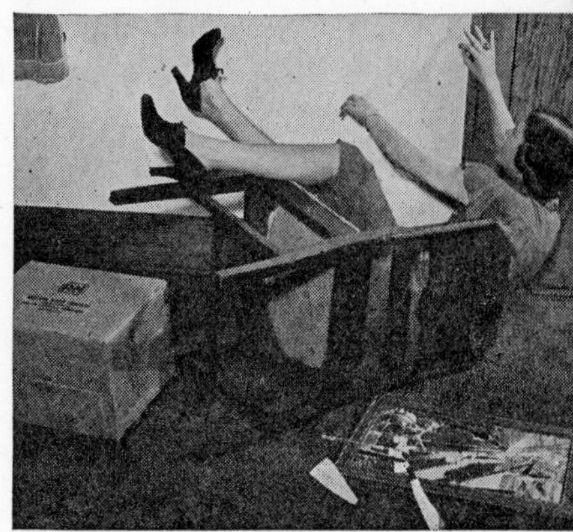

To hang a mirror or picture on a wall requires extreme care. Falls like this are a result of using chairs instead of stepladders.

Is the floor dry? Are her hands dry? Does her washing machine have sound electrical connections? In other words, how safe is she at her work?

The *electricity* which makes our lives comfortable and convenient is the cause of many accidents, including fire. The following things should be observed in its use:

1. Use cords for electrical equipment only when they are in good condition.
2. Disconnect all equipment from the wall or floor sockets when you are through using it.
3. Do not touch electric fixtures or switches when the hands or body are wet or are in contact with a metal object. Check especially the risks of such contacts in bathrooms and at all sinks and lavatories, and get your parents interested in making these safeguarding changes.

Other precautions that should be taken in preventing accidents in the home are the following:

Most of the accidents occurring in homes can be prevented. Family members have a responsibility to see that safe conditions are provided and maintained.

1. See that all gas burners are turned off as soon as you are through using them, and check them before retiring.
2. Turn out gas lights and other open lights before retiring.
3. Leave no needles, scis-

sors, pins, or other sharp-pointed objects on chairs or other furniture.

4. Promptly dispose of broken glass, used razor blades, and broken crockery in the rubbish can or box.

5. Keep poisons labeled and in a special place—well marked and away from regularly used drugs.

Activities:

1. Make a list of changes in the care of your home that would make your home a safer place.

2. Do you have any practices that might easily result in fire accidents? If so, what are they? Could you change your practices?

3. Give examples of accidents that you know that resulted from the care of the house.

REFERENCES FOR THE UNIT

Balderston, Lydia Ray, *Housekeeping Workbook.* Chicago: J. B. Lippincott Co., 1936.

Calvert, Maude Richman, *The New First Course in Homemaking.* Atlanta: Turner Smith Co., 1932.

Donovan, Dulcie Godlove, *The Mode in Dress and Home.* Boston: Allyn and Bacon, 1935.

Jensen, Milton B., Jensen, Mildred R., and Ziller, M. Louisa, *Fundamentals of Home Economics.* New York: The Macmillan Co., 1935.

Kinyon, Kate W., and Hopkins, L. Thomas, *Junior Home Problems,* Revised Edition. New York: Benj. H. Sanborn and Co., 1938.

Trilling, Mabel, Williams, Florence, and Reeves, Grace G., *Problems in Home Economics.* Chicago: J. B. Lippincott Co., 1939.

U. S. Bureau of Standards, *Safety in the Household.* Washington, D. C.

SUGGESTED HOME EXPERIENCES

1. Repeat at home the cleaning jobs done at school: sweeping and dusting; cleaning magazines, books, and accessories; cleaning the bathroom or parts of it; cleaning the pantry and cupboards; cleaning silverware; and other jobs.

2. Assume the responsibility for certain jobs in caring for the house.

3. Try to make your home freer from the likelihood of one or more accidents.

UNIT 13

FUN FOR THE FAMILY

IT IS HARD TO DEFINE FAMILY FUN, since it differs with families and family members. In one home, the father returning from work is seized about his knees by his three-year-old daughter who pleads, "Daddy, daddy, let's have fun!" Fun in this case is playing "big growly bear" on the floor, reaching its height when mother stops her work to round up the players and announce that it is time to wash for dinner. In another home, the family gathers about the fireplace to read aloud or play authors or Chinese checkers. As the young daughter completes her book of authors or jumps her last marble into place, she shouts, "And do we have fun!" In still another home, such as that of your grandparents, perhaps family fun means listening to grand opera over the radio or playing a quiet game of chess.

In each case, there is shared enjoyment, highly satisfying to the family members concerned. Family fun gives color and warmth to the memories people carry from their home life. If we listen to our elders talk of the fine times they had in "the good old days," we will find they recall most frequently perhaps pleasures shared with the family group.

If the family is really to have fun, each member must have some share in the hours of recreation. This sharing builds happiness now and pleasant memories later. By means of it a fine spirit of family loyalty is developed.

The best hour of the day comes when Daddy is home and ready for fun with the children.

Problem 1: HOW SHALL THE FAMILY PROVIDE FOR ITS FUN?

We all know that the joyous mirth, the jokes, and the gay laughter that we associate with fun cannot be provided like a bag of flour or sugar. We cannot place an order for a certain amount of family fun two hours beforehand and be sure that it will be delivered. Provision for family fun, though just as necessary as provision for food, is much more difficult.

First we must understand the tastes and interests of the family members. If reading aloud contributes to the pleasure of the group, it may be a means of providing family fun. If reading aloud seriously annoys one or more members, this means of entertainment should be counted out. If several members of the family are musical and enjoy playing together, the family orchestra or chorus may be a means of family fun. If the musical sense is lacking in the group, discords of several kinds may attend such efforts. If one's idea of hiking is a walk out to the front sidewalk, active outdoor sports will have little appeal or interest.

Even when we know the tastes and interests of our own family, the matter of moods may make a game of chance of the planning for family fun. An unhappy day may leave one in no mood for a lively adventure story or for losses in chess or some other game. Of course we all want to master our moods, but we need help in doing this. At any rate, we can see that sensing the family's mood is important in making successful provision for family fun.

Plans for fun should be such that all members of the family, from the youngest to the oldest, can share in some part of it. This may mean that a variety of games should be included in the playtime. Before Sammy and Jo go up to bed, a game of "pick-up-sticks" and a chapter in *Huckleberry Finn* may be enjoyed by them and the other family members. After they are gone, father, mother, and the older school daughter and son may enjoy contract bridge or rummy, or may listen to a favorite radio program. The evening's enjoyment, thus, has been shared by everyone.

The development of family members may come through sharing in family fun. Does this seem strange? If you stop and think for a moment you may realize how much of your sense of fair play has come through home games. Cheating at checkers just is not done. Playing out of turn soon puts you out of the game. Peeking at cards or dominoes quickly brands you as a spoil-sport. Thus your sense of fair play and respect for the rules of the game have grown as you have played. In the same way your knowledge of books and music may be increased through hours of family fun spent reading aloud or listening to music.

Family fun may help us to share in the fun of other families and in the fun of the community. If we learn how to sense the moods of our own family members we will be better able to understand the moods of people outside our family and will be more willing to fit into the plans others may make for fun. Also, having played games at home, we know the rules, and are not shy about playing games with others. If we have had our share of winning and losing at home, we do not feel too victorious or disappointed over our share of winning and losing away from home. In other words, we learn not to take the game too seriously.

A wide variety of activities should be included in the provisions for family fun. Already we have mentioned several games, and there are many others. Ping-pong is another of those suitable for indoor enjoyment. Out-of-door games include archery, croquet, horseshoes, and miniature golf.

Many families find the fun of growing things extends long after the summer is over. Seed catalogues, plans for borders and flower gardens, and books on gardening keep this kind of family fun going throughout the year.

Interest in making things has prompted many families to have workshops in their homes. The hobby of refinishing furniture or weaving rugs may be shared by the whole family. If one can plant, weave, play games, read, and create or listen to music, happily sharing the experience with other family members, there is little danger of these persons finding their family life monotonous or boring.

Provisions for family fun should be in keeping with the family funds. Fortunately, there is no direct relationship between the amount of money spent and the amount of fun enjoyed. We may have a merry time and spend very little. Common expenditures for fun include those made for a radio, books, magazines, games, game table, tools and supplies for gardening, and tools and supplies for wood and metal work. We may pay as little as $9.95 for the radio. We may spend as little as ninety-eight cents for a game table and ten cents for a game of dominoes. Other games, such as anagrams or bingo, may cost one dollar. A homemade ping-pong table may be built for a few dollars, or a ready-built one may be bought at a higher price. Usually it is lack of thought rather than lack of money that prevents adequate provision for family fun.

> By playing together regularly, family members come to know each other better, to have great satisfaction in their family, and to build pleasant memories. All these things are well worth making provision for family fun.

A definite time should be set aside for family fun. In some families the hour directly after dinner is the most satisfactory. In other families certain evenings of the week are held for family fun, and no engagements are accepted by family members for those times. Being together as a family is held to be quite as important as a meeting of father's service club or mother's card club.

Activities:

1. Select a family that you know. Show how the tastes and interests of the members influence the family fun.
2. Select a family consisting of adults and children. Plan in a general way this family's fun for one month.
3. Plan a score card for judging the family's provision for fun.
4. How much should a family spend for fun?

Problem 2: HOW CAN CONVERSATION CONTRIBUTE TO FAMILY FUN?

The ability to carry on good conversation is regarded as the mark of an educated person. Unfortunately, this ability is far too rare at the present time. The many short cuts used to convey ideas prevent us from speaking "clearly, pointedly, and exactly" as our grandfathers tried to do. The use of "whatch-you-ma-call-it" and "thing-a-ma-jig" as the main part of a sentence does not make a brilliant conversation that gives pleasure to the listener and growth to the speaker. One might as well try to express noble ideas in baby talk. If we are to converse well, where shall we get our practice and who shall help us?

The family has an important responsibility in developing in its members the ability to carry on good conversation. Its opportunity for doing this is greater than most of us realize. The members are together frequently. The group is small and an informal situation exists. Members are so interested in each other that they bring to the group the news with which they are all concerned. There are many subjects that may be the basis of most interesting conversation. Current topics of the day; books; magazine and newspaper articles; music, plays, and movies; and local events all furnish such fine possibilities that some families feel justified in levying a fine on members whose talk drifts to the "he said this" and "I said that" level.

It requires time to develop the ability to carry on good conversation—it cannot be done over night. For this reason, children at an early age should be encouraged and given opportunity to have a part in the talk. When a timid one fails to enter in, he should be brought in by questions directed to him. Children very soon show the effect of such training, and often because of it they can express themselves better than many grownups.

Good manners should always be observed in conversation; bad manners should never be allowed. One person should not take up the whole conversation, but all members should have a part. Each should wait his turn and not begin until the speaker is through. Perhaps one of the satisfactions of listening is knowing that sooner or later the speaker will stop and your turn will come. Voices should be kept pleasing and all loud talking be avoided. Sneering and cutting remarks are always out of place. Those engaging in the conversation should not lose their tempers and become angry. When differences of opinion arise, they should be discussed in a friendly way. If conversation cannot be carried on thus, the subject should be changed entirely.

Further "don'ts" for good conversation include the following:

1. Don't ask personal questions.
2. Don't tell off-color stories.
3. Don't boast of yourself or your family.
4. Don't gossip.
5. Don't seem curious about the affairs of others.
6. Don't argue or contradict flatly.

Opportunity for conversation should be provided often in the family, even if the periods are for only a short time. Sometimes it is well to appoint someone to be responsible for directing the conversation. This gives family members good experience, and the opportunity should be passed around.

Activities:

1. (*Class activity*) Divide into "family" groups and practice carrying on a conversation.
2. Evaluate the conversation and make suggestions for improvement.
3. Try to improve your conversation for a given length of time. Report the results to the class.

Problem 3: HOW CAN MUSIC AND READING BE A MEANS OF FAMILY FUN?

Music is a valuable means of family fun. It serves as both recreation and education. Enjoyment can come from taking part or from listening and being entertained.

Music is furnished by various family members by the playing of some musical instrument, such as the piano, the

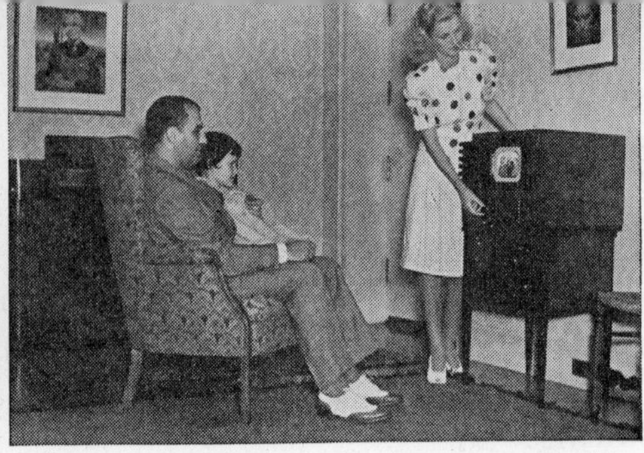

The radio is an important source of family fun for both farm and city families. Television may some day bring us even more enjoyment.

violin or clarinet, or by singing. One person may furnish all the music, or several may contribute. In some families all the members play instruments or sing, and a "family orchestra" or chorus is carried on.

The radio furnishes opportunity for the family to enjoy music together. The musical programs and the comments of the critic may be listened to and then followed by family discussion. The phonograph, too, offers a good means of learning to appreciate music. The records are selected by the family members and can be played again and again, followed by discussions of them.

Although reading is often considered a personal activity, it, too, can be made a family activity and a means of family fun. Like music, reading may be a means of both education and recreation. The reading together of books, plays, and magazine articles is most enjoyable. Each member can take his turn at reading aloud. If a play is read, a good plan is for the various family members to be responsible for reading the parts of different characters. The play then becomes more real to the readers. After not having been done so much as it used to be, reading aloud is again becoming a popular pastime. Certain evenings in the week or month can be set aside for a period of reading together. These need not be long. Some families prefer frequent short periods rather than the longer occasional ones.

A certain family organized itself into a reading club which

met twice each month and was conducted as a real reading club. This proved a source of much pleasure to the family members and also contributed to their education. It was started when the children were young and continued until they were grown. As a result of this family reading club, all the members now have a wide knowledge and appreciation of literature. Discussion by the family of what was read together was a source of much pleasure.

Some families prefer individual reading to reading together. In this case each member reads the same book, play, magazine, or article. When all have finished it, a discussion is held and plans for the next reading are made.

Families should make larger use of music and reading for family fun. Music and literature speak a language which all can come to understand and love, and they can add much to the joy of daily living.

Activities:

1. What radio musical programs would you recommend for family fun? Give reasons for your choice.
2. Make a list of phonograph records that would be a means of the family learning to appreciate music.
3. (*Class activity*) Imagine that the class is a family. Plan and hold a music-appreciation half-hour.
4. What books would you recommend for a family reading club?
5. (*Class activity*) Form into a family reading club and hold a session of the club.

Problem 4: HOW SHALL WE PLAN A PICNIC FOR THE FAMILY?

Some families enjoy picnics so much that they have them often throughout the summer months and on into the fall. The long days make it possible to go in the afternoon and stay until late in the evening.

To start the picnic as a family affair, the plans should be made by the group. The responsibilities that each member will have should be agreed upon and everyone, even the youngest, should have some task assigned to him. The time and place for the picnic should be decided upon in relation to the desires of the whole family rather than to those of any one member. Guests should be invited only upon decision of the group as a whole.

The activities that will be carried on for fun should be planned either by the group or by certain members. Any equipment that will be needed for fun and comfort should be assembled and taken along. Cushions and blankets needed for rest should be included in the list. Games that are suitable for the family picnic include indoor baseball, for which a ball and a bat are needed; the ever-popular game of "catch"; horseshoes, for which 4 or 6 horseshoes and two stakes are needed; and speed-ball or basketball, for which the proper ball is needed. Tag and hide-and-go-seek can be played by a small group. Such games as drop-the-handkerchief and London's bridge are also enjoyable, although the number of people required to play them is more than we find in families today; these games are good for those times when two or more families go together for a picnic.

The means of going to the picnic spot, whether by walking, by car, or by bus, should be decided upon by the group. Some members may wish to go one way and some another. In any case, plans should be so made that people, equipment, and food arrive on time at the place agreed upon.

The clothing to be worn may have to be discussed, unless regular picnic outfits are owned by the family members. The clothing should be comfortable and of the sports type. One should never wear her best clothes on a picnic.

Matches, always, and usually kindling are needed for a picnic. One person should be given the responsibility of providing these.

The food is an important part of the picnic, so the menu

should be carefully planned. Appetites are usually greater in the open, so plenty of food should be provided. Foods that are easily packed, carried, and eaten should be chosen. Most of the food is prepared and made ready to serve before the lunch is packed. The meal should be sufficient in quantity and well balanced. The essential foods should be included. The food should be well prepared and made as attractive as possible. Drinking water should be taken from the home unless one is sure that safe water can be obtained at the picnic site.

Here are two picnic menus:

Meat Sandwiches
Jelly Sandwiches
Potato Salad
Carrot and Celery Strips
Apples and Bananas
Lemonade

Fried Chicken
Potato Chips
Combination Vegetable Salad
Bread-and-Butter Sandwiches
Pickles Olives
Ice Cream Cookies
Coffee or Milk

Families who have picnics often should have special equipment in the way of baskets, vacuum jugs, dishes, and silverware for this purpose. It will make the picnic meal much easier to prepare, pack, and serve. Many use paper dishes and napkins, thus lessening the dishwashing. Some families use special coffeepots, broilers for steaks and weiners, or pancake griddles, so that the cooking of favorite picnic foods may be done without damage to regular household equipment.

The picnic is not over when the food is eaten. There are yet many "kitchen-police" jobs to do in order to clear the food away and pack up. In this work, each family member should share.

Activities:

1. (*Class activity*) Divide into family groups and each group plan a picnic for the "family."
2. Plan a picnic for your own family.

Problem 5: HOW SHALL WE PLAN A PARTY FOR THE FAMILY?

A party for the family! What could be more fun? We think of a party as an entertainment to which we ask guests. Here is one for just the family. Some families have found parties such fun that they have them often.

As was the case in preparing for the family picnic, the group should make the general plans. The responsibilities are then divided among the different members of the family. The time for the party should be suitable for all. After these things have been agreed upon, each should feel it imperative to reserve that time for the family fun. The party should be such that all members can enjoy it. The amount of money to be spent should be discussed and the plans should be so made that the party expense is kept within that allowance.

The entertainment for the party should be carefully planned. If games are to be played, the needed equipment should be assembled. If contests are to be used, they should be prepared and any needed equipment provided. If group singing is to be included, the words and music should be either known or copies made ready.

Suggestions were made on pages 359–364 for the entertainment at a party for guests. Many of these suggestions are suitable for a family party. Contests are especially enjoyed, and many families use them frequently, even without a party. Other contests than those previously described may be planned. Contests may deal with any and all types of subjects: history, geography, current events, art, music, and science. Some families use current events contests to check their information on the events of the day, or they use a music contest to test their knowledge of music. After completing the reading of a book or play, a contest on it is great fun.

A guessing contest is popular. There are all kinds—one guesses the number of beans in a jar, where some object is hidden, or what is wrong with a certain picture. Matching contests are interesting. They consist of two lists of words, the like ones being put together. Sometimes objects are matched with words that describe them. The contest is made more difficult by adding to the list extra words that do not match. An example of a matching contest is given here:

Write in each blank the word from the right-hand column that belongs with the word at the left of the blank.

Needle	__________	Water
Bread	__________	Point
Crackers	__________	Cake
Ice cream	__________	Eye
Hook	__________	Ear
Soap	__________	Cheese
Tree	__________	Butter
Box	__________	Bark

A completion contest is one in which words are omitted and a blank placed there instead. The problem is to supply the missing word. These may be a series of unrelated statements, or a little story can be made in which the correct words are to be inserted in the blanks. The words to be supplied may be all of one type or they may be varied.

The refreshments should be planned and then prepared before the time of the party. Refreshments for a family party are kept very simple. Sometimes only one food is served, such as popcorn, apples, fruit juice, or candy. If more is desired, some pleasing combinations are cider and cookies; cocoa and graham crackers; fruit salad and whipped cream; and caramelized milk and cup cakes. Whatever the refreshments are, they should be attractive and correctly served, as in any other party.

Activities:

1. (*Class activity*) Divide into family groups and each group plan a party for the "family."
2. Plan a party for your own family.
3. Plan and prepare a contest that would be suitable for a family party.

Problem 6: WHO IS RESPONSIBLE FOR THE FAMILY'S FUN?

Family fun has been described as including the joyous mirth, the jokes, and the gay laughter of the home, as well as the quiet enjoyment of just being together. Fixing the responsibility for so much of all that makes life worth living is not easy.

In ancient times, the responsibility of providing the mirth, the jokes, and the laughter of a large household or a court was assigned to a jester or fool. This person had a cap with bells and a mock scepter, from which his own face grinned back at him in a silly manner. He was allowed great freedom of speech, and he was regarded as successful if he could keep everyone merry and gay. No one but the jester was supposed to act the fool. Then, as now, young people were told, "Now don't act the fool." Today in our homes, we have no jester to provide our fun and we are not willing that any one member of the family play such a part. The task of making family fun, then, belongs to no one person, but to the whole family group. As was the case long ago, all family members must help by their attitudes, so that what is meant to be fun will be fun. A clever joke, stunt, or story may be spoiled by the way it is received.

Each member of the family must believe so sincerely in the importance of having fun together that he will be willing to take time and make an effort for it. Small brother, who sadly wonders why no one has time to play a game with him; father, who would like someone to play for his singing;

and grandfather, who wants an opponent in chess—all are expressing a desire for a share in our time for family fun. If we really believe in it, we will find no great difficulty in making time for doing these things together. For our family fun we must be willing to carry any responsibility, either large or small, for the sake of the pleasure of the group. We must share in the variety of tasks that make for family fun.

> We must each be eager to serve as a member of the group—not as the king, nor yet as the jester, but just as a family member. Today we know that family fun is something that must be shared and carried on by every family member if it is to be truly family fun.

Activities:

1. (*Class activity*) Select a "family." Decide what responsibilities for family fun each member could assume.
2. (*Class activity*) Make a plan for the assignment of these responsibilities for a given length of time. Be sure that one person does not do the same thing all the time.
3. Decide what responsibilities for family fun you could assume in your own family.

REFERENCES FOR THE UNIT

Calvert, Maude Richman, *The New First Course in Homemaking.* Atlanta: Turner Smith Co., 1932.

Jensen, Milton B., Jensen, Mildred R., and Ziller, M. Louisa, *Fundamentals of Home Economics.* New York: The Macmillan Co., 1935.

Kinyon, Kate W., and Hopkins, L. Thomas, *Junior Home Problems,* Revised Edition. New York: Benj. H. Sanborn and Co., 1938.

Talbot, Nora, and Others, *Practical Problems in Home Life for Boys and Girls.* New York: American Book Co., 1936.

Trilling, Mabel, Williams, Florence, and Reeves, Grace G., *Problems in Home Economics.* Chicago: J. B. Lippincott Co., 1939.

Lawson, Arthur, *Fun in the Back Yard.* New York: Thomas Y. Crowell and Co., 1938.

Meyer, Jerome S., *Fun for the Family.* New York: Greenberg, Inc., 1938.

SUGGESTED HOME EXPERIENCES

1. Participate in conversation at home and other places outside of school.
2. Score your family's provision for fun.
3. Conduct a family reading club at home.
4. Conduct a music appreciation contest at home.
5. Interest the family in a family night and help put it over.
6. Participate in a family picnic.
7. Participate in a family party at home.
8. Plan and make some games for your family to play.

UNIT 14

SELECTING AND PREPARING THE SCHOOL LUNCH

MANY HIGH SCHOOL PUPILS EAT THEIR noon meal away from home, because they live a long distance from school and the noon period is short. Some schools furnish a room in which lunches brought from home are kept and eaten. Some schools provide cafeterias where a whole meal can be purchased for a small amount of money. In other schools it is possible to buy a part of the lunch, perhaps one food, and bring the rest from home. These plans are all much more satisfactory than the light lunch snatched at a commercial lunch counter or hot dog stand. In such places the quality of the food is often uncertain, the price is usually high, the cleanliness is commonly doubtful, and the chance of obtaining a balanced meal is extremely poor. Unfortunately, there are many pupils who go without food at noon. This is a dangerous practice and very harmful to their health.

Pupils and their parents do not always realize the importance of the school lunch and often give too little attention to the provisions made for it. One needs just as nourishing a noon meal when he is at school as when he is at home. In fact, the demands of his body may be greater. The trip to and from school, the class work at school, and the games in the gymnasium all require much energy, which must be supplied by food. The other food needs of the body continue, regardless of where the pupil is. Successfully meeting these needs in two meals is almost impossible. There is a need for us to know how to select and plan school lunches so that we may protect our health.

Problem 1: WHAT IS A GOOD SCHOOL LUNCH?

Perhaps most of us give less thought to the standard of our school lunch than we do to that of our other meals. If we buy lunch at the school cafeteria, we may have to choose the foods ourselves. The sight of a thick wedge of chocolate pie may cause us to forget the importance of a bowl of vegetable soup or a glass of milk. If we bring our lunch from home, we may grow weary of the daily task of planning lunch, packing it, and carrying the box.

It is so easy to say, "An ice cream cone will be enough for me; I'll not bother with taking a lunch" or "I'll get a hot dog and a bun this noon." However convenient these foods may be to obtain, they do not furnish the proper lunch, and the person who makes this a practice will suffer eventually. Although it requires more effort, thought, and care, the time spent in studying the values of a school lunch and putting good standards into practice brings rich returns.

The school lunch, regardless of where it is obtained, should be sufficient in quantity for our needs. This means that it should contain about one-third of the day's food. The quantity should be as much as we would have if we were eating the meal at home. School lunches are commonly lacking in respect to quantity.

All the essential foods should be well represented. These foods, as you will recall, are milk; vegetables; protein foods, such as eggs, cheese, and meat; fruit; butter; grain products; and water. Recalling what we ate for breakfast and checking the menu for dinner will help us make a wise selection of our lunch. A one-sided or unbalanced meal at lunch time makes it difficult to obtain the needed foods for the day.

The school lunch, like all other meals, should be attractive, appealing to the appetite, and well prepared. Often we fail to apply this rule to the school lunch because it is not a formal meal. This, however, should never make us forget good standards. Unless the food is attractive, appealing, and well prepared, a sufficient amount of it may not be eaten. The conditions under which the lunch is eaten often add little to the pleasure of the meal. Unless the food is very tasty, the quantity eaten may not be sufficient.

The school lunch should have at least one hot dish. In some places school cafeterias make this easy; in others, special lunch box equipment solves the problem. No one needs to be without one hot dish if careful planning is done. If the hot food is purchased at the cafeteria, there is only the problem of selecting it. If it is brought from home, cocoa, caramelized milk, and soups of all kinds can be kept hot in special jars that fit in the lunch box.

The school lunch should contain a variety of foods, and its menu should be changed from day to day. Obtaining variety in the school lunch is more difficult than in the meals served at home. The cafeteria menu may include only a small list of foods. Then, too, the foods suitable for a lunch box are quite limited. Even under these circumstances, most of us could have better school lunches than we do, with a little more thought and effort.

Activities:

1. Plan a good school lunch for an active girl.
2. Plan a good school lunch for a boy who is a member of the basketball team.

Problem 2: HOW SHALL WE SELECT OUR LUNCH AT THE SCHOOL CAFETERIA?

When one eats lunch at the school cafeteria, the responsibility of obtaining a satisfactory lunch falls quite largely upon her. Especially is this true when the right foods may be had at the cafeteria.

Lunch in this modern school cafeteria may be chosen from a tempting array of healthful foods.

In many cafeterias a wide range of food is served. Often suggestions are given for combinations of foods that make good lunches, for a stated price. In other cafeterias a small range of food is served, perhaps not more than three items. Choice here is greatly limited. Some cafeterias provide one regular lunch and also one or more foods for adding to the lunch box brought from home. In still others, only a few simple foods to add to the lunch brought from home are served.

One of the first considerations in choosing a lunch is the amount of money we have to spend. We wish, of course, to get the most for our money in what we buy. School cafeterias usually are operated to accommodate school children and not to make money, so their prices are not high. Even so, if we have only a small amount to spend, we must select carefully to obtain an adequate lunch. We should remember that the most expensive foods are not always the most nourishing ones.

A salad-sandwich plate for lunch may be an attractive combination of color and flavor contrasts, such as the one shown here of a spiced apple, cheese balls, and various kinds of sandwiches.

Our lunch should be selected with other meals of the day in mind. In most families the meal pattern tends to be always much the same, so it is not difficult to know in a general way what will be served for dinner. If for any reason the breakfast was light or not adequate, the lunch should help to make up the lack.

We should select a well-balanced meal with all the essential foods represented in it. The quantity should be sufficient to provide for carrying on the afternoon's schoolwork satisfactorily. If we are having strenuous activity, such as physical education class or basketball practice, we may need a heavier lunch than that required on days with a lighter schedule.

If part of the lunch is brought from home, the choice of food bought at the cafeteria should be made in relation to this. We should know what the lunch from home contains and the food or foods needed to make a satisfactory lunch. It may be milk, soup, vegetables, fruit, sandwiches, ice cream, or other food. Knowing what we should have and what money we have to spend, our choice of food should not be difficult.

Activities:

1. Here are some school cafeteria menus with the prices of the foods; from these select good lunches for ten, fifteen, and twenty cents:

	MAIN DISH	VEGETABLE	SALAD	DESSERT
Monday	Hot Tamale Pie	Buttered Apples *Cauliflower	Head Lettuce * Pear-grape Salad	Melba Peach * Peanut Brittle Fluff
Tuesday	Spanish Omelet	Buttered Peas * Brussels Sprouts	Cole Slaw * Mixed Fruit	Jello with Ice Cream * Date Torte
Wednesday	Beef and Noodles	Creamed Turnips * Broccoli	Perfection Salad *Tomato-Lettuce	Glorified Rice * Whole Apricots
Thursday	Creamed Ham and Celery	Baked Potato * Fried Pineapple Rings	Waldorf Salad * Spanish Peach	Gingerbread * Fruit Plate (banana and grape)
Friday	Boston Baked Beans	Cabbage au Gratin * Banana Scallops	Carrot-raisins * Grapefruit-orange	Baked Apple * Coconut Pie

Four items for 15¢, except those marked with an asterisk (*), which are 5¢ extra.

Chocolate milk, whole milk, or orangeade may be substituted for any item on the 4-for-15¢ plate.

Sandwiches are always available at 5¢.

2. Judge the following lunches which were selected by some pupils at school:

Menu 1

2 "hot dog" sandwiches
1 glass of milk

Menu 2

Cream of tomato soup
Crackers
Lemon pie
Chocolate bar

Menu 3

Chop suey
Baked potato
Cabbage and pineapple salad
Bread and butter
Custard

Menu 4

Baked beans
Head lettuce salad
Bread-and-butter sandwiches
Canned peaches
Milk

Problem 3: HOW SHALL WE PLAN THE SCHOOL LUNCH BROUGHT FROM HOME?

When a group of school children swing up a country lane to the little white schoolhouse or load into a school bus bound for the near-by high school, there is usually a wide variety of lunch baskets, pails, boxes, and bags. If by some magic, all these were suddenly to become transparent, their contents would show even more variety, but in a way the lunches would be more alike than different. The reason for this is that the choice of food for the school lunch brought from home is limited in a number of ways. The food must be prepared several hours ahead of time, packed in a container, carried some distance, and stored awhile before eaten. Many foods are not suitable for a lunch that must be so treated.

Modern lunch boxes offer conveniences for packing and carrying a satisfying lunch. Covered jars and cans and vacuum bottles are features that enable us to carry cooked food and beverages so important in making the meal pleasing. There are many new foods now on the market which can add variety. Our knowledge of what the school lunch should be has also increased. Even so, the variety of foods that can be used is limited. Foods that are generally considered suitable for a lunch box are sandwiches, cold meats, fruits, cookies, cakes and pies, beverages, soups, custards, cheese, and vegetables.

The school lunch should be planned as carefully as any other meal. It should appeal to the appetite as much as possible. Although the lunch is packed for only one family member, or possibly two, it is a meal, and it should be planned as any other one. A balanced meal should be planned. The essential foods should be represented. Provision should be made for one hot dish. This can be done by use of the vacuum bottle or jar in the lunch box or by

Many schools provide rooms for those students who bring lunches that have been prepared at home.

purchasing a hot dish at school. If the lunch is not carefully planned, too often cold leftovers may be hastily collected with no thought of the importance of an attractive and tasty meal. Cold soda biscuits, cold corn bread, cold boiled potatoes or cold baked sweet potatoes can scarcely be combined with other foods to make a pleasing lunch.

Plans for the lunch box should be made well ahead of the time for putting up the lunch, Its preparation need not be difficult if plans are carefully made. Often the lunch food can be prepared along with other meals. Sandwich fillings and salad dressings may be made in quantity sufficient for the week. Salad, meat, and dessert are often the same as those served at the family's noon meal. Often it helps with our planning to provide a lunch box shelf which will hold two or more kinds of sandwich spread; two or more kinds of cookies; nuts; and chocolate bars. Fruit, of course, should always be on hand; of these, a big red or yellow apple is one of the most popular. On the shelf are kept also the paper napkins and the oiled paper needed for packing.

Activities:

1. Judge the following menus for some school lunches brought from home:

Menu 1

Plain raisin-bread sandwiches
Cheese sandwiches
Carrot strips

Menu 2

Hard-boiled egg
Ham sandwiches
Cucumber pickles
Apple pie

Menu 3

Bread-and-butter sandwiches
Meat loaf
Celery stalks
Cottage cheese
Oatmeal cookies
Orange

2. Plan a menu for a schoolgirl's lunch box.

Problem 4: HOW SHALL WE PREPARE MEAT SANDWICHES?

Sandwiches are one of the most common foods in the school lunch. Since they are made of bread, butter, and some kind of filling, they may be substantial and nourishing. A wide variety of sandwiches can be made. Different kinds of bread may be used: rye, whole wheat, nut, raisin, and white. Although peanut butter, jelly, egg, and cheese sandwiches are popular, perhaps those with meat filling are the favorites.

Meat sandwiches are good for the lunch box. They help provide the needed grow or protein foods. Meat used as the filling may be sliced, ground, or chopped with other foods. Beef; pork, including ham; or chicken—in fact, almost any meat—may be used as filling. Meat sandwiches as well as other sandwiches for the lunch box are called closed sandwiches. A closed sandwich is made by spreading a filling, or by placing thin slices of meat or other food, on one slice of buttered bread and covering it with another slice of buttered bread. Bread for sandwiches is better if it is twenty-four hours old. For lunch-box sandwiches the bread is cut 1/3 to 1/2 inch thick and the crusts are not removed. Butter spreads more easily if it is creamed first.

The utensils

Bread knife or butcher knife	Measuring cup
Bread board	Measuring spoons
Spatula	Mixing bowl
Food chopper	Mixing spoon

The recipes for meat sandwiches

Plain meat sandwiches:

Slice in thin pieces cold roast or boiled beef, ham, pork, lamb, or chicken. Place between buttered slices of bread.

One girl—1 sandwich.

Ground meat sandwiches:

Grind 1 c. of pieces of cold cooked meat or fowl. Mix with salad dressing until of consistency to spread on buttered slices of bread. Two small sweet pickles, 1/4 of a green pepper, or 1/2 pimento ground may be added to the mixture if desired.

One girl—1/4 recipe.

Bacon and pickle sandwiches:

6 slices crisp broiled bacon, chopped
3 medium dill pickles, chopped fine or ground in food chopper
1/4 c. cooked salad dressing

Combine and spread on buttered slices of bread

One girl—1/3 recipe

Deviled ham sandwiches:

1/2 c. deviled ham	Salt to taste
1/3 c. ground peanuts	Cooked salad dressing to moisten
2 T. chopped pickle	

Spread on buttered slices of bread.

One girl—1/3 recipe.

Liver sandwiches:

½ lb. cooked liver, ground
4 T. chili sauce
Salt and pepper to taste
½ c. celery chopped fine
2 T. melted butter

Combine and spread on buttered slices of bread.

One girl—¼ recipe.

A sandwich made of two full slices of bread is too large for convenience in eating, so it is usually cut in two. Sandwiches are wrapped in waxed paper if they are to be carried in the lunch box. They are eaten with the fingers. If the sandwich is large, it is broken in several pieces before eating.

Activities:

1. (*Class activity*) Prepare various kinds of plain and ground meat sandwiches.
2. Estimate the cost of each sandwich.
3. Bring other recipes of meat sandwiches to class.

Problem 5: HOW SHALL WE PREPARE EGG AND CHEESE SANDWICHES?

Eggs and cheese and combinations of these with other foods make good lunch-box sandwiches. These foods, too, are high in grow or protein content. They make tasty and colorful sandwiches which help make the meal attractive and appetizing.

The utensils

Mixing bowls
Measuring cups
Measuring spoons
Mixing spoon
Knife
Food chopper
Grater
Spatula
Fruit juicer

The recipes

Egg sandwiches:

1 hard-cooked egg	1/8 t. mustard
1/4 t. salt	3/4 t. salad dressing

Chop the egg and mix with the other ingredients. Spread between buttered slices of bread.

One girl—entire recipe.

Egg-yolk sandwiches:

3 hard-cooked egg yolks	1 t. lettuce, parsley, or other greens, chopped
2 T. butter or substitute	3 T. lemon juice
Salt and pepper to taste	

Mash the egg yolk and mix thoroughly with the other ingredients. Spread between buttered slices of bread.

One girl—1/3 recipe.

Egg and ham sandwiches:

1/2 c. chopped or ground cooked ham	Salt and pepper to taste
4 hard-cooked eggs, chopped	Salad dressing to moisten
2 T. chopped green pepper or olives	

Mix and spread between buttered slices of bread.

One girl—1/4 recipe.

Egg and pickle sandwiches:

1 hard-cooked egg, chopped fine
1 T. chopped pickle (cucumber, onion, or beet)
Salt and pepper to taste
Salad dressing to moisten

Mix and spread between buttered slices of bread.

One girl—entire recipe.

Scrambled egg sandwiches.

Spread scrambled eggs between buttered slices of bread, allowing one egg for each sandwich.

One girl—one egg or one sandwich.

Plain cheese sandwiches:

1. Spread Philadelphia cream cheese between buttered slices of bread.
2. Spread cottage cheese between buttered slices of bread.
3. Mix grated cheese with enough salad dressing to moisten. Spread between buttered slices of bread.

One girl—one sandwich.

Combination cheese sandwich fillings:

1. 2 T. grated cheese
   1 t. chopped olives
   Salad dressing to moisten
2. 2 T. grated cheese
   1 t. chopped pimento
   Salad dressing to moisten
3. 2 T. grated cheese
   2 t. chopped nuts
   Salad dressing to moisten
4. 1 hard-cooked egg, chopped
   1 T. grated cheese
   1 t. chopped pickle
   Salad dressing to moisten

Mix and spread between buttered slices of bread. The amount given in each recipe will fill one sandwich.

One girl—one sandwich.

Many other combinations of both eggs and cheese can be made for sandwiches. Any of us will find it easy to work out some interesting sandwich fillings ourselves. Egg and cheese sandwiches are wrapped and eaten in the same manner as meat sandwiches.

Activities:

1. (*Class activity*) Prepare various kinds of egg and cheese sandwiches.
2. Compare the cost of the different sandwiches.
3. Suggest other combinations of egg and cheese sandwich fillings.

Problem 6: HOW SHALL WE PREPARE SWEET SANDWICHES?

Sweet sandwiches introduce another flavor and type of food into the school lunch. As a rule, the sweet sandwich is a popular one and makes a pleasing variety in the lunch. Whole wheat bread is generally used for sweet sandwiches.

The utensils

Mixing bowls
Measuring cups
Measuring spoons
Mixing spoons
Spatula
Knife
Fruit juicer
Food chopper
Grater

The recipes

Raisin and peanut butter sandwiches:

1 c. raisins
1/8 t. salt
1/3 c. peanut butter
6 T. orange juice

Put raisins through the food chopper. Mix all the ingredients together thoroughly. If the mixture is too thick to spread, add more orange juice. Spread the filling between buttered slices of bread. This filling will keep several days if stored in a cool place.

One girl—1/6 recipe.

Fig and nut sandwiches:

1 c. dried figs
1/4 c. chopped nuts
4 T. strained honey
1 T. lemon juice
2 T. cooked salad dressing
Salt to taste

Grind the figs. Combine with other ingredients and mix thoroughly. Spread between buttered slices of bread. This filling will keep several days if stored in a cool place.

One girl—1/6 recipe.

Cheese and marmalade sandwiches:

1/2 c. grated cheese
1/2 c. orange or other marmalade
1/4 c. cream or cooked salad dressing

Combine cheese and cream or cooked salad dressing. Spread one slice of bread with this mixture. Spread the other slice with marmalade. Put the two slices together.

One girl—1/6 recipe.

Date and pineapple sandwiches:

1/2 c. chopped dates
3 T. grated or crushed pineapple

Combine thoroughly. If the mixture is too thick to spread, add pineapple juice until it is of spreading consistency. Spread between buttered slices of bread.

One girl—1/4 recipe.

Pineapple and peanut sandwiches:

1/3 c. grated or crushed pineapple
4 T. peanut butter
Salt to taste

Mix until well blended. Spread between buttered slices of bread.

One girl—1/3 recipe.

Banana and nut sandwiches:

1 banana
1 T. peanut butter
Cooked salad dressing to moisten

Mash the banana to a pulp. Mix with the other ingredients thoroughly. Spread between buttered slices of bread.

One girl—1/3 recipe.

Sweet sandwiches are wrapped and eaten in the same manner as the other sandwiches.

Activities:

1. (*Class activity*) Prepare various kinds of sweet sandwiches.
2. Determine the cost of each sandwich.
3. Suggest other combinations for sweet sandwich fillings.

Problem 7: HOW SHALL WE PREPARE EGGS FOR THE LUNCH BOX?

Eggs are always a good lunch-box food. If we are to have one egg daily, we should include them often in the school lunch. Plain, hard-cooked egg is perhaps most commonly prepared for use in the school lunch box. Eggs so prepared are easy to carry and are also pleasing to the taste. However, if the school lunch menu includes them regularly, they become tiresome. Ways of varying the hard-cooked egg are important and desirable in giving interest to the lunch.

The utensils

Two pans
Measuring cup
Measuring spoons
Mixing bowl
Spatula
Mixing spoon
Fruit jar

The recipes

Hard-cooked eggs: see page 217
Deviled or stuffed egg:

1 hard-cooked egg
¼ t. salt
⅛ t. mustard
¼ t. butter, melted
⅓ t. vinegar or cooked salad dressing

Remove the shell from the egg. Cut the egg in half and remove the yolk. Mash the egg yolk and add other ingredients. Mix thoroughly. Refill the egg whites with the mixture. Put halves together and hold in place with two toothpicks.

One girl—1 egg.

Pickled eggs:

Hard-cooked eggs
Liquor from pickled beets to cover

Remove the shells from the eggs; put the eggs in a fruit jar. Heat beet-pickle liquor and pour over the eggs. Put the lid on the jar and set it aside in a cool place for 24 hours, or longer if necessary, for color and flavor to penetrate the eggs.

Pickle liquor from cucumber pickles, either sweet or sour, makes good-flavored pickled eggs, but the color is not so pleasing as when the beet liquor is used.

One girl—1 egg.

The serving

Hard-cooked, deviled, and pickled eggs are wrapped in waxed paper. When a part of the lunch-box meal, they are eaten with the fingers.

Activities:

1. (*Class activity*) Prepare eggs in various ways for a school lunch box.
2. What is the cost per egg?
3. Find other ways of preparing eggs for a lunch box.

Problem 8: HOW SHALL WE PREPARE MEAT LOAF?

Meat loaf is a frequently served food at luncheon and dinner and is also widely used as a lunch-box food. It is as good cold as it is hot. It slices nicely and is eaten plain or in sandwiches. There are various recipes for meat loaf. These vary in the meats used, in the spices and seasoning required, and in the other foods added. Most of the recipes include raw egg and milk to help hold the ingredients together in a loaf. The recipe given here is simple and easily prepared.

Meat loaf is good either hot or cold.

The utensils

Mixing bowl
Measuring cup
Measuring spoons
Mixing spoon
Baking pan or roaster

The recipe for meat loaf

Ingredients:

- 2 lbs. ground beef
- 4 t. melted butter or substitute
- 2 eggs, slightly beaten
- ⅓ t. pepper
- 2 c. coarsely broken crackers
- 2 c. milk
- 2 t. salt
- 4 slices bacon

Method:

Combine all ingredients but the bacon. Mix well and form into a loaf. Place in a pan or roaster. Lay slices of bacon across the top. Bake in a moderate oven (375°F.) 1½ to 2 hours.

Two girls—¼ recipe.

The serving

Just before packing the lunch box, cut slices ⅓ inch thick from the cold loaf and wrap each in waxed paper. When it is a part of the lunch-box meal, the meat is eaten with the fingers.

Activities:

1. (*Class activity*) Prepare meat loaf.
2. Practice cutting loaf in slices suitable for a lunch box.
3. Determine the cost per slice.
4. How does your mother's recipe for meat loaf differ from this one?

Problem 9: HOW SHALL WE PREPARE RAW VEGETABLES AND FRUITS FOR THE LUNCH BOX?

Raw vegetables and fruits are being eaten more and more. This is partly due to our knowledge of their food value. It is also due to the fact that many vegetables and fruits are more pleasing raw than cooked. The frequent use of raw vegetables and fruits in the lunch box helps us balance our diet. They also have the advantage of being easy to prepare and carry. Some of the vegetables commonly eaten raw are tomatoes, onions, carrots, celery, radishes, cabbage, and cauliflower. Some fruits commonly eaten raw are oranges, apples, pears, plums, and peaches.

The utensils needed for the preparation of these raw foods are brushes and bowls for cleaning and washing; paper or cloth towels for drying; and knives for cutting. The preparation required for fruits and tomatoes carried whole includes cleaning, washing, and drying. Sometimes oranges are pared, but as a rule they are not.

Many vegetables must be cut or broken into small pieces. The vegetables are cleaned and washed, scraped if needed, dried, and cut in convenient and attractive shapes and sizes. Carrots and celery are cut in strips. Cauliflower is broken into small pieces, and cabbage is cut into squares, rectangles, or strips. Radishes are usually left whole. Raw vegetables are wrapped in waxed paper for the lunch box. They are eaten with the fingers. If salt is desired for vegetables and other foods in the school lunch, a jar or can that closes tightly should be used.

Activities:

1. (*Class activity*) Prepare various raw vegetables for a lunch.
2. Why should raw vegetables and fruits be carried frequently in the lunch box?

Problem 10: HOW SHALL WE PREPARE BAKED BEANS?

Baked beans were a common food in Colonial days. Taken hot from the oven for Saturday night supper, they were a tasty dish. Warmed over and served with codfish cakes Sunday morning, they were still enjoyed. If there were any boys and girls who failed to find them good on Tuesday or Wednesday when the leftovers were warmed up again or made into soup, history does not tell us. Cooked all day in the community oven or bean hole, the beans developed a nutty flavor and a rich brown color. That we still like the flavor of the colonial bean is shown by the advertising appeal of "Boston Baked Beans" or "Bean Hole

A dish of baked beans is a tasteful and delicious meal in itself.

Beans" used by the commercial canners. Though the time of cooking has been shortened, several hours are still necessary to prepare baked beans. Today, as then, they are good hot or cold and boys and girls find them a tasty lunch-box food.

The utensils

Mixing bowl
Kettle
Measuring cup
Measuring spoons
Knife
Deep baking dish or bean pot

The recipe for baked beans

Ingredients:

2 c. navy beans
⅓ lb. salt pork sliced thin, or bacon
¼ c. molasses
¾ t. mustard
2 t. salt
1 c. boiling water

Method:

Wash the beans. Cover them with warm water. Place them on the fire and simmer until the skins are easily pierced. Drain off the water. Place several slices of salt pork or bacon on bottom of baking dish or bean pot. Add the beans.

Place the remainder of the meat on top of the beans. Mix molasses, salt, mustard, and boiling water. Pour this over the beans. Add boiling water to cover. Cover the baking dish or bean pot. Bake in a slow oven (325°F.) 6 to 8 hours. Uncover and bake 15 or 20 minutes.

Two girls—¼ or ⅓ recipe.

The serving

Baked beans are carried in the lunch box in an individual covered glass or jar. They are eaten with a fork.

Activities:

1. (*Class activity*) Prepare baked beans.
2. Determine the cost of the recipe.
3. Estimate the number of servings in the prepared dish.
4. Check several recipes for baked beans. Note how they are alike, and how they are different.

Problem 11: HOW SHALL WE PREPARE FILLED COOKIES?

Filled cookies are made by spreading a fruit paste between two layers of cookie dough, and then baking them.

The utensils

Mixing bowl
Measuring cup
Measuring spoons
Cooking spoon
Mixing spoon
Wooden spoon
Saucepan
Sifter
Rolling pin
Breadboard
Spatula
Baking sheet or pie pans
Cake rack

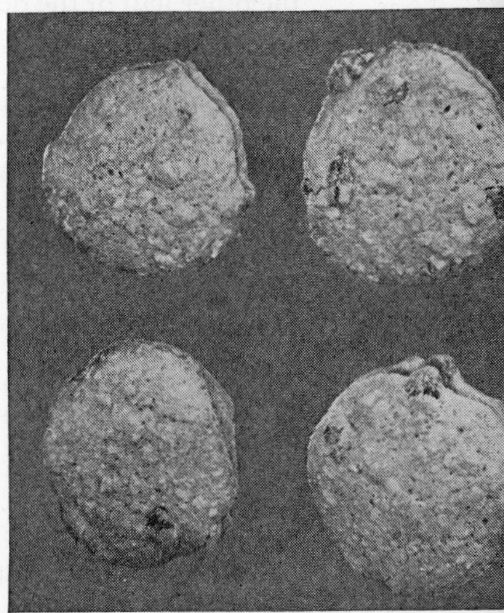

Filled cookies are always popular in the school lunch.

The recipe for filled cookies

Ingredients for the filling:

1 lb. dates
½ c. sugar
½ c. water

Method:

Remove the seeds from the dates. Add sugar and water. Cook to a paste over a low flame, stirring constantly. When done, remove from fire to cool.

Two girls—¼ recipe.

Ingredients for the cookie dough:

2½ c. oatmeal
2½ c. white flour
1 c. butter or substitute
1 t. salt
½ c. water
1 t. soda
1 c. brown sugar

Method:

Cream the butter; add sugar and salt. Cream until smooth. Mix soda and water. Mix flour and oatmeal. Add the two mixtures alternately to the butter and sugar.

Flour the board and roll the dough out thin. Spread one-half the rolled dough with the fruit filling, using a spatula. Turn the other half of the dough over that spread with the filling, using a spatula.

Cut in strips 3 or 4 inches long and 1 to 1¼ inches wide. If preferred, cut the dough with a round cookie cutter. Spread with filling and cover with another round cut piece of dough.

Place on an ungreased baking sheet or on pie pans. Bake in a hot oven (400°F.) until a golden brown. Remove with a spatula to a cake rack to cool.

Two girls—¼ recipe.

The serving

Filled cookies are wrapped in waxed paper for the lunch box. They are eaten with the fingers.

Activities:

1. (*Class activity*) Prepare filled cookies.
2. Determine the cost of these cookies.
3. How many cookies can be made from the recipe.

Problem 12: HOW SHALL WE PREPARE BROWNIES?

Brownies are another type of cookie greatly enjoyed. They are not dropped from a spoon as the oatmeal cookies, nor rolled and cut as the filled cookies were. They are baked in a shallow pan and are cut after baking. They are rich cookies and remind one somewhat of chocolate nut fudge.

The utensils

Mixing bowl	Knife
Measuring cup	Double boiler
Measuring spoons	Mixing spoon
Sieve	Dover egg beater and bowl
Spatula	Shallow baking pan, pie pan, or cake pan

The recipe for brownies

Ingredients:

2 sq. chocolate	½ c. flour
½ c. butter or substitute	1 c. chopped nuts
3 eggs	⅛ t. salt
1 c. sugar	¼ t. fat for oiling pan

Method:

Melt chocolate and butter over hot water. Separate eggs, beat yolks until light. Add sugar, salt, melted chocolate, and butter to egg yolks. Mix well.

Mix flour and nuts. Add to the other mixture. Beat whites of eggs until stiff and fold into the mixture. Pour into oiled pan in a thin layer. Bake in a moderate oven (375°F.) about 15 minutes. Cut into squares. Cool. Remove from the pan.

Two girls—⅓ recipe.

The serving

Brownies, like filled cookies, are wrapped in waxed paper for the lunch box. They too are eaten with the fingers.

Activities:

1. (*Class activity*) Prepare brownies.
2. How do brownies differ from other cookies we have made?
3. Compare the cost of brownies with the cost of other cookies.

Problem 13: HOW SHALL WE PREPARE INDIVIDUAL RAISIN PIES?

Perhaps the first you ever learned about pies was from the old nursery rhyme about blackbirds in a pie:

Sing a song of sixpence,
Pocket full of rye.
Four and twenty blackbirds
Baked in a pie.
When the pie was opened, the
birds began to sing.
Wasn't that a dainty dish to
set before the king?

There are, so far as we know, no recipes for blackbird pie. You wouldn't want it in your school lunch if there were. Like the sadly disappointed king, you would like a pie with crust tender and flaky and filled with tasty fruit, well-sweetened and flavored. For a lunch-box meal you would want the filling so firm that it would not run and be difficult to handle. Raisin pie is pleasing in flavor and also has these other qualities.

The utensils

Mixing bowl	Breadboard
Measuring cup	Saucepan
Measuring spoons	Cooking spoon
Knives or spatulas	Double boiler
Sifter	Individual pie pans or muffin tins
Rolling pin	

The recipe for individual raisin pies

Ingredients for pie dough or pastry:

1½ c. flour	½ c. lard or similar fat
¼ c. cold water	½ t. salt
¼ to ½ t. baking power	

Method:

Sift flour, salt, and baking powder together. Cut in the fat with two knives or spatulas until mixture is coarse and granular. Add water gradually, working it in lightly with spatula or finger-tips until the small grainlike balls hang together in one large ball. Use no more water than necessary to hold the mixture together. Turn half of the dough onto a lightly floured board.

Roll out 1/8 inch thick. Cut in pieces about the size of pie or muffin pans. Line pans with dough.

Roll the remainder for top crusts. When filling has been placed in lower crust, put the top crust in place. Using a fork, crimp the edges together, thus binding the two crusts together. Cut small slits or holes in top to allow steam to escape.

Two girls—1/2 recipe.

Ingredients for raisin filling:

3/4 c. raisins	3 t. flour
4 t. lemon juice	1 t. butter
1 c. sugar	1/8 t. salt
1 c. hot water	

Method:

Combine sugar, salt, and flour in the top of the double boiler. Add hot water slowly, stirring constantly. Cook over hot water until clear and thick. Add lemon juice, butter, and raisins. Stir well. Fill pastry-lined pans with mixture. Cover with top crust. Bake in a hot oven (425°F.) about 25 minutes until a golden brown. Use a spatula to remove from the pan.

Two girls—1/2 recipe.

The serving

The pie should be placed on a small paper plate and, when cold, wrapped in waxed paper for the lunch box. It is eaten with a fork or with the fingers.

Activities:

1. (*Class activity*) Prepare individual raisin pies.
2. Determine the cost of each pie.
3. Is this a light or heavy dessert? Why?

Problem 14: HOW SHALL WE PACK THE LUNCH BOX?

The packing of the lunch box is a most important part of preparing the school lunch. Even though suitable foods have been selected and properly prepared, the packing

These boys know that they will enjoy their school lunch. Good things to eat are being carefully and attractively assembled.

should be given special attention if the lunch is to be entirely satisfactory. The lunch should be so packed that the food will be kept clean and free from spoiling. Its normal flavor, texture, and form should be preserved. The content of the lunch box receives such bouncing and bumping as to shake it almost to pieces unless it is carefully packed. If the lunch box is not tightly closed, dust may sift in, and cockroaches or flies may share the meal.

There are many convenient and attractive lunch boxes that are not expensive in which the safe carrying of the food is possible. These offer many advantages over the "dinner pail." A lunch box that can be thoroughly and easily cleaned should always be bought. The box should be equipped so that milk and a hot dish can be carried in good condition if these cannot be obtained at school. Some boxes have food jars and cans and vacuum bottles as a part of their equipment. These are light in weight and fit exactly in the box.

The lunch should be so packed in the box that the food remains in good condition. Nothing is more unpleasant than food mashed into bits, or one food spilled over the rest of the lunch. Almost all solid foods not packed in a special closed jar or can will remain in better condition if wrapped separately in waxed paper. This applies to sandwiches, cookies, meat, and eggs. Fresh fruit should be wrapped, too, if soft and if the skin is easily broken. Prepared foods or foods of a liquid nature should be carried in covered jars. Milk, chocolate, soup, fruit juices, sauces, baked beans, and custards require this type of packing.

Those foods which are to be kept hot should be placed in a vacuum bottle or the vacuum division of the box. Foods and jars heavy in weight should be placed at the bottom of the box; those lighter in weight should be placed on top.

The packing should be such that the lunch is appealing and attractive in appearance. Colored waxed paper and paper napkins help in this. If the daily lunch box can look as pretty as the picnic lunch prepared for a special occasion, it will bring similar satisfaction and pleasure.

Activities:

1. (*Class activity*) Working in groups, pack several lunch boxes.
2. Determine the cost of each lunch packed.
3. Judge each lunch according to the standards for a good lunch.

REFERENCES FOR THE UNIT

Calvert, Maude Richman, *The New First Course in Homemaking.* Atlanta: Turner Smith Co., 1932.

Jensen, Milton B., Jensen, Mildred R., and Ziller, M. Louisa, *Fundamentals of Home Economics.* New York: The Macmillan Co., 1935.

Matthews, Mary Lockwood, *The New Elementary Home Economics.* Boston: Little, Brown and Co., 1937.

SUGGESTED HOME EXPERIENCES

1. Prepare at home the recipes and dishes prepared at school for the school lunch.
2. Assume responsibility for preparing food at home for school lunches.
3. Assume responsibility for packing lunch boxes.

UNIT 15

HELPING TO SELECT AND PURCHASE OUR CLOTHING

YEARS AGO, MUCH OF THE CLOTHING worn was made from cloth woven in the home. The girl of those days was familiar with the weaving process and knew the history of the fibers used.

Flax from the field yielded the linen; the fleece from the flock, the wool; and in the deep south, the white fluff of the cotton plant was picked and torn from its seeds for use in making thread and fabric. Of course, the girl herself did not share in every process, but she knew firsthand what was required to make good cloth.

Today we buy our materials in the store or we buy the garment ready-made, lacking personal experience with the weaving process and often knowing little about the fiber and almost nothing about the conditions under which the garments were made. We find it necessary to have some guides as to the best kind of material to buy, either in the piece goods or in the factory-made garment. Substitution of poor yarns has become so common and successful a practice in weaving many fabrics that the experienced shopper is many times deceived in what she buys. As schoolgirls, we are inexperienced shoppers. Unless we study and work to become well informed, we will find our inexperience a real handicap in the important business of getting what we want.

Problem 1: HOW CAN WE BE GOOD SHOPPERS?

We have often seen the shopper who looks for a dress with no idea as to the color, size, or style of dress desired. She has not estimated the amount of money that she can spend for the dress, nor has she studied her wardrobe to know the kind of a dress that she needs. Because of lack of information she takes an undue amount of the saleswoman's time, perhaps delays you or others in their shopping, and finally goes home with a garment that she does not want.

A good shopper has a clear notion of what she wants to buy. She knows that the skirt she is looking for is one she plans to use for all-service wear. She will wear it to school and to the all-school picnic; it may be the same skirt that is a part of her costume for Sunday School on Sunday morning. She will recall her experience with a previously purchased garment, which was soft and woolly and snagged on all the bushes when worn to the picnic.

A good shopper will be familiar with the guides that we have in our buying. A good shopper knows how much money she has to spend; she is only one part of a family, no doubt sharing the family's money. So the money to be spent for clothing is limited, and it cannot be increased without unfairness to others. She will recognize that the heavy material filled with starch, after laundering, will be a sleazy, thin, and loosely woven material. She will know that the fabric free from starch and firmly woven will not have its present appearance destroyed by laundering.

The good shopper will know that such factors as labor conditions—such as the young child doing an adult's work but working for extremely low wages—influence the price one pays for ready-made garments. The blouse she can buy for 59 cents may be a product of child labor. As a good citizen she wishes to discourage child labor, and seeks

A code of the shopper may well cover the following points:

1. Shop early.
2. Know what you want.
3. Know what you can spend.
4. Be courteous.
5. Know how to judge quality.
6. Know factors influencing cost.
7. Do not ask for unusual privileges.

labels that indicate the garment was made under good labor conditions.

The shopper should remember at all times to be courteous and well-mannered. Even though we may feel that the salesperson is a public servant, our own good breeding should keep us from being rude. The courteous shopper is one who buys or shops at the time of day when the crowds are smallest and the salesperson is less busy. Only a poor and thoughtless shopper would buy Christmas gifts on Christmas Eve.

Salespeople enjoy waiting on the person who knows what she wants, the price she can pay, and how to ask for or about the goods being sold. The traits necessary to become a good shopper can be developed in each individual.

Activities:

1. Make a list of the things you would do if you were going to town to buy a dress for yourself.
2. Write a paragraph describing a good salesperson.
3. Write a paragraph describing a good shopper.

Problem 2: WHAT INFLUENCES US IN PURCHASING CLOTHING?

Our desire to be like others often leads us to make unwise purchases; the bright blue dress, in so popular a color, when purchased is unbecoming to the wearer and she soon tires of the color. Because the small hat bought by our chum is

We may choose slips with shoulder straps or with shaped shoulders. This is one of the many buying problems which we must be able to solve.

becoming to her does not mean that we, too, should make a similar purchase. Too often we are influenced by the opinions and choices of our friends. The dress we bought because Mary admired it may not be the one we would enjoy the most, or could afford to buy. Sometimes our friend's ideas are valuable, but we should learn to make our own decisions.

Fashion often directs our purchases of clothing and often proves a poor guide. However, adaptations of prevailing fashion may be purchased and worn successfully by the average individual. Although each season has one or more prevailing colors which are recognized as good style, our selection must be governed by what we can wear. A slight change in the prevailing fashion not only suits us, but is also a way of lengthening the possible wear of a garment. Extreme styles soon go out of fashion. However, one should be careful when buying and not permit high-powered salesmanship to influence one's choice of clothing. Flattering words and flowery compliments often influence our choice. We want to believe we are like our favorite moving picture star and we accept such statements without questioning.

We should remember that the salesperson's business is to sell, not necessarily to direct us to a wise choice. She is not informed about our family income nor about the rest of our wardrobe. Hence she cannot advise us fully or well.

We well know the saying "a dollar down and a dollar when you have it" has sold many an article that should not have been purchased. At the time the purchase is made, it seems an easy way to buy additional things. But as the payments come due, stretching our money to meet all our obligations becomes difficult. We should remember that articles sold on the "easy payment plan" must cost more in the end than those sold for cash. We must pay cash value plus an additional carrying charge. We should not be swayed by appeals to buy now and pay later.

Money influences us in purchasing clothing. A limited amount of money necessitates careful consideration of the articles on hand and those to be bought. We know a low-priced article does not always mean a saving of money. The value of a garment can only be estimated by the satisfaction it gives the wearer and the amount of service it may render. To buy highly advertised goods may mean that we pay in excess of what the garment is worth—some of this money must go for advertising.

Each individual has a standard of living which influences her expenditures for clothing as well as for other items. "Keeping up with the Joneses" is a saying too often true of many people in their standard of living. Because the Joneses make a large outlay for dress, others tend to ape the Joneses and do likewise. This may mean that they will do without something else really of greater value to them.

The desire for show and display is clearly shown in those cases where garments are purchased which will give an appearance of wealth and no signs of work. The best influence for purchasing clothing is an understanding that directs us to buy the articles that we need at a price that we can afford to pay. Our needs are governed by our activities and the standard of living that we maintain.

Activities:

1. Why did you buy the coat you now have? Do you consider your reasons good? Why?

2. Secure some samples of cotton material of different prices and compare their qualities.

Problem 3: WHAT SHALL WE DO BEFORE WE SHOP?

There is a big difference between window-shopping and real shopping. Almost anyone can window-shop with some satisfaction. The window display can be approved or criticised as something quite apart from our own life. It may show a party on the sands of a winter resort in Florida, and we look at it and comment, "I don't like the green bathing suit" or "Oh, isn't that large bright sunshade and matching beach cape clever!" If the window presents a skiing scene, we pass judgment on the snowsuits lightly, saying, "Oh, I like the red one" or "I wouldn't have the brown one." Prices, good wearing qualities, needs based on activities, wardrobe lacks, suitability, and many more things can be disregarded when we window-shop. There are no bills to pay, no clothes that must be worn for a season or more, and no wardrobe plan to influence our choices. We "spend" our preferences freely and carelessly.

Real shopping is quite a different matter. Our decisions or choices are final, and we will well be reminded of our wisdom or folly day after day. We cannot, therefore, proceed as if we were window-shopping. We find that fact rather than fancy is the sound basis of choice. Before we shop we should analyze our needs.

We will list what we do both in and out of school hours, both work and play; we will include what we do on Saturday and Sunday and also any unusual occasions which bring special clothing needs. Before we say our list is complete we will check it to see that the activities include rest; out-of-door recreation in rain, storm, and wind; hiking and swimming; cooking; or gardening. Then, we will list the clothing needed for each activity, underscoring the items that we will use most. Our list will range from anklets to zipper galoshes and from galoshes to hats.

If we owned no wardrobe this list would be our shopping guide. Fortunately most of us have a wardrobe that makes provision for many of our activities. We should now check our present wardrobe, following the list previously made. We may find that we have aprons, swim suits, berets, and galoshes to spare, but that we lack stockings, school dresses, and underwear. These lacks will make up the list of items to be bought. If the list of needs is long, it may have to be checked again to determine what items are to be purchased immediately and what items may be purchased later.

Now we must turn to the money we have to spend for clothing. If we have a clothing allowance, we will plan its division among the various items. Perhaps our division among the items of the list would be like the following:

Shoes (tan)	$4.00
Hose (2 pair brown)	1.50
Dress (brown wool)	5.00
Kerchief (rust-green)	.25
Scarf (brown-green)	.50
	$11.25

This plan for spending will not be the same for any two individuals, and will be subject to change, of course. Before we shop, we will check our plan, as we checked our list, by looking at newspapers and magazines, and at displays in shops, to know what are acceptable styles for us, and whether or not our price range is accurate and our color choices good. Last, but not least, we will study available information on labeling so that we can know what we are buying. There are many kinds of labels. Some tell us much; some tell us little. We will try to find labels that are informative. The first label we will see probably will be the brand name under which the goods is sold—such as, for example, "Betty Brown Shoes," "Step Hi Hose," and "Dainty Lady Dress." If we have had satisfactory experience with a brand, we are glad to buy articles bearing that brand again. But brand names give us little information. We find a label that tells something about the fabrics, such as "preshrunk," "sunfast," or "100% wool." Some articles are labeled to indicate that good working conditions existed in the factory where the article was made. Some articles such as dresses and hats are labeled indicating that the design is registered and hence not to be widely copied. Shoes, hats, dresses, coats, and many other articles are labeled more or less correctly as to size. So we can see that there are many kinds of information which we will need if we are to buy wisely, and which we should have before we go to shop.

Activities:

1. How do you decide how much to spend for various articles of clothing?
2. What is meant by being "systematic in buying"?
3. Make a shopping list for your next shopping.

Problem 4: HOW SHALL WE SELECT AND PURCHASE OUR UNDERGARMENTS?

We know that the material for underwear should be easy to launder and fast in color. Our choice of material will no doubt be influenced by personal preference and the price we can afford to pay. Woven and knit fabrics are used for underwear. Woven materials familiar to all include cotton, rayon crepe, and silk crepe. Cotton batiste and longcloth are common examples; these fabrics come in many colors, in plain and crinkle weaves.

The following qualities are desired in woven undergarments:

1. Turned-under, double-stitched flat fell seams.
2. Strong plackets and fastenings.
3. Reinforced crotches.
4. Strong double trimmings.
5. Shaped well to fit the body.

Knit garments with their stocking-like construction are even more popular. This is no doubt caused by the ease of taking care of the knit underwear. Knit underwear, in addition to the ease in laundering, is more elastic than the woven, fits better, allows more freedom of motion, and wrinkles less. The following qualities are desired in knit undergarments:

1. Flat-locked seams.
2. Plain hem or facing.
3. Reinforced crotches, underarms, and edges.
4. Simple, durable trimmings.

The cost of garments depends upon the kind and quality of material from which they are made, the construction and type of workmanship, and the exclusiveness of the design. The slip that sells for $2.95 may not be made of any better material than one selling at $1.95, but the workmanship and design may be such as to cause the difference in price.

The labels on undergarments should be read carefully. The laundering process recommended should be followed to insure the best wear of the garment. Different methods of denoting size are used for various articles of underwear. Slips may be labeled by specific bust size; panties are labeled as small, medium, and large. The purchaser should know not only her size, but also the class grouping of small, medium, and large in which her size will place her. The following items should be considered when purchasing undergarments:

1. Wearing qualities.
2. Appearance.
3. Ease of laundering.
4. Fit.
5. Cost.
6. Fastness of color.
7. Season and occasions on which to be worn.
8. Type of garment to be worn under.

Activities:

1. What do you take into consideration when you buy your underwear? How does your list of qualities compare with the one given?
2. What size slips and panties do you buy? How did you decide upon this size? What indications do you have that the size is correct?

Problem 5: HOW SHALL WE SELECT AND PURCHASE OUR DRESSES?

Unlike the selection and purchasing of underwear, the choice of dresses is a responsibility which we may wish to share with our mother or older sisters. The choice of a dress brings up certain questions. Again, we must know how much money we have to spend and the wear that we expect to get from the garment. The dress we purchase should fit in with the rest of our wardrobe. The dress should not require the purchase of complete new accessories, unless this has been planned. It should be attractive, suitable to our needs, and becoming to us.

The material, construction, and workmanship should be

carefully examined before trying on the dress. Such practice saves time for both the customer and the salesperson. Much time is lost if after you have tried on a dress and are about to purchase it you discover that it is made with narrow seams and has poor workmanship. In addition to such examination of the dress, one should inquire about the fiber used, the possible shrinkage, the weighting, color fastness to sun and water, the effect of perspiration, and the method of cleaning recommended. Some of this information may be found on labels. The salesperson may be able to answer these questions. But full information should be obtained about as many of these points as possible.

The purchase of the ready-made dress presents a different problem from that which is met in buying material for a dress. We have no opportunity to make any tests on the material of the ready-made dress. Ready-made garments give us the advantage of being able to see how we look in them before buying. Thus we can determine the becomingness of style, color, and fit.

Extreme styles, color, and fabrics often limit the satisfactory wear of a garment to one season. It is never wise to invest much money in such a garment. The amount of care a garment will need should also be considered when purchasing a dress. A delicate blue wool dress to be worn to school will require much more care than a navy blue one and the chances are that the latter will look well for a longer time.

Certain dresses on the market are made of guaranteed materials and with guaranteed workmanship. The manufacturer agrees to stand back of his product according to the terms of his label. In buying such a dress, we must expect to pay more for it than for a dress which is not guaranteed. Although the first cost may be greater, the service given by the dress may prove to be enough to justify the added expense.

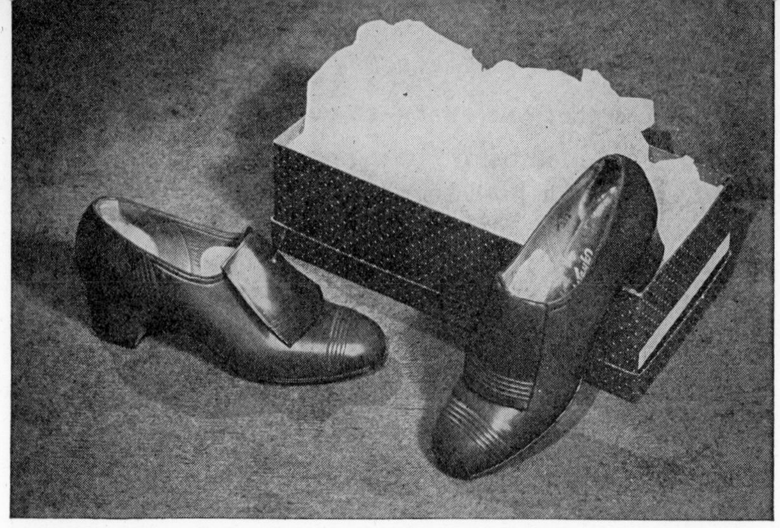

Even new shoes should feel comfortable if they have been purchased intelligently.

Activities:

1. Who helps you to select and buy your dresses?
2. What procedure do you follow before you go to town to buy a dress?
3. When buying a ready-made dress what information do you require before making the purchase? Why?

Problem 6: HOW SHALL WE SELECT AND PURCHASE OUR FOOTWEAR?

Footwear includes all the articles worn on the feet: hose, short and long, sturdy and sheer; shoes, some broad of sole and heel, well-built of heavy leather, and others daintily patterned of silver kid bands; rubbers, which cover the sole and cap the toe; and zipper galoshes, which enclose the whole foot and much of the leg. There is much information with which we should be familiar if we are to be able to select footwear wisely. First of all, we should know the characteristics of our own feet. Our feet are the foundation of our bodies. They should support the weight of the body in standing and walking without aches or hurt. The arches of the foot give it strength and elasticity, and make possible the long hours of walking and standing in comfort, especially if we are wise in our choice of footwear. Not all people are wise in their choice. The complaint "My feet are so tired" can be heard among sight-seers almost anywhere. "These shoes don't fit" or "This stocking bunches" usually follows as the next statement from the weary person.

Let us see what are the important considerations in choosing comfortable covering for our feet. Stockings come next to the skin, so we will consider them first. The matter of the size of hose is important, both in comfort and in durability. Hose should be long enough in the foot to be comfortable and should just fit the foot without stretching the hose. The leg of the hose should extend at least six inches above the knee. Common hose sizes are 8½, 9, 9½, and 10. If the hose is too short, it makes the foot uncomfortable by its pulling, and the prospects of a good wearing record are very poor. Hose should be free from rough seams, knots, and irregular places which might press on the foot.

The fit of hose is largely determined by the way in which they are made. The full-fashioned hose are knitted flat, being shaped for the leg. The flat piece is then seamed up at

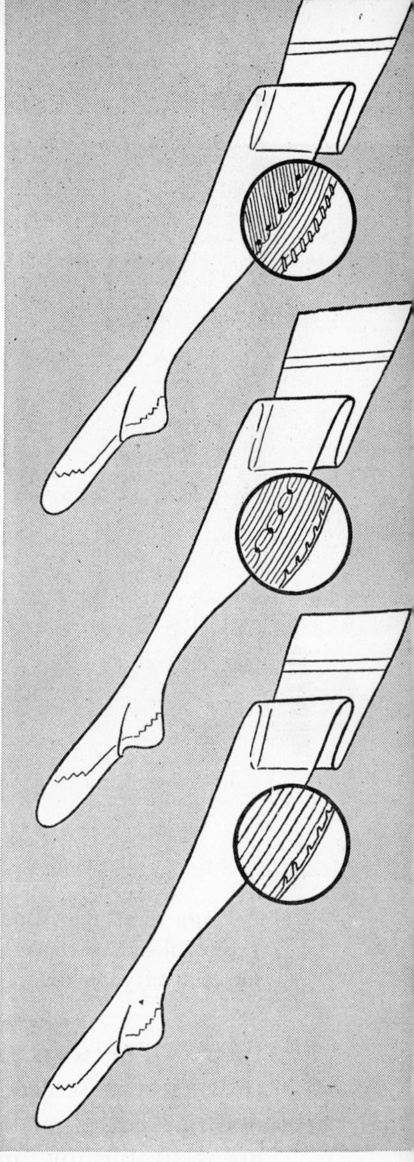

Three methods of stocking construction are shown here: the full-fashioned (top); the semifashioned (center); and the circular-knit (bottom).

Be sure that the widest part of the shoe comes at the joint of your foot.

the back of the leg. The shaping is done by dropping stitches. Full-fashioned hose fit better than the circular-knit or the semi-fashioned hose. Circular-knit hose are knit in one piece, having the same number of stitches at the top as at the ankle. Children's ribbed hose are usually circular-knit. Semi-fashioned hose look like the full-fashioned, but the seam at the back is a "make-believe" one and the dropped stitches are made as a decoration rather than for shaping. The absence of fit is evident after laundering. The full-fashioned hose cost the most, but they give satisfaction in fit and appearance.

Hose are made from cotton, silk, rayon, and wool. Cotton hose cost less than silk, rayon, or wool hose and they wear better than those of silk or rayon. Silk hose appear much more attractive and the majority of people prefer to wear them. The wear the hose will receive should determine the material selected. Cotton hose are desirable for outdoor activities such as hikes or tennis games; wool hose are desirable for long mountain tramps; and silk hose are used for dress wear.

Silk hose are purchased according to the thread. A two-thread hose is a very sheer hose and rarely gives long service. These are suitable for "dressy" wear, and if carefully used they will give satisfactory service. Three-thread hose are slightly heavier and are considered by many as a satisfactory sheer all-purpose hose. Four-thread hose are next in weight and give good service for everyday wear. The count goes on up to seven-thread hose, which are very heavy hose. Silk hose are also purchased as chiffon, semiservice, and service weight.

Some silk hose are woven with cotton at the heel and toe. Such construction gives better wear, but the appearance of the hose may be less pleasing. It is economical to buy two matching pairs of hose at one time. In case one stocking of each pair fails to give good service, you will still have one good pair.

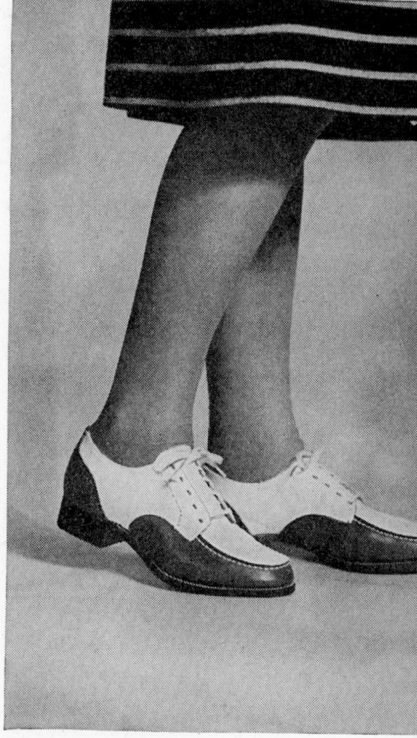

Wide toes and heels low enough for comfort need not detract from smart appearance.

Shoes are bought according to size and last. The size is denoted by numbers and the last by letters. Sizes two, three, and four are small; sizes eight, nine, and ten are large. Width A is average; width AAAA is as narrow as shoes usually can be purchased; width B is wider than average.

The shoe should be long enough to extend about a half-inch beyond the large toe, and wide enough to allow the toes to fall into normal place without cramping. If the shoe is too short, or if it is not properly shaped, the large toe may be forced inward, out of line, and this may lead to a bunion. The heel of the shoe should fit the foot closely, without pinching or rubbing at any place. The soles should be flexible enough to respond to the movement of the foot.

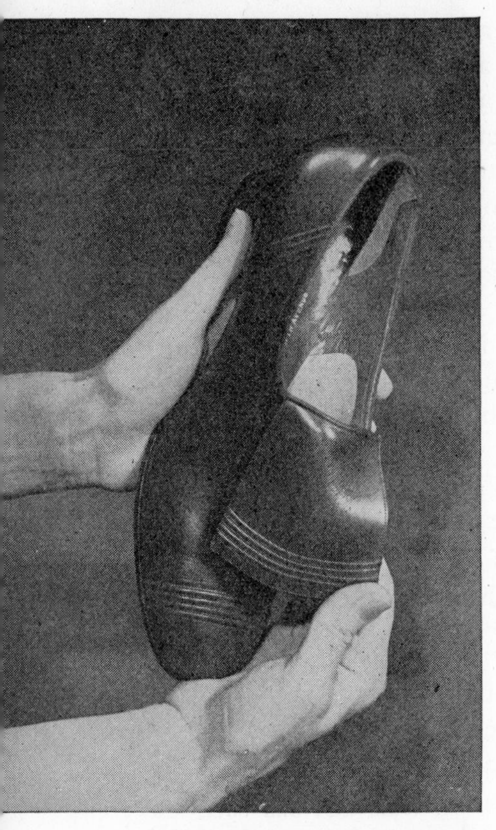

Good leather and workmanship can be easily noted by the buyer who knows what to look for.

Heels of shoes for daily wear should not be more than one and one-fourth inches high and they should be as broad at their base as is the heel of the person wearing them. High-heeled shoes that send the wearer tottering down the street do not add to her grace and charm; they point to her lack of good taste. For dancing, perhaps high heels are suitable; for lounging, heelless sandals may be our choice; but for the business of daily living, we want shoes that can "go places" and help us to "do things." Rubber caps on the heels make the "going" more pleasant. *Size, width, heel*—when we have considered these, let us look at the leather.

A sturdy calfskin or buckskin shoe wears well and looks well for school and play. For dress wear, kid, suede, and patent leather are popular. The current styles and popular use of perforations make the discomfort of patent leather shoes far less than was formerly experienced. Whatever the leather chosen, the lining of a shoe should be carefully examined to note that it is free from wrinkles, rough places, or poor seams. A good shoe will have a good lining. Buying a good make of shoe, made from good material with good workmanship, is usually much more economical than the purchase of a low-priced shoe.

The choice of rubbers and galoshes should be made according to one's needs. In the snowy winters of the North, a high overshoe may be needed; in sunny Arizona, even a toe rubber is unnecessary. In the colder climates, a fleece lining may be needed by many for adequate warmth; galoshes and rubbers thus lined are somewhat higher in price. Whatever is needed, the rubber selected should give the required protection. The heels of the rubbers or galoshes should be right for the heels of the shoes, and sizes should be carefully checked before buying.

Activities:

1. Why do we usually like to buy our footwear at one or two certain places, rather than just any place?
2. What qualities do you require in your hose?
3. What qualities do you require in your shoes?
4. Rate these qualities in relation to their importance.

Problem 7: HOW SHALL WE SELECT AND PURCHASE OUR HEADWEAR?

Headwear includes hats, berets, caps, scarfs, and other articles to cover the head as designed by fashion. In determining the quality of a hat, beret, or cap, it is necessary to examine the material and the workmanship used in its construction.

Headwear may be made from felt, velvet, yarn, silk, linen, piqué, straw, and many other materials. Fashion usually plays a large part in determining the material used, as well as the style and shape of hats. Our choice of color is influenced by the popular color of the season and by our own coloring. The amount of money to be spent for headwear should be determined in relation to the rest of the clothing costs. The purchase of a five-dollar hat to be worn with the three-dollar dress is unwise. Berets, caps, and scarfs are usually inexpensive.

We should choose clothes suitable to the occasion. A study of the activities we take part in will show the occasions for which we should have suitable headdress. School, church, trips to town, skating, hiking, and Girl Scout events may be on our list. As the season changes from winter to spring and then to summer our activities change, but the nature of the occasion in which we participate remains much the same. In the winter we need a trim felt hat for wear to church and town, and a beret and one or more scarfs for school and sport. In the spring we need a straw hat for church and town, and a beret and scarfs of different material than those worn in winter for school and sports. The informal scarf or kerchief for wear to a steak-fry or a class picnic is still a necessity. The headdress should be suitable to the occasion and to the costume with which it is worn.

In selecting headwear one should stand before a full-length mirror and note the relation of the hat or cap to the figure and to the entire costume. A hat may be becoming as far as its relationship to the face is concerned, but when viewed with the dress it is worn with one may find that the total effect is not good.

The following questions should be answered before buying headwear:

1. Is it becoming?
2. Is it in good fashion, yet not extreme?
3. Is it appropriate to the occasions for which it will be worn?
4. Is it suitable in color and effect to the costumes with which it will be worn?
5. Is it suitable in every way to the individual?
6. Is it within the cost range planned?
7. Will it be durable under the conditions of wear expected of it?

Activities:

1. What kind of headwear do you like to wear? Why? When do you wear this headwear?
2. What guides do you follow in buying headwear?
3. What difficulties do you have in selecting and purchasing headwear? How could these be lessened or overcome?

Problem 8: HOW SHALL WE SELECT AND PURCHASE OTHER ACCESSORIES?

Accessories are articles which add to the costume without actually being a part of it. Sometimes shoes, hats, gloves, and purses are classified as essential accessories; such things as jewelry, flowers, scarfs, and handkerchiefs are grouped as nonessential accessories.

Accessories should be chosen to complete the costume and harmonize with it. They should be attractive in design and appropriate to the occasion. The cost of accessories should be determined in relation to the money spent for the entire wardrobe. For the person whose dresses do not exceed ten dollars each in expenditure, $1.50 is out of proportion for a flower. However, a relatively large expenditure may be justified if the accessory purchased is to be worn with several costumes.

In buying *gloves* it is wise economy to select those of a color to fit in with several costumes. The gloves should be of good quality so that good wear can be expected from them. Knit woolen gloves are practical for school and sports in winter, while kid and nicely finished fabric gloves are suitable for dress wear. In the summer, washable gloves of sheer fabric or open weaves are desirable. Pigskin makes a fine all-service glove.

The *purse* we buy should be of such material, size, and color that it will go well with the costumes with which it will be used and with the individual using it. The large envelope purse is not a good choice if carried by an unusually small girl. If the purse is not wisely chosen, one may see it before seeing the girl, especially if it is too large, too extreme in style, or too bright in color. Purses are made from various kinds of materials. Leather, fabric, wood, straw, and beads are all used. The season of the year helps to determine both the material and the color to buy. Purses vary greatly in price, and unless one plans to carry a purse for more than one season, a large expenditure is unwise.

Costume jewelry is effective if wisely purchased; it may be barbaric if selected without good judgment. Costume jewelry should be purchased to harmonize in color and texture with the garment worn; it should accent a color or some particular part of the costume; and it should be in keeping with the personality of the wearer. If the costume jewelry is more vivid than the wearer, it tends to discount her attractiveness.

Scarfs play an important part in our dress today, and if correctly chosen they are a definite part of the costume and add to its attractiveness. They are particularly useful in accenting a color note, and in softening a neckline that may be too severe. Although they are commonly knotted around the neck, they are also frequently worn around the head.

Handkerchiefs should be selected to harmonize with the costume and should be well made of good material. Linen handkerchiefs are preferred by most people. They are easily laundered, absorb moisture, and are not excessive in price. If well cared for, handkerchiefs will last a long time. A supply of one or two dozen is regarded as adequate to meet our requirements.

In buying accessories, a relatively large expenditure of money for nonessentials is unwise, since their period of use may be rather short. The essential accessories are usually selected to be worn with more than one costume, so more money may be spent for them.

Activities:

1. What accessories do you have? Which of these can you wear with more than one costume?
2. How much do you spend for accessories in a year?
3. Do you have accessories that you can exchange with other members of the family? Is this a good practice to follow? Give reasons for your answer.

Problem 9: HOW SHALL WE PURCHASE OUR COATS AND SWEATERS?

The purchase of a coat usually involves a larger expenditure of money than we make for other articles in our wardrobe. The service expected from the coat is much greater. Usually, two or more seasons' satisfactory wear is expected. As the expenditure is larger and the length of service greater than that made for other articles of clothing, it is important that the choice of a coat be wisely made. This is true of winter coats, which we expect to protect us fully from chilly winds and falling snow, and to stand the stress and strain of being put on and taken off many times daily.

The first step in the choice of a coat is to determine the type which we should buy. Coats are classed as dress, tailored or sport, and in-between, depending upon the material used, the style, and methods of construction employed. Dress coats are usually made from soft materials in dark colors, and for winter wear usually have fur collars. Usually, plain, pressed-open seams are used. Sport coats are made from rough and coarser materials. They are usually cut along swagger lines, and may or may not have a fur collar. The seams are generally finished as a flat fell seam with no stitching showing on the right side. The cloth is often of heavy material and gives interesting color combinations. The sports coat is worn for school, for sports, as its name suggests, and for general wear.

Many wardrobes do not include a dress coat and a sports

This buyer will not be satisfied until she finds the facts from the label. The label should give information about the kind of cloth used and the conditions under which the garment was made.

coat but an in-between or "all-season" coat, which has some of the characteristics of each of the two coats we have discussed. The in-between or all-season coat may be made of rough-textured materials with plain seams; it may or may not have a fur collar. In cut, construction, and color, it is suitable for either dress or sports wear. We will decide on the type of coat we wish to buy after consideration of what we have in our wardrobe. If it contains a leather jacket in good condition, perhaps a dress coat would be a wise purchase. If the new coat is to serve for all kinds of wear, perhaps an all-season coat should be our choice.

When the type of coat to be purchased has been determined, the next step is to choose a style and color well suited to us and to our individual needs. Coats are worn with several dresses, perhaps of widely different colors and styles. Hence, the coat itself should be of a color that seems to fit into the wardrobe generally. Selection of a color somewhat darker than that of the dresses in the wardrobe is desirable. That is, a brown coat may be worn with tan, beige, or brown dresses and would seem to complete the costume as a lighter color would not do. Bright greens, strong yellows, and off-colors of rose are not desirable colors for coats, since they are too definite to combine with other colors easily, and, also, we would easily tire of them.

The fabric used in the coat and in the lining, if a lining is used, should be of the best quality that we can get for the amount of money available. We should look for labels indicating that the coat fabric is all wool, and that the lining is of one of the fabrics known to stand the sort of wear to which linings are subjected. Both silk and rayon are used for linings. Certain makes of satins (rayon or silk) wear very well. Often there is no relationship between the wearing quality of a lining and the price paid for the coat or the lining.

Inexpensive coats with fur collars are rarely ever wise purchases. Cheap fur, such as cat or rabbit fur, is short-lived and tends to look "ratty" long before the fabric of the coat is worn out.

The construction processes and the cut of the coat are also important in making a wise choice. The seams and joinings of a well-made coat are ample, yet do not show or attract attention. Also, the stitching is strong throughout the length of the seam. Buttonholes or loops should be neatly made or applied. The cut of the coat should provide for a liberal lap at the front closing. A coat with a skimpy lap gives poor protection from cold and wind. The cut should be simple, with no unusual bunches of fur or elaborate fastenings difficult to keep in order.

When buying a coat, the fit should be carefully studied. The coat that fits well allows for freedom of movement of the body, hangs straight, sets smoothly on the figure, and has the right sleeve and body length. The full-length coat should be about one inch longer than the dress worn beneath it. The finger-tip- or three-quarter-length coat comes midway between the hip line and the knees. This length coat is most commonly worn for sport wear by women.

Jackets of wool or lined leather are commonly purchased by the schoolgirl for sport wear.

Sweaters, so commonly worn by girls today, should be selected carefully and wisely. In purchasing sweaters, girls must consider the amount of money they have to spend, the color that is best for them to buy, and the workmanship of the garment. A sweater of poor quality yarn soon sags, pouches, and loses its shape; and it will not wash well. The sweater of good quality will have the wales running lengthwise on the face and crosswise on the back. Certain brand names have come to indicate a sweater of good quality.

The price of sweaters is based on the quality of yarn used and the cost of production. The handmade sweater is priced higher than the machine-made, but it does not always give better service. The size of sweater to buy should be decided upon before going shopping. They are purchased according to bust size, and should be large enough not to appear stretched when on the figure. Sweaters are worn for school or sports.

Activities:

1. What would you list as important considerations in buying a coat? In buying a dress?
2. How are the seams in your coat made? Are they satisfactory?
3. How are the seams in your sweater made? How do they differ from the seams in your dress? Why do they differ?
4. How much money should one spend for a winter coat? How much money should one spend for a light-weight coat?

REFERENCES FOR THE UNIT

Donovan, Dulcie Godlove, *The Mode in Dress and Home.* Boston: Allyn and Bacon, 1935.

Friend, Mata Roman, and Shultz, Hazel, *Junior Home Economics: Clothing.* New York: D. Appleton-Century Co., 1933.

Kinyon, Kate W., and Hopkins, L. Thomas, *Junior Clothing,* Revised Edition. New York: Benj. H. Sanborn and Co., 1938.

Kinyon, Kate W., and Hopkins, L. Thomas, *Junior Home Problems,* Revised Edition. New York: Benj. H. Sanborn and Co., 1938.

Matthews, Mary Lockwood, *The New Elementary Home Economics.* Boston: Little, Brown and Co., 1937.

Todd, Elizabeth, *Clothes for Girls.* Boston: Little, Brown and Co., 1935.

SUGGESTED HOME EXPERIENCES

1. Observe the various store windows downtown and note how many articles you see which you need in your wardrobe.
2. Estimate the amount of money that would be required to purchase these needed articles.
3. Check your wardrobe and see if you have special clothing for all your activities. Do some of your clothes serve more than one purpose?
4. Figure the amount of money you spent for clothing last year.
5. Check your ready-made clothes for their labels. Note what information each label carries. Decide what labels would be helpful to you in buying the garment.

UNIT

16

EXPRESSING FRIENDSHIP FOR OTHERS

IF YOU WERE TO LOOK UP THE WORD friendship in the dictionary you would find the definition worded something like this: "Friendship—mutual liking, esteem, or regard; being friends." As you read this you realize that the mutual liking or esteem which we often call friendship is not really friendship, but only a beginning upon which friendship might grow if both persons work to keep the budding plant alive and flourishing. Emerson warns us that "Our friendships hurry to short and poor conclusions because we make them of the texture of wine and dreams instead of the tough fiber of the human heart. Too often we aim at a swift and petty benefit, to a sudden sweetness. We snatch at the slowest fruit in the whole garden of God which many summers and many winters must ripen. The end of friendship is for aid and comfort through all the relations and passages of life and death. It is fit for serene days and graceful gifts and country rambles but also for rough roads and hard fare and shipwreck. It should never fall into something usual and settled, but should be alert and inventive and add rhyme and reason to life itself."

In order to keep the friendship vital and significant there must be a sharing together of many things—ideas, confidences, dreams, and courage, quite as much as candy, pencils, and popcorn.

Problem 1: HOW CAN WE EXPRESS FRIENDSHIP?

The ways we may use to express our friendship include almost every means of communication that is known. The most common means is perhaps conversation. We can express our friendship in our talk. Words of affectionate regard and approval are appreciated by everyone; they bring us courage and assurance. Some girls and boys feel that such expressions are "sissy" and so are to be avoided as embarrassing. This, of course, is a mistake. Sincere statements of our pleasure and satisfaction in our friendships show strength rather than weakness.

Letters and notes are a means of expressing friendship. These can be written and sent at any time and for any purpose. In joy or sorrow, in health or illness, in success or misfortune, a letter or note seems to bring the sender to us. Cards, too, may express our interest. The sending of cards on vacation trips and at different times of the year, such as Christmas, New Year's Day, Easter, and Mother's Day, has now become a regular custom. Cards are more enjoyed if they bring a personal message. Sometimes on some special occasion we use the telegram to carry our greetings.

Since long, long ago, even before the Three Wise Men came "bearing gifts of gold, frankincense, and myrrh," regard and affection have been expressed through gifts. Our gifts may not be as rare and costly as those the Wise Men brought, but they carry the same message. If our gifts are to express our friendship, we should remember that the important thing in giving is

> Not what we give, but what we share,
> For the gift without the giver is bare.

Our gifts may be either objects or deeds. As long as they are given in the spirit of friendship, they will have meaning. The giving of things is the most common. There is almost no limit to the objects which serve as gifts. Gifts may be made or purchased. The great variety of articles displayed at the holiday season as "gifts for Mother" or "gifts for Brother" show the importance of *things* in our scheme of giving.

The giving of service is common among friends. Examples of such are helping with the general housework, preparing food, assisting in the serving of meals, and caring for a small child when the need arises. Many times, giving a service is the most appropriate gift possible. When friends are moving to a distant place or going on a long journey, or when they have guests visiting in their homes, gifts of service are greatly appreciated.

In times of sorrow and misfortune, thoughtful friends may give one courage to face matters and carry on. The gift of courage is not small. It can be given only by one who has both courage and the ability to share it. No gift is finer.

Certain events, such as Christmas, Valentine's Day, birthdays, Mother's and Father's Days, and graduation, have come to be generally accepted as times for gifts. Occasions of special joy and happiness, or of special honors and recognition for a person or family, merit expressions of affection from relatives and friends. The pleasure in such an event is always more enjoyed when we know others, too, are interested in our good fortune.

So expressing our friendship becomes a real way of adding to the joys of others and also to our own. We can say with the poet Whittier:

For somehow, not only for Christmas,
  But all the long year through,
The joy that you give to others is
  The joy that comes back to you;
And the more you spend in blessing
  The poor and the lonely and sad,
The more of your heart's possessing
  Returns to make you glad.

Activities:

1. What means do you use to express your friendship for others? Why do you use these means?
2. Make a list of guides to help us express our friendship in a good way.
3. Choose five of your friends and suggest desirable ways of expressing your friendship for them. Give reasons for the means you use.
4. Write all the ways during the past year that your friends have shown their friendship for you. How do they compare with the ways you have used to show your friendship for them?

Problem 2: HOW SHALL WE CHOOSE OUR GIFTS?

Time and thought should be given to selecting a gift if we are to make a wise choice. The gift should be suitable for the person to whom it is to be given. Many times we choose something we ourselves want instead of considering what our friend might like. In such cases, we may chance to choose a gift our friend will enjoy too, or we may add another "white elephant" to her collection. Considering the tastes and interests of our friends is a safe guide to a wise choice.

A gift that expresses the personality of the giver is especially nice. Whenever we see or use such gifts we recall the giver. A gift that expresses the personality of the receiver is nice, too. A gift that expresses the personality of both the giver and receiver is almost an ideal one. Such gifts are only possible when time and thought are given to their selection. They are the kind that are lasting in the joy and pleasure given.

The amount of money spent for the gift should be in keeping with what we can afford. It is considered bad taste to give expensive and costly gifts. Much harm can come from such a practice, and the giving of gifts is no longer a pleasure. The amount of money spent has little or no relation to the joy and pleasure that a gift brings. The spirit that goes with the gift is much more important, as is also the ability to choose wisely.

Deciding just what we shall give is not an easy matter. Our choice of gifts will not be the same for everyone. We want our gifts to be interesting and unusual. We sometimes prefer a gift that is useful, possibly something for which the person has much need. Whatever the type of gift, we do want it to be enjoyed.

Careful planning should be done before the time of shopping. Various articles that seem suitable to the person may be listed. Shopping then is done for these. When we find what seems best for what we can afford to pay, our choice is made. One of the less busy hours of the day is a better time for shopping. If a Christmas gift is to be chosen, the earlier part of the season is the best time to do it.

Many people enjoy making their gifts. They feel that such gifts express much more of the giver than does a purchased gift. Usually the gifts we make cost less money but require more time and effort than those we buy. In planning for the making of gifts, the time we can give to the work should be considered. Gifts that can be made in the time we have free should be chosen. Our ability in making gifts should affect our choice. We have more enjoyment in what we can do well. Trying to make a gift that is too difficult for our abilities may take away from our pleasure in giving it.

There are many gifts that we can make. We may work in the crafts and make desk sets, greeting cards, textile prints, and decorative centerpieces. We may prepare various foods, such as cake, candy, preserves, and puddings. We may use our sewing skill in making gifts such as pot holders, aprons, shoe bags, and handkerchiefs. All sorts of original and different ideas can be used. Giving gifts may be a joy and a pleasure if we make it so. Whether purchased or made, the gift should express our sincere friendship.

Activities:

1. Decide upon gifts that would be suitable for the members of your family.
2. Select five of your friends; decide upon one or more gifts that would be suitable for each person.
3. What do you think are five most important considerations in choosing gifts? List them in the order of their importance.

Problem 3: HOW SHALL WE MAKE A DECORATIVE CENTERPIECE?

Decorative centerpieces make pleasing gifts. They are much used now for the dining room or library table, buffet, or desk. They add color and interest to the room and may help carry out the spirit of the particular season of the year. Such a gift can be distinctive and can be enjoyed by the entire family.

Various things are used in making centerpieces; flowers, potted plants, weeds, greenery, fruit and vegetables, colored paper, candles, and miniature objects are among the most common.

The plan for the centerpiece is influenced by the season and by the occasion. Certain things and ideas have been accepted as belonging to certain events and times. Halloween, Thanksgiving Day, Christmas, Washington's Birthday, St. Patrick's Day, Easter, and Fourth of July all have characteristic colors and symbols. Birthdays, weddings and wedding anniversaries, graduation, and Mother's Day, too, have characteristic symbols or colors. In each case, some idea becomes the main note of the centerpiece. Original ideas are most valuable in planning a successful decorative centerpiece.

Attractive centerpieces can be made of potted plants, flowers, weeds, or greenery. Little needs to be done to the potted plant except to decorate the pot in some way with paper and ribbon. Real flowers make nicer centerpieces than artificial ones, although these too may be used. Flow-

See how beautifully fruits and vegetables can be combined to make an artistic centerpiece. This would make a pleasing gift.

ers should be arranged artistically in a bowl or vase. Artificial flowers may be arranged in a basket. Straw flowers are particularly attractive so used. Weeds and greenery of various types make pretty centerpieces. Each locality has its lovely wild plants which are usually not hard to get. The holly, pokeberry, bittersweet branches, pussy willows, and cattails all make attractive decorations.

Fruits and vegetables make interesting centerpieces. Those of high color and rounded form can be used. They are first polished with an oiled cloth to give them a high luster, and then arranged on a platter or in a bowl in a pleasing way. A pumpkin or squash from which a slice has been cut at the top and the pulp and seeds removed is good to hold the fruit and vegetables. Cornucopias made of lacquered brown paper are also used for this purpose.

A nest of shredded paper filled with colored eggs, with cotton chickens, ducks, and rabbits placed near by, makes a centerpiece well suited to the Easter season.

The Yule-log centerpiece is always a popular one for Christmastide. An oak log four or five inches in diameter is cut sixteen or eighteen inches long. The log is laid on several thicknesses of newspapers. Candles of various colors, the more the better, are allowed to melt over it until the wax is thick over the top of the log, and the colors are blended. Holes are made in the wax to hold six or more candles. A sheet of asbestos paper protects the tray upon which the log is placed. The centerpiece, including the tray, is then placed on the buffet or table. The candles are lighted and the log is kept burning throughout the Christmas season. The melted wax runs down on the log, adding more color all the time. As the candles burn down, new candles are put in their place.

Centerpieces are sometimes made to represent scenes. Winter scenes are always pretty. A mirror can be used for a pond, cotton and "diamond dust" for snow and frost, evergreen branches and twigs for trees, and toy figures for people, animals, and buildings. Appropriate for the Christmas season is the Nativity scene. A Pilgrim scene is suitable for Thanksgiving. A miniature wedding scene is appropriate as a centerpiece for a wedding reception, wedding anniversary, or bridal shower.

The time and effort spent in making such gifts as these are well repaid by the appreciation of our friends.

Activities:

1. (*Class activity*) Plan and make a decorative centerpiece.
2. (*Class activity*) Divide into groups, each group planning and making a decorative centerpiece.

Problem 4: HOW SHALL WE MAKE CANDY?

Nearly everyone has a "sweet tooth," so candy is always an acceptable gift. Homemade candy is especially well liked. Stuffed dates, peanut brittle, and fudge are popular and easy to make. They differ widely from each other in the ingredients and method used and in the finished products.

Stuffed Dates

The utensils

Mixing bowl	Measuring spoons
Plate or pie tin	Cooking spoon
Measuring cup	Paring knife

The recipe for stuffed dates

Ingredients:

1 package dates	½ c. granulated sugar
¾ c. walnut or pecan meats in large pieces	

Method:

Remove seeds from the dates. Fill the cavity with nut meats and close the date around it. Roll in sugar until completely covered.

One girl—4 dates.

Peanut Brittle

The utensils

Saucepan or kettle	Measuring spoons
Cooking spoon	Platter, pan, or candy slab, well oiled
Measuring cup	

The recipe for peanut brittle

Ingredients:

2 c. sugar	2 c. raw peanuts
1 c. white corn syrup	1 t. vanilla
½ c. water	2 t. soda
2 T. butter or butter substitute	2 t. butter or other fat for oiling

Method:

Cook sugar, syrup, and water until the crack stage. (This is determined by dropping a drop of the syrup in cold water.) Add butter and peanuts. Cook, stirring constantly, until the syrup becomes brown in color.

Remove from the fire. Add vanilla and soda, stirring until

For a friend with a "sweet tooth," no gift could be finer than homemade fudge.

the soda is thoroughly dissolved. Pour on a platter. When set, slip from the platter and turn. When cold, break into pieces.

One girl—¼ recipe.

Chocolate Fudge

The utensils

Saucepan or kettle	Measuring spoons
Cooking spoon	Table knife
Measuring cup	Candy pan or pie pan, oiled

The recipe for chocolate fudge

Ingredients:

2 c. sugar	⅔ c. milk
6 T. cocoa or 2 sq. unsweetened chocolate	2 T. butter or butter substitute
⅛ t. salt	1 t. vanilla
	1 t. butter or other fat to oil pan

Method:

Put the sugar, milk, salt, and cocoa, or chocolate cut in small pieces, in a pan or kettle and mix well. Place on the fire and cover until the boiling point is reached. Cook to the soft-ball stage (234° to 238°F.). Add butter and flavoring, and cool to room temperature without stirring. Beat until the mixture is

Homemade candy is an impressive gift when it is wrapped attractively.

creamy and thick. When it has lost its glossy appearance and will hold its shape when dropped from a teaspoon, pour into the oiled pan. When cold, cut in squares.

Two girls—½ recipe.

Activities:

1. (*Class activity*) Prepare stuffed dates, peanut brittle, and fudge. (If time permits make this Problem into three Problems and give three days to it instead of one.)
2. Determine the cost of each kind of candy.

Problem 5: HOW SHALL WE WRAP GIFTS?

"Why not glorify your Christmas gifts this year?" reads an advertisement for a company that makes fancy paper and wrappings. "Dress them up and make them more alluring" it further says, offering suggestions for wrapping gifts. The

Beautiful wrappings can add much to the charm of gifts which are exchanged at Christmas.

idea of "dressing up" gifts is not limited to Christmas. We try to make every gift package lovely, regardless of what it is or when it is given. In the wrapping of gifts we have a fine opportunity to be original and clever.

The wrapping of the gift may add to or take away from its attractiveness. A beautiful package interests us more than one tied up in an ordinary way. The pot holder, the glass of jelly, or the string of lacquered pods appear to much better advantage when done up in an attractive package.

The gift itself should influence the choice of wrappings, and the two should be somewhat in harmony. Dainty and delicate wrappings should be used for gifts of this type. Sturdy and colorful wrappings are suitable for utility gifts.

The occasion of the gift should also be considered in its

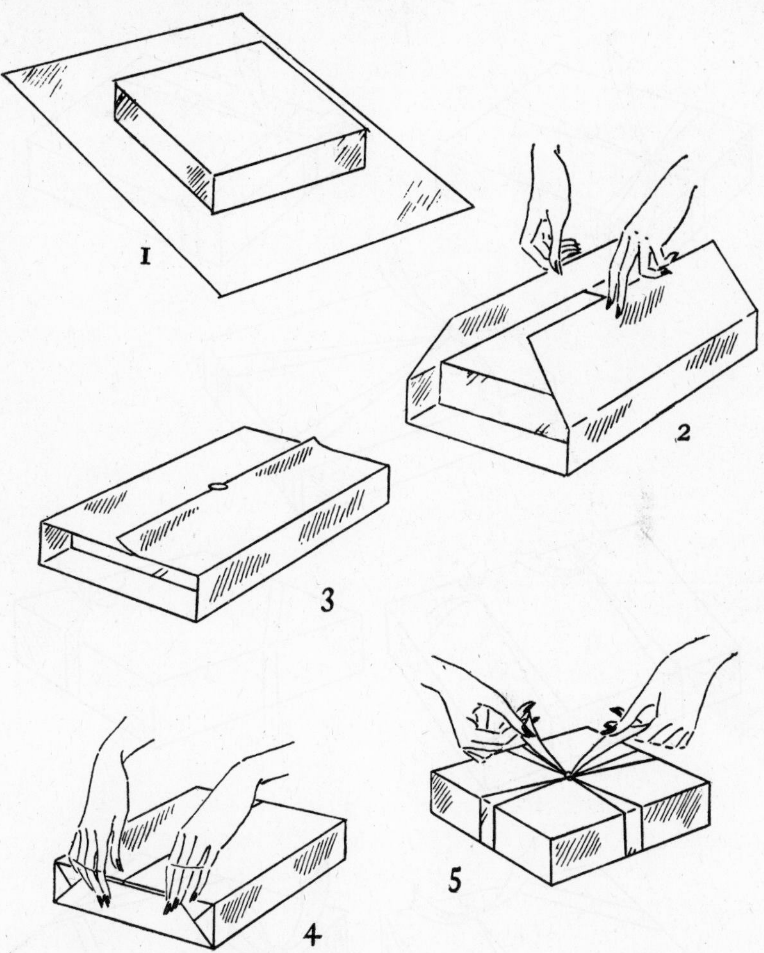

These five steps will insure a neatly wrapped package, whether the material used is simple or elaborate.

wrappings. Emblems and colors characteristic of the occasion or season are nice to use. Christmas trees, Santa Clauses, stars, stockings hung on a fireplace, and the colors red and green belong to Christmas; hearts and cupids, and the colors red and white belong to Valentine's Day;

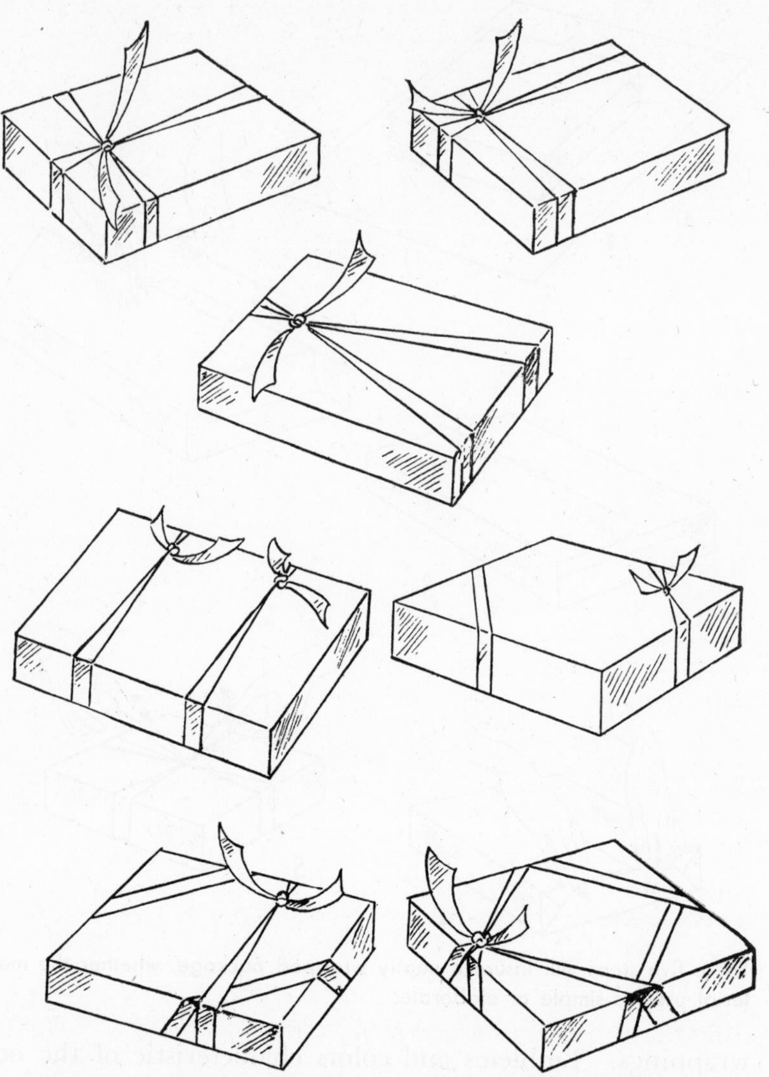

Ribbon can be tied on gift packages in many different ways. The methods shown here may be copied with a little practice. You may enjoy originating some styles of your own.

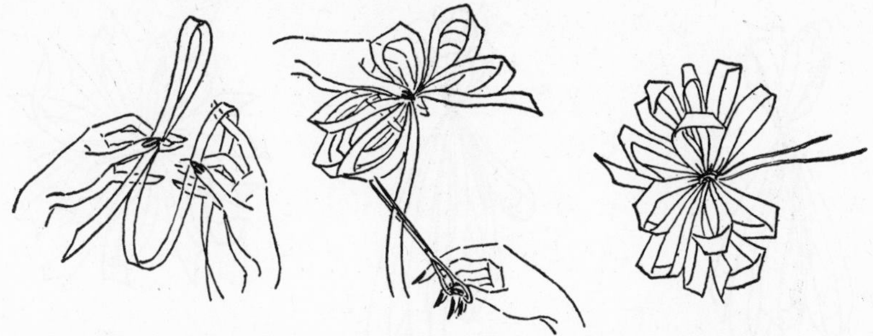

These are the three simple steps in making a multiple bow.

and shamrocks, pigs and pipes, and the color green are for St. Patrick's Day.

Too much money should not be spent for wrappings. With all the numerous and lovely things in the stores, it is easy to make the wrapping of a gift absurdly expensive. The cost of the wrapping should certainly never exceed, and would ordinarily be much less than, the money value of the gift.

Things needed for wrapping gifts are boxes, paper, cards, ribbon, seals, paste, pins, and scissors. Before selecting the materials, the color scheme should be decided upon and the general plans should be made for the wrapping. Colors that go well together should be selected. Combinations of figured and plain materials are more pleasing than are combinations of all figured ones. Sometimes it is desirable to choose colors for the wrappings that are in harmony with the colors of the gift.

Some guides that have been found helpful in wrapping packages are suggested:

1. The box to be wrapped should be placed top down on the paper in order to have the smooth surface on top.
2. All seams and joints should come on the bottom of the package.

Decorative bows can be varied in many ways in the manner in which they are tied or put together.

3. The paper should be cut the correct size with 1-inch overlap left in the middle, and a little over half the depth of the box left on the ends.
4. The ends of the paper are brought around the box and then fastened with paste or seals, forming the bottom of the package.
5. The ends of the paper sticking out should be folded in neatly on both sides and fastened down with paste or seals to the box.
6. The box is then decorated as desired with ribbon, seals, or other materials.
7. When two differently colored papers are used for a tailored effect, they are pasted together before wrapping. The seam is then covered with ribbon.
8. Cellophane paper is used over a plain paper, usually white.

Some interesting ways of wrapping gifts are shown on page 490. These will give you some ideas for planning the wrapping of your packages. Remember that neatness is the most important factor in obtaining a beautifully wrapped gift package—one that you are proud to give or send.

Activities:

1. (*Class activity*) Divide the class into groups of two or three members. Bring gifts and wrappings. Plan wrappings for the gifts.
2. Wrap packages according to the plans.
3. Exhibit and judge the packages.
4. (*Class activity*) If a longer unit is desired, other problems could be added, such as the following: How shall we make a peasant apron? How shall we make textile prints? How shall we make a desk set? How shall we make a linoleum-block cut?

REFERENCES FOR THE UNIT

Jensen, Milton B., Jensen, Mildred R., and Ziller, M. Louisa, *Fundamentals of Home Economics*. New York: The Macmillan Co., 1935.

Matthews, Mary Lockwood, *The New Elementary Home Economics*. Boston: Little, Brown and Co., 1937.

SUGGESTED HOME EXPERIENCES

1. Practice expressing your friendship for others in various ways.
2. Plan the gifts you will give your family members for Christmas; for their birthdays.
3. Make gifts at home.
4. Make candy at home.
5. Wrap some packages attractively.

UNIT 17

WHEN THERE IS SICKNESS IN THE HOME

ON YOUR WAY TO SCHOOL THIS MORNING you may have seen many homes that showed signs that some family member was sick. Perhaps one house had an orange-colored sign, warning of mumps, another farther down had the red danger sign of scarlet fever tacked on it, and still another had the quarantine sign for measles.

Perhaps you saw a man hobbling about the porch on crutches, or a tired, pale-faced child lying in the sunlight on the lawn. Perhaps you heard a mother call, "Johnny, remember you have a cold! Now come back here!"

If your mind had not been on the brightness of the morning or the basketball game at school, you may have thought, "Almost every other home has someone sick in it! They must be lots of bother. I hope I don't get sick." Perhaps at some time or other you have had an argument with your mother as to whether or not you were sick. When all the words were exhausted, your mother may have answered, "Now, young lady, I know sick people when I see them. You march right up to bed." If you were not too cross at being sent to bed, you may have wondered how she knew how badly you really felt, and you were grateful for her decision after you were safely in bed and receiving the care that you needed.

Problem 1: HOW CAN WE TELL WHEN A PERSON IS SICK?

You have all seen people whom you thought looked ill, yet you could not say just why you thought so. Many things combine to give this impression. Illness is shown in one's appearance by flushed cheeks, unusually bright eyes, and by the impatience and crossness of the person. It is also shown by complaints of the sick person and of a feeling of nausea, general aching, headache, sore throat, chilling and burning sensations, pain, and drowsiness. If a person seems ill, she should be watched, placed in a room by herself, and made as comfortable as possible. This is for her sake, because quiet and rest will hasten her recovery, and for the sake of others, for she may have a contagious disease.

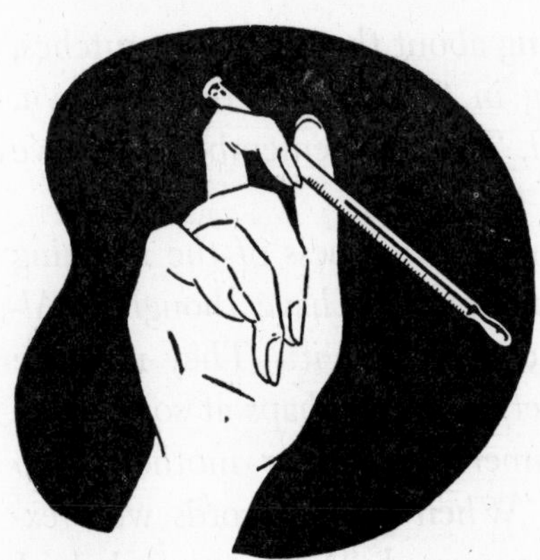

The thermometer may be used to tell us whether or not the body temperature is normal.

The person having a fever will have a flushed appearance, her lips will be dry and her forehead will feel hot to your hand. Every home should have a clinical thermometer and each member of the family should learn to take body temperature as early as possible. The temperature is taken with the thermometer in this manner:

1. Place the thermometer in alcohol and rinse it in clean water.
2. Shake the mercury down below 95°.
3. Place the bulb of the thermometer under the patient's tongue and have the patient close his lips. Let it remain three minutes, unless it is a one-minute thermometer.

4. Remove the thermometer from the patient's mouth, read it, and record the temperature.

5. Clean the thermometer by rinsing it in water and dipping it in alcohol; wipe it, and put it in the case.

The seriousness of some diseases may be lessened if we notice the signs at the very beginning and have the sick person go to bed and rest; then we call a physician if rest and quiet do not bring improvement.

Activities:

1. Try to read a thermometer. Report any difficulties encountered.

2. List the different indications of sickness that may be seen on your way to and from school.

3. What various colors of quarantine signs are used? Why are the different colors used?

Problem 2: HOW CAN WE HELP CARE FOR THE SICK PERSON?

Whenever there is sickness in the home, you should try to help in every possible way. The ways in which you can help depend upon the nature of the sickness. If mother has a sick headache, she will want quiet more than anything else and you can help to obtain that for her. If little brother is quarantined with mumps in some other part of the house, and you have never had the disease, you can help by staying away from him. It may be that you can take a larger share in the household tasks in order to give mother free time to serve as his nurse.

If you can share directly in the care of the sick person, you will find many ways in which you can help. It may be that you can stay in the sick room and thus let the one in charge get a short rest, take a walk, or attend to some personal matter. While you are staying with the sick person you may read to her, you may tell her of amusing incidents

Pillows are more comfortable if well "fluffed."

that happened at school, or entertain her in some other way. Some sick persons may like to play games or be amused by guessing contests, crossword puzzles, or checkers.

You may give the sick person fresh, cold water to drink and help to serve his food. The food may be prepared by you or by someone else, yet you may take the entire responsibility of serving it.

When we are sick, we find the pillows get hard and lumpy and the sheets pull and twist into hard knots; then we like to have the pillows "fluffed" and covers straightened. This you can do for the sick person in your home. In fluffing the pillows, one should be careful not to annoy the patient or to seem rough in the task. The pillow may be turned and the feathers shaken to be evenly distributed in the pillow. In straightening the covers, you should pull the sheet to the bottom of the bed and tuck it in firmly, then you should pull it up at the top, being careful not to uncover the sick person. The top covers are then straightened and the top end of the sheet turned back over the covers.

You can always watch the light and ventilation and make sure that those are satisfactory to the sick person. Light in our eyes makes us uncomfortable even when we are well, and is of greater disturbance to a sick person. Artificial light should be placed according to the patient's desire and in a proper manner. Light for reading should fall on the material being read, and not on the patient's eyes.

Whatever you can do for the patient should be done thoughtfully and willingly. You should always bear in mind that illness may come to any of us, and you should attempt to give the same type of care that you would like to have. You should run errands and meet other requests cheerfully, even though they may seem unreasonable to you.

Activities:

1. What are some interesting stories you would read to a boy eight or ten years old? What stories would be enjoyed by girls six, eight, and ten years old?
2. List the ways in which you can help care for one who may be ill in your home.

Problem 3: WHAT CARE SHALL WE GIVE THE SICK PERSON'S ROOM?

The room occupied by the sick person should be cheery and bright, and it should be kept clean and orderly. Only those articles should be in the room which add to its cheer or are needed. Dressers and tables covered with unnecessary "things" are hard to care for, bring confusion to the room, and are dust-catchers.

In arranging the furniture and ornaments, the sick person should be consulted and her likes or dislikes considered. The arrangement should be made to be as easy as possible for the sick person as well as for the one caring for her. For example, if the sick person is able to read, books and papers should be so placed on a table near the bed that she can reach them.

Flowers and plants add much to the appearance of the sick room. They require special care. Depressing to the patient are wilted flowers with falling blossoms and dead leaves, or plants dying from lack of water. Each day cut flowers should be removed from the vase, the vase should

On the bedside table may be placed a clock, lamp, and other articles needed in the sick room.

be emptied and washed, and fresh water placed in it. The stems should be cut off one-half inch, any dead blooms or leaves should be removed, and the flowers returned to the vase. Plants should be watered as needed, and any dead leaves removed. Sometimes it is wise to remove the flowers and plants from the sick room at night. The return of the flowers in the morning creates new interest in them. Good care of plants and flowers may aid in lengthening their life.

The bed should be kept clean and well made. We have already learned how to do this. A clean, orderly bed gives comfort and satisfaction to a patient. More changes of bed linen are necessary for a sick person than for one who is well. Tossing and turning wrinkle the linen and take away its freshness.

The floors and coverings should be swept and dusted daily; then the room should be aired. In sweeping and dusting, care should be taken that as little dust as possible is set in motion in the room. This can be avoided by the use of a vacuum sweeper, or by the use of well-oiled mops or cloths to take up the dust. If a broom is used in sweeping, it may be slightly moistened before starting to sweep. The woodwork and windows should be washed and dusted as needed. Frequent dusting keeps them in good condition, and does away with much of the need for washing.

When airing the room, the windows may be lowered from the top, but great care should be taken that a draft does not hit the patient. The raising and lowering of the windows for fresh air should be watched carefully. Specially made screens are often placed on the window sill to prevent direct draft, if the window is opened from the bottom. The shades should be adjusted to shut out glaring light, to darken the room, or to make it light for reading, as desired. The light should not fall on the patient's eyes, nor should it cause a glare any place in the room.

Activities:

1. Why might you like to have a different arrangement of furniture in your room than you have now if you were ill? What might the arrangement be?
2. Arrange some flowers in a vase that would look well in the sick room.
3. Suggest ways of fixing a flower pot to make it attractive when placed in a sick room.
4. Ask your father to make a window board for your room to protect against a draft when you have your window raised a few inches for ventilation. This may be used in any room for ventilation in case of illness.

Problem 4: WHAT FOODS ARE SERVED TO THE SICK?

The food served to the sick depends upon the kind and seriousness of the illness. In those cases where a physician has been called, he may tell us the foods which the sick person may have and the method of preparation that may be used. In times of sickness, likes and dislikes should be considered. The sick person usually does not care a great deal about food, so it is necessary that the food be prepared and served in an attractive way. The physician may ask that liquid foods or soft foods be prepared and served. Liquid foods which are commonly served to sick people are fruit juices, soups, beverages, and milk. These may sometimes be served with crackers or toast, and at times they are served alone.

Soft foods commonly served to the sick are more substantial. They include creamed and scalloped dishes, custards, milk toast, eggs, fruit sauces, and baked and steamed vegetables. This gives a large group to choose from. If soft foods are used, the same dish is often prepared for the family meal, thus lessening the work. Meat is sometimes served to the sick; the kind and method of preparation should be carefully considered, unless it has been prescribed by the physician. In planning meals we must remember that the finished appearance of the meal plays a large part in preparing and serving food for the sick.

Activities:

1. Make a list of foods you would enjoy having if you were sick.
2. What sicknesses would prevent you from having some of these foods?
3. List the different ways in which you can serve milk. Can it be served attractively in these ways? How?

Problem 5: HOW SHALL WE PREPARE AND SERVE FRUIT AND MILK BEVERAGES FOR THE SICK?

Fruit and milk beverages commonly served to sick people are easily prepared and simple to serve. Some pleasing fruit beverages are lemonade, fruit punch, and grape punch. The recipes for these beverages follow:

Lemonade

The utensils

Paring knife or butcher knife	Fruit juicer
Measuring cup	Pitcher
Measuring spoons	Tablespoon

The recipe for lemonade

Ingredients:

¾ c. sugar
1 qt. water
3 lemons

Method:

Make a syrup of ½ c. of the water, sugar, and a slice of lemon. Cool, add lemon juice and remainder of water. Chill.

Two girls—⅓ recipe.

The serving

Lemonade is served in a tumbler or iced-tea glass. It may be placed on a dessert plate or a tray. A teaspoon, iced-tea spoon, or straws may be used.

Fruit Punch

The utensils

Same as for lemonade.

The recipe for fruit punch

Ingredients:

2 oranges	½ c. sugar
2 lemons	3¼ c. water

Method:

Squeeze juice from the fruit and strain. With ½ c. of the water and the sugar make a syrup. Cool. Combine syrup, fruit juice, and remaining water. Add a small amount of ice if an extra cool drink is desired.

Two girls—¼ recipe.

The serving

Same as for lemonade.

Grape Punch

The utensils

Same as for lemonade.

The recipe for grape punch

Ingredients:

1 c. fruit punch
2 c. grape juice

Method:

Mix the fruit punch and grape juice. Chill.

Two girls—½ recipe.

The serving

Same as for lemonade.

Two pleasing milk beverages for the sick are eggnog and malted milk. The recipes for these beverages follow:

Eggnog

The utensils

Small mixing bowl or pitcher
Measuring cup
Measuring spoons
Dover egg beater

The recipe for eggnog

Ingredients:

1 egg
¾ T. sugar
⅔ c. milk
Few grains salt
½ t. extract

Method:

Beat the egg thoroughly, add sugar, salt, and flavoring, mixing well. Add milk gradually. Strain, and chill.

Two girls—entire recipe.

The serving

Eggnog is served in a tumbler, placed on a dessert plate or a tray. A teaspoon may be used if desired.

Malted Milk

The utensils

Small mixing bowl or pitcher
Measuring cups
Measuring spoons

The recipe for malted milk

Ingredients:

⅔ c. milk
1 T. malt

Method:

Mix the malt with 2 T. of the milk; add the remainder of the milk. Chill and serve.

Two girls—entire recipe.

The serving

Malted milk is served in a tumbler or iced-tea glass placed on a dessert plate or a tray. A teaspoon or iced-tea spoon may be used if desired.

Activities:

1. Prepare fruit beverages for the sick.
2. Prepare milk beverages for the sick.
3. Figure the cost of what you will make.

Problem 6: HOW SHALL WE PREPARE AND SERVE MEAT BROTH?

Meat broth is a clear liquid made by cooking meat in water with any desired seasoning. When served to the sick, it is usually seasoned only with a small amount of salt.

The utensils

Kettle and cover	Measuring spoons
Measuring cup	Cooking spoon

The recipe for meat broth

Ingredients:

1 lb. meat and a small bone
1 qt. cold water

Method:

Cut the meat in small pieces and have the bone cut in pieces. Soak 1 hour or more. Heat gradually to the simmering point and cook at this temperature from 1 to 2 hours. Strain and cool quickly if not to be used at once. Keep in a cool place.

Two girls—½ recipe.

The serving

Meat broth is served in a bouillon cup or soup dish placed on a luncheon plate or a tray. The broth is eaten with a bouillon spoon or dessert spoon. A napkin is placed on the plate or tray.

Activities:

1. (*Class activity*) Make a quart of meat broth.
2. How would you vary the seasoning of meat broth?

Problem 7: HOW SHALL WE PREPARE AND SERVE JUNKET CUSTARD?

The utensils

Mixing bowl, medium size
Measuring cup
Saucepan
Measuring spoons
Sherbet dishes or cups

Soft custard or junket can be varied and made attractive in many ways. Chopped fruit may be used to give a pleasing contrast of tastes.

The recipe for junket custard

Ingredients:

1 tablet of junket
1 T. cold water
1 pt. fresh milk
3 T. sugar
1 t. vanilla extract

Method:

Have sherbet dishes or cups ready. Put the junket tablet in a mixing bowl. Add cold water. Crush the tablet and dissolve thoroughly.

Put milk in a saucepan. Add sugar and vanilla. Warm slowly, stirring constantly until *lukewarm,* not hot. Remove from the stove. Test to be sure it is only lukewarm. Add to the dissolved tablet. Stir quickly for a few seconds only. Pour at once into sherbet dishes or cups. Do not move the dishes until the custard is firm. This takes about ten minutes. Chill.

Two girls—entire recipe.

The serving

Junket custard is served in the dishes in which it set. The dish is placed on a dessert plate or a tray. It is eaten with a teaspoon. Sometimes a cherry is placed on top of the custard just before serving.

Activities:

1. (*Class activity*) Divide into two groups, one group preparing junket from the tablet form and the other group preparing junket from the powder form.
2. Vary the serving of junket, stressing its attractiveness.

Problem 8: HOW SHALL WE SET UP A TRAY FOR A SICK PERSON?

Health is one of the joys of life, yet it seems that at some time we all will have sickness in some degree. In most sicknesses we care very little for food, and many times it is the attractiveness of the tray that tempts us to eat at all. Most homes have some sort of a tray that may be used for serving the sick. The tray should be covered with a white or gayly colored cloth or paper doily. It should be clean and free from spots. Attractive, clean dishes and silver should be used. These should be easily handled and suitable in every way for a tray prepared for a sick person. The use of dishes or glasses that tip easily, or any heavy dishes, should be avoided.

We should plan an arrangement of the dishes on the tray so that it will be convenient for the sick person. It is often a good plan to place something on the tray to give a bit of life or color. A flower or a bit of green brightens the tray. Sometimes a surprise such as a small gift or a note from a friend may be taken in on the tray to add to its interest. The patient's mealtime should be quiet, restful, and free from visitors. Anything that may disturb the patient while eating should be avoided. Eating time should bring pleasure to the sick person, and we must plan carefully for it.

When one of the family members is ill, a neat and attractive tray will make the meals more appetizing.

Activities:

1. Prepare some food suitable for a sick person and arrange it on a tray as you would to take it to a sick person.
2. Suggest some things that could be used in place of a tray. Show how these could be used satisfactorily.
3. Make a list of surprises that could be placed on the sick tray if it were for your mother.

REFERENCES FOR THE UNIT

Kinyon, Kate W., and Hopkins, L. Thomas, *Junior Home Problems,* Revised Edition. New York: Benj. H. Sanborn and Co., 1938.

Matthews, Mary Lockwood, *The New Elementary Home Economics.* Boston: Little, Brown, and Co., 1937.

SUGGESTED HOME EXPERIENCES

1. Prepare various foods that would be suitable to serve to a sick person.
2. Practice reading a thermometer until you can do it easily.
3. Make a plan for arranging a bedroom in your home for a sick person.
4. Plan several surprises for a person who is sick in bed.

UNIT 18

THE FAMILY'S MONEY

LONG, LONG AGO THERE WAS NO SUCH thing as money. People bartered or traded what they had plenty of for what they lacked and needed. The man who was successful at trapping animals traded his skins for grain which someone else had harvested, and the man who had a dog or a pony he did not need traded it for shells to sew on his belt and feathers to decorate his headdress. Later, certain things that were desirable, scarce, uniform, and easily counted out and divided into parts came to be used in buying and selling. In this way, the use of money was begun. As you can see, trading was made much simpler by having money.

Many things have been used as money. In Burma, lead is used; in Siam, cowrie shells; in certain sections of Africa, beads; and as you know, the early settlers in this country used the wampum or shells that served the Indians as their money. We know best the money of our own country. We recognize the five- and ten-dollar bills, and we know well the one-dollar bill, the large round silver dollar, the half-dollar, the quarter, the dime, the nickel, and the copper cent. We know that money can be used to buy things we want and things we need. We know that sometimes there isn't enough for all our wants and needs. So we are interested in our family's money—where it comes from, how we use it, and what we get for it.

Problem 1: WHERE DOES THE FAMILY GET ITS MONEY?

The fairy stories you read as a child told of many strange and wonderful ways, always easy, by which people got money. A rub or two of Aladdin's lamp brought him the riches of kings; a fish, grateful that it was thrown back into the sea, gave wealth to the kind fisherman; and the "good sister" found pieces of gold falling from her mouth when she spoke. In real life, there is no such easy way of getting money. In most cases, someone must work hard to get money for the family's needs. Usually the father is the family member who is the wage earner. He may follow any one of many occupations to earn money for his family. If we were to make a list of the occupations men follow in our community to earn money for their families, it would be long and varied. Doctors, lawyers, merchants, and teachers; engineers, chemists, and druggists; plumbers, mechanics, and shoemakers; farmers, dairy men, and bus drivers—all might be included. The salaries or wages for these occupations differ widely.

Sometimes the money the father earns is not enough for the family's needs. Then the mother or one or more of the children may also work for wages and contribute their earnings to the family's money.

Some families have invested money which was earned by their members in other years, or perhaps money inherited from the grandparents or other relatives, in land, buildings, or other property for which rent is received. The rent collected then becomes part of the family's money. Some families invest their savings in stocks and bonds which bring an annual return in cash. Such returns, like rent, serve to increase the amount of money the family receives.

The sale of goods produced by the family is also a source of money for it. Most farm families find this the main source of their money. The goods raised may be corn, cotton, turnips, tomatoes, pigs, or pecans. It may have required the work of the father alone, or the work of father, mother, and children. The money return for crops raised is not always a fair return for the labor spent. Droughts, floods, or an oversupply of the product raised may all affect the money the family receives for the goods it raises. Some families raise food for their own use. No money is received for this, but it means no money need be spent. This frees money for other purposes so that the family's money is really increased by home production. Green vegetables from the garden, chickens, and milk from the cow are foods commonly produced for home use. Almost all families carry on work at home which in effect stretches the family's money. The canning of fruits and vegetables, the baking of bread, and the making of clothing at home result in a saving for the family.

Salary or wages; rents and returns on investments; crops and animals sold; food raised for home use; and home production, such as canning and sewing, are sources of the family's money in cash or its equivalent.

Activities:

1. Select ten or twelve of your friends and list the occupations of their fathers and mothers. How many have the same occupation? How many different occupations are listed?
2. Write down sources of your family's money. How many sources do you have? How many persons in your family help earn the family's money? How does your family compare with other families in these items?
3. Why do not two families whose fathers have the same salary or wages always have the same amount of money?
4. How can children add to the family's money?

Problem 2: FOR WHAT IS THE FAMILY'S MONEY SPENT?

For what is the family's money spent? If you were to ask your mother this question she might reply, as she offered you a freshly baked cookie and a glass of milk, "Much of it must go for *food*." Perhaps she might tell you that the amount spent for food for each person in your family averaged thirty cents or fifty cents each day. If you check the rules you had for your daily food, you can see why much of our money must be spent for food.

Money must be spent for *shelter*. If the family does not own the house or apartment in which it lives, part of its money must be paid out in rent. If the family owns its home, part of the money must go to pay taxes on the property, and to keep it in repair. As much as fifteen to twenty per cent of every dollar of the money belonging to the average American family often goes for shelter.

Part of the family's money must go for *clothing*. It is hard to say just what share clothing will take. So much depends upon the interests and habits of the family and upon the location of the home. Usually, if the family's money is not enough to go around to all its needs and wants, the members try to spend less on clothing than they had first expected to do.

The *operating expenses* of the home take part of the family's money. Under this head we would list the expense of lighting and heating the house, supplying fuel for the cook stove, and supplying ice or electricity for the refrigerator, as well as the cost of clean linen for the household and the family members. Operating expenses vary with families. Carelessness may make these costs so large that they take money that might yield more satisfaction spent in some other way.

The *automobile* requires some of the family's money. The amount depends upon the kind of car, its age and condition, and the extent to which it is used. Gasoline, oil, tires, and repairs all must be paid for from the family's money. It is very easy for the auto to take more than its rightful share and thus crowd out the meeting of other important needs.

Every family spends money on *health, recreation,* and *education.* Expenses for health include such items as straightening teeth, operations, inoculations, vaccinations, annual health examinations, and the filling of medical prescriptions when necessary. Expenses for recreation include the cost of the family vacation, money spent for picture shows, for memberships in organizations, and for other means for family fun. Money spent for education will be greater in some families than it is in others. It may cover only the cost of school books, pencil and paper, and music lessons for the school girl; it may cover the expenses for education in college or in a professional school.

Some of the family's money is spent to support the *church* which the family attends. In some churches, as much as a tenth of the family's income is expected as a pledge to church support.

Some of the family's money may be set aside for *savings.* Money may be saved to buy a home, to provide for the education of the children, or to assure security for the old age of the father and mother. Also, some money must go for taxes to support the city, state, and federal governments.

Activities:

1. Talk with your parents and find out how much your family spent last month for different items such as shelter, food, clothing, automobile, and recreation. For what items has the most money been spent?
2. Do all families spend their money in the same way? Give examples of differences in family spending.
3. What expenditures of your family would you list as operating expenses?

Problem 3: WHAT INFLUENCES THE FAMILY'S SPENDING?

We have seen that the family's money goes for food, shelter, and clothing for the family members; to cover the operating expenses of the household; to provide for the health, recreation, and education of family members; to support the church or other organizations in which the family is interested; and for savings. Now we are interested to find out what influences the family's spending among these items. Why does one family spend much for shelter and little for education, and another spend little for shelter and much for education?

Perhaps the first thing that influences the family's spending is the amount of money it has to spend. If the amount is too small to provide for all the family's needs, then some of these will receive little. If there is only enough money for actual needs, the family cannot live in a mansion, wear expensive clothing, and have large automobiles. Its spending must be simple. If the amount of money is great enough to provide liberally for all the family's needs, then the family's spending will be freer and more lavish.

The size of the family, the age of its members, and the state of their health influences the family's spending. The size of the family directly affects its spending. If there are ten people to be supported on $100 per month, more money must be spent for food, shelter, and clothing than would be necessary if there were only three in the family. When more money is spent for food, shelter, and clothing, less remains for education, recreation, health, and savings.

The age of the family members affects the family spending more than is usually realized. It costs much more to feed, clothe, educate, and provide recreation for a high school girl or boy than it does to meet the same needs for a two-year-old child or an aged grandmother. If a family of five has three members in high school or college, it may find it difficult to make any saving during the years of their going to school.

The state of health of the family members also influences the family's spending. If one member has a sudden illness requiring an operation, the cost may be so great as to limit all other spending of the family for some time. In some families, some member, perhaps the mother or father, suffers from a long illness which requires frequent attention from a physician and possibly expensive treatments. The family's spending is influenced by this situation. The other members cheerfully trim their own wants to provide for the needs of the person dear to them.

The family's standard of living influences its spending. If the family takes it for granted that a month's vacation trip for all its members is to be expected; that the family car should be traded in each year; that the house should have new furniture frequently to bring it "up to the minute," its scale of living may lead to extravagance and overspending. If a family's standard of living is simple and sensible, the family spending will be simple and sensible.

Of course, the ideals and interests of the family and the activities it enjoys influence its spending. If the family members enjoy music and books, they try to see that these are bought. If they enjoy gardening, they want money spent for bulbs, plants, and seeds. If they are interested in antiques, some money is spent for things that another family would regard as "rubbish." If the family is interested in community organizations, money will be spent to support the Camp Fire Girls, the Boy Scouts, the church, the community library, and other organizations important in good community life. We will spend money to obtain those things which we believe to be important to a good life.

Family spending is also influenced by the spending habits of friends and acquaintances. You may have said to your mother, "Well, I don't care, *all* the other girls have new party dresses (or something else) and I think I should, too!" Such a demand shows what effect the spending habits of others can have on the way your family spends its money. If we stop to consider matters thoughtfully, we prefer to have what is best for *our* family determine our spending habits.

Activities:

1. In a column write five things that your family has purchased during the past week or month. Write the reasons why each purchase was made. Compare the reasons to see what were influences in your family's purchasing of these things.

2. To what extent have you or your family been influenced by others in your spending? Give examples.

3. What does the saying "Money burns her fingers" mean?

Problem 4: WHY SHOULD THE FAMILY PLAN ITS SPENDING?

Perhaps as you read this Problem you are thinking, "We don't have to plan to spend! Spending is *easy*. Saving is what takes planning." If spending were just getting rid of money, surely that could be done without any planning or effort. There is something more than this to the family's spending. There are several people in the family to be supported. The money must serve the real needs of the family, and not just the passing whims of one or two members. Wise spending requires planning. If all needs are to be met as well as possible from the money to be had, they must be considered before any of the money is spent.

Making plans for the family's spending is like studying road maps before we set out on a trip. We find out the direction we will travel, the distances to be covered, the road markings that we will follow, any detours we may have to make, and then we make our plan for the trip based on our study of the map. The family is to travel through a year. It wishes to provide for all its members, pay its bills, and have something saved for education, old age, or a home. It must be sure to follow markers that will keep all its members well fed, adequately clothed, comfortably housed, with necessary attention to health, recreation, and education. A long illness or the loss of the home through fire, earthquake, or cyclone is like a bad detour. It upsets the schedule for the trip and causes many changes in the plans of the group.

Planning makes sure that everything has been considered fully and even some provision made for an emergency.

Family planning helps to keep the spending balanced. If the amount to be spent for the various needs is left to chance, it is quite possible that so much will be spent for one need or want that there will not be enough for other needs. For example, one family wanted, and thought it needed, a number of pieces of new electrical equipment, and made the purchase on the installment plan. When the monthly payments proved difficult to manage, the family members sat down and figured up the family spending. They found that the provisions they had made for their needs were not balanced. After the food and rent bills were paid, all that was left had to go to pay for the new equipment. Had they planned *before* instead of *after* the purchase was made, they might have saved themselves trouble.

You may have heard one family member say, "Well, she gets everything and I get nothing!" Sometimes it is true that some one person gets far more than his or her share. This usually happens when there is no planning and the loudest speaker wins. If the family plans its spending, the needs of all members are studied and a fair division can result.

Family planning places the responsibility on the whole group. It is no one person's fault but the fault of all if the spending does not bring the satisfaction expected. Concern with getting your money's worth out of services and things you buy becomes more real if you share the responsibility for the purchases.

A better understanding of family finances comes through family planning. Most of us know many, many things we want. If we help in the family planning, we also know just what money the family receives that may go for all the wants and needs of all its members. One girl who shared for the first time in the family planning said, after there was a discussion of family needs and money, "But where is the rest of our money—to do with what we please?" When she found that there was no special source for extra money, she was much surprised and disappointed. We all find it hard to give up our belief in fairies and easy money, but that is a part of growing up. Helping plan the family's spending helps us to grow.

Family planning makes for working together with satisfaction on the part of the family members. If we understand what the situation is, we are interested in helping. We are eager to work together. The money problems are not "father's and mother's," but the whole family's, and their solution gives satisfaction to all the members.

Family planning helps bring about the growth and development of the family members. Do you see how this can be? The five-year-old who shares in one of the planning sessions may understand far less than does the fifteen-year-old, but he learns that his family works together, that its members are thoughtful in their consideration of problems, and that they willingly adjust for the good of all. The fifteen-year-old may understand far less than her parents do about the whole matter of family finances, but her understanding is far greater than that of her five-year-old brother. She has learned the difficult lesson that if you have four apples and eat two, you then have only two apples. She has developed her interest in the group. By being willing to share, she has gained a sense of values through sharing in the family's plans for its spending.

Activities:

1. What things have been purchased by your family recently that would not have been purchased if plans had been made before?
2. What plans should be made before buying a refrigerator, a chair, groceries, or a dress?
3. How old should a child be before he has a part in helping in the planning?

Problem 5: HOW SHALL THE FAMILY PLAN ITS SPENDING?

If the family is to plan its spending, a time should be set for the planning conference when all the members can be together. The planning is so important to family success that sharing in the planning should be placed above any personal plans or interests, such as a picture show or skating.

If everyone remembers that the goal is to provide for family needs and get the most satisfaction possible from the money spent, then the planning seems very important to each one. Planning for spending is so interesting and profitable that no one could regard it as a chore.

The first point which the family will discuss will be "How much money will our family have to spend this year?" You will recall that the family's cash money came from earnings of the father, and perhaps other members; rents and dividends; and food produced at home. The money received from each of these sources last year will show what may be expected for the coming year. Perhaps the report on the family's money for the past year would look like this:

Father's salary . . .	$1200.00
Rent from land . . .	200.00
Poultry and garden .	100.00
	$1500.00

Then the family will consider its needs, and the amount of money which will probably be necessary for each. Questions which the family will answer will be similar to the following: What did we spend for food last year? What did our rent cost us? What did we spend for clothes? What did we spend for the car? What did Junior's music lessons cost? What did we spend for fuel, laundry, and electricity? What should we allow for a vacation? How much shall we try to save? Perhaps the yearly spending plan made at first will be like the one at the top of the next page.

Food	$460
Rent	240
Clothing	
Father	50
Mother	30
John	35
Lucy	35
Zoe	10
Operating expenses	275
Car	175
Education	
Music lessons	20
Schoolbooks	20
Gifts	10
Vacation	25
Church	20
Other expenses	95

After the first estimates are made, some member of the family may say, "Well, we must have new tires this year." Junior may say, "Well, I don't want to take music any longer." Perhaps mother may agree, saying "Well, Father must have a new overcoat." So the planning would go. It may be found necessary to reduce expenditures for certain things in order to provide for others. Certain expenses, such as food and rent, are difficult to reduce, so the planning for spending becomes an exciting game. Perhaps when the family's spending plan is finished it would be somewhat like this:

Food	$460
Rent	240
Clothing	
Father	60
Mother	30

John	35
Lucy	35
Zoe	15
Operating expenses	225
Car	150
Education	
Schoolbooks	20
Gifts	25
Vacation	20
Church	20
Other expenses	165

Activities:

1. Plan the spending of a family with an income of $1000. Of $800. Of $600.
2. Suggest ways in which your family could improve its spending.

Problem 6: WHAT RESPONSIBILITY DOES EACH MEMBER HAVE FOR THE FAMILY'S SPENDING?

If we turn the pages of a newspaper to the personal and "want ad" section, we may find a brief statement: "To whom it may concern: I will not be responsible after this date for any debts other than those of my own making.—Sam Jones." Such a statement usually shows that the family is not happy, and often money matters are the cause. It also shows that the father and husband is held responsible for the debts caused by the spending by family members unless he announces to the world that he no longer accepts that responsibility. We say he is legally responsible for his family's spending.

The other members of the family are not *legally* responsible; however, they should share with the father certain responsibilities for family spending. Each member who shares in the planning has the responsibility of planning wisely and well. It is *his* plan quite as much as it is that of other family members, and he cannot escape his responsibility.

Each member has the responsibility of helping the family to live within the plan. We have had enough experience with team work to know that one person who will not pull with the others can cause the team to lose the game. One family member who will not be responsible may cause the family to spend far more than their plan provided. Perhaps we can give several examples of this. The son or daughter may wreck the family car through careless driving. To provide the money necessary to replace it, all saving must be stopped for the year; sister's music lessons must be given up; perhaps the clothing purchases may have to be much less. Often the family members who fail to live within the family income have less drama in their failures than there would be in a car wreck. They simply spend *a little more here and a little more there* than the plan provided. Of course, they are failing to carry their responsibilities, too. The success of a spending plan depends quite as much on day-by-day efforts to make the plan work as it does on avoiding some large act that will surely make the plan fail. Some of us find it easy not to wreck cars, or burn down garages, or become mixed up in an accident suit. We may find it hard to keep faith with the spending plan in the many little happenings of every day. Both are our responsibilities.

Each member is responsible for making needed adjustments in the spending plan. Sometimes the father of the family may be out of work for a month, and the money the family has to spend is far less than was expected when the plans were made. Sometimes an emergency arises which must be met. In such cases, adjustments are necessary. These cannot be made by any one or two members alone. They should be shared by all the family's members.

Each member has the responsibility of seeing his own needs in their true relation to the needs of other family members. Babies and little children think only of themselves. They think what they want is the most important thing. As we grow and share in family living we should come to see ourselves as one, not as *the one*. If we can do this, we can meet our responsibility to be fair in family planning.

Each member should accept the family plan in a helpful and happy spirit. If we are honest in our thinking, this should be easy. We will see that the plan is a statement much like $2 + 2 = 4$.

If we can accept the spending plan our family makes in a happy spirit, without soreness of heart, perhaps we will learn to face the rest of Life's arithmetic in the same way!

Activities:

1. List ways in which you can help your family improve its spending plan.
2. When is a family member spending more than her share of the income?
3. How do money matters bring unhappiness to the family? Can you give examples of this?

Problem 7: HOW SHALL WE PLAN OUR PERSONAL SPENDING?

Personal spending is something which we all do. We may spend our money for a malted milk or an orangeade; for a ticket to the music recital or the ball game; for a book or a picture show; for a postage stamp or a phone call. Perhaps not a day goes by without our doing some personal spending.

We get money that is ours for personal spending in one of three ways. We may *coax* it out of our parents: "Please, will you give me a dime?" There is a sort of a gamble in this way of getting money, because their mood may not be "right," the thing we wish to buy may seem silly to them, and therefore the money may not come forth;

furthermore, the money may be needed so badly for other expenses that our requests are not taken seriously. We may have an *allowance*. In some families, the family spending plan provides that each child has a definite sum each week, the sum becoming larger as the child grows older. This plan gives the girl or boy a feeling of assurance about what he or she can count on. We may *work* to earn money. Many schoolgirls "tend babies," read aloud to invalids, or run errands to earn their spending money. Usually their chances for work are much alike from week to week, so they know how much to count on. Of these three ways, perhaps having to ask or coax is the least satisfactory, as it is hard to know what you will get.

The usual personal spending of schoolgirls includes the purchases of school supplies; "treats," such as candy, popcorn, ice cream, and sodas; recreation, including school parties and picture shows; hose and handkerchiefs and other accessories; and gifts. If our personal spending is to be wisely done, it should be planned. You recall that when we discussed the family's plan for spending we considered, first, what money there was to spend, and next, what things there were that we needed to buy. We should do the same way in planning our personal spending. If we plan well, our money will cover our needs for the week or month for which it is allowed. The girl who is "rich" for two days and out of funds for five has many bad moments. We have no desire to be in her shoes, so planning seems a good idea.

Following the plan is as important in personal spending as it is in family spending. There will be many times when we will be tempted to forget the plan, but if we can follow it through, we will have more satisfaction in the end.

Setting aside small amounts to grow into a larger fund enables us to satisfy some desire that takes a sum of money larger than our allowance. Perhaps we want a radio for our room, a bicycle, or a dressing table. It is really fun to save toward such a goal, and after the first week or two, the holding fast of some part of our money for the purchase will not seem at all hard. We will have established the habit of saving. We will also have developed our ability to defer our satisfaction which is very important in growing up.

If we make a plan for our spending for a month, it might look something like this:

Allowance	$3.00
Expenditures:	
Hose, 2 pair	$1.50
Pencils	.10
Paper	.10
Class dues	.10
Comb	.10
Saving for our share of bicycle	.25
Church collection	.20
Movies	.50
Popcorn	.05
Candy	.10
	$3.00

If we could plan to give our hose such care that they would last longer, we could have money free to spend for something else.

Our personal spending has been wisely planned if it has met our needs, has given us satisfaction, and has contributed to our growth and development. What we learn in managing our personal spending will help us to be wiser in family spending. What we learn in planning family spending should help us to do a better job in our personal spending. In each case, the problem is to get the most satisfaction possible out of the money.

Activities:

1. Plan your own expenditures for one month.
2. List expenditures that you made last month that were wise; list those that were not wise.
3. When is our money well spent?

REFERENCES FOR THE UNIT

Calvert, Maude Richman, *The New First Course in Homemaking.* Atlanta: Turner Smith Co., 1932.

Donovan, Dulcie Godlove, *The Mode in Dress and Home.* Boston: Allyn and Bacon, 1935.

Jensen, Milton B., Jensen, Mildred R., and Ziller, M. Louisa, *Fundamentals of Home Economics.* New York: The Macmillan Co., 1935.

Kinyon, Kate W., and Hopkins, L. Thomas, *Junior Home Problems,* Revised Edition. New York: Benj. H. Sanborn and Co., 1938.

Talbot, Nora, and Others, *Practical Problems in Home Life for Boys and Girls.* New York: American Book Co., 1936.

SUGGESTED HOME EXPERIENCES

1. Plan your own expenditures for each month and follow the plan. Enter in an account book the items of spending as they take place and compare your actual spending with the plan you had made. Include in your items what is spent for you—for example, the purchase of a dress—as well as the money you handle personally.
2. Help in the family planning of family expenditures.

UNIT 19

HELPING TO CARE FOR YOUNGER CHILDREN

CHILDREN ARE A LONG TIME IN GROWing up. Many years must pass from the time they are born, when they are entirely helpless, before the time comes when they can take complete care of themselves. The number of things they first do for themselves is very small. Gradually these increase, until, as grownups, they can do everything for themselves. Nothing is more interesting and fascinating than watching children develop. The tiny baby waving his arms and legs, the older baby toddling here and there looking for new experiences, and the six-year-old child starting off to school all furnish plenty of interest, ever new and enjoyable.

Guiding and directing young children in their growing and learning is an important responsibility of the older family members. It is essential that this be done in the right way. Much of our happiness and later success depends upon how we are directed during these first years of life. The chief responsibility of caring for children falls upon the mother. However, other members of the family should share in this too. Besides helping the mother, assisting in caring for the younger members brings about happy and pleasant relationships within the family. Helping in the care of children should be regarded as a privilege and should be done in this spirit.

Problem 1: WHAT CARE DO CHILDREN NEED?

Caring for children is a big job which is made up of many small ones of all types and kinds. It requires much time. Studies show that as much as five or six hours daily are given by mothers to the care of infants. This time is not all given at one part of the day, but stretches out during the whole twenty-four hours. In addition to the care the mother gives, other members of the family give as much as one and one-half hours daily. The babies in these studies were in good health. Sick ones would require even more time. The care does not end with babyhood. The toddler makes demands on the mother and the other family members. The need for care continues through the preschool days, decreasing little by little as school days begin.

Children have definite needs that must be cared for properly if they are to grow up as they should. It is the responsibility of the older members of the family to see that these needs are met and that the children receive the right kind of care.

Children need the right amount of good, wholesome food. It should be well prepared and served at the correct time. The children should be considered in the planning of the meals and their food needs provided for in an adequate manner. The children should be included in the plans for serving the meals. Some families find it desirable to have a special table for the young child or children. Others prefer to seat the young children at the family table.

Children need a good home, one that permits their best growth and development. The house should be clean and properly cared for. They need a warm place to live in the winter and a cool one in the summer, with plenty of fresh air and sunshine all the time; they need a place to romp and play; they need rest and sleep; they need a place where complete rest and sound sleep may be possible.

Children must be properly clothed. Their clothing should be comfortable and should permit freedom of movement. It should be easily laundered and cleaned. It should protect them from the cold in the winter and help keep them cool in the summer.

Children must be kept clean, but without making cleanliness, instead of the happiness of the child, the goal. Play and all the many things children must do in order to know the world in which they live seem to bring them dirty hands and dirty clothing. Before we call, "Now, don't get yourself dirty," we must remember that for the child a certain amount of dirt goes with enjoyment. The way the child feels about being too clean has been described thus:

> Over the daisies and through the long grass,
> Dirty but happy, gay little lass.
> Dressed up for company, dull hours pass,
> Clean but so wretched, poor little lass.

Children should be kept reasonably clean, but not to the extent that they are not permitted to play and do the things which children like to do.

Children must be protected from danger. Danger is not a wolf hiding by the door, but it is the thousand and one chances for harm that come in everyday living. The home and community should do everything possible to prevent harm coming to children. The number of accidents to children in the home and the community is far too large for us to feel satisfied with present conditions. Young children should be watched during their waking hours. They do not know that fire burns them, water drowns, and cars crush. They must have personal attention if they are to be safe.

Children need to be out-of-doors. Those who live in cities and large towns may not have a safe place to play close by. It may mean that some one must take them to a park or playground and watch to see that they are in no

The small child's birthday party has simple food, but the occasion is filled with splendor for him. He feels his importance and is pleased with the good wishes of his friends.

danger. Even in one's own yard it may be necessary to watch a child at his play.

Children need help in their play. Play is essential in the development of children, and they should engage in the right kind. Children ought to have stories read and told to them. Through these their lives are enlarged and enriched, their imagination is developed, and many ideals are established. The child must wait some time before he can read for himself. He needs this training long before he can do it.

Good habits must be formed, and desirable personal qualities must be developed. The little child has no sense of "mine or thine"—he does not know the difference between his things and those that belong to others. He does not quite understand the difference between what he imagines and what is true. To his mind, the big, black, growling bear which he says he saw in the closet is real. He must have help if he is to understand the difference between real and unreal. Perhaps you have seen classmates who sulked and pouted when they could not have their own way, or others who wanted to be the "whole show" all the time. They had lacked the help they needed to make them develop desirable personal qualities as they grew up. The child must learn to obey and live with others successfully. The right type of direction makes all this possible.

Children need love and affection. They are sensitive to our attitudes. Disapproval, teasing, and making fun of them make them unhappy and hurt their growth. We must learn to be affectionate and considerate without indulging and spoiling them. It may seem strange to include showing affection as a job to be done, but placing it here may emphasize the need for it; to show affection wisely, thought and effort are required.

Activities:

1. Observe a young child for several hours. Make a note of all the things that were done for him by others.
2. Of all the things that must be done for young children, which are the most important? Why?
3. Describe a well-cared-for child according to your idea.

Problem 2: WHAT IS OUR RESPONSIBILITY WHEN THERE ARE CHILDREN IN THE HOME?

One of the first responsibilities in regard to children in our home is that of helping in such ways as we can with their care. There are so many jobs included in this that no one need lack a means of helping. Perhaps help in washing hands is what is needed, or taking the child for a walk, teaching him a new game, or staying nearby while the child naps. Whatever the job is, the doing of it will be interesting and of value to us if we will allow it to be. Sometimes the child needs care that can best be given by the mother. In such case, we should relieve her of some other responsibility and thus give her time for the task. Some of these things that we can do to free time for the mother are setting the table, washing and putting away the dishes, preparing part of or all the meal, mending hose, helping with the laundry, cleaning the house, and marketing for food. Often the mother finds it gives her rest and joy to turn from household tasks to those of child care. So we can help her, and also carry our own responsibility.

We all have a responsibility to help carry out the parents' plans for the training and directing of the children. Our help in this is absolutely important if the children are to develop into well-adjusted persons. For the parents to act one way toward a child and for us to act in just the opposite way is very bad. Even though parents have not planned too wisely, a child should not be upset by conflicting directions from others. Any changes in the child's management should be made as easily as possible and by the parents. Talking about these changes should not be done in the child's hearing.

We should avoid teasing children. Nothing disturbs a family more, and nothing is worse for a child's disposition. The child does not quite understand whether the teasing is truth or pretending. He is embarrassed because he is being laughed at. He is upset, and his actions are not his best. Even most grownups find it difficult to take teasing gracefully and happily. Children certainly should not be expected to do so.

Needless irritating of children is bad practice. Teasing often causes this, but other things irritate, too. Among these are rudeness, loud talking, hitting, and continually saying, "don't." The irritated child is cross, sulky, and ugly in disposition. We should not do things to make children so unhappy.

We should accept the fact that children have certain rights that should be respected. We should feel our responsibility to safeguard these rights. Children have a definite place in the home. They, too, are members of the family, and are just as important as we are.

We should have the correct attitude toward children.

We should not be jealous of them. Family life is not a contest for favors. If the younger children seem to have more time and attention from the parents, it is because they need it. We should try to be understanding and helpful. A helpful spirit should prevail between the younger and older members of the family.

All this does not mean that the younger members should rule the family, nor does it advocate the spoiling of children until they are not fit to live with others. It does mean that the older members have a responsibility in directing and guiding the younger members of the family so that they can take their place in the home satisfactorily.

Helping to care for younger children is good training for us all. It is a means of increasing our interests, as well as educating ourselves. It helps us to understand ourselves better. It aids us in improving our own personalities. It may be a means of earning some money in caring for a neighbor's child. It helps us to be better family members, through an increased understanding of some of the problems of the home.

Activities:

1. Make a list of the things you can do in your home or another's to free the mother's time to care for a young child.
2. Name some specific ways in which you can help in training and guiding some young child.
3. What rights does a young child have that should be respected by the older children and grownups?

Problem 3: WHAT SHALL BE OUR GUIDES IN CARING FOR CHILDREN?

If we are to care for children we want to do our task well and have it contribute to the happy, rounded growth of the child. Here are some guides to help us to this end:

1. The routine of a child's life should be followed. By routine we mean those necessary activities that are done regularly, and sometimes often, throughout the day. These include eating, sleeping, bathing, and playing. Routine is established early in the child's life. Any change from this will disturb the child and may harm him. We should do our best to keep the child in the established routine.

2. Desirable habits should always be encouraged, and bad habits, never. Sometimes an action appears cute and funny in a small child, but would be punished severely in an older one. It is a mistake to encourage this action until it becomes a habit, for later the child will be forced to break it and suffer from its results.

3. The child should learn to help himself as early as possible and to the extent that he is capable. He should never be made a helpless individual, expecting everything to be done for him.

4. The child should be permitted to develop as an individual, but he should also learn to be a willing worker in a group. It is surprising how early a child can learn this.

5. The child should develop a respect for the property of others, and also for his own, as soon as possible. Learning this takes a longer time than some other things, but is an important thing for every child to know.

6. The child should be let alone as much as possible and given freedom for development. Constantly scolding a child to let this alone, or not to touch this, or to come away from that, are poor ways to train him. Positive methods with children are much better than negative ones. "Don't" should be excluded from one's list of words and "do" substituted. "Don't this" and "don't that" soon fall on closed ears. The child soon has little regard for the "don't" rules.

7. Punishment should be withheld until absolutely necessary. Preventing the need of punishment is always the better plan. When used, punishment should be construc-

Children should be regarded as intelligent human beings. The methods used in caring for them should be based upon this idea.

tive. That is, it should help the child be a better person and to fit in his group and its rules. The child who finds that others will have nothing to do with him when he takes all the toys to himself, or when he scratches and bites his playmates, is usually more effectively punished than if he is spanked for his bad habit.

8. The child should not be told falsehoods. If it is not wise to tell a child the truth, then the subject should be changed. Lying to a child destroys his faith in the person. It is always a dangerous thing to do.

9. The child should not be urged constantly to hurry. Young children have no idea of time. For them it has no meaning. They do not understand what is wanted, and they are likely to become cross and irritated.

10. The cause of a child's behavior should always be sought. There is usually a reason for it. Sometimes he has not understood what was desired of him. Sometimes he may not like the way the request was made. Sometimes more was demanded than he could do. Other reasons, too, may be found.

The relations between children and those caring for them should be such that the children are calm, peaceful, and not greatly upset or disturbed. This means that they should not be frightened or teased.

Activities:

1. What other guides would you add to the above list?
2. Which of the above guides are easiest to follow? Why?
3. What is likely to result if children are greatly upset and disturbed?

4. Give an example of a child's misbehavior being caused by an older person's actions.

Problem 4: HOW CAN WE HELP CHILDREN TO FORM GOOD FOOD HABITS?

Good food habits are the basis of good health in children. These habits should be formed very early so that the child may have the right start in health. Children need help in acquiring good food habits. Here we older members of the family can assist greatly.

Good food habits on our part do much to help children in the family form good food habits. Children are great imitators. They especially want to do as the grownups do. If father and big sister drink milk and eat vegetables, little brother follows their example happily. The "do-as-I-do" plan works much better with children than the "do-as-I-say" plan.

Regular and adequate meals are important in the forming of good food habits by children. This practice should be adopted at the beginning of a child's life and followed as he grows up. His meals should come at a definite time. They should be sufficient in amount for his needs and should contain all the essential foods. His food needs are changing all the time. These needs should be known and provided for as he grows and develops. As a tiny baby, he needs six feedings of milk per day. Later, he needs four feedings. Orange juice, vegetables, cereals, and cod liver oil are included, as well as milk. When he becomes a schoolboy he needs three full meals. The amount of food he needs increases as he grows. Milk, orange juice, vegetables, and whole grain cereals will always be important in his diet, even after many other foods are added.

Well-prepared and attractive food helps in forming good food habits, and helps to avoid fickle appetites. Children's food should not be highly seasoned and flavored. The food should be attractive, so that the child is interested and wants to eat it. Often the way the food is served determines whether it is attractive. A pretty dish or a gay napkin may increase his desire for the food. A "mother goose" spoon or fork, or a bowl with a picture in the bottom, has been known to interest many a youngster in eating his food.

The child's food may be made more interesting by unusual and attractive tableware.

Another aid is for every family member to eat the food as it is prepared and served. If it is the family custom for everyone to accept the meal without comment, the children will do so, too. Almost without effort this food habit is established. Little or no discussion of the food by the family members is a good plan to follow, unless one wishes to compliment or praise. Talking about our likes and dislikes of food at the table makes the meal unpleasant and helps in forming bad habits. If a family member does not care for a food he should leave it alone and say nothing about it. Many a young child has been "talked" into a food dislike by older family members.

No eating between meals by the family members except for the drinking of milk or orange juice is a good food habit to form. The children will copy the grownups. They can so easily acquire the habit of wanting candy and other sweets or soda pop between meals. Such things prevent them from eating a wholesome meal at the regular time.

Introducing new foods and new ways of preparation from

time to time is a desirable plan. If this is not done, the habit of eating only a few foods will be formed, and we do not want this to happen. Children should be willing to try new foods and to learn to enjoy flavors and other qualities that are somewhat different.

The constant refusing of certain foods by a child may develop into a harmful habit, since in this way important foods may be omitted. We should try to find the reason for a child's refusal and then remove the cause. The refusal may be due to the child's desire to imitate an older person; it may be due to the things about him; and it may be due to the way the child is feeling.

Knowing the food habits which children should form is not enough. We should help them eat as they should until good eating habits are formed. We should discourage any exceptions and encourage only those food habits which are good.

Activities:

1. Observe a young child and see how much alike or unlike are his and his parents' food habits. What may be the reason for this?
2. Make a plan for helping a young child form a desirable food habit.
3. Talk with some mother and find out the method she used to help her children develop their food habits.

Problem 5: HOW CAN WE HELP CHILDREN IN THEIR PLAY?

Play is essential to children. In addition to furnishing them fun, play helps them to grow physically, mentally, and socially. Children need help in their play so that it may do the most for them. If we are to give this help we must understand the part which play takes in lives of children and the right way to help them.

We should avoid bossing children in their play. When children are bossed they lose interest and come to depend

Little children enjoy fitting very simple puzzle pieces together, with a little help. Constructive play of this kind is excellent training for them.

upon others. Children should have the pleasure of planning and doing for themselves. If everything is all worked out for them, little is left for them to do.

We can take part in the games of children. This makes fun for both. In doing this, we should become members of the group and do the parts we are given. Nothing gives children more pleasure than for daddy or big sister to join in their fun.

We can help children learn new games and new ways of playing. This help is always well received by children. A game or way of playing is good to the extent that it helps the child develop physically, mentally, or socially. It is good to the extent that the child can have a part in the activity himself. Games that help children develop physically are finger games, stick horse, ring-a-round-a-rosie, hide-and-seek, relays, races, and prisoner's base. Games that help children develop mentally are animal sounds; hunt-the-thimble; guessing games, such as hot or cold; card games, such as authors; lotto; pit; parchesi; pollyanna; and who's who. Games that help children develop socially are those in which several take part. Relays, card games of many types, baseball, soccer, clap-in-and-clap-out, and Captain Jinks are good for social development.

We can help by obtaining new and different play materials for children. This is something they cannot do for themselves. Play materials should be such that they encourage some type of activity on the part of the child. If the playthings require an older person to operate, they are not good. If they are complete in themselves, or if they merely repeat performance and do not encourage progress, they are not desirable. If they are too difficult for the child to operate, or if they have sharp edges or small parts that are easily pulled off, they are poor playthings.

Children should be encouraged to play by themselves. This ability should be developed as early as possible, as it is an important one for both children and grownups. Grown people who cannot entertain themselves are in a difficult situation. Children must also learn how to play with others. The child who lives in a group of people much older than himself especially needs help in this, and it should not be left for him to learn when he starts to school.

We can encourage children to be good sports. It is most important that children learn early to accept success and failure in the right spirit. Children must be made to realize very soon that they cannot always have their own way. They should know how to give in to others and how to be good sports about it. Sometimes the family, eager to have only the best things for its members, prevents them from being good sports by emphasizing the rewards of success instead of the satisfactions from playing the game.

Whatever we do to help children in their play, we should not do so much for them that they become on-lookers only.

We should not interfere with them. As long as they are engaged in profitable play, as little help as possible should be given them. Even that little is better given when requested by the children themselves. The important thing is to provide a good place to play, interesting playthings, and protection from harm or injury.

Activities:

1. What games would you recommend for a two-year-old; for a three-year-old; and for a four-year-old?
2. What playthings would you recommend for a baby; for a two-year-old; and for a three- or four-year-old?
3. Give some examples of ways of encouraging good sportsmanship in children.

Problem 6: HOW CAN WE HELP TO KEEP CHILDREN CLEAN?

We want children to be clean, but only comfortably so. Keeping the house clean is a great aid in keeping children clean. A clean house helps to prevent children from becoming dirty. It is almost impossible for children to be clean in a dirty house.

The playthings of children should be kept clean. This is important for both health and appearance. Playthings which are easily washed or cleaned are the most desirable. The cleaning should be done just as often as is needed.

Objects which will make the child especially dirty and which are of no particular value to him should be kept out of reach. Cleaning brushes, sooty pans, and dust cloths are examples of such articles. Shoe polish equipment and even garbage cans have been known to interest small children and make them very dirty.

Providing a reasonably clean place for children to play, both indoors and and out-of-doors, is helpful. Sometimes people who keep a very clean house pay little attention to the conditions of the place where the children play. Harm

Knowing how to wash his own hands is fun for the child and helps him to develop habits of cleanliness.

to health may result if the place of play is not a clean one.

Good habits of cleanliness in the family are most helpful in keeping children clean. So much is learned through imitation and example that we cannot emphasize too much the influence of the habits of the other family members. If good habits of cleanliness are a part of the family life, everyone comes to adopt them as a matter of course and to do as the other members do.

We can help children to have a desire to be clean. We can also help them to establish regular habits of washing and bathing. Children must learn to wash, bathe, and dress themselves. At first this is done for them. After a while the responsibilities are gradually turned over to them until, as school boys and girls, they are able to do much of this for themselves. We can help in this training. Washing, bathing, and dressing should be done for children only as long as it is absolutely necessary.

Certain methods will be found desirable in washing, bathing, and dressing children.

Washing the Hands

1. Fill the lavatory, wash bowl, or pan about three-fourths full of warm water.
2. Use a soft washcloth and towel and toilet soap.
3. Have the child put his hands in the water and wash off the loose dirt by rubbing his hands together in the water.
4. Wring the washcloth from the water and rub it over the soap several times.

5. Wash the child's hands with this as many times as are needed to remove all the dirt and soil.

6. When the hands are clean, rinse in clear water, either cold or warm.

7. Dry the hands thoroughly and gently with the towel.

Washing the Face

1. Prepare the water as for washing the hands.
2. Use a soft washcloth and towel and toilet soap.
3. Wring the washcloth from the water and wash the face gently with the cloth, removing all the dirt and soil. If necessary, rub the wet cloth over the soap several times and wash the face with the soaped washcloth. In either case, wash well around the hair line. Wash the ears and neck, too, if needed. Take care that no soap gets into the eyes.
4. Rinse by holding the face over the bowl and using the hand to throw water over the face. Rinse the neck and ears with the washcloth which is dipped in clear water.
5. Dry thoroughly and gently with a towel.

Bathing

1. Turn warm water into the tub to a depth of six, eight, or ten inches, as desired. Test the water with the hand to see that it is not too hot.
2. Use a soft washcloth and towel and toilet soap.
3. Have child sit in the tub.
4. Wash the face, neck, ears, and hands as directed above.
5. Wash the legs and feet with the soaped washcloth, giving attention to any especially dirty places, such as the knees. It may be necessary to rinse the cloth in the lavatory and resoap it once or twice.
6. Wash the rest of the body, using the washcloth lightly soaped.

7. Rinse the soap from the body, using the water in the tub.

8. If desired, the hair may be washed at this time. In this case, the hair is washed with the soaped washcloth or by applying the soap directly to the wet hair and rubbing well with the hands. The hair is well rinsed with water from the tub and then further rinsed with clear, cool water poured from a pan or pitcher.

9. When the bath is over, help the child from the tub to a mat and dry him thoroughly with a towel. The hair requires a longer time for drying.

10. If preferred, the washing of the child's hair may be done at the lavatory before or after the bath. The procedure followed is practically the same as given above.

Changing Clothes

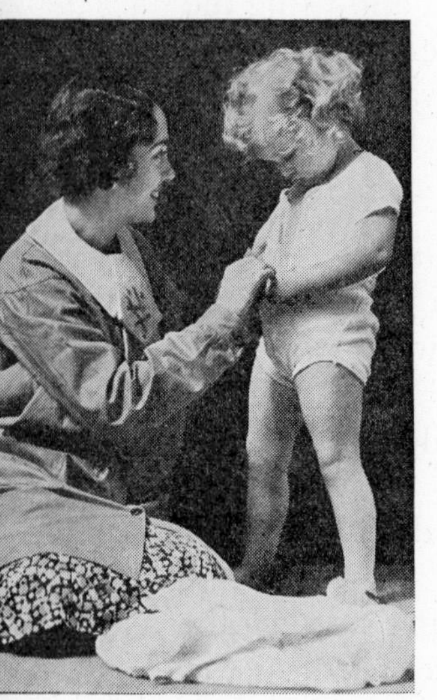

Children like to fasten their own buttons, with just a little help.

1. Remove all soiled clothing. If a complete change is to be made, remove the shoes and stockings.

2. Wash the face, hands, and any other parts of the body which are dirty.

3. Unbutton or unfasten all placket openings. If the garment is a slip-over style have the child put the arms up, and slip the dress or shirt over the head with the arms going into the sleeves. If the garment is coat style, have child hold out the arms and put on the dress or shirt as a coat.

4. Put on the trousers, bloomers or panties.

5. Fasten all openings; fasten the trousers to the shirt.

6. Put on the hose and shoes.

7. Brush and comb the hair.

In all these operations the child should be encouraged and helped every time to do as much as he can, until finally he reaches the place where he can do all for himself.

Activities:

1. Make a list of the reasons for keeping children clean.
2. To what extent should a child be kept clean?
3. Make a plan for helping a young child form some habit in keeping himself clean.
4. Make a list of easily-cleaned playthings.

Problem 7: HOW SHALL WE READ AND TELL STORIES TO CHILDREN?

All children enjoy stories; whether these are read or told makes little difference, just so they have a story. This desire appears early. At first the stories must be simple, scarcely more than a three- or four-line nursery rhyme. Gradually the child develops, until before long he wants an incident or event of some kind.

Some people are good at story telling; others are poor. When a person can tell stories well, she should by all means tell them. If she cannot do so, it is better to read them. When stories are read, they should be read well. Practice in reading aloud may be necessary to make us successful readers. The ability to tell and read stories can be developed, and a poor storyteller or reader can become a good one if she tries hard enough.

We often think of reading and telling stories as being primarily a means of entertaining children. It also is an important means of educating them. A number of years must pass before the child is able to read for himself. During this time he needs to be introduced in some way to literature and history. This can only be done through the help of older people. The child who is early interested in stories usually becomes a reader himself later on.

Even after these children learn to read they will still like to have Mother read or tell a story to them.

Some families have a regular story time set aside in the day. Often this hour is in the evening, and it serves as a "calming down" time before bedtime. As soon as a child is old enough, he shares with the other family members in this hour. Very young children can share in this good time.

Suitable stories should always be selected. The suitability, of course, depends upon the age of the children. Nursery rhymes please the very young. As children become older the fables interest them. Animals and toys that are pictured as people who live and do the things that children do are fascinating to them. Fairy stories are all right if the child is old enough to understand what is real in the story and what is not. Flights of imagination are good for children as long as they do not try to turn them into reality.

When reading a story we should try to make it sound as much like *telling* the story as possible. We should put ourselves into the reading and make the story seem real to the listener. When reading to a group of children, we may sit in a circle with them. When reading to one or two, we may sit with the children so that they can look at the book as it is being read. This is an especially good plan if there are pictures in the book. Children sometimes like to help in turning the pages, and may even want to stop and look at the pictures. The reading should be slow enough so that the children can understand what is being said. Expression should be given to the reading. If possible, a change of voice should be made for the different characters in the story. If a surprise of any kind is coming at the end, interest should be built up for it. Sometimes children wish to talk about a story after it has been read. Opportunity should be given for this. We should be patient if they wish the story reread immediately—this shows that they like the story.

Telling stories requires more skill than does reading them. Fewer people can tell stories well than can read them well. In telling a story we must trust to our memory and ingenuity. These must be good, because children insist that the story be repeated exactly the same each time. Even slight changes in the words of *Red Riding Hood* or another favorite story bring protest from children. The storyteller usually sits in the group of children with everyone in a comfortable position. She plans her story in interesting steps so that she can hold the attention of all until the end. She tells the story as if she were interested in it and wants everyone else to be. She tells it slowly enough for those listening to understand, but not so slowly that they lose interest. She avoids making the story too long, for she wants to keep their interest to the end. She does her best to make the story real. When she comes to the end, if the children want to ask questions or talk about the story, time should be given for this.

The books in the following lists have been found to be successful choices for the story time:

For children from two to three and one-half years:

A Day with Betty Ann, D. Baruch
Two Wooden Soldiers and a Hobby Horse, G. Muter
About Bunnies, G. Muter
Three Little Kittens
The Here and Now Story Book, Lucy S. Mitchell
The Little Red Chair, M. Walker
The Little Family, Lois Lenski
The Tale of the Wee Little Old Woman, Elsa Beskow
Millions of Cats, Wanda Gag

For children from three and one-half to five years:

Snapp, Snapp, Snurr and the Red Slippers, M. Lindman
Peter Rabbit, Potter
Little Black Sambo, Bannerman
Angus and the Cat, M. Flack
Chummy Corner Stories, Hutchinson
The Three Little Pigs, A. Dolgliesh
Round the World, Esther Brann
The Farmer in the Dell, Elmer and Berta Hader
The Toy Animals and Tinkle, the Tired Fairy, Florence Bourgeois
The Little Engine that Could, Mabel Bragg
Wynkin, Blynkin, and Nod, Eugene Field

There are hundreds of other books which children find enjoyable. Information about them can be obtained at your library.

Activities:

1. Bring to class a story that you consider good for a child of a certain age.
2. The class may read the story and judge your choice.
3. Tell or read your story to the class, and have them judge your ability.
4. Examine a number of story books. Decide whether they are good or poor, and for whom they would be suitable. Give reasons for your decisions.

Problem 8: WHAT SHALL WE DO WHEN WE STAY WITH CHILDREN?

Most of us at one time or another have the responsibility of staying with children. If there are younger brothers and sisters in the family, we may be called upon to do it frequently. Sometimes we find it necessary to help out a friend or neighbor by staying with the children for a while. High school girls often stay with children in order to earn money. Whatever may be our reason for having this responsibility, we wish to do the job as well as we can.

When staying with children we should try our best to carry out the desires of the parents in regard to the children. We should listen carefully to the instructions given us and write down any that we think we might forget. There will be many times when we must use our own judgment, but we should make our decisions in relation to what we think the parents would wish done.

We should tend strictly to the business of caring for the children. It is for this purpose that our services have been asked. We should not invite personal guests to be with us unless we have been specially requested to do so. If any of our friends call, it would be better to explain what we are doing and excuse ourselves. Visiting over the telephone with friends should not be done, either; nor is going off in a corner or room to read or write letters a desirable thing to do.

We should conduct ourselves in such a manner that people respect us and trust us. We should also act so that they have confidence in our honesty and ability. We should betray no family secrets or happenings; neither should we attempt to pry into the family's private affairs. We should leave household and personal things strictly alone, using only those needed in the care of the children.

We should do our best to keep the children happy and

contented. If they are disturbed by the parents' absence, we should try to divert their minds from the situation and get them to forget that their parents are away. A pleasant time with the children will make both them and their parents our friends.

It is very important that we help the children in following their regular schedule. The mother usually gives us the schedule and if she does not, we should ask for it. The schedule should include the time for food, play, rest, and sleep, according to the length of time that we are caring for them. Parents appreciate greatly our ability to follow the children's regular schedule.

We should remember that punishment is not to be given by us. This is the parents' responsibility, not ours. So many difficult situations are likely to arise if we do the punishing that we cannot afford to take such a risk. If the child cannot be managed and directed into doing the right thing, we should not attempt to stay with him.

We should treat children well when staying with them. We should not threaten, frighten, or hurt them in any way. We should do our best to make them like us and want us to stay with them again.

To be successful in staying with children we should enjoy doing it. In addition, we should be a happy individual with a good disposition. We should know the right things to do and should do them in a satisfactory manner. A good recommendation for any of us is that children like us.

Activities:

1. Plan what you might say to a friend who wished to call on you while you were staying with a young child. Why is it better that the friend not call on you at this time?
2. What are some ways by which you can keep children happy and contented when staying with them?
3. Is it good for children to be left sometimes in the care of others than their parents? Give reasons for your answer.

Matches are dangerous in the hands of children of any age. They should never be permitted as playthings.

Problem 9: HOW CAN WE HELP TO PREVENT ACCIDENTS TO CHILDREN?

A large portion of all accidents, whether in the home or elsewhere, happen to children. The older members of the family are all responsible for the reduction of these accidents and for the provision of safer conditions for children.

The home should be made as safe as possible for children. Everything should be done to prevent accidents. All the safety measures that were discussed on pages 401–405 apply here. A home that does not prevent accidents to grownups is certainly not a safe home for children.

Fire is one of the most common causes of accidents to children. Many homes are not properly protected from fire. Children love to play with matches. Often these are kept where children can easily get them. Matches should be kept in metal cans or boxes, and should always be well out of the reach of children. Children should be taught early the dangers in lighting matches. Fireplaces should be

Poisons should be kept well out of the reach of small children. This is one of the most important rules of safety for the home.

protected with fire screens. Children should never be permitted to play near a fireplace that is not protected. Children should learn that they should not throw paper and other trash in the fireplace or even the stove.

Toddlers too young to understand should not be permitted to be in a room alone with a gas stove, lest they turn on the gas. As soon as possible, they should be taught not to touch the parts that turn on the gas. Some of the newer gas stoves have switch buttons for turning the gas on and off, which make the stoves much safer.

The handles of utensils in which food is cooking should be turned so that children cannot pull them off the stove. Many serious burns have resulted from children upsetting hot food on themselves. Another bad practice is leaving tubs or large pans of hot water where children can fall into them.

Keys should be kept out of the door locks. Children frequently lock themselves in rooms and become badly frightened. Especially dangerous in this case is the bathroom, where water can be turned on and a child can easily slip or fall into the full tub.

Electric cords which lie on the floor are dangerous. The child may trip himself and have a bad fall, or he may cut or break the cord in two. He may receive a bad shock, or a short-circuit fire may result.

Carelessly dropped rakes have been responsible for injury to many children who fall on the upturned teeth. All articles of this kind should be put away when not in use.

Only toys which are safe should be given to children. Toys with sharp edges, those painted with soluble paint, those with buttons, pins, trimmings, or small parts that can be pulled off and swallowed should never be used. Sometimes children like to play with knives, forks, scissors, pencils, and sharp-pointed sticks. This should never be allowed.

Highly polished floors with rugs that slip and slide are as bad for children as for older people. Some method of holding the rugs fast should be used. Toys and other articles should not be left on the stairs or in the middle of the floor. Children should be taught very early to put away their toys, and older members should put their own things away, too.

All poisons and medicines should be well labeled and kept far out of the reach of children.

In the yard where children play, boxes and boards containing nails sticking out should not be left lying around. Tools with sharp edges, such as hoes, rakes, and spades, should be put away as soon as they are no longer being used. Tricycles and bicycles should be kept in their places and not left on the walks or in the pathways. Children should play in their yard and not in the streets. They should be taught how and when to cross the street.

In helping in the prevention of accidents to children, we do not want to make them cowards who are afraid of everything. We want them to be cautious and to know the right things to do for safety. We want our homes to be such that accidents are not possible.

Activities:

1. Inspect your home and list the things that might cause accidents to young children.
2. Decide in each case what could be done to remove the possible cause.
3. What guides would you suggest to parents for training children to avoid accidents and still not become cowards or "fraidy cats."
4. Talk with a mother and find out how she trained her child to leave matches alone; not to leave his playthings in the middle of the floor; not to play in the street; and not to turn on the gas.
5. Do you consider her method a good or poor one? Why?

REFERENCES FOR THE UNIT

Donovan, Dulcie Godlove, *The Mode in Dress and Home.* Boston: Allyn and Bacon, 1935.

Goodspeed, H. C., and Johnson, E., *Care and Guidance of Children.* Chicago: J. B. Lippincott Co., 1938.

U. S. Bureau of Standards, *Safety in the Household.* Washington, D. C.

Zechlin, Ruth, *How to Play With Your Child.* New York: Barrows Mussey, Inc., 1937.

SUGGESTED HOME EXPERIENCES

1. Care for a young child in your own family.
2. Care for a young child for a friend.
3. Assist at a children's party.
4. Assist a group of children in their play.
5. Read and tell stories to children.
6. Teach a group of children a new game.

UNIT

20

PLANNING AND MAKING A SCHOOL DRESS

PLANNING AND MAKING A SCHOOL DRESS can be fun. The lovely, colored prints displayed in the shops give a wide assortment of materials in color and design from which to choose our cloth.

There are prints gay with pictures of the barnyard, or cocks strutting and announcing the rising sun with "cock-a-doodle-do." There are others that show scenes from vacation land, or suggest the romance of life in the South Seas, or the glory that belonged to kings centuries ago. These may seem amusing and may appeal to us because they are "different." Perhaps we may find them too different to be satisfactory. There are striking checks and plaids that seem to promise a smart as well as a "highly visible" dress.

The many bright or dark colors and the charming pastel ones may make a choice difficult. The style books are filled with many designs suitable for wash dresses.

The simplicity of line is kept, and yet the design is made by some detail, often of neckline, of collar and cuff, or of pockets or plackets.

As we study these, we should find one that is becoming to us and yet not too difficult for us to make in the time we plan to spend sewing.

Problem 1: WHAT DESIGN AND PATTERN SHALL WE CHOOSE FOR OUR SCHOOL DRESS?

In the wise choice of a design for our school dress, study of ourselves is important. Only as we understand the shape of our bodies can we plan or select good dress designs for them. If we are tall—too tall, perhaps we think—we will not want to choose a design that emphasizes our tallness, nor do we want one that denies it. If we are short and round, perhaps tubby, we will not want to emphasize our roundness. Our choice of a design should be one that will be becoming to us. Nor will we be fooled into accepting a design by the familiar words "This is the newest pattern shown," or "Everyone is wearing this design this season. It is really awfully good."

The design for a school dress, like that of a morning dress, should be simple, so that the dress will be easily cared for and suitable for the activities of school. Some new problems in construction, such as sewing the waist and skirt together, setting in sleeves, and perhaps making pleats in the skirt, may be presented. The plain set-in sleeve and the raglan sleeve are often used for a school dress. The dress with the waist and skirt sewed together at the waistline is good for school wear. Fullness, pleats, and darts may be used in the skirt and in the waist.

The trimmings used on the school dress may be contrasting materials, buttons, decorative fastenings, or braid. The type of trimming chosen will no doubt be governed by the design selected for the dress.

We may select a design from pictures in a paper or magazine, or we may draw it ourselves. The pattern we buy to use as our guide in cutting out the dress should be as nearly like the design selected as possible. The pattern should be purchased in the correct size, and altered to fit us and to make the chosen design.

There is a large variety of attractive designs to choose from when selecting clothes for school wear. It is easy to see that "duty" clothes may also be "beauty" clothes if we choose wisely.

Activities:

1. Measure your height, and the width of your shoulders. Draw to scale a rectangle with these measurements, to help you judge your type of figure.
2. Select a picture of a dress which you think you can wear.
3. What design of material will be good for the style of this pattern?

Smartness is not sacrificed in this sturdy cotton school dress of simple design.

Problem 2: HOW SHALL WE CHOOSE AND BUY OUR MATERIAL?

The dress we wear to school should be made from material that is durable, of fast color, easily laundered, and not too difficult to work with. We learned in making our morning dress that material which was free from starch and not sleazy but closely woven and firm was a wise choice for a dress expected to give good service. We should know how much we can spend for our materials and for the other necessities needed for construction. At the present time, satisfactory prints may be purchased for as low as fifteen cents per yard, and as high as thirty cents may be paid for other prints.

We will want to select a material suitable for the

dress design chosen. The color selected should be one that is becoming to us, one that fits into our wardrobe, and one that we will not tire of easily. The design, too, should be pleasing, evenly distributed over the cloth, and not too striking. Suitable materials for a school dress are percale, various prints, gingham, seersucker, linen, and cotton challie. Percale and gingham will give good service and will perhaps be best suited for our purpose. Next, we must decide how much material to buy. To determine this, we must figure twice the length of the waist front, plus twice the length of the skirt back, plus the length of the sleeve. If the sleeve has much fullness at the top, and the pattern for it measures wider than one half the width of the material, it will be necessary to have twice the length of the sleeve. The extra pieces, such as collar, belt, and cuffs, can be cut from surplus material coming from the sides of the skirt and waist lengths.

The purchase of an adequate length of material enables one to avoid piecing, which is difficult to do and not always satisfactory. Where expensive material is used, one often finds it economical to piece. The purchase of excess material is wasteful. The money spent for a half-yard length that is not used brings no returns.

Activities:

1. Examine several samples of material and determine which one would be best for your dress.
2. Determine how much material you will need for your dress.
3. Keeping in mind the money you can spend for your dress, decide how much you can pay per yard for the material.

Problem 3: HOW SHALL WE STUDY OUR PATTERN?

When we studied the pattern for our kimono-sleeve dress we found that it had just two main pieces. The pattern for our school dress will have several main pieces: the front and back waist, the front and back skirt, and the sleeve. The pattern guide must be carefully studied and each pattern piece needed laid aside. Pattern markings should be noted. It would be wise to use with this pattern the study questions given on pages 108 and 109. It is a good practice to pin the pattern together to make half the dress. This aids us in knowing how the dress will go together.

Activities:

1. Examine the pattern and decide what pieces you will want to use.
2. Pin the pattern pieces together according to the markings.

Problem 4: HOW SHALL WE CHECK AND ALTER OUR PATTERN?

In checking the pattern for the two-piece dress with set-in sleeves, we will find it necessary to take more measurements than were required for the kimono-sleeve dress, as there will be more pattern pieces to check. The measurements to be taken are bust, waist, hip, waist front, back, and underarm; skirt length—front, back, and side; sleeve length–both underarm and from the armscye at the shoulder seam; around the arm, midway between the shoulder and elbow; width of the chest, taken about four inches down from the shoulder line, and extending from one armscye to the other; width of the back, taken the same as the chest measurement, but across the back; and shoulder seam length, taken from the base of the neck in a straight line on the highest part of the shoulder to the armscye.

When we have taken and recorded these measurements we are ready to check them against the corresponding measurements on the pattern. We may find that our measurements are larger or smaller. Alterations may be needed in the width or length of the pattern pieces, or in both. The alterations made on the pattern for width and length will be

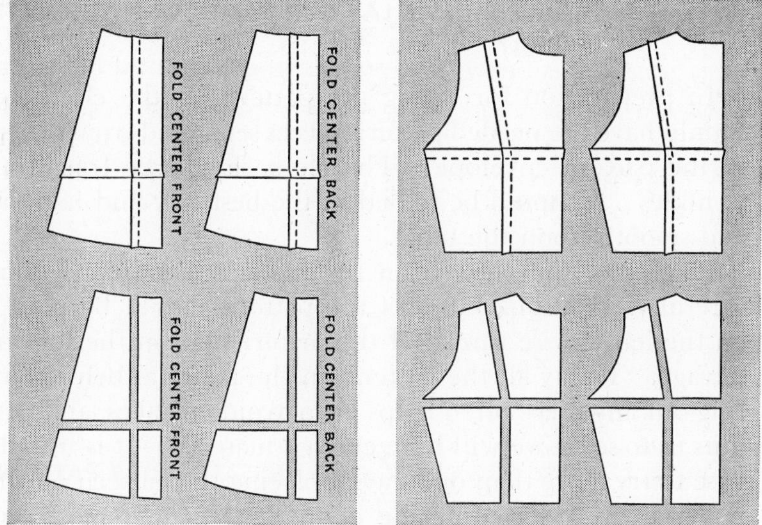

Necessary pattern alterations may include either increasing or lessening the width or length of the skirt or waist.

made by folding over or cutting and spreading the pattern pieces the desired amount as shown in the above diagram. In this dress, the waist and skirt are altered separately.

You will have a sleeve to alter in addition to the other pieces. If the sleeve is too narrow it may be added to on each side seam line. If the sleeve is too large, a small amount may be taken from the sides, or a pleat may be folded in the length of the sleeve to remove the surplus. All alterations of the pattern should be carefully made and rechecked with one's own measurements.

Activities:

1. Have your partner take your body measurements and record them.
2. Check the measurements of your pattern with your body measurements.
3. Alter the pattern to fit your body measurements.

Problem 5: HOW SHALL WE LAY OUR PATTERN ON THE MATERIAL?

In preparation for laying the pattern on the cloth, we should have the needed pattern pieces separated from others in the pattern envelope. The cloth should be free from wrinkles. It should be folded in the best way and laid flat and smooth upon the table.

Placing of the pattern on the material should be done carefully. The markings of the pattern should be placed on the lengthwise thread of the material, as on the fold or selvage. To lay all the pattern on the material before cutting out any piece often helps us to avoid mistakes, and permits us to see if we will have enough material. It is usually wise to try more than one way of placing the pattern on the material, in order to decide upon the best and most economical arrangement. The "up and down" and "crosswise" in weave and design should be carefully noted and considered in laying the pattern. With the pattern pieces placed on the material, our next step is to pin them in place. Any alterations not actually made on the pattern, such as seam allowance or increase in length, should be indicated with pins on the material.

Activities:

1. Try more than one way of placing the pattern on the material to determine which way will be the most economical.
2. Lay your pattern on the material and pin it in place.

Problem 6: HOW SHALL WE CUT OUR DRESS AND REMOVE THE PATTERN?

In the Unit on the morning dress we learned the best way to use our scissors or shears, and the precautions to take in cutting. It is well to recall again the rules for cutting given in that Unit:

1. Cut on the edge of the pattern or alteration line.
2. Cut notches out from the pattern.
3. Keep the material flat on the table while cutting.
4. Use the entire blade of the scissors or shears when cutting a long straight or curved edge; use the points when cutting a short edge or turning a corner.

This dress will present some problems in cutting not found in the first garment. We may find it necessary to cut out certain pieces first, such as the front and back of the waist, and then to fold the material again and place the other pieces on and cut. The center front and center back of the skirt and waist should be marked with long basting threads. Darts, pleats, and tucks should be marked with tailor tacks. These we learned to make in Unit 5, Problems 9 and 10.

Following the marking, the pins are removed, the pattern folded and put away. Each piece of the dress is then marked with its correct name. This may be done by writing the name, such as waist front, on a piece of paper and pinning it to this piece of the dress. Sometimes it may be advisable to leave the pattern pinned to the pieces until these are basted together.

When all pattern pieces are placed back in the envelope, it may be put into the sewing box for later use. The cut pieces of the dress are folded neatly and laid away until our next lesson.

Activities:

1. Cut out the dress and make all the necessary markings on the material.
2. As you remove each pattern piece, label the piece of material with the name.
3. Fold each of the pattern pieces and place them in the envelope.

Problem 7: WHAT PROCEDURE SHALL WE FOLLOW IN MAKING OUR DRESS?

In making a dress we will find that there are definite processes to be completed before others are undertaken. This being true, it is wise to analyze our dress and decide upon the best plan of procedure.

The following is a suggested plan of procedure:

1. Pin and baste in all darts, pleats, and tucks in the separate pieces of the dress.
2. Baste the waist together for the first fitting.
3. Fit and make necessary alterations.
4. Baste the skirt together for the first fitting.
5. Fit and make necessary alterations.
6. Stitch darts, pleats, and tucks, and finish the seams.
7. Baste the waist and skirt together.
8. Fit and make necessary alterations.
9. Stitch the waist and skirt together.
10. Make the placket.
11. Finish the neck.
12. Set in the sleeves.
13. Make the belt and pockets.
14. Sew on the fasteners.
15. Hem the garment.
16. Press the garment and score your work according to the score card suggested in Problem 27 (page 586).

Not all of us will find necessary all the items listed in the suggested plan of procedure in making our dress. Therefore, we will each make our own plan of work, listing in order the work we see to be done.

The dress should be given the proper care during the making. Folding the material carefully when the work is put away is important. As soon as it is possible, the garment should be placed on a hanger. Clean hands and a clean place to work are necessary to keep the garment in good condition during construction.

Activities:

1. Study the pattern guide and the cut-out pieces of your dress.
2. Set up a plan of procedure to follow in making your dress.
3. How does your plan compare with that of your partner?

Problem 8: HOW SHALL WE BASTE THE WAIST FOR THE FIRST FITTING?

To make the waist, the pieces of the dress are placed with the right sides together and pinned on the line of seam allowance at the shoulder and underarm seams. One should be sure that the waistline of the front and back pieces of the waist come together exactly at the side seam. The seams are then pinned and basted, with stitches from 1/8 to 1/4 inch long. Pins may now be removed and the waist turned to the right side. To aid in keeping the neck from being stretched, it is a wise plan to put a basting thread around the neckline, about 1/4 inch from the edge.

Activities:

1. Check your waist to see that all pleats, darts, and tucks are basted into place.
2. Baste the pieces of the waist together.
3. Put a basting thread around the neckline.

Problem 9: HOW SHALL WE FIT THE WAIST?

We learned when we made our morning dress how to fit the shoulder and underarm seams. This waist will require additional fitting, since there are more pieces. Also we will want this dress to fit more closely to the lines of the body than our morning dress did.

Put the waist on, right side out. Be sure the center front and center back are in the middle of the front and back, and perpendicular to the floor. The shoulder seam should be a straight line from the highest part of the shoulder, bisecting the arm at the shoulder.

The underarm seam of the waist should fall in a straight line from the armpit to the floor.

The threads of the material going across the bust should be parallel to the floor.

In fitting the neck of the dress, it is always well to have the back high. The correct neckline may be found by draping a string around the neck at the place where the string seems to rest easily. Do not draw it too tight. A pin line may be placed here and the neck trimmed to within 3/8 inch of the seam allowance.

The front of the waist usually has some fullness to be eased in when joining it to the skirt. It is well for this fullness to come just below the points of the bust. The fullness may be adjusted by gathers or by darts.

When the alterations are pinned in place, the waist is removed, alterations are basted in, and the waist is again fitted.

Activities:

1. Put the skirt on and pin it as you will wear it.
2. Fit the shoulder and underarm seams.
3. Locate the neckline and mark it with a line of pins.
4. Baste the alterations.

Problem 10: HOW SHALL WE FIT THE SKIRT?

After the front and back pieces of the skirt are basted together, the skirt is put on, right side out, for fitting. The waistline of the skirt is placed at the waistline of the body. The center front and center back should fall perpendicular to the floor. The threads of the material going across the abdomen and across the back should be parallel to the floor.

The underarm seam of the skirt, like that of the waist, should fall in a straight line to the floor.

The skirt should be fitted smoothly, but not too closely. Allowance must be made so that sitting and moving about do not throw strain on the seams.

Activities:

1. Put the skirt on and pin it as you will wear it.
2. Have your partner fit the side seams and the waistline.

Problem 11: HOW SHALL WE MAKE THE SEAMS OF OUR DRESS?

In the morning dress, we made a plain seam stitched twice. This was simple to do and made a satisfactory seam. However, in this garment we want a seam that does not have raw edges, so we will make the false French seam. The steps in making this seam are as follows:

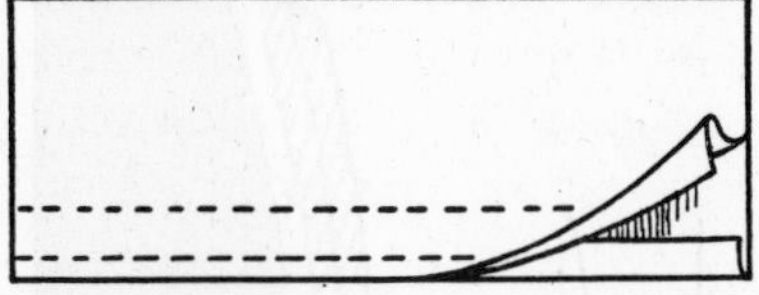

This shows how the false French seam is made.

1. Stitch close to the basted line.
2. Trim so that the seam is ½ inch wide.
3. Turn the edges of the seam in toward each other ¼ inch, and baste into place.
4. Press and stitch on the machine close to the edge of the fold.
5. Remove the bastings and press the seam.

Stop the stitching of the left side seam of the waist three inches from the waistline. A similar opening is made three inches from the top of the left side seam of the skirt. When the waist and skirt are joined, this opening of six inches will provide for the placket.

Activities:

1. Practice making a false French seam.
2. Make the seams in your dress.

Problem 12: HOW SHALL WE BASTE AND STITCH THE WAIST AND SKIRT TOGETHER?

If the waist or the skirt has darts, pleats, or tucks, these should be basted in according to the markings, thus making ready the two sections to be basted together.

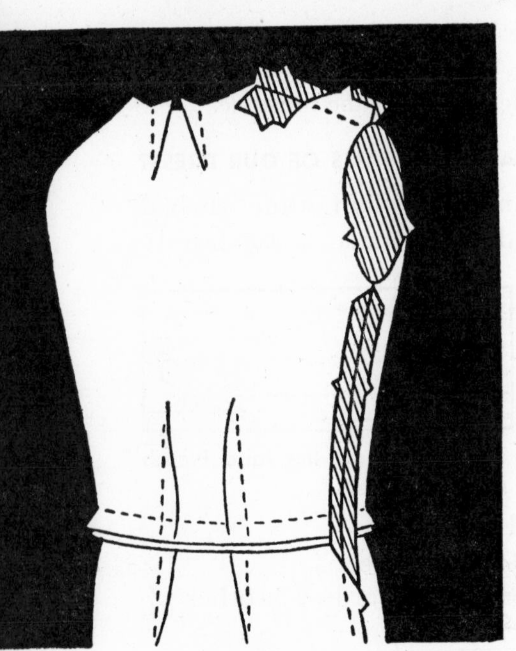

Baste the waist and skirt together very carefully.

In making this dress, the pieces of the waist are sewed together and fitted. Then the pieces of the skirt are sewed together and fitted. Then the waist and skirt are joined together in the following way:

1. With the right sides together, pin the center front of the waist to the center front of the skirt. Pin again at the notches on the waistline.
2. Adjust the fullness between pins and pin it into place.
3. Baste the pieces together with a $3/8$-inch seam and remove the pins.
4. Join the back of the waist and the skirt in same manner, pinning, adjusting, and basting.
5. Try on and make needed alterations.
6. Stitch along the line of basting.

If the measurements for our waist lengths have been carefully and correctly made, the basted seam line will be in the right place. If this has not been correctly done, some adjustment may need to be made when one fits the dress. For this reason, the seam is not stitched until after the fitting.

Activities:

1. Check the waist and skirt to be sure all seams, darts, and pleats have been stitched.
2. Place the right sides and center front of the waist and skirt together. Pin into place.
3. Place the right sides and center back of the waist and skirt together. Pin into place.
4. Baste the waist and skirt together.
5. Try on and have partner check any needed alterations.
6. Make alterations needed.
7. Stitch the waist and skirt together.

Problem 13: HOW SHALL WE MAKE THE PLACKET?

Plackets are necessary in many of our dresses to permit us to put them on or take them off. The placket is an

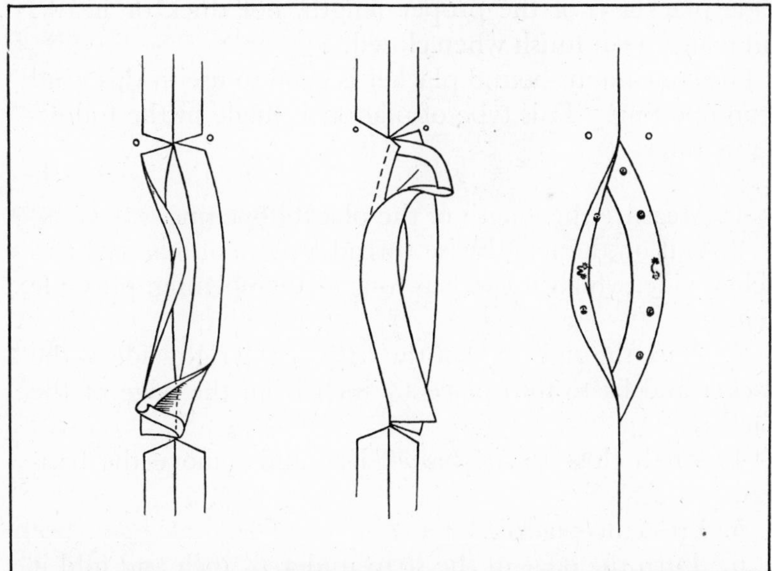

Here are the steps in making the faced and extension placket.

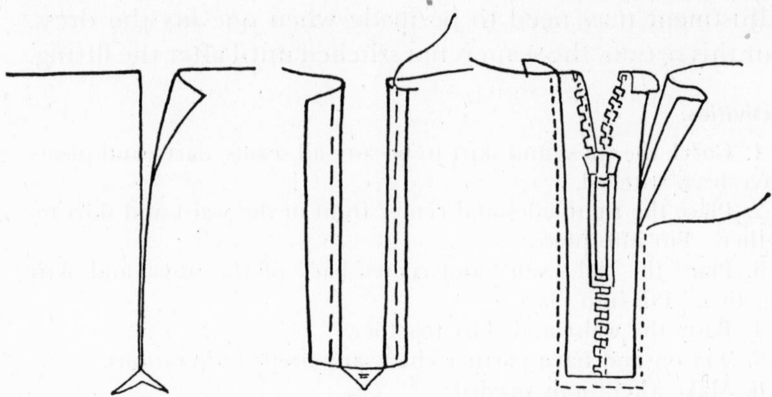

This zipper is set into a slash and is visible from the outside of the garment.

opening which, when open, gives more room in putting the garment on or taking it off, and when closed, will make the garment fit closely to the lines of the body. The well-made placket is of the proper length, not thick or heavy, and makes a flat finish when closed.

The continuous-bound placket is good to use in this kind of an opening. This type of placket is made in the following manner:

1. Measure the length of the placket opening.
2. Cut on the lengthwise thread a piece of material two inches wide, which is twice as long as the opening, plus one inch.
3. Place the right side of the strip to the right side of the placket and baste into place ¼ inch from the edge of the placket.
4. Stitch close to the basted line and remove the bastings.
5. Press the placket.
6. Turn the edge of the strip under ¼ inch and fold it over to the stitched line.

7. Baste on the line of stitching.
8. Fasten it down by hand stitching.
9. Remove the bastings.
10. Press the finished placket.

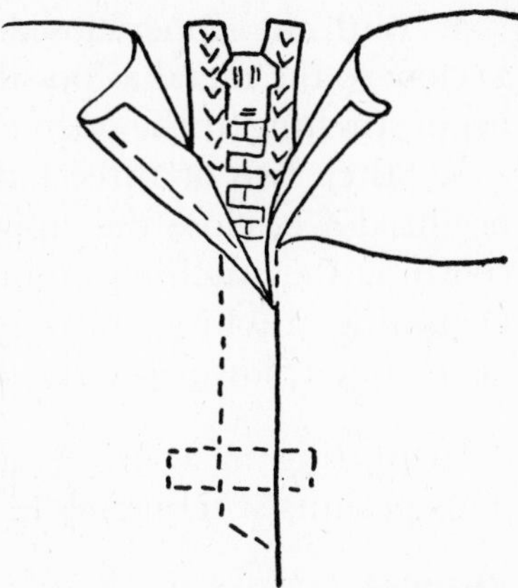

This is how the zipper is stitched in place on a seam so that the zipper does not show from the outside.

If the material is firm and of good quality, some may want to use a zipper in the placket. The zipper may be put in the placket in either of two ways. When the zipper is to show, the method is as follows:

1. Have the opening the exact length of the metal.
2. Slit crosswise at the end the width of the seam allowance.
3. Turn under the edge and press.
4. Baste the zipper tape (with the metal at the end of opening) to the folded edge.
5. Stitch close to the basted line, with the seam as near the metal as possible.

When a zipper is placed in a seam, the zipper should continue in the line of the seam. When the zipper is to be hidden, the method is as follows:

1. Be sure that the seam is at least one-half inch wide, with opening one-fourth inch longer than the metal.
2. Press each side of the opening back, to appear as a regular seam.
3. Place the zipper on the wrong side and baste it in place so that the center of the zipper is a continuation of the seam and the folded edges just meet.

4. With the zipper closed, the machine stitching is made, as close to the metal as possible. Have the zipper open and begin stitching at the open end.

5. Stitch two or three inches, raise the presser foot with needle down, close the zipper, lower the presser foot, and continue the stitching around to within two inches of the beginning stitching, raise presser foot with needle down, open zipper, lower presser foot and complete the stitching.

In putting in a zipper, a cording foot should be used. This permits stitching close to the metal.

Activities:

1. Practice making a continuous-bound placket on a short opening closed at each end.
2. Make the placket in your dress.

Problem 14: HOW SHALL WE MARK THE NECKLINE?

It is true that two dresses alike in all other respects may appear quite unlike if their necklines are decidedly different. We will recall from Unit 5, page 129, that common neckline finishes include various shapes. Our choice among these will have much to do with the appearance of our dress.

In marking the neckline of this dress, we will do it as we did on the morning dress, or we may use the string, as suggested on page 127.

Activities:

1. Put on your dress and adjust it correctly in place.
2. Have your partner mark your neckline.

Problem 15: HOW SHALL WE FINISH THE OPENING AT THE NECK OF OUR DRESS?

In making the school dress we may either bind or face the opening at the neck. If we choose to finish the opening by binding, we will proceed in the same way as we did in making the morning dress. If we choose to face the opening, the procedure will be as follows:

1. Cut a piece of cloth from the straight of the material, long enough to be stitched into the shoulder seam and one inch longer than the opening.
2. Place the center of the facing over the opening, with the right sides together.
3. Baste the facing to the neck edge $\frac{1}{8}$ inch from each side of the opening.
4. Stitch close to the basted line, slanting to a point at the end of the opening, and stitch in the same manner on the opposite side.
5. Cut the facing at the opening almost to the stitching at the point.
6. Remove the bastings.
7. Turn the facing to the wrong side.
8. Baste and press so that none of the facing shows on the right side.
9. The cut edge of the facing may be turned under once and stitched, or it may be overcast.

Activities:

1. Finish a short opening by facing in a piece of material.
2. Finish a short opening by binding in a piece of material.
3. Compare the two openings and decide which you will use for your dress.
4. Finish the opening at the neck of your dress.

Problem 16: HOW SHALL WE MAKE THE COLLAR?

Collars made of contrasting material are often used as a decoration or trimming on a dress. Collars may be of various shapes and sizes, may be double or single, and finished with braid, rickrack, bias binding or facing, or hemming.

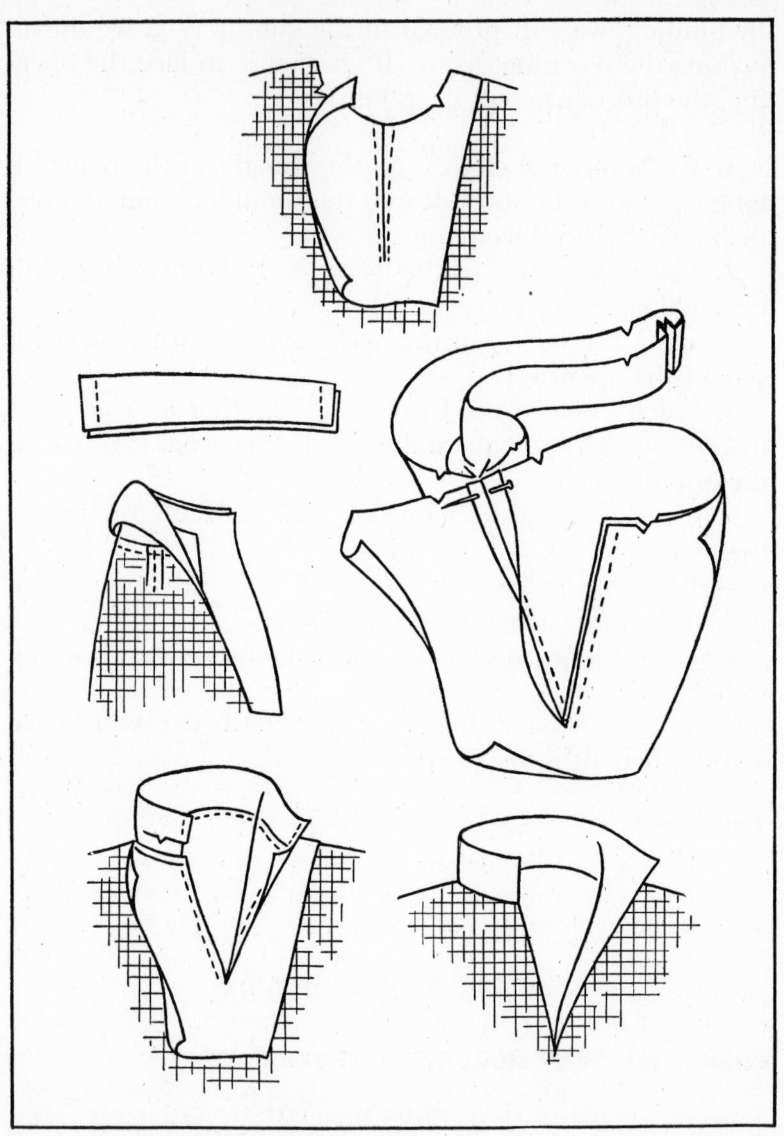

These are the steps in facing the opening at the neck and in making and attaching the convertible collar. The collar may be worn open or fastened at the neckline.

In making the morning dress, we used a plain double collar. In making this dress, we may use the convertible type of collar, which is made in the following way:

1. Check the collar pattern with neck of the dress and make any necessary alterations on the pattern.
2. Cut out the collar according to the markings on the pattern.
3. Fold and pin into place.
4. Baste the ends together with a 1/4-inch seam and stitch close to the basted line.
5. Remove the bastings, turn, and press the collar.

Activities:

1. Check the collar pattern with the neck of your dress.
2. Cut the collar out of the material.
3. Make the collar.

Problem 17: HOW SHALL WE ATTACH THE COLLAR TO THE DRESS?

Perhaps some of us will choose to use the same type of collar on this dress as was used in making the morning dress. If this is the case, the collar will be attached in the same way as was described in Unit 5, page 131.

If the collar is the convertible type, the method of attaching it is as follows:

1. Pin the right side of the collar to the wrong side of the dress, with the center back of the collar and neck of the dress coming together.
2. Pin the right side of the collar and the neck together at both fronts, being sure that the seams of the collar opening meet exactly.
3. Pin firmly into place, easing in any fullness of the neck to the dress.

4. Baste into place with a ¼-inch seam.
5. Stitch, remove the bastings, and tie the thread ends.
6. Press the seam upward and flat.
7. Fold under the edge of the wrong side of the collar ¼ inch and pin it to the first seam, making the edge of the fold just cover the machine stitching.
8. Baste this into place, remove the pins, and press.
9. Fasten this down with the overhand stitch to the machine stitching.
10. Remove the bastings and press the collar.

Activities:

1. For practice, make a small convertible type of collar and attach it to a small neck opening.
2. Attach the collar you have made to your dress.

The dress is put on and the armscye is marked with pins.

Problem 18: HOW SHALL WE MARK THE ARMSCYE IN THE DRESS?

Marking the armscye in the dress is a task requiring exact work and care. It must be carefully done if a well-fitted and comfortable sleeve is to be obtained.

To mark the armscye, the dress is put on and adjusted properly to the figure. The neck is fastened or pinned into place just as it is to be worn.

The armscye line is located in the following way:

1. Locate the high point on the shoulder where the arm and shoulder meet.
2. Place a line of pins perpen-

dicular to the shoulder seam line for 4 inches each way, front and back.

3. Then follow the natural curve of the arm until the two lines meet, making sure that enough room is allowed for freedom of movement.

A row of pins is then placed marking the armscye line. When both armscyes have been marked, the dress is removed, the pin line is checked, a basting thread is placed on the line of pins, and the pins are removed.

Activities:

1. Put on your dress and have your partner mark the armscye lines according to the directions.
2. Remove the dress and place a basting thread along the line.

Problem 19: HOW SHALL WE MAKE AND SET IN THE SLEEVE?

In order to be comfortable and look well, a dress must have well-fitted sleeves. If the sleeves bind, the wearer will be uncomfortable; if they are baggy, the dress will not look well. We will take care to have well-fitted sleeves in our dress.

In making the sleeve, we will sew the underarm sleeve seam together as a plain seam and finish as a false French seam, the same width as the other seams of the dress.

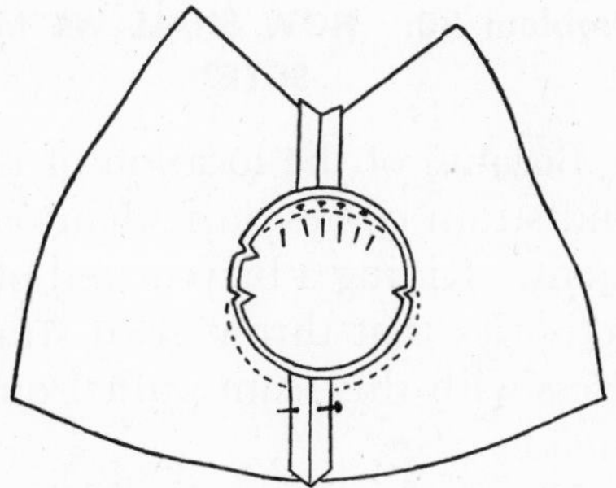

The sleeve is stitched in, after it has been carefully set in place with pins and basting thread.

When the sleeve seam is made and the armscye line is marked, we are ready to set in the sleeve. This will be done in the following way:

1. Trim the armscye to within ¾ inch of the basted line, marking original notches if cut off.

2. Place the sleeve in the armscye with the inside of the sleeve toward the worker.

3. Place a gathering thread in the top of the sleeves between the notches.

4. Match and pin the notches at highest and lowest points of the sleeve and armscye.

5. Adjust the gathers of the sleeve to fit the armscye; pin them in place.

6. Easing, but allowing no fullness in the lower half, pin the remainder of the sleeve to the armscye, changing the underarm seam as necessary.

7. Baste the sleeve in place and remove the pins.

The dress should be tried on, alterations made as needed, the dress removed, and alterations basted into place.

Activities:

1. Make the sleeve seam.
2. Set the sleeves into the dress.
3. Try on the dress and make any necessary alterations.

Problem 20: HOW SHALL WE MAKE THE SEAMS OF THE ARMSCYE?

Because of the location of the armscye seam, more stress and strain comes on it than on the other seams of the garment. Riding a bicycle and playing tennis are examples of activities that throw great strain on the armscye seam. A dress with this seam pulled out is unattractive and hard to mend.

Hence the sleeve should be stitched to the armscye in as strong a way as possible. The seam should not be bunglesome or appear heavy. The twice-stitched plain seam is practical for the armscye. This is made in the same way as it was made in the morning dress. The first stitching is made close to the line of basting, and the second stitching $\frac{1}{4}$ to $\frac{3}{8}$ inch from the first stitching. Trim the edge of the seam to within $\frac{1}{8}$ inch of the second stitching. Tie the machine thread ends, remove the bastings, and press the seam down to the sleeve.

Activities:

1. Examine a dress and note how the armscye seam is made.
2. Make the seams in the armscye of your dress.

Problem 21: HOW SHALL WE MAKE THE CUFFS FOR OUR DRESS?

The cuffs of a dress serve as a finish for the bottom of the sleeve, and may be decorative. Cuffs may vary in shape and size, but should correspond to the collar, if a collar is used.

The pattern of the cuff should be checked with the bottom of the sleeve to make sure it is the correct size. If alterations are necessary, they should be made in the same manner as alterations on the collar. In cutting out the cuffs, the material is folded right sides together and the pattern placed according to the markings. Two exact pieces are cut for each cuff.

Cuffs may be open or closed. If an open cuff is desired, the pieces are sewed together in the same way in which the collar was sewed.

If a closed cuff is to be made, the following procedure is used:

1. Place the right sides together and baste a $\frac{1}{4}$-inch seam along the outside edge of the cuff.

2. Stitch, remove the bastings, and open it out as one piece.

3. Fold over, with right sides together and seam ends meeting.

4. Pin into place and baste along the line of seam allowance.

5. Check with the bottom edge of the sleeve and make the necessary alterations.

6. Stitch the seam, remove the bastings, and press it open.

7. Fold the cuff together on the line of first stitching, baste it into place, and press.

Activities:

1. Cut out the cuffs for the dress.
2. Make the cuffs to your dress by the method given.
3. How does this method compare with other methods?

Problem 22: HOW SHALL WE ATTACH THE CUFFS TO THE SLEEVES?

Cuffs should be attached to the sleeves with a smooth, flat finish that does not show on the right side. The best way to do this is to use a bias facing.

The bias facing is cut 1¼ to 1½ inches wide, and as long as the distance around the cuff plus enough to join the two ends. The ends are joined and the seam is pressed flat.

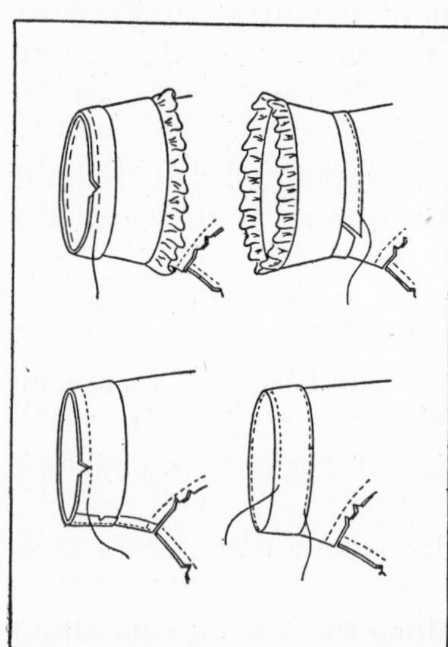

A cuff and a facing are applied.

The cuff is attached in the following way:

1. Matching the notches, place the wrong side of the cuff to the right side of the sleeve and pin into place.

2. Baste into position with a ¼- to ⅜-inch seam, and remove the pins.

3. With the right side of the bias facing to the right side of the cuff, pin the bias into place.

4. Baste into position with a 1/4- to 3/8-inch seam, and remove the pins.

5. Stitch close to the line of basting, remove the bastings, and tie the thread ends.

6. Crease and press the bias flat to the sleeve.

7. Baste into place, close to the sleeve.

8. Turn down 1/4 to 3/8 inch of the raw edge of the bias and baste it flat to the sleeve.

9. Stitch on the edge of the bias fold, remove the bastings, and tie machine thread ends.

Activities:

1. Cut the bias facing for attaching the cuffs.
2. Attach the cuffs to the sleeve.

Problem 23: HOW SHALL WE MAKE THE BELT AND BELT KEEPERS?

You will recall how we made the belt for our morning dress. This belt will be made in the same way. The steps in making the belt are as follows:

1. Place the right sides together and fold lengthwise so that the edges are exactly even.
2. Pin into place.
3. Baste with a 1/4-inch seam, starting at the folded side of one end, going across the end and entire length, leaving the other end open.
4. Stitch close to the basted line.
5. Remove the bastings.
6. Clip the corners 1/8 inch from the stitching to avoid bulkiness.
7. Turn the belt to the right side, using a safety pin or yardstick to pull or push the material through.
8. Crease at the seam, and fold and baste into place.
9. Turn in the unstitched ends 1/4 inch, baste into place, and stitch in by hand.

10. Sew on the hooks and eyes for fastening, using the methods given on pages 132 to 134.

11. Press lightly, remove the bastings, and press again.

The belt keepers are made to hold the belt in place, one keeper being placed on each side seam at the waistline. The belt keepers are made as follows:

1. Cut a piece of material 1¼ inches wide and in length twice the width of the belt plus 1½ inches.
2. Fold lengthwise with the right sides together, and baste in a ¼-inch seam the length of the piece.
3. Stitch close to the basting line and remove the bastings.
4. Using a safety pin, turn the keeper to the right side.
5. Fold so that the seam is in the center of the keeper, and press it.
6. Cut it in two equal lengths.
7. Turn the ends in, baste into place, and overhand stitch them together.

The dress is put on and the proper position of the belt keepers is marked. The keepers are then basted into place and fastened to the dress at the ends by overhanding or by machine stitching.

Activities:

1. Make the belt for your dress.
2. Make and attach the belt keepers for your dress.
3. Press the belt and the keepers on the dress.

Problem 24: HOW SHALL WE SEW ON FASTENERS?

For fastening this dress we will find it good to use a hook and eye at the waistline on the placket, and snaps along the placket. We learned to sew on the hook and eye when we made our morning dress. Now we will learn to sew on snaps.

Snaps are sewed on in the following way:

1. Place a pin at each point where the ball part of the snap is to be placed. The ball part is placed on the upper side of the placket. Place a pin on the lower part of the placket where the socket part of the snap is to be placed.

2. With a knot in a single heavy thread, take a stitch where the pin is located.

3. Place the ball part of the snap over the knot, and take several stitches through each hole of the snap.

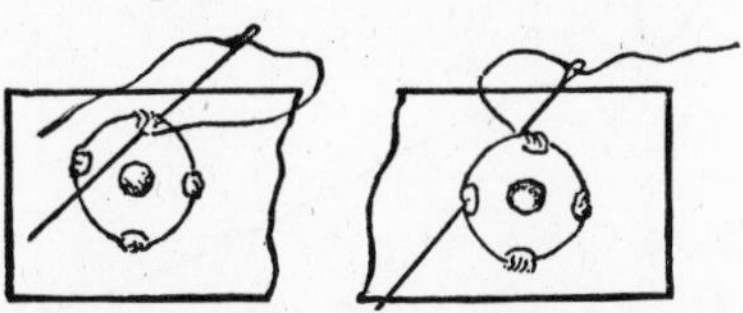

Snap fasteners sewed on in this manner will stay secure.

4. Pass the needle to the underside and fasten the thread with two or three small stitches.

5. Sew on the socket part of the fastener next.

6. Sew the remainder of fasteners on in the same manner.

Activities:

1. Examine fasteners used on some of your dresses and see how they are sewed on.
2. Sew the snap fasteners on the placket of your dress.
3. Sew the hook and eye at waistline on the placket of your dress.

Problem 25: HOW SHALL WE PUT IN THE HEM?

The evenly made hem line adds much to the appearance of a well-made dress. We will mark the hem line in the same way as we did the one in our morning dress. We will also follow the same procedure in putting in the hem. However, if our skirt happens to be a circular one, a much narrower hem will be used.

Shall we recall the steps in marking and putting in the skirt hem? These are as follows:

1. Decide how many inches from the floor the dress will be.

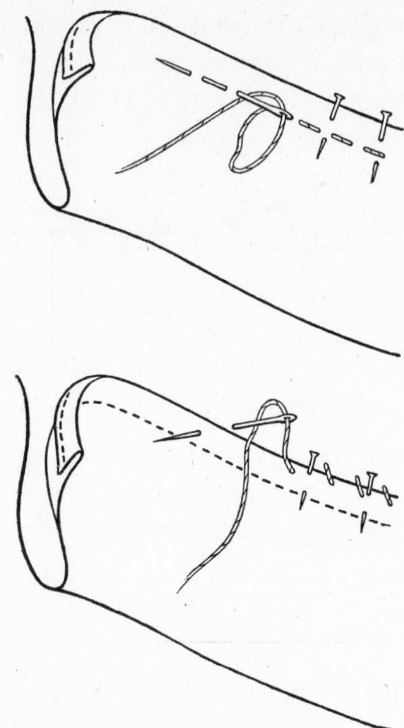

The hem is first basted (top) and then sewed in by hand (bottom).

2. Mark this number on the yardstick with chalk or a rubber band.

3. Hold the yardstick, perpendicular to the floor, against the dress.

4. Place pins in the dress at the point even with the mark on the yardstick and parallel to the floor.

5. Pins should be placed about 3 inches apart.

6. Recheck the line of pins.

7. Remove the dress, turn the hem on the line of pins, and crease.

8. Pin the hem into place.

9. Put on the dress and check.

10. Make any needed corrections.

11. Remove the dress.

12. Baste the hem line in place 1/4 inch from the lower edge, removing all pins when you have completed the basting.

13. With a gauge, measure up from the hem line the desired width of hem plus 3/8 inch for a turn-in. Measurements should be made at intervals of two inches and marked with a pin at each point.

14. Trim along the line of pins and remove the pins.

15. Turn under the edge of the hem 3/8 inch and baste with small basting stitches, starting with a new thread at the center front, center back, and each side seam.

16. Pin the hem into place at the center front, center back, and each side seam.

17. With basting thread, adjust fullness between the pins and pin the hem into place.

18. Baste the hem into place and remove all pins.

19. Try on the dress and make any needed alterations.

20. Press the hem.

21. Stitch close to the edge of the hem.

22. Remove the bastings, tie the threads of the machine stitching, and press the hem again.

If desired, the hem can be put in by hand. When this is done, the stitching is practically invisible on the right side. This method requires a longer time than does stitching with the machine.

Activities:

1. Have your partner mark the hem line of your dress.
2. Put the hem in your dress.

Problem 26: HOW SHALL WE PRESS OUR DRESS?

We noticed that pressing the morning dress added much to its appearance and made our work look much better. Pressing will have the same effect on this dress. Our school dress will be pressed in much the same way as our morning dress. We will use a damp cloth to brush over the dress as we press, being certain that the iron is not too hot for the fabric.

However, this dress has the set-in sleeve, and we must press each side of the sleeves and be sure that we give special attention to cuffs, before putting the dress on the ironing board. The seams at the armscye and waist are heavy, so they require special pressing. Next, the waist is pressed. Begin pressing at the shoulder seam and press down to the waist seam. If the neck has an opening, it should be well pressed. In pressing the skirt of the dress, begin at the waist and press down. The skirt may be too long to press its entire length at one time on the ironing board, so we will press all the way around the upper part of the skirt and then press its lower part, being sure that the hem is well ironed. When the pressing is completed, the dress is placed on a hanger and hung in a closet.

Activities:

1. Press your dress as directed.
2. Why are some dresses harder to press than others?

Problem 27: HOW SHALL WE JUDGE OUR DRESSES?

When we chose our material and pattern we considered the design and color carefully, so that our dress would be attractive. Now that our dress is ready to wear we will check it to see if it has worked out as we had planned. We will also wish to check or judge our workmanship, the fit of the garment, and our carefulness in keeping the garment clean.

An easy way to check or judge a dress is to use a score card. A basis for a score card which we might make follows:

Design:

Pattern
Material

Material:

Color
Weight

Workmanship:

Seams
Hem
Neck and sleeve finishes
Fasteners
Pressing

Fit:

Neck
Sleeves
Shoulder seams
Side seams

Cleanliness

Activities:

1. Make a score card that would total 100 on the basis of the points listed above.
2. (*Class activity*) Score your own dresses.
3. Judge some dresses of classmates.
4. How can you improve on the next garment you make?

REFERENCES

Donovan, Dulcie Godlove, *The Mode in Dress and Home.* Boston: Allyn and Bacon, 1935.

Friend, Mata Roman, and Shultz, Hazel, *Junior Home Economics: Clothing.* New York: D. Appleton-Century Co., 1933.

Jensen, Milton B., Jensen, Mildred R., and Ziller, M. Louisa, *Fundamentals of Home Economics.* New York: The Macmillan Co., 1935.

Kinyon, Kate W., and Hopkins, L. Thomas, *Junior Clothing,* Revised Edition. New York: Benj. H. Sanborn and Co., 1938.

Matthews, Mary Lockwood, *The New Elementary Home Economics.* Boston: Little, Brown and Co., 1937.

Todd, Elizabeth, *Clothes for Girls.* Boston: Little, Brown and Co., 1935.

SUGGESTED HOME EXPERIENCES

1. Make a plan for buying your clothes for the remainder of the school year.

2. Make another school dress for yourself, using a more difficult design.

3. Make a wash dress for some member of your family.

4. Plan a dress with the accessories which it would need for some member of your family.

5. Take the measurements of your mother and decide what size pattern she should buy.

6. Make a slip to wear with your school dress.

INDEX

Accessories, 469–470
Accidents
  to children, 551–554
  in the home, 401–405
Apples, baked, 264–265
Armscye
  marking the, 576–577
  seam, 578–579

Baked dishes
  apples, 264–265
  beans, 441–442
  custard, 263–264
  hash, 255–256
Basting
  dresses, 119–120, 565, 567–569
  pillowcases, 70–71
  tea towels, 66–67
Bathroom, care of the, 393–395
Beans, baked, 441–442
Belt, making the, 135–136, 581
Belt keepers, making, 582
Beverages
  chocolate, 208–210
  cocoa, 208–210
  coffee, 210–212
  eggnog, 504
  fruit punch, 378, 503
  grape punch, 503
  lemonade, 502
  malted milk, 504–505
  for the sick, 502–505
  tea, 377–378
Bias strips
  cutting, 124–125
  joining, 130–131
Biscuits, 225–226
Bobbin, winding a, 62
Body
  care of the, 312–314
  food needs of the, 31–34
Boiled
  dressing, 253–254
  eggs, 217–218
Books, care of, 391–393
Bows, for packages, 490, 491, 492
Bread pudding, 297–298, 299
Breads
  biscuits, 225–226
  griddle cakes, 223–225
  plain muffins, 259–260
  serving, 222, 223, 225, 226, 260, 261
  toast, 221–223
  whole wheat muffins, 260–261
Breakfast
  importance of, 199–200
  judging, 237–238
  patterns, 202
  planning, 227–228
  preparation of, 203–226, 236
  score card for judging, 237–238
  serving, 203–226, 236
  setting the table for, 228–232
  standards for, 200–202
Broth, meat, 505–506
Brownies, 444–445
Butter cake, 294–296
Buying
  canned foods, 279–282
  clothing, 452–453
  coats, 471–474
  dresses, 460–461
  fruit, 276–277, 278–279
  material for a morning dress, 103–106

Buying—(*Continued*)
material for a pillowcase, 69
meat, 282–285
patterns, 106–108

Cabbage, scalloped, 248–249
Cafeteria, school, 425–427
Cake
butter, 294–296
cup, 266–267
devil's food, 366–368
seven-minute icing for, 368
sponge, 293–294
uncooked icing for, 296–297
Campfire Girls' laws, 88
Candy
chocolate fudge, 486
peanut brittle, 485–486
stuffed dates, 485
Canned food, 279–282
Care of
bathroom, 393–395
body, 312–314
books, 391–393
children, 527–554
clothing, 322–325, 331–338
cupboards, 395–397
hair, 315–316
hose, 326–327
house, 384–391, 401–405
magazines, 391–393
nails, 314–315
ornaments, 391–393
pantry, 395–397
sick person, 497–499
sick room, 499–501
silverware, 397–398
undergarments, 325–327
Centerpiece, making a, 482–484
Cereals
Cream of Wheat, 216–217
ground, 216–217
ready-prepared, 213–214
rolled oats, 214–215
Cheese sandwiches, 433–435
Children
care of, 528–531
cleanliness for, 541–545
games for, 539–540
good food habits for, 536–538
guide for care of, 533–535
play for, 538–541
preventing accidents to, 551–554
reading to, 545–548
responsibility of, 19–21
responsibility to, 531–533
staying with, 549–550
Chocolate, 209–210
Cleaning
house, 389–397
odd jobs of, 398–400
silverware, 397–398
Clothing
accessories, 469–470
caring for, 321–339
choosing, 317–320
coats, 471–474
dresses, 460–461
footwear, 462–467
headwear, 467–468
purchasing, 452–456, 471–474
shopping for, 452–453
undergarments, 458–460
Coats, purchasing, 471–474
Cocoa, 209–210
Code for the shopper, 453
Coffee
boiled, 211
drip, 212
filtered, 212
percolated, 211
preparation of, 211, 212
serving, 212
Collar
attaching a, 131–132, 575–576
making a, 128–130, 573–575
Combination salad, 252–253
Conduct
away from home, 76–78, 91–94
in homes of others, 84–86

Conduct—(*Continued*)
in public, 89–91
at school, 86–89
when traveling, 94–98
Conversation, 411–413
Cookies
brownies, 444–445
filled, 443–444
oatmeal, 267–269
Cooking methods, 196–199
Corn soup, 241–242
Cream of Wheat, 216
Creamed dishes
dried beef, 245–246
green beans, 246–247
Cuffs
attaching, 580–581
making, 579–580
Cup cakes, 266–267
Cupboards, care of, 395–397
Custard
baked, 263–264
floating island, 261–263
Cuts of meat, 284–285
Cutting
a bias strip, 124–125
the morning dress, 114–115
the school dress, 562–563

Darning, 327–330
Desserts
baked apples, 264–265
baked custard, 263–264
bread pudding, 297–298, 299
cookies, 267–269
cup cakes, 266–267
floating island, 261–263
fruit in gelatine, 289–291
junket custard, 506–507
lemon sauce for, 299
raisin pie, 445–447
vanilla ice cream, 369–370
Deviled eggs, 438, 439
Devil's food cake. 366–368
Diagram of
breakfast table, 230
dinner table, 300, 301, 302
luncheon table, 272
supper table, 272
tea table, 379, 380
Dinner
patterns, 286
planning, 286–288
serving, 303–305
setting table for, 299–303
Dishwashing, 194–195
Dresses
basting, 119–120, 565, 567–569
cutting out, 114–115, 562–563
judging, 142, 586–587
morning, 102–103
practice in making, 118–119
pressing, 141–142, 585–586
procedure in making, 564–565
purchasing, 460–461
school, 556
selecting, 556. 558–559
steps in making, 117–118, 564–565
stitching, 122–124, 567–569
Dressing, boiled, 253–254
Dried
beef, creamed, 245–246
fruit, 207–208
Dusting, 163–164, 389–391

Egg sandwiches, 433–435
Eggnog, 504
Eggs
boiled, 217–218
cooked in water, 217–218
deviled, 438, 439
fried, 219–220
hard-cooked, 217–218
pickled, 438–439
poached, 218–219
scrambled, 220–221
soft-cooked, 217–218
stuffed, 438, 439
Environment, 8

Equipment
  dishwashing, 194–195
  school-kitchen, 191–194

Family
  conversation, 411–413
  fun, 408–411, 420–421
  generations in the, 4–6
  groups, 3
  influence, 9
  inheritance, 5
  meals, 189–191
  members, 21–23
  music, 413–415
  parties, 418–420
  picnic, 415–418
Fasteners, 132–134, 582–583
Father, responsibility of, 12–15
Filled cookies, 443–444
Fitting
  shoulder, 121–122
  skirt, 567
  waist, 566–567
Floating island, 261–263
Food
  classification, 33–34
  customs, 25
  groups, 31–32
  habits, 50–53, 536–538
  requirements, 35–37
  for sick person, 501–502
  source of, 26–29
  use of, in the body, 29–31
  variety of, 40–42
Footwear, 462–467
French dressing, 252
French toast, 222–223
Fried eggs, 219–220
Friends
  choosing, 172–174
  importance of, 167
  keeping, 177–182
  making, 174–177, 180–182
  reasons for, 168–169
Friendships
  building, 169–172
  expressing, 478–479
Frosting (*see* Icing)
Fruit
  baked apple, 264–265
  buying, 276–277, 278–279
  dried, 207–208
  punch, 378, 503
  raw, 203–206, 440–441
  salad, 289–290
  stewed, 206–207
Fudge, 486

Games
  for children, 539–540
  for parties, 359–364
Gelatin fruit salad, 289
Gifts
  choosing, 480–481
  wrapping, 487–492
Girl Scout laws, 87–88
Gloves (*see* Accessories)
Go foods, 33
Grape punch, 503
Green beans, creamed, 246–247
Griddle cakes, 223–225
Ground cereals, 216–217
Grow foods, 33
Guests
  attitudes toward, 344–345
  entertaining, 345–348, 359–364
  inviting, 351–354
  reasons for, 342–343
  responsibilities of, 78–80
  week-end, 355–356
Guide
  for care of children, 533–535
  for selecting food, 38–39

Habits, good food, 51
Hair, care of, 315–316
Handkerchiefs (*see* Accessories)
Hard-cooked eggs, 217–218
Hash, baked, 255–256

Hats (*see* Headwear)
Headwear, 467–468
Hem
  marking, 138–140, 583–584
  for morning dress, 138–141
  for school dress, 583–585
  for tea towel, 65–68
Heredity, 5
Hose
  care of, 326–327
  choosing, 463–465
  darning, 328
Hostess responsibilities, 349–351
House, care of, 384–391, 401–405

Ice cream, 369–370
Icing
  seven-minute, 368
  uncooked, 296–297
Ideals and attitudes
  toward family, 21–23
  toward guests, 344–345
  toward life, 10–12
Individual pies, 445–447
Informal invitations, 81–82, 353
Invitations
  accepting, 80–83
  declining, 81–83
  extending, 82
  informal, 81–82, 353–354
  oral, 81
  semiformal, 82–83, 354
  written, 81

Jewelry (*see* Accessories)
Junket custard, 506–507

Lemon sauce, 299
Lemonade, 502
Liver and gravy, 256–257
Loaf, meat, 439–440
Lunch
  from home, 429–446
  packing, 447–449
  school, 424–425, 447
  in school cafeteria, 425–427
Luncheon
  judging the, 275–276
  menus, 239
  planning the, 269–270
  preparation of, 274–275
  serving the, 272–275
  setting the table for, 272
  types of, 238–240

Malted milk, 504–505
Manicure (*see* Nails)
Manners (*see* Table Manners and Conduct)
Marking
  armscye, 576–577
  hem, 138–140, 583–584
  neck, 127–128, 572
Material for
  morning dress, 103–106
  pillowcase, 69–70
  school dress, 558–559
  tea towel, 65, 69
Meal patterns
  for breakfast, 202
  daily, 42–44
  for dinner, 286
  for luncheon, 238–240
  for supper, 238–240
Meals
  importance of, 184–186
  influence on, 186–188
  judging, 46–48, 275
  responsibility for, 189–191
Meat
  baked hash, 255–256
  balls, 258–259
  broth, 505–506
  buying, 282–285
  creamed dried beef, 245–246
  cuts, 284–285
  liver and gravy, 256–257
  loaf, 439–440
  pie, 291–293
  sandwiches, 431–433

Menus
for daily meals, 42–44
luncheon, 239
school-cafeteria, 428
Methods of cooking, 196–199
Milk toast, 222
Money
influences for spending, 513–515
personal spending of, 523–525
planning to spend, 516–521
responsibility for spending, 521–523
source of, 510–511
spending, 511–513
Morning dress, 101–143
Mother, responsibility of, 15–18
Muffins
plain, 259–260
whole wheat, 260–261
Music in the home, 413–415

Nails, care of, 314–315
Neck
cutting the, 127–128
fastening the, 132–134
finishing the opening for the, 125–127, 572–573
marking the, 127–128, 572

Oatmeal cookies, 267–269
Overeating, dangers of, 39

Pantry, care of, 395–397
Parties
family, 418–419
games for, 359–364
planning, 357–359, 418–420
refreshments for, 364–366
Patch pockets, 137–138
Patching clothing, 330–331
Patterns
altering, 109–111, 560–561
breakfast, 202
buying, 106–108
checking, 109–111, 560–561
Patterns—(*Continued*)
choice of, 102–103, 556
dinner, 286
laying out, 113–114, 562
removing, from material, 116–117, 562–563
studying, 108–109, 559–560
supper, 238–240
Peanut brittle, 485–486
Pickled eggs, 438–439
Picnic, family, 415–417
Pie
meat, 291–293
raisin, 445–447
Pillowcases
basting, 70–71
judging, 73
making, 69–73
Placket, making the, 569–572
Play
for children, 538–541
in the family, 408–411
Poached eggs, 218–219
Pockets, making and sewing, 137–138
Posture
sitting, 310–311
standing, 310
walking, 311
Pressing
a morning dress, 141–142
a pillowcase, 72–73
a school dress, 585–586
a tea towel, 68
Preventing accidents
to children, 551–554
in the home, 401–405
Protecting foods, 34
Purses (*see* Accessories)

Raisin pie, 445–447
Raw
fruit, 203–206, 440–441
vegetables, 440–441

Reading
to children, 545–548
in the home, 413–415
Ready-prepared cereals, 213–214
Refreshments
for parties, 364–366
for teas, 373–375
Regulating foods, 33
Requirements
food, 35–39
for looking our best, 308–309
Responsibilities
for care of house, 387–389
of children, 19–21
to children in the home, 531–533
of father, 12–15
of guests, 78–80
of mother, 15–18
Rolled oats, 214–215
Rooms
attractive, 146–147
convenient, 146–147
daily care of, 161–162
furnishing, 147–150
improving, 147–150
personality of, 153–156
rearranging, 156–158
seasonal care of, 163–165
for sick people, 499–501
storage space in, 158–161
weekly care of, 163–165

Salad
combination, 252–253
dressings for, 252, 253–254
gelatin fruit, 289–290
tuna fish, 253–255
Salmon, scalloped, 247–248
Sandwiches
cheese, 433–435
egg, 433–435
meat, 431–433
sweet, 436–437
tea, 375–377
Sauce, lemon, 299
Scalloped dishes
cabbage, 248–249
salmon, 247–248
Scarfs (*see* Accessories)
School
cafeteria, 425–428
dress, 556, 586–587
kitchen, 191–194
lunch, 423–425, 429–449
Score card for judging
a morning dress, 142
a pillowcase, 73
a school dress, 586–587
breakfasts, 237–238
foods, 47
Scrambled eggs, 220–221
Seams
armscye, 578–579
for a morning dress, 122–124
pillowcase, 70–71
school dress, 567
shoulder, 122–124
underarm, 122–124
Semiformal invitations, 82–83, 354
Setting the table for
breakfast, 228–232
dinner, 299–303
luncheon, 272
tea, 379–380
Sewing machine
parts, 56–58
stitching, 60
threading the, 63–65
treadling the, 58–59
winding bobbin of the, 62–63
Shampoo, 315–316
Shoes (*see* Footwear)
Shopping, 452–453
Shoulder, fitting the, 121–122
Sick people
beverages for, 502–505
care of, 497–499

Sick people—(*Continued*)
food for, 501–502
room for, 499–501
symptoms of, 496–497
tray for, 507–508
Silverware, care of, 397–398
Skirt, fitting a, 567
Sleeve
finishing edge of, 134–135
making the, 577, 578
setting in the, 577–578
Soft-cooked eggs, 217–218
Soup
cream of corn, 241–242
cream of tomato, 243–244
Sponge cake, 293–294
Standards
for care of the house, 384–386
for school lunch, 424–425
Stewed fruit, 206–207
Stockings (*see* Hose)
Storage
of clothing, 334–337
space in room, 158–161
Stories for children, 545–548
Study table, 156–157
Stuffed
dates, 485
eggs, 438, 439
Supper
judging the, 275–276
patterns, 238–240
planning the, 269–270
preparing, 274–275
serving, 272–274, 274–275
types of, 238–240, 272–274
Sweaters, buying, 471–474
Sweeping, 163–164, 389–391
Sweet sandwiches, 436–437

Table appointments for
breakfast, 229
dinner, 300, 301, 302
luncheon, 272
teas, 372, 379, 380
Table manners, 233–236
Table service for
breakfast, 228–232
dinner, 299–303
luncheon, 272–274
teas, 370–373, 379–380
Tea
beverages for a, 377–378
food for a, 373–375
with fruit juices, 378
hot, 377
iced, 377–378
invitation to a, 82–83, 354
planning a, 370–373
Russian, 378
sandwiches for a, 375–377
table arrangements for a, 379–380
Tea towels
basting, 66–67
hemming, 65–68
material for, 69
pressing, 68
Toast
buttered, 222
dry, 222
French, 222–223
milk, 222
preparing and serving, 221–223
Tomato soup, 243–244
Traveling conduct, 94–98
Tray for sick person, 507–508
Tuna fish salad, 253–255

Undereating, dangers of, 39
Undergarments
caring for, 325–327
purchasing, 458–460
Used garments, obtaining service from, 337–338

Vegetables
baked beans, 441–442
buttered, 250–251
canned, 279–282

Vegetables—(*Continued*)
creamed, 246–247
fresh, 276–279
guide for, 278
raw, 440–441

Vitamins, 34

Waist, fitting the, 565–566
Washing dishes, 194–195
Wrapping gifts (*see* Gifts)